This volume brings together article

the Laboratory of Comparative Hu

benchmarks in the recent history of research and theory on the cultural and contextual foundations of human development. The central theme of this discussion can be posed as a question: How shall we develop a psychology that takes as its starting point the actions of people participating in routine, culturally organized activities? The discussion is organized in terms of a set of overarching themes of importance to psychologists and other social scientists: the nature of context; experiments as contexts; cultural-historical theories of culture, context, and development; the analysis of classroom settings as a socially important context of development; the psychological analysis of activity in situ; and questions of power and discourse.

Mind, culture, and activity

Mind, culture, and activity

Seminal papers from the Laboratory of Comparative Human Cognition

Edited by

MICHAEL COLE
University of California at San Diego

YRJÖ ENGESTRÖM
University of California at San Diego

OLGA VASQUEZ
University of California at San Diego

CAMBRIDGE
UNIVERSITY PRESS

PUBLISHED BY THE PRESS SYNDICATE OF THE UNIVERSITY OF CAMBRIDGE
The Pitt Building, Trumpington Street, Cambridge CB2 1RP, United Kingdom

CAMBRIDGE UNIVERSITY PRESS
The Edinburgh Building, Cambridge CB2 2RU, United Kingdom
40 West 20th Street, New York, NY 10011-4211, USA
10 Stamford Road, Oakleigh, Melbourne 3166, Australia

First published 1997

Printed in the United States of America

Typeset in Ehrhardt

Library of Congress Cataloging-in-Publication Data

Mind, culture, and activity : seminal papers from the Laboratory of
    Comparative Human Cognition / edited by Michael Cole, Yrjö
    Engeström, Olga Vasquez.

    p. cm.

Includes index.

    ISBN 0-521-55238-9 (hardcover). – ISBN 0-521-55823-9 (pbk.)

    1. Ethnopsychology. 2. Cognition and culture. 3. Social
psychology. I. Cole, Michael, 1938– . II. Engeström, Yrjö,
1948– . III. Vasquez, Olga A.
GN502.M55   1997
155.8'2 – dc21   96–38956
                                       CIP

*A catalog record for this book is available from
the British Library*

ISBN 0-521-55238-9 hardback
ISBN 0-521-55823-9 paperback

Contents

v

Cognition in the wild

Power and discourse

Contributors

Michael Akiyama
4260 Washtenaw Avenue
Ann Arbor, MI 48104

Alonzo B. Anderson
Educational Psychology &
  Technologies
School of Education
University of Southern
  California
Los Angeles, CA 90089

Kathryn Hu-Pei Au
College of Education
University of Hawaii
1776 University Avenue,
  WA-226
Honolulu, HI 96822

Erik Axel
Psykologisk Laboratorium
Koebenhavns Universitet
Njalsgade 90
Copenhagen 2300
Denmark

David Bakhurst
Department of Philosophy
Queen's University
Kingston, Ontario K7L 3N6
Canada

Ernest E. Boesch
University of Saarbruecken
or:
62 Boulevard St. Michel
75006 Paris
France

Ann L. Brown
Graduate School of Education
University of California,
  Berkeley
4533 Tolman Hall
Berkeley, CA 94720

Katherine Brown
Department of Communication,
  0503
University of California,
  San Diego
La Jolla, CA 92093

Courtney B. Cazden
School of Education
Harvard University
Cambridge, MA 02138

L. Carol Christopher
Department of Communication,
    0503
University of California,
    San Diego
La Jolla, CA 92093

Michael Cole
Department of Communication
Department of Psychology
Laboratory of Comparative
    Human Cognition, 0092
University of California,
    San Diego
La Jolla, CA 92093

Judy S. DeLoache
Department of Psychology
University of Illinois,
    Urbana–Champaign
Champaign, IL 61820

Esteban Diaz
School of Education
California State University,
    San Bernardino
San Bernardino, CA 92404

Yrjö Engeström
Department of Communication,
    0503
University of California,
    San Diego
La Jolla, CA 92093

Frederick Erickson
Graduate School of Education
University of Pennsylvania
3700 Walnut Street
Philadelphia, PA 19104

Elette Estrada
3507 River Way
San Antonio, TX 78230

Charles O. Frake
Center for Cognitive Science
652 Baldy Hall
State University of New York at
    Buffalo
Buffalo, NY 14260

Anderson F. Franklin
Department of Psychology
City College – CUNY
Convent Avenue at 138th Street
New York, NY 10031

Ronald Gallimore
Department of Psychiatry
University of California,
    Los Angeles
760 Westwood Plaza
Los Angeles, CA 90024

Esther Goody
Department of Social
    Anthropology
Cambridge University
Free School Lane
Cambridge CB2 3DZ
England

Judith Gregory
Kaiser Permanente, SCPMG
Clinical Systems Development
393 East Walnut Street,
    7th Floor
Pasadena, CA 91188

Giyoo Hatano
Faculty of Letters
Educational Psychology
Keio University
2-15-45 Mida, Minato-ku
Tokyo 108
Japan

Michael Holquist
C-105, WLH 311
Yale University
New Haven, CT 06520

Lois Hood (now Holzman)
East Side Institute
500 Greenwich Street
New York, NY 10013

Edwin Hutchins
Cognitive Science Department,
    0515
University of California,
    San Diego
9500 Gilman Drive
La Jolla, CA 92093

Keiko Kuhara
Department of Psychology
Tokyo Women's Christian
    University
2-6-1 Zempukuji
Suginami-ku
Tokyo 167
Japan

Laboratory of Comparative
    Human Cognition
c/o Michael Cole
LCHC, 0092
University of California,
    San Diego
La Jolla, CA 92093

Alfred Lang
Institut für Psychologie
Universität Bern
Unitobler, Muesmattstr. 45,
    CH-3000
Bern 9
Switzerland

Jean Lave
Graduate School of Education
University of California,
    Berkeley
Berkeley, CA 94720

Bonnie E. Litowitz
180 N. Michigan Ave. Suite
    2220
Chicago, IL 60601

Lawrence M. Lopes
Del Mar, CA

Harry Markowicz
English Department
Gallaudet University
800 Florida Avenue, N.E.
Washington, DC 20002

Raymond P. McDermott
Department of Education
Stanford University
Stanford, CA 94305

Hugh Mehan
Teacher Education Program,
    0070
University of California,
    San Diego
La Jolla, CA 92093

Norris Minick
Louisville, CO

Luis C. Moll
Division of Language, Reading
    & Culture
College of Education
University of Arizona
Tucson, AZ 85721

Denis Newman
BBN Systems & Technologies
    Corporation
10 Moulton Street
Cambridge, MA 02138

Ageliki Nicolopoulou
Department of Psychology
Lehigh University
17 Memorial Drive East
Bethlehem, PA 18015
or
61 Paradise Road, #6
Northampton, MA 01060

Carol Padden
Department of Communication,
    0503
University of California,
    San Diego
La Jolla, CA 92093

Marilyn G. Quinsaat
Educational Development
    Center
55 Chapel Street
Newton, MA 02158

Geoffrey B. Saxe
Graduate School of
    Education
University of California,
    Los Angeles
405 Hilgard Avenue
Los Angeles, CA 90024

Yutaka Sayeki
Faculty of Education
University of Tokyo
7-3-1 Hongo, Bunkyo-Ku
Tokyo 113
Japan

Jeffrey Schultz
Professor & Chair of
    Education
Beaver College
450 S. Easton Road
Glenside, PA 19038

Sylvia Scribner
Deceased

William H. Teale
College of Education
The University of Illinois at
    Chicago
1040 West Harrison Street
Chicago, IL 60607

Olga Vasquez
Department of Communication,
  0503
Laboratory of Comparative
  Human Cognition
University of California,
  San Diego
La Jolla, CA 92093

James Wertsch
Department of Education
Washington University,
  St. Louis
Campus Box 1183
One Brookings Drive
St. Louis, MO 63130

1   Introduction

Michael Cole, Yrjö Engeström, and Olga Vasquez

The *LCHC Newsletter* articles that are contained in this volume are important benchmarks in the history of a discussion of context, culture, and development. The central theme of this discussion can be posed as a question: How shall we develop a psychology that takes as its starting point the actions of people participating in routine cultural contexts? This question engenders a second: What kind of methodology does the study of human behavior in context entail?

In retrospect it is possible to identify the late 1970s and early 1980s as a time when many students of human development began to express the need for a new unit of psychological analysis, one which attributed to that elusive concept, context, a central role in the constitution of human nature. Several publications at the time gave voice to this convergence.

In her article on cognitive development in the 1978 *Annual Review of Psychology*, Rochel Gelman reviewed the emerging evidence that changes in the way Piagetian concepts were investigated – changes in context – produced apparently dramatic changes in the cognitive competence preschoolers display. Uri Brofenbrenner's classic monograph, *The Ecology of Human Development*, appeared the following year, providing a workable heuristic for contextually oriented developmental psychologists. Up to that time, the research group associated with LCHC had concentrated its efforts in the area of cross-cultural research, arguing for what we called a "cultural-contexts" approach to development. As Gelman noted, our demonstrations of a critical role of experimental procedures in children's expression of cognitive competence had

1

implications for cross-age, within-society research. New approaches to research and theorizing about human development were called for. Answering that call seemed no easy matter.

Especially important to work presented in this volume was the appearance, in 1978, of Vygotsky's *Mind in Society*. Although not explicitly contextualist in its world view, *Mind in Society* provided a way to link American ideas about context and the heterogeneity of mind across settings with Russian ideas about the historical nature and social origins of higher psychological function and a deep appreciation for the centrality of cultural mediation in the constitution of human psychological processes. At present, as a result of intense interaction among psychologists, anthropologists, linguists, sociologists, and mixes of scholars from other disciplines, new "interdisciplines" are popping up and in some cases becoming institutionalized. Cognitive Science and Communication are two such hybrids. Cultural Psychology is a third.

Although the idea of Cultural Psychology is older than the discipline of Psychology itself (Cole, 1990), the idea reemerged in the late 1970s as one expression of context as a central constituent of human mind. Douglas Price-Williams, who gained prominence for his cross-cultural research, defined Cultural Psychology as "that branch of inquiry that delves into the contextual behavior of psychological processes" (Price-Williams, Gordon, and Ramirez, 1979, p. 14). Suggestions were made by a number of psychologists, some emphasizing the intimate relation between context and meaning, others the equally intimate relations between context and emotion, and all concerned with the study of development. (See Bruner, 1990; Shweder, 1990; and Valsiner, 1995, for summaries.)

Whatever one's entry point into the study of culture and development, a commitment to a unit of analysis that includes individuals and their sociocultural milieu immediately entails a series of major methodological problems to anyone who would seek to embody the resulting theoretical notions in empirical practice. To begin with, such an enterprise cannot proceed entirely on the basis of experimental methods, nor can it draw theoretically only on psychology. It must be multimethod and interdisciplinary.

Interdisciplinarity is a fashionable buzzword that evokes warm feelings in right-thinking scholars, but it is a whole lot easier said than done.

Disciplines are paradigms, ways of seeing and interpreting the world. To mix disciplines is to ensure that the way data are collected and interpreted is certain to offend as many members of a research group as there are disciplines represented. What an interdiscipline such as Cultural Psychology calls for is its own methodology, its own "disciplined" way of linking theory and evidence.

Despite their diversity, the authors of the articles contained in this volume are distinguished by the ways in which their work combines insights from the cultural historical psychological tradition of Vygotsky, Luria, and Leont'ev, the American Pragmatist tradition as exemplified by scholars such as Dewey and Mead, and the work of sociocultural anthropologists and sociologists. The resulting discussion, therefore, is a blend of American cultural anthropological approaches and Russian historical approaches infused with ideas from other disciplines and other national traditions including a number of participants from European countries and Japan.

Evidence for the contemporary relevance of these articles comes from examining the questions that arise when we juxtapose the ideas of James Wertsch, Jean Lave, Barbara Rogoff, and A. N. Leont'ev, all of whom are important to the development of Cultural Psychology.

Jim Wertsch and his colleagues carry forward the tradition of Vygotsky by starting with the idea of mediation of behavior through signs and other cultural artifacts. This starting point is enhanced and enriched with Bakhtin's notions of social language, speech genre, and voice (Wertsch, 1991, 1994, 1995; Wertsch, del Rio, and Alvarez, 1995). Wertsch and his colleagues choose mediated action as the proper unit of psychological analysis. Starting in this manner requires them to find a way to go beyond mediated action to specify the "something" ("the context") with respect to which that mediated action becomes meaningful. Wertsch (1995, pp. 71–72) turns to Burke's (1962) pentad of literary analysis (act, scene, agent, agency, and purpose).

Another important example of cultural–contextual theorizing is the situated learning (or legitimate peripheral participation) approach promoted by Jean Lave and her colleagues (Lave, 1988; Lave and Wenger, 1991). The central concepts and unit of analysis in this line of inquiry are practice, community of practice, and participation. While acknowledging the importance of mediational means, this unit is decidedly broader than individual action. Moreover, practical object-oriented work is investigated on a par with interaction and sign-mediated communication.

Barbara Rogoff's current thinking complements the perspectives of Wertsch and Lave. For Rogoff, development is participation in sociocultural activity. Activities are made up of the active and dynamic contributions of individuals, their social partners, historical traditions and materials, and their (mutual) transformations. Any activity, according to Rogoff, must include the analysis of three forms of change: Change in the child's participation (personal plane), changes in the relationships between participants (interpersonal plane), and historical changes in technologies and institutions (community plane). Even a cursory consideration of Rogoff's ideas makes clear the methodological challenge of her position, and by implication, all of the varieties of cultural–contextual approaches of which hers is one prominent variant. Experimental psychology, discourse analysis, ethnography, and microsociology (to name a few) are all involved.

A fourth direction in recent cultural–psychological research represented in this volume is the theory of activity, initiated by Leont'ev (1978, 1981). Activity is here seen as a collective, systemic formation that has a complex mediational structure. Activities are not short-lived events or actions that have a temporally clear-cut beginning and end. They are systems that produce events and actions and evolve over lengthy periods of sociohistorical time. The subject and the object are mediated by artifacts, including symbols and representations of various kinds. The activity system incessantly reconstructs itself through actions and discourse. As a consequence, activity theory calls for historical analysis of the collective activity system, a point also made by Rogoff.

Recent work in activity theory (Engeström, 1987) emphasizes that activity systems contain a variety of different viewpoints or "voices," as well as layers of historically accumulated artifacts, rules, and patterns of division of labor. This multivoiced and multilayered nature of activity systems is both a resource for collective achievement and a source of compartmentalization and conflict. Contradictions are the engine of change and development in an activity system as well as a source of conflict and stress.

Although each of these perspectives extends the new understanding of culture, context, and cognitive development that began to emerge in the late 1970s, each of them also poses acute questions of how to convert methodological and theoretical programs into doable projects. For example, while a variety of scholars such as Wertsch are drawing upon Burke and his use of the dramatic metaphor, there is as yet no generally agreed upon way to embody Burke's ideas in a way that cognitive psychologists would find acceptable as a source of empirical data.

Psychologists who wish to build upon Lave's work face similar methodological problems. The theory of legitimate peripheral participation investigates learning and development primarily as movement from the periphery occupied by novices to the center inhabited by experienced masters of the given practice. But it is position in the group, not properties of individuals qua individuals, that are of concern. Are psychologists to give up on the analysis of individuals altogether and abandon psychology's traditional mission? On the other hand, if researchers want to attribute aspects of action to individuals as well as supra-individual units, how can they do so given the intimate dialectical constitution of action which situated action theorists take as primary? How does one mix historical analysis with experimental analysis or discourse analysis? What role does experimentation play in the tool kit of methods? What role should ethnography or discourse analysis play when experiments are also used?

These and many allied questions are taken up in the articles presented below. While there are no definitive answers to the many questions entailed by allegiance to a cultural psychology, there is a good deal of accumulated experience, detailed maps of blind alleys, and perhaps some wisdom that can be appropriated to deal with the tasks at hand.

The problem of context

Since the *Quarterly Newsletter of the Laboratory of Comparative Human Cognition* began with the question of context, it is fitting to start this collection of articles by addressing this seminal concept.

The work by members of the research group that evolved into LCHC began with cross-cultural research on cognitive development in Liberia. The basic impulse in that research was to take the doings of people in their everyday lives (of which tests and schools are one class of doings) as the starting point of psychological analysis. "Context" functioned as an omnibus category that allowed the analyst to point to factors outside of the psychological task itself as contributors to performance. In the logic of that early work, context could be considered a "stimulus variable," a "proximal cultural medium," that could be related to performance as dependent variable. Over time, however, it became clear that it is inadequate to conceive of context merely as a preset environment that influences behavior. The two articles included in the section on context both represent clear and persuasive arguments for thinking about context in more complicated ways than we did in the late 1970s, as many psychologists are wont to do today. Fred Erickson and Jeff Schultz articulate the idea that contexts are not given, they are mutually constituted, constantly shifting, situation definitions that are accomplished through the interactional work of the participants. Erickson and Schultz begin by reviewing relevant research from sociolinguistics. They then present a five-stage strategy for the study of context through an analysis of the changing organization of face-to-face interaction using videotapes of strips of interaction as their basic source of data.

Charles Frake (1977) discusses contexts as cultural frames of interpretation. He modifies the idea of culture as a script for the production of social occasions, recasting cultural scripts as sets of principles for constructing (perhaps co-constructing is a better term) social events. He emphasizes the crucial point that culture is more than a fixed set of interpretive frames that people acquire; rather, it is a set of resources for creating culture and cognition. Frake's formulation provides one promising starting point for those seeking to use the dramatic metaphor as a heuristic for working out a contextual, activity-based psychology.

Experiments as contexts

Given the starting point of LCHC in the experimental study of culture, mind, and development, it should come as no surprise that a great many of the articles published during its early years addressed the problematic nature of experiments as instruments for reaching conclusions about culture and cognitive development.

One of the few concepts used by psychologists to address the issue of experiments as contexts is the idea of ecological validity, normally thought of as the extent to which the conclusions drawn from experimental and test methods are applicable outside of the procedure itself and the extent to which they are representative of psychological functioning in everyday life. The article by Cole and his colleagues (1978) traces out some of the history of discussion of ecological validity, pointing out that despite rhetorical gestures toward satisfying this criterion in cognitive research, the problem is more difficult than psychologists have ordinarily thought.

The difficulties of using experimental studies as if they were context-free indices of cognitive processing are the topic of Jean Lave's (1980) article. Lave's concern is to undo the asymmetrical analytic power accorded to experiments as revealed by the question, "Does this experimental result generalize to everyday life?" In its place she proposes a more symmetrical question: "Is there any hope we may learn from contrasting performances in contrasting situations?" She gives an affirmative answer to this question, drawing upon the first results of the work she and her colleagues conducted on arithmetic practices in supermarkets and weight watcher clubs (see Lave, 1988; or Lave and Wenger, 1991, for accounts of the later evolution of these ideas).

A major concern of researchers at LCHC has been to bring critical analyses to bear on claims of ethnic or racial cognitive inferiority based upon performances in cognitive psychological tasks. A. F. Franklin's (1978) study of word recall memory is representative of one genre of critical methods. Franklin notes the use by Arthur Jensen of category clustering in free recall to make claims that African-Americans are deficient in higher-level, transformative remembering. Franklin draws upon extant research to argue that the African-American students are placed at a disadvantage because of their relative lack of familiarity with the categorical structure of word lists created on the basis of Anglo norms. He demonstrates how manipulation of list contents can reverse the direction of deficits, taking the deficit out of his subjects' heads and placing it in differences in everyday language which previous researchers had ignored.

Despite the difficulties, not only members of LCHC but many developmental researchers began to create methods for the study of cognitive development in a variety of settings. Judy DeLoache and Ann Brown's (1979) study of young children's ability to remember the location of objects using a delayed response will come as no surprise to anyone who has been a parent, but it came as a distinct surprise to psychologists who had been drawing conclusions for years about preschoolers' deficient memories. In subsequent years, research such as this has led to a radical reevaluation of early cognitive development in which the crucial role of context in performance is widely recognized (see Cole and Cole, 1993, Chapter 9, for a recent summary).

Sayeki (1981) argues persuasively that the human body provides a rich source of intellectual resources that can be brought to bear for the solutions of intellectual problems. His emphasis on an embodied point of view as a fundamental aspect of thinking and ways in which it can be harnessed to aid problem solving is an important early contribution to the current discussion on the situated nature of culturally mediated thought processes.

The article entitled "Paradigms and Prejudice" authored by a group at LCHC (1983) takes up another aspect of the way that research on ethnic group differences is practiced in the United States. The provocation for writing this article was a request for assistance from an African-American colleague. Her grant application for studying a feature of language acquisition was rejected when two reviewers argued that such research should first be conducted on middle-class Anglo children to establish the appropriate normal profile against which data from African-American children could be analyzed. Unfortunately, the difficulties to which this article is addressed remain relevant to the present day.

Exploring cultural historical theories

At the time that LCHC came into being in the early 1970s, the focus of its efforts was largely methodological. Insofar as a theoretical position could be said to characterize the work, that theory was derived largely from American psychological, sociological, and anthropological sources. The first article representing Russian ideas was by L. A. Abramyan (1977), a student of Luria's. Its point was interpreted in the context of questions about developing experimental methods.

In the late 1970s, as noted earlier, there were marked changes. The articles in this section provide a snapshot account of several different lines of theory that take cultural mediation and the historically contingent nature of human thought as their starting points. Norris Minick

(1986) traces changes in the ideas of Vygotsky and his colleagues in the late 1920s and 1930s. According to Minick, it is possible to see a shift from a focus on social interaction as the locus of mind to a concern for including the sociocultural context, or activity, of which the interaction is a part as an essential constituent of mind.

Erik Axel's (1992) narrative picks up, so to speak, where Minick's ends. He traces the development of the activity theory proposed by Vygotsky's student and colleague, A. N. Leont'ev. Axel also considers the way in which various features of Leont'ev's approach can be improved upon by taking into account the Critical Psychology tradition that came to prominence in Germany and other European countries in the 1970s.

David Bakhurst (1988) explores the ideas of another, less well known, contributor to the cultural–historical, activity-centered approaches that flowered in the 1960s and 1970s, the Soviet philosopher Evald Ilyenkov. Bakhurst presents Ilyenkov's ideas as an important resource for making the transition from Cartesian theories of mind to a nondualistic, cultural-mediational, communitarian theory. It is sometimes thought by American social scientists that commitment to cultural–historical approaches derives exclusively from the work of Russian scholars. In fact, however, the key notion of cultural historical approaches that human beings engage in a species-specific form of mediated action through the appropriation of the resources bequeathed by prior generations has adherents in many countries.

Ernest Boesch, whose (1993) work draws upon Piagetian ideas, presents a vivid account of cultural–historical thinking in his discussion of the kinds of evidence that one must bring together in a fully realized cultural mediational approach to culture and cognition. The material and the ideal, the historical and the contemporary, the individual and the social, are all simultaneously present in his finely wrought thought experiment.

Alfred Lang's (1993) major inspirations for developing a cultural mediational theory of cognition are derived largely from German and American sources, not Russian ones. It is elaboration and wedding of ideas from Kurt Lewin and C. S. Peirce that motivates his discussion of how to develop a non-Cartesian, ecological approach to thinking about culture and mind.

Historical analysis

A basic tenet of cultural–historical approaches to cognition is that mental functioning in the present emerges from the interplay of different developmental domains including cultural history, ontogeny, and microgenesis. Actual historical analysis or the use of historical materials as an object of study has been rare among scholars interested in culture, context, and development. The papers in this section represent two quite different attempts to carry cognitive psychological analysis beyond the study of individual ontogeny to make history a usable resource for psychologists.

Ageliki Nicolopoulou (1989) draws upon the work of the German psychologist Peter Damerow and his colleagues, who analyzed a large corpus of texts taken from the ancient Middle Eastern city of Uruk in what is currently called Iraq. A major goal of Damerow's work has been to see if it is possible to determine when and if the material representation of cognitive structure influences the process of cognitive development. Nicolopoulou concludes that the availability of new media for representing number may enter directly into the process of epigenesis by promoting the crystallization of arithmetic operations in a form that opens up new developmental horizons.

James Wertsch's (1987) contribution addresses the issue of collective memory as it is conceived within the theoretical tradition of Vygotsky and Leont'ev. Wertsch believes that while Vygotsky's analysis was strong in illuminating the dynamics of higher psychological function in dyads, it needs to be supplemented by approaches that link to the activity settings in which people function if it is to become a comprehensive theory of mind in society. Wertsch suggests that one way to deal concretely with questions of the cultural–historical conditioning of mental processes is to focus on the mediational means involved, which carry with them histories of which they were a part. As he puts it, what is available in particular people's tool kits depends in a central way on their sociohistorical and cultural situation.

Focusing on language as a tool, Wertsch examines the writings of sociologists such as Robert Bellah and his colleagues, pointing out how certain language genres are privileged over others, entering into the creation of communities of memory where constitutive narratives are central into the creation of both one's social world and the ability to communicate and think within it. Many of these ideas can be found playing themselves out in the recent volume published by Wertsch and his colleagues, *Sociocultural Studies of Mind* (1995).

Classroom settings

By far the largest corpus of research on the nexus of issues indicated by the notions of context, culture, activity, and cognitive development has been conducted in educational settings. Given the importance of cultural–historical theories in the development of this research enterprise, the heavy emphasis on educational settings in the LCHC *Newsletter* is no surprise, but it presents the editors with difficult problems of selection because there is so much from which to select. We begin this section with a contribution by Hugh Mehan (1976), whose work on the social organization of classroom interactions had brought him into contact with psychologists interested in bridging between experimental studies of individuals and the naturally occurring interactions that constitute knowledge acquisition in naturally occurring classroom interactions. Mehan's contribution looks at what can be learned (by both analysts and children) when whole-group lessons are broken up and replaced by small-group working sessions, each headed by one of the students. Mehan's analysis suggests that researchers can learn about useful pedagogical practices from seeing how adult-led lessons are transformed (not necessarily for the worse) when they are carried out as small-group, child-led lessons.

Ron Gallimore and Kathy Au (1979) also concern themselves with displays of competence in elementary school classrooms. In their case, the focus is on ethnic Hawaiian children who have long been reported to experience difficulty in early reading instruction and in other basic academic settings, although ethnographic reports of their behavior at home suggests that they are perfectly competent in ways not in evidence in the classroom. Their chapter provides a concise report of the KEEP reading program, which takes advantage of the ethnographic evidence to help reorganize classroom discourse on a more effective basis.

The simultaneous existence of competent and incompetent intellectual performances is also the focus of work by Luis Moll and his colleagues (1980). Their work with bilingual Latino children who were instructed in both Spanish and English at different times in the school-day led to two important findings:

1. A reductionist theory of reading produces bilingual student failure in English-only instructional environments and
2. Student failure is supported in a number of subtle ways by institutional arrangements.

Hatano and his colleagues investigated the important problem of the way that language is represented in the writing system. These authors made it clear that the current Japanese writing systems each have some definite advantages over Latin orthography with respect to certain cognitive tasks. The entire issue of "kinds of literacy" associated with different technologies, different language systems, and different social systems is a topic that needs far greater attention in a world that believes there are important social and mental differences associated with different kinds of literacy. It also helps to counteract oversimplified theories that place the alphabet at the apex of a developmental pyramid of written language power.

Further opportunities arose for researchers to study mediated learning and development when microcomputers began to come into the lives of children, teachers, and researchers in the early 1980s. This line of work is represented here by Denis Newman (1985), who, along with Jim Levin and Margaret Riel, spearheaded the application of cultural–historical, contextual approaches to the use of microcomputers in classroom settings. Especially noteworthy in this work is emphasis of the potential to reorganize classroom interactions where computers are used as communication media.

When researchers move out of the experimental setting and into the classroom they lose power over the contexts of observation in many ways. At the same time, they raise issues of power for the teachers whose classrooms they visit. Marilyn Quinsaat (1980) reports on this process from the perspective of a teacher whose classroom has been made the site of cognitive psychologists interested in the contexts of learning and development. Through her concern to represent the interests of the children while respecting those of the researchers, Quinsaat reveals a number of important contrasts between classroom and tests as sites of cognitive analysis. Any psychologist interested in the possibility of seeing her work contribute to classroom practices would do well to consider carefully the lessons of Quinsaat's experience. (See Newman, Griffin, and Cole, 1989, for the larger context of this article.)

The final chapter in this section, by Courtney Cazden (1981), is an early elaboration of the implications of the idea of zone of proximal development, proposed by Vygotsky, for the analysis of child–adult discourse and the role of the social interaction in the process of cognitive and linguistic development. Her linking of the idea of zone of proximal development to overcome the shortcomings of theories which demand competence before performance has lost none of its relevance in the years since it was published.

Cognition in the wild

The authors of *Newsletter* articles have increasingly moved into studies of cognition and mediated action outside of classrooms and laboratories. Their interests in everyday practical activity as a source of empirical data has led them to homes, streets, and workplaces. This trend reflects the increasing confidence in a new generation of scholars motivated by more than the need to test the generalizability of findings obtained in constrained settings. Above all, the move was born of increasing opportunities to explore human mental functioning and development in the full richness of its social and artifactual texture. As Clifford Geertz (1973, p. 83) pointed out, "man's mental processes indeed take place at the scholar's desk or the football field, in the studio or lorry-driver's seat, on the platform, the chessboard, or the judge's bench."

An early example of this move was a study conducted by Anderson, Teale, and Estrada (1980) of low-income children's preschool literacy experiences at home. The authors used natural observations, self-report diaries, and controlled behavior samplings to analyze events in which the children were involved with production and/or comprehension of print. This early study is the direct ancestor of later work on "emergent literacy" (Teale and Sulzby, 1986). It also inspired research on home and community literacy resources carried out by Moll (1992) and Vasquez (1993) among others.

Another pathway into the realm of cognition in the wild is represented by Geoff Saxe's (1989) study of Brazilian children who sell candy in the streets. Saxe used ethnographic observation of candy selling, interviews involving mathematical tasks, and comparison between sellers' and non-sellers' mathematical understanding. He found that goals of mathematical problem solving emerged in bargaining and negotiating between sellers and buyers. Children's construction of new understandings and solution strategies was interwoven with their participation in the social practices (see also Saxe, 1994; and Nunez, Schliemann, and Carraher, 1993).

Cognitive anthropological approaches inspired Ed Hutchins's work on mediation and automatization (1986) outside of "White room" conditions, exemplifying the challenge posed by the notion of cognition in the wild. They examine the ways humans use and internalize external checklists in skilled actions. They conclude that what we know and what the culture knows for us are "hunks of mediating structure." For Hutchins, thinking consists of bringing these structures, both external and internal, into coordination with each other. This line of work reached its fruition in Hutchins's recent book (1995).

Sylvia Scribner's (1983, 1992) studies on work activities in a milk-processing plant opened up the world of industrial work to students of cognitive development. Again, a combination of methods was used: extensive ethnographic observation, modeling and simulation of key tasks in experimental sessions, and comparisons between experienced workers and novice outsiders. Scribner found qualitative differences and developmental shifts in the workers' construction and use of mediating symbol systems and solution strategies in their daily tasks. Work was recognized as playing a formative and educative role in the lives of the workers.

Engeström and his colleagues (1991) approached work from another angle, focusing on the developmental significance of disturbances in activity. The authors studied legal work in complex trials, using observations, interviews, and analysis of discourse recorded in the sidebar conferences devoted to the collaborative handling of disturbances. They identified expansive transitions, qualitative shifts in the mode of interaction, as responses to disturbances. The findings were interpreted against a framework of historical change and emergence of a collective zone of proximal development for work in courts.

Power and discourse

Increasingly over time, as issues of polyphony, multivoicedness, conflict, and contestation began appearing in the pages of the *Newsletter*, American researchers in a number of disciplines were problematizing gender, race, and other forms of "otherness" in identity politics and theorizing. Three examples of articles treating these topics are included in this section. In them we can see threads that are very familiar in the current tapestry of ideas that are associated with current postmodern theorizing on multiplicity of voices, the multiply constituted subject, the social and historical construction of ethnicity and its role in the distribution of power, and so on.

Michael Holquist's (1983) paper on the politics of representation marked the advent of Mikhail Bakhtin's dialogism in the *Newsletter*. Holquist's paper, which appeared concurrently with Emerson's paper on Bakhtin and Vygotsky (1983) contrasts dialogism with personalism and constructionism. Dialogism holds that meaning is made as a product of polyphonic collaboration. One can appropriate meaning for one's purposes only by ventriloquating others. Moreover, each utterance is unavoidably a contest, a struggle.

Ray McDermott (1985) analyzes the ethnographic dramas of John Millington Synge. Drawing on Bakhtin's notion of voice, McDermott examines how Synge's plays reconstructed the tension between the core and the periphery of Irish society. McDermott observed that people locked away from core culture may, by virtue of their marginalization, also have something powerful to say about that very core.

Carol Padden and Harry Markowicz (1982) took the issue of struggle to a concrete level, examining conflicts between hearing and deaf cultures in America. The authors trace the experiences of a group of young deaf adults who entered Gallaudet College, a college for deaf students, without having socialized with other deaf people before that. None of the subjects were prepared to find a minority with its own culture and its own language.

Esther Goody (1987) directs the analysis of power and morality to a macrolevel analysis of the relations between men and women. Goody examines South American Indian origin myths, the initiation rites of Australian aborigines, and African witchcraft. She identifies in each an ideology of legitimate power based on the premise that women are originally or fundamentally antisocial or evil. She finds the same thread woven into Judeo-Christian traditions. Ideological support for containing and controlling the essentially errant woman manifests itself dramatically in the widespread practices of domestic violence.

Goody delves into behavioral psychological theory for components of a general model of domination that might explain the reward/punishment system that helps maintain some women's complicity with systems of their own oppression. There is, she writes, a sense of guilt and lack of confidence in many women that arises from conflicting messages about women's worth in cultural and family norms. This factor is linked to a second source of the experience of female inferiority: built-in contradictions in the nature of roles which women face as they define goals. A third grim factor in this equation is this: women know from experience and observation in their daily lives that in most instances of violent or potentially violent conflict with men, "might is right" in the moment of face-to-face interaction. Most women will act (or act passively) to avoid being hurt. These sources of beliefs about women's inferiority produce and reproduce inequality in social interaction and on an institutional level for most women at some point in their lives.

Finally Bonnie Litowitz (1990) redirects the focus to Vygotsky's concept of the zone of proximal development and its problematic interpretations and implications. She points out that the scenario of sociocultural learning is typically based on adultocentric assumptions. These assumptions lead to an image of perfectly orchestrated dyads for smooth acquisition of adult wisdom. Resistance, conflict, and creation by the child are all but excluded from such an image.

Each of these authors points out in their own way, using different literatures and units/levels of analysis dynamic relations between and within identity-formation processes that disrupt the ascription of dichotomous categorical terms (core/periphery, insider/outsider, powerful/powerless).

The *Newsletter* as context

Over the decade and a half of its existence, the *Newsletter* itself constituted a context within which the interdisciplinary discussions needed to develop deeper insight into questions of context, cognition, and culture could be explored. Thanks to generous support from

Rockefeller University, the University of California at San Diego, and several foundations (and, of course, the willing collaborations of hundreds of scholars), an unusual forum was created within which psychologists, anthropologists, linguists, sociologists, literary theorists, and representatives of many other disciplines could test out their ideas. By designating the publication a *newsletter*, and not a journal, we sought to create an intermediate space where ideas still in the process of formulation could be tried out and already worked out ideas that had appeared in sources unlikely to come to the attention of specific disciplines could be introduced. As the selections in the current volume amply testify, it would be difficult to think of another forum containing such a concentration of important openings, paradigmatic statements, and bold empirical instantiations of cultural–historical mediational theories of mind than in the sixteen volumes of the *Quarterly Newsletter of the Laboratory of Comparative Human Cognition*. By bringing many of the most stimulating articles together in this volume, we hope to provide the reader with a synoptic view of the origins, early formative studies, and intertwined developmental paths that constitute current explorations of the cultural nature of human psychological processes.

The current historical context of the discourse summarized in this volume is, of course, markedly different from that in which the *Newsletter* arose. When we began, the ideas of the Russian cultural–historical school were barely on psychology's radar screen, and issues of method between anthropological/sociological and psychological approaches to cognition were the focus of attention. Now the ideas of the Russian school are broadly respected and institutionally recognized and genuine new hybrid forms of inquiry are proving feasible and useful. The disappearance of the USSR, the advent of a wired-up, in-your-face world, and many dislocations that are ensuing has provided those interested in cultural theories of human nature unparalleled opportunities for interaction even as they recoil at the social problems that are the object of their concern.

References

Abramyan, L. A. (1977). On the role of verbal instructions in the direction of voluntary movements in children. *The Quarterly Newsletter of the Laboratory of Comparative Human Cognition, 1*, 1–7.

Anderson, A. B., Teale, W. H., and Estrada, E. (1980). Low-income children's preschool literacy experiences: Some naturalistic observations. *The Quarterly Newsletter of the Laboratory of Comparative Human Cognition, 2,* 59–65.

Axel, E. (1992). One developmental line in European activity theories. *The Quarterly Newsletter of the Laboratory of Comparative Human Cognition, 14* (1), 8–17.

Bakhurst, D. (1988). Activity, consciousness and communication. *The Quarterly Newsletter of the Laboratory of Comparative Human Cognition, 10* (2), 70–76.

Boesch, E. (1993). The sound of the violin. *The Quarterly Newsletter of the Laboratory of Comparative Human Cognition, 15* (1), 6–15.

Brofenbrenner, U. (1979). *Ecology of human development.* Cambridge: Harvard University Press.

Bruner, J. (1990). *Acts of meaning.* Cambridge: Harvard University Press.

Burke, K. (1962). *The grammar of motives and a rhetoric of motives.* Cleveland: World Publishing Co.

Cazden, C. (1981). Performance before competence: Assistance to child discourse in the zone of proximal development. *The Quarterly Newsletter of the Laboratory of Comparative Human Cognition, 3,* 5–8.

Cole, M. (1990). Cultural Psychology: A once and future discipline? In J. J. Berman (Ed.), *Nebraska Symposium on Motivation, 1989: Cross-cultural perspectives, vol. 37,* 279–336. Lincoln: University of Nebraska Press.

Cole, M., and Cole, S. (1993). *Development of children* (2nd ed.). New York: Scientific American.

Cole, M., Gay, J., Glick, J., and Sharp, D. W. (1971). *The cultural contexts of learning and thinking.* New York: Basic Books.

Cole, M., Hood, L., and McDermott, R. (1978). Concepts of Ecological Validity: Their differing implications for comparative cognitive research. *The Quarterly Newsletter of the Laboratory of Comparative Human Cognition, 2* (2), 34–37.

DeLoache, J., and Brown, A. (1979). Looking for Big Bird: Studies of memory in very young children. *The Quarterly Newsletter of the Laboratory of Comparative Human Cognition, 1* (4), 53–57.

Emerson, C. (1983). Bakhtin and Vygotsky on internalization of language. *The Quarterly Newsletter of the Laboratory of Comparative Human Cognition, 5* (1), 9–13.

Engeström, Y. (1987). *Learning by expanding: An activity-theoretical approach to developmental research.* Helsinki: Orienta-Konsultit.

Engeström, Y., Brown, K., Christopher, L. C., and Gregory, J. (1991). Coordination, cooperation and communication in the court: Expansive transitions in legal work. *The Quarterly Newsletter of the Laboratory of Comparative Human Cognition, 13* (4), 88–96.

Erickson, F., and Schultz, J. (1977). When is a context? Some issues and methods in the analysis of social competence. *The Quarterly Newsletter of the Laboratory of Comparative Human Cognition, 1* (2), 5–10.

Frake, C. O. (1977). Plying frames can be dangerous: Some reflections on methodology in cognitive anthropology. *The Quarterly Newsletter of the Laboratory of Comparative Human Cognition, 1* (3), 1–7.

Franklin, A. F. (1978). Sociolinguistic structure of word lists and ethnicgroup differences in categorized recall. *The Quarterly Newsletter of the Laboratory of
Comparative Human Cognition*, 2 (2), 30–34.

Gallimore, R., Au, K. Hu-Pei. (1979). The competence/incompetence paradox in
the education of minority culture children. *The Quarterly Newsletter of the
Laboratory of Comparative Human Cognition*, 1 (3), 32–37.

Geertz, C. (1973). *The interpretation of cultures. Selected essays.* New York: Basic
Books.

Gelman, R. (1978). Cognitive development. *Annual Review of Psychology*, 29, 297–
332.

Goody, E. (1987). Why must might be right? Observations on sexual herrschaft. *The
Quarterly Newsletter of the Laboratory of Comparative Human Cognition*, 9 (2),
55–76.

Hatano, G., and Inagake, K. (1987). Everyday biology and school biology: How do they
interact? *The Quarterly Newsletter of the Laboratory of Comparative Human
Cognition*, 9 (4), 120–128.

Hatano, G., Kuhara, K., and Akiyama, M. (1981). *Kanji* help readers of Japanese infer
the meaning of unfamiliar words. *The Quarterly Newsletter of the Laboratory
of Comparative Human Cognition*, 3 (2), 30–33.

Holquist, M. (1983). The politics of representation. *The Quarterly Newsletter of the
Laboratory of Comparative Human Cognition*, 5 (1), 2–9.

Hutchins, E. (1986). Mediation and automatization. *The Quarterly Newsletter of the
Laboratory of Comparative Human Cognition*, 8 (2), 47–58.

Hutchins, E. (1995). *Cognition in the wild.* Cambridge: MIT Press.

Lang, A. (1993). Non-Cartesian artefacts in dwelling activities: Steps towards a semiotic
ecology. *The Quarterly Newsletter of the Laboratory of Comparative Human
Cognition*, 15 (3), 87–96.

Lave, J. (1980). What's special about experiments as contexts for thinking. *The Quarterly
Newsletter of the Laboratory of Comparative Human Cognition*, 2 (4), 86–91.

Lave, J. (1988). *Cognition in practice. Mind, mathematics and culture in everyday Life.*
Cambridge: Cambridge University Press.

Lave, J., and Wenger, E. (1991). *Situated learning: Legitimate peripheral participation.*
Cambridge: Cambridge University Press.

LCHC. (1983). Paradigms and prejudice. *The Quarterly Newsletter of the Laboratory of
Comparative Human Cognition*, 5 (4), 87–92.

Leont'ev, A. N. (1978). *Activity, consciousness, and personality.* Englewood Cliffs:
Prentice-Hall.

Leont'ev, A. N. (1981). *Problems of the development of the mind.* Moscow: Progress.

Litowitz, B. (1990). Just say no: Responsibility and resistance. *The Quarterly Newsletter
of the Laboratory of Comparative Human Cognition*, 12 (4), 135–141.

Lucariello, J. (1995). Human development, mind, culture, person. Elements in a Cultural
Psychology. Commentary. *Human Development*, 38 (1), 2–18.

Mehan, H. (1976). Students' interactional competence in the classroom. *The Quarterly
Newsletter of the Laboratory of Comparative Human Cognition*, 1 (1), 7–10.

Minick, N. (1986). The early history of the Vygotskian school: The relationship between mind and activity. *The Quarterly Newsletter of the Laboratory of Comparative Human Cognition, 8* (4), 119–125.

Moll, L. C. (1992). Bilingual classroom studies and community analysis: Some recent trends. *Educational Researcher, 21* (3), 20–24.

Moll, L., Estrada, E., Diaz, E., and Lopes, L. M. (1980). The organization of bilingual lessons: Implications for schooling. *The Quarterly Newsletter of the Laboratory of Comparative Human Cognition, 2* (3), 53–58.

Newman, D. (1985). Functional environments for microcomputers in education. *The Quarterly Newsletter of the Laboratory of Comparative Human Cognition, 7* (2), 52–57.

Newman, D., Griffin, P., and Cole, M. (1989). *The construction zone: Working for cognitive change in school.* New York: Cambridge University Press.

Nicolopoulou, A. (1989). The invention of writing and the development of numerical concepts in Sumeria: Some implications for developmental psychology. *The Quarterly Newsletter of the Laboratory of Comparative Human Cognition, 11* (4), 114–124.

Nunez, T., Schliemann, A. D., and Carraher, D. W. (1993). *Street mathemetics and school mathematics.* New York: Cambridge University Press.

Padden, C., and Markowicz, H., (1982). Learning to be deaf: Conflicts between hearing and deaf cultures. *The Quarterly Newsletter of the Laboratory of Comparative Human Cognition, 4* (4), 67–71.

Price-Williams, D., Gordon, D., and Ramirez, W. (1979) Skill and conversation: A study of pottery making in children. *Developmental Psychology, 1,* 769.

Quinsaat, M. G. (1980). "But it's important data!" Making the demands of a cognitive experiment meet the educational imperatives of the classroom. *The Quarterly Newsletter of the Laboratory of Comparative Human Cognition, 2* (3), 70–74.

Saxe, G. B. (1989). Selling candy: A study of cognition in context. *The Quarterly Newsletter of the Laboratory of Comparative Human Cognition, 11* (1 & 2), 19–22.

Saxe, G. B. (1994). Studying cognitive development in sociocultural context: The development of a practice-based approach. *Mind, Culture, and Activity, 1* (3), 135–157.

Sayeki, Y. (1981). "Body analogy" and the cognition of rotated figures. *The Quarterly Newsletter of the Laboratory of Comparative Human Cognition, 3* (2), 36–40.

Scribner, S. (April 1983). *Mind in action: A functional approach to thinking.* Invited address at the Biennial Meeting of the Society for Research in Child Development, Detroit, MI.

Scribner, S. (1992). Mind in action: A functional approach to thinking. *The Quarterly Newsletter of the Laboratory of Comparative Human Cognition, 14* (4), 103–110.

Shweder, R. A. (1990). Cultural Psychology – what is it? In J. W. Stigler, R. A. Shweder, and G. Herdt (Eds.), *Cultural Psychology: The Chicago Symposium on Culture and Human Development.* Cambridge: Cambridge University Press.

Teale, W. H., and Sulzby, E. (1986). *Emergent literacy*. Norwood, NJ: Ablex Publishing Corp.

Valsiner, J. (1995). Irreversibility of time and the construction of historical developmental psychology. *The Quarterly Newsletter of the Laboratory of Comparative Human Cognition, 1* (1 & 2), 25–42.

Vásquez, O. A. (1993). A look at language as resource: Lessons from La Clase Mágica. In B. Arias and U. Casanova (Eds.), *Bilingual education: Politics, research, and practice*, pp. 119–224. Chicago: National Society for the Study of Education.

Vygotsky, L. S. (1978). *Mind in society*. Cambridge: Harvard University Press.

Wertsch, J. V. (1987). Collective memory: Issues from a sociohistorical perspective. *The Quarterly Newsletter of the Laboratory of Comparative Human Cognition, 9* (1), 19–22.

Wertsch, J. V. (1991). *Voices of the mind: A sociocultural approach to mediated action.* Cambridge: Harvard University Press.

Wertsch, J. V. (1994). The primacy of mediated action in sociocultural studies. *Mind, Culture, and Activity, 1* (4), 202–208.

Wertsch, J. V. (1995). The need for action in sociocultural research. In J. V. Wertsch, P. del Rio, and A. Alvarez (Eds.), *Sociocultural studies of mind*. Cambridge: Cambridge University Press.

Wertsch, J. V., del Rio, P., and Alvarez, A. (1995). Sociocultural studies: History, action, and mediation. In J. V. Wertsch, P. del Rio, and A. Alvarez (Eds.), *Sociocultural studies of mind*. Cambridge: Cambridge University Press.

2 When is a context? Some issues and methods in the analysis of social competence

Frederick Erickson and Jeffrey Schultz

In order to know whatever they need to know to operate in a manner acceptable to others in society, children and adults must know what forms of verbal and nonverbal behavior are appropriate in which social context. This requires knowing what context one is in and when contexts change. We think that the capacity for monitoring contexts must be an essential feature of social competence (Hymes, 1974). We will detail some theoretical and methodological issues in our ways of studying how people are able to decide *when* a context is, as well as *what* it is.

How do persons assess what context they are in? What features of context do they seem to be attending to? Contexts are not simply *given* in the physical setting (kitchen, living room, sidewalk in front of drug store) nor in combinations of personnel (two brothers, husband and wife, firemen). Rather, contexts are constituted by what people are doing and where and when they are doing it. As McDermott puts it succinctly (1976a), people in interaction become environments for each other. Ultimately, social contexts consist of mutually shared and ratified definitions of situation *and* in the social actions persons take on the basis of those definitions (Mehan et al., 1976).

These interactionally constituted environments can change from moment to moment. With each change, the role relationships among participants are redistributed to produce differing configurations of concerted action. Sociolinguists have been studying such configurations, called participant (or participation) structures by Philips (1972, 1974), and have shown them to be marked by ways of speaking, ways of

22

listening, ways of getting the floor and holding it, ways of leading and following. Differing participation structures may not only be juxtaposed back to back across time in getting from one social occasion to the next, e.g., from playing cards to riding the fire truck, but differing participation structures can also alternate within a single occasion, e.g., a card game may contain the primary constituent "slots": /getting ready/, /playing/, and /winding up/ (Mathiot, 1976; Pike, 1967; Goffman, 1974). Each slot can be expected to be marked by different distributions of speech events and speech functions.

Language-centered analysis here articulates with the postural-kinesics (body motion) research of Scheflen, whose pioneering "context analysis" of group psychotherapy interviews (1973, 1974) stands to date as the most comprehensive treatment of the sequential juxtaposition of differing participation structures within a single interactional occasion. Scheflen identified differences in interactional activity from one principal part of the therapy session to the next, and identified the major junctures between primary parts. He found, as did Kendon and Ferber (1973), McDermott (1976a, 1976b), Schultz (1976), and Bremme (1976), that during junctures between principal parts of occasions, major reorientations of postural configurations (positions) occur among participants, and that across the duration of a principal part, these positions are sustained collectively. We have reported a related finding for changes in interpersonal distance (proxemic shifts) between speakers (Erickson, 1976a).

Postural and proxemic configurations are instances of a general class of culturally conventional signals, termed contextualization cues by Gumperz (1976). These signal how messages are to be interpreted from moment to moment. Some cues usually apply as diacritical marks to behavioral slots of relatively short duration, such as words or phrases. Other cues, such as postural shifts, seem to mark the boundaries of slots that are longer in duration. At any rate, what one sees and hears at the junctures between principal slots is a redundancy of contextualization cues (Fitzgerald, 1975). The multimodal nature of communication produces great modality redundancy across the verbal and nonverbal channel (Cook-Gumperz and Gumperz, 1976). Many dimensions of difference in performance form, in addition to the postural and the proxemic, can have contrastive relevance as contextualization cues – changes in voice tone, pitch, and other features of speech prosody; changes in linguistic code, style, and topic; changes in the tempo and rhythmic organization of speech and body motion; changes in gaze direction and facial expression; changes in the number of speakers and listeners (cf. Hymes, 1974; Birdwhistell, 1970).

In addition to modality redundancy, participants can also rely on the sequential relationships among different behaviors to inform them of their context. It is only in sequential context that shifts in performance form, such as rate of speech, can have potential for contrastive relevance; a shift to "faster" speech is only a shift in terms of the rate of speech immediately prior to the faster rate. The combination of temporal and modality redundancy in contextualization cueing seems to function as an interactional fail-safe mechanism. It insures that, despite individual differences in interactional competence, whether due to difference in culture, personality, or level of acquisition of competence (cf. Cook-Gumperz and Corsaro, 1976), and despite differences in individual variation in focus of attention at any given moment, members of the interacting group are likely, both collectively and individually, to "get" the socially important message that something new is happening.

Despite the redundancy of cues, it usually is not possible to determine (in informal occasions in the United States, at least) an exact moment when the definition of situation has changed. It is only after the cues for a change in context have occurred that it is possible to determine that something has indeed changed. Thus, it would seem that it is by retrospective evaluation that persons determine that the context has changed. While the change is developing, persons may perceive that something new is happening and that a change in their behavior may be called for. They may infer expectations of what will happen next. Then subsequent events may help progressively to make the definition of situation unambiguous; their expectations will be progressively confirmed or disconfirmed (Mehan and Wood, 1975; Bremme, 1976). There are limits to the range of options for what can appropriately happen next. Once the selection is made and the context changes, what follows may be entailed in the selection itself.

Some evidence suggests that not only is social behavior hierarchically organized from large slots down to small, embedded slots of microsecond durations, but that processes of interactional inference or social cognition are similarly organized. As experienced in social performance, hierarchically organized activity can be apprehended only as relationships of succession across time. The relatively undifferentiated complexity of the myriad slots of activity of short duration that are strung together in interactions, like beads, in succession across time is reduced by a *plan* into a simpler order; into *slots* of proportionally long duration and high social salience within the whole occasion.

In the inferential work of interactional competence, it is as if the string of constituent events, while continuous in time, were made by social salience discontinuous in mass and texture across time. Interactional inference could be compared with fingering one's way along a rosary, rather than along a string of perfectly matched pearls.

But, because interaction is not an object but a social accomplishment, interactional performance cannot be compared with the rosary itself. Rather, it is as if all participants in interaction collectively create and sustain the rosary in feeling along it with their fingers – by what ethnomethodologists call reflexivity (a mutually constitutive interplay between expectation and action, Mehan and Wood, 1975) – the *participants become the rosary*; their collaborative doings constitute the social organization of the event. By identifying differences in the texture of their activity across time and by specifying the alternative choices that are culturally appropriate at the points of change in texture, the analyst can describe the inferences which participants make in producing a social occasion. Recent attempts at such modeling can be seen in the analysis by Sacks, Schegloff, and Jefferson of turn-taking in conversations (1974), in McDermott's analysis of the organization of classroom reading lessons (1976a, 1976b), in Mehan's studies of teaching sequences (1976), and in Erickson's analysis of the social and cultural organization of paying attention and explaining in counseling interviews (1976b).

A research group at the Harvard Graduate School of Education has been working in this area, as well, studying the social organization of such classroom activities as playing a board game (Shultz, 1976), talking with the teacher in the "circle" at the beginning of the school day (Bremme, 1976), and being interrupted during classroom events by visitors (Florio, unpublished). Recently, we have been interested in identifying shifts in participation structure within such occasions and within lessons, shifts from less formal and instrumental activity to more formal and instrumental, and back again. We find these shifts occurring between principal parts within occasions that both observers and participants in the classroom label as undifferentiated wholes when they give an initial answer to the question "What /time/ is it now?" – /lesson time/, /snack time/, /first circle time/. Within the occasion, e.g., /lesson/, we find constituent "times" of differing participation structure, with differing rules of appropriateness for paying attention, getting the floor, maintaining topical relevance, fidgeting. When children "miss" such situational shifts within an occasion, especially the shifts from less instrumental to more instrumental activity that can be glossed as "getting down to business," they are sanctioned for situationally inappropriate behavior by the teacher and by other children.

Essentially, our procedure for discovering the constituent structure of occasions consists of making judgments of *same/different* and *next* across real time. We work from audiovisual behavior records – sound film or videotape that is shot continuously with the camera moving as little as possible, keeping all the participants in the occasion within the visual frame. Usually, we begin our recording at least five minutes before the occasions we are studying begin and continue recording until after those events of interest end.

If we are using videotape, the behavior records collected at a site arrive back at the laboratory as one-hour or half-hour reels of tape. We then begin a six-stage process of viewing the tapes analytically. (These are listed in abbreviated form here. A fuller account is available from the authors.)

Stage I.   This stage follows the pattern by which the material was shot in the first place. We view each reel throughout, stopping it only very occasionally, taking most notes as the tape is running continuously. These intentionally sparse notes become an index of all the major occasions on the tape, showing (by tape-deck counter numbers) the approximate location of occasions and of the transitions between occasions. At this stage, we may index a number of reels before moving on to the next stage.

Stage II.   After a corpus of tapes is indexed, it is searched for analogous occasions of theoretical interest, e.g., all /lessons/, all /snacks/, or whatever. We choose one instance of a kind of occasion for more detailed analysis, record it on a copy tape, and use a time-date generator to print digital-clock numbers on the tape to insure an accurate analysis of timing. At this stage, we attend mainly to the junctures between parts, rather than to the parts themselves, both because the junctures have theoretical salience for us and because the pile-up of temporal and modality redundancy at junctures makes these moments discontinuous in interactional texture from those preceding and following them in time. During the juncture, one sees the most intuitively obvious shifts in com-munication behavior form, nonverbally and verbally, including changes in postural configuration.

The following two procedures have proven useful at this stage of analysis. First, we organize our descriptions on a chart with a continu-ous horizontal time line, indicating on the chart the approximate tem-poral location of junctures between principal parts and characterizing the parts themselves in terms of very general features of participations structure and topic, or main, activity. This chart provides a synoptic "wide-angle" picture of the structure of the whole occasion.

Second, we interview participants in the occasion in a *viewing session*, asking them to stop the tape as often as they can while viewing it with us, as often as they sense something new is happening. As they stop the tape, we elicit their characterizations of what is happening and what could reasonably be expected to happen and *not to happen* next. By this procedure we get a sense of the participants' points of view as members.

Stage III. Here we locate precisely the junctures or transition sections between primary parts of the occasion, and identify specifically the dif-ferences in participation structure across the junctures. We note the changes in postural position, speech prosody, and any other features of speech style and topic that occur before, during, and after the juncture. Often we diagram the postural positions and distance relationships among the participants, the direction of gaze and shifts in gaze, and tran-scribe along a time line the speech of all participants. All this inform-ation is organized onto a second chart, which is like an enlargement or close-up photograph of one portion of the wide-angle picture of the whole occasion that was provided by the synoptic chart prepared at Stage II of the analysis.

Stage IV. Here we attend primarily to the participation structures ahead of the junctures we have focused on in detail in Stage III. We go to each principal juncture of interest and rewind the tape back to the next previous principal juncture. In replaying the whole segment between the two junctures, we characterize the participation structure between them in fairly broad strokes, relative to the level of detail with which the subsequent juncture and its immediate surround was described, i.e., we may not transcribe all the speech or chart all the gestures of all participants for the whole participation structure between junctures. Rather, we try to attend to the intuitively "biggest" things that are happening – what postural positions are sustained, what the topics of talk are, who does most of the talking and listening, what general interactional strategies are occurring across the whole segment that can be glossed in ordinary language, e.g., /getting ready to start/, /dealing with the main issue/, /taking time out/. We do not attempt exhaustive description, but analytic description for the purpose of model construction.

Stage V.   At this point, we attempt an initial test of the validity of our model of interactional structure. In the previous stages, we have been constructing a model derived from analysis of a single case – a *type-case analysis*, in the terminology of Gumperz (personal communication). In the type-case model, we propose to show principles of social organization underlying the surface form of communication behavior in interaction. In particular, we are interested in demonstrating the contrastive relevance to participants of contextualization cues at principal junctures within an occasion.

   There are four types of evidence from which inferences can be drawn as to the social significance manifested in particular configurations of performance form. These are the requisite testing points for a single case-derived model of interaction:

   1. During those moments the model designates as moments of transition, descriptively specifiable shifts in interactional performance form are occurring.
   2. After a moment of transition, specific forms and functions of communication behavior – ways of listening and speaking, topics, postural positions, etc. – are differently distributed in contrast to their frequency of presence or absence and their sequential position of occurrence during the time prior to the moment designated by the model as a moment of transition.

3. After the moment of transition, kinds of interactional behavior, which, before the juncture were sanctioned if present (or absent), are no longer sanctioned by participants if these behaviors are present (or absent), and kinds of behavior previously not sanctioned are now sanctioned, i.e., participants behave as if rules of appropriateness differ from before the juncture to after it (Mehan and Wood, 1975; McDermott, 1976b).

4. If, in a viewing session, the participants themselves or other informants are shown the juncture and its immediate surround, their accounts of what is socially appropriate before and after the juncture agree with analytically descriptive evidence of types (2) and (3) above.

Stage VI. This final stage involves establishing the generalizability of the single case analysis conducted in the previous five stages. Here we search our indexed corpus of tapes for analogous instances of whatever kind of occasion we were investigating. We view all the occasions and locate all instances of whatever phenomenon we are investigating, e.g., all shifts from less instrumental to more instrumental activity within a lesson. Then we examine all instances in the corpus (or a systematically selected sample of them), noting the distribution of communication forms and functions before, during, and after the juncture, as in Stage III, above, but now limiting our attention only to those communication forms and functions that had structural salience in the model derived from the single case. If, in the analysis of multiple instances, the same types of evidence obtain as those discussed in Stage V, the generalizability of the analytic model has been initially demonstrated, i.e., we have shown that the single case is typical at least within the corpus investigated.

Conclusion

We have described a theoretical and procedural approach to the study of the social organization of interaction. We have specified methods of working analytically from the top down through the structure of interactional behavior to construct models of social organization of behavior. We think these models are congruent with the ways participants in interaction must be construing interaction as it happens, attending first to longer segments as gestalts and then to shorter ones embedded within the larger frames. Type-case models of interactional structure point to what a collectivity of members needs to know in order to produce the interaction.

The methods we have described can apply to a range of problems in the analysis of communication structure and interactional competence.

A theory of the interactional construction of social contexts is crucial to an understanding of how communication forms come to manifest social, as well as referential, meaning. One way of studying how contexts are socially generated and sustained in face-to-face interaction is to study the processes of organization by which contexts change from moment to moment and the processes of social cognition – interactional inference by which participants monitor verbal and nonverbal indicators of such change.

References

Birdwhistell, R. L. 1970. *Kinesics and Context*. Philadelphia: University of Pennsylvania Press.

Bremme, W. 1976. Accomplishing a Classroom Event: A Microethnography of First Circle. Working Paper #3, Newton Classroom Interaction Project, Harvard Graduate School of Education.

Cook-Gumperz, J., and Corsaro, W. 1976. Social-Ecological Constraints on Children's Speech. In: *Papers on Language and Context*. Working Paper #46, Language-Behavior Research Laboratory, University of California at Berkeley.

Cook-Gumperz, J., and Gumperz, J. 1976. Context in Children's Speech. In: *Papers on Language and Context*. Working Paper #46, Language-Behavior Research Laboratory, University of California at Berkeley.

Erickson, F. 1976a. One Function of Proxemic Shifts in Face to Face Interaction. In: A. Kendon, R. Harris, and M. R. Key (Eds.), *The Organization of Behavior in Face to Face Interaction*. The Hague: Mouton/Chicago: Aldine.

Erickson, F. 1976b. Talking Down and Giving Reasons: Hyper-Explanation and Listening Behavior in Inter-Racial Interviews. Paper delivered at the International Conference on Non-Verbal Behavior, Ontario Institute for Studies in Education, Toronto, Canada, May 11, 1976.

Fitzgerald, D. K. 1975. The Language of Ritual Events among the *Ga* of Southern Ghana. In: M. Sanches and B. Glount (Eds.), *Sociocultural Dimensions of Language Use*. New York: Academic Press.

Florio, S. 1976. *Learning How to Go to School: An Ethnography of Interaction in a Kindergarten/First Grade Classroom*. Harvard Graduate School of Education. Unpublished dissertation.

Goffman, E. 1974. *Frame Analysis.* New York: Harper Colophon Books.

Gumperz, J. 1976. Language, Communication, and Public Negotiation. In: Peggy Reeves Sanday (Ed.), *Anthropology and the Public Interest.* New York: Academic Press.

Hymes, D. 1974. *Foundations in Sociolinguistics.* Philadelphia: University of Pennsylvania Press.

Kendon, A., and Ferber, A. 1973. A Description of Some Human Greetings. In: R. Michael and J. Crook (Eds.), *Comparative Ecology and Behavior of Primates.* New York: Academic Press.

Mathiot, M. 1976. On Building a Frame of Reference for the Analysis of Face to Face Interaction. Paper delivered at the annual meeting of the American Anthropological Association, Washington, D.C., November 19, 1976.

McDermott, R. P. 1976a. *Kids Make Sense: An Ethnographic Account of the Interactional Management of Success and Failure in One First-Grade Classroom.* Stanford University. Unpublished dissertation.

McDermott, R. P. (with K. Gospodinoff and L. Aron). 1976b. Criteria for an Ethnographically Adequate Description of Activities and their Contexts. Paper delivered at the annual meeting of the American Anthropological Association, Washington, D.C., November 19, 1976.

Mehan, H., and Wood, H. 1975. *The Reality of Ethnomethodology.* New York: John Wiley & Sons, p. 103.

Mehan, H., Fisher, S., and Maroules, N. 1976. *The Social Organization of Classroom Lessons.* Technical Report submitted to the Ford Foundation.

Philips, S. U. 1972. Participant Structures and Communicative Competence: Warm Springs Children in Community and Classroom. In: C. Cazden, V. John, and D. Hymes (Eds.), *Functions of Language in the Classroom.* New York: Teachers College Press

Philips, S. U. 1974. *The Invisible Culute: Communication in Classroom and Community on the Warm Springs Reservations.* University of Pennsylvania. Unpublished dissertation.

Pike K. 1967. *Language in Relation to a Unified Theory of the Structure of Human Behavior.* The Hague: Mouton.

Sacks, H., Schegloff, E., and Jefferson, G. 1974. A Simplest Systematics for the Organization of Turn-Taking for Conversation. *Language,* 50 (4): 696–735.

Scheflen, A. E. 1973. *Communicational Structure: Analysis of a Psychotherapy Transaction.* Bloomington: Indiana University Press.

Scheflen, A. E. 1974. *How Behavior Means.* New York: Anchor Books.

Shultz, J. 1976. It's Not Whether You Win or Lose, It's How You Play the Game: A Microethnographic Analysis of Game Playing in a Kindergarten/First Grade Classroom. Working Paper #1, Newton Classroom Interaction Project, Harvard Graduate School of Education.

3 Plying frames can be dangerous: Some reflections on methodology in cognitive anthropology

Charles O. Frake

What is written here is not so much a "paper" addressed to a reader as it is a representation of a "talk" presented to an audience. Some of the discussion refers to the audience's shared experience as listeners to the talk. It would be helpful if the reader could imagine that he or she were a member of that audience. Accordingly, he or she will henceforth be addressed in the second person. Remarks addressed to you as a "reader" rather than as an "audience member" will be placed in parentheses.

Cognitive anthropologists, sometimes known as "ethnoscientists," are said to be people who listen to what the natives have to say. I do not claim to be one of the experts among cognitive anthropologists, but I do claim to be a native. This occasion, then, can be taken as an opportunity to assess the interest of listening to a native's point of view about the activities of his own group.

The research tradition that has come to be known as "cognitive anthropology," like most labeled schools of thought, includes such a diversity of approaches and perspectives that it is difficult to find much, apart from the label itself (and, maybe, the attacks of Marvin Harris), that holds the tradition together. Probably the most apparent common theme has been a concern for methodology, inspired by an admiration for the supposedly greater rigor of sister sciences, either psychology or linguistics. The value of the various methods proposed may be debatable, but the effort of pursuing them has succeeded in giving the field of cognitive anthropology a bag-of-tricks image among both adherents and critics. Some adherents seem to feel that the problems of the field, problems of lack of coherent theory or of substantial descriptive accounts, can be solved by evermore diligent pursuit of new methods.

Somehow, with tighter frames, more dimensional scales, and more flaw-less flow charts, the cognitive maps of our informants will be brought into focus. Critics, on the other hand, have pointed to the danger of this kind of excessive methodological tinkering. The scope of the data narrows to accommodate the methods. A pursuit of methods that work for something – anything – replaces the search for a theory that expli-cates what we want to know.

I am not about to suggest that cognitive anthropology abandon its methodological concerns. I do not recommend following the route of some linguists, freeing oneself for theoretical flights by cutting off ties with empirically grounded data. Nor do I advocate joining the hermeneutic circle, burying data under repetitive interpretations of "what it means (to me)," a tactic that produces thick books, but does not necessarily deepen understanding.

Methodology, some theoretically motivated notions of *what to do* when faced with the real world, is as necessary in science as it is in every-day life. Methods link data – what we construe to be observations of some particular reality – with theory, our proposals for understanding reality in general. When methods fail, the answer may be not only to tinker some more with the methods, but also to rethink the theory. My purpose here is to reflect upon some of the methodological successes and failures of cognitive anthropology in terms of their implications for general conceptions of the relations among behavior, verbal descriptions of behavior, cognition, and culture.

I will focus on what is certainly one of the best-known items in the cognitive anthropologist's bag of tricks: the frame. This methodological device was lifted out of the distributional model of structural linguis-tics, and shares kinship with similar notions of the same ancestry: paradigmatic/syntagmatic, slot-filler, contrast/contiguity, alternation/co-occurrence. Some element, A, is specified by its contextual con-straints, X–Y, and by its relation to other elements, B, that can occur in the same context,

The unique, and still poorly appreciated, contribution that the cognitive anthropologist made to this contextual model was that the context was

not limited to portions of single, isolated sentences. A frame was construed as an inquiry matched with a set of responses. The unit of analysis was a question–answer sequence, a conversational exchange.

This extension of the range of linguistic context beyond single speakers uttering isolated sentences was made in an effort to find a context that would frame semantic, rather than grammatical, relations (the latter being the sole concern of both structural and transformational linguists at that time). Inquiries specify informational contexts, constraining the semantic domain of the response. Speakers of language were seen as question askers and answerers, not simply as sentence producers. This pursuit of meaning by relating sentences produced by different speakers together as part of a discourse was an advance over the sentence-bound semantics practiced until recently by linguists. (Compare the analysis of "bachelor" in Katz and Fodor's much-heralded 1963 paper on linguistic semantics with what was being done at that time in ethnographic semantics. Katz and Fodor's analysis would have allowed a married man to answer a woman's question "Are you a bachelor?" by "Yes," on the grounds that he was (1) a holder of a BA degree, or (2) a seal.)

The notion of frames proved to be a powerful and useful methodological tool. It provided ways of obtaining and organizing certain kinds of data so that they made certain kinds of sense in convincing ways. But, as critics have been quick to point out, not all kinds of data proved to be equally tractable and, more significantly, the results, while they may have made some kind of sense, often did not seem to answer very interesting or important questions. In contrast to the essays of symbolic anthropologists, not so hampered by methodological constraints, the output of cognitive anthropology often seemed compartmentalized and trivial. One might counter that one person's trivia is another's eureka, and, moreover, a secure little truth is as useful as a wobbly grand theory. Nevertheless, cognitive anthropology ought to aspire to bigger truths, to go beyond offering tiny fragments of cognitive maps from here and there, to offer an overall view of the landscape.

More upsetting to cognitive anthropologists than the triviality issue have been problems of inducing people to verbalize in consistent question–response fashion about many topics of interest to the investigator and of obvious relevance to the people being studied. Why is it easier to get a taxonomy of birds than of social roles?

The other problem that has arisen from applying frames and other, more experimental, methods in cognitive anthropology has been the high degree of informant variability that is so often manifest. This result, to my mind, reveals a strength, not a weakness, of the methods. It reflects the way the world is, a reality less methodologically oriented approaches in anthropology have obscured. The last thing we should do is to flee from this reality or to tinker with our methods to eliminate it. But there remains the question of how to account for variability. The traditional use of the frame as a question-response device leads to what I think is the wrong answer: that we each go around with unique cognitive ideo-lects in our heads, each of which must be separately described and somehow summed up to equal culture.

These methodological difficulties have arisen from a failure to exploit fully the interactive aspects of the frame model, to widen the frame so as to capture a context that more fully specifies how human behavior comes to have meaning. Instead, attention was focused on questions and responses as chunks of verbiage isolated from their settings and their speakers. The specter of the stimulus–response model of behavior hung over many early programmatic statements. Some investigators empha-sized that the idea was to *discover* the questions (stimuli) that evoked the answers (responses) we were trying to describe. But this notion that the answers are there, that the job is to find the questions, while often cited, did not seem really to take hold. Frames began to be called *eliciting* frames, to be thought of not as contexts for behavior but as prods to behavior. The ethnographer, rather than the informant, thus becomes the questioner.

Of course, one tries to elicit the questions from the informant, but this process can amount to little more than finding out how to translate into the informant's language the questions the ethnographer wants to ask. Both the prevalence and the hopelessness of this procedure have become apparent to me in classroom informant-eliciting exercises, both those I have staged and those I have witnessed. In cases where I had some knowledge of the language and culture (and I quickly restricted this game to such cases), it was clear that the only way to discover useful questions was to specify inquiry contexts within which such questions could be asked. Doing this in English without a knowledge of the culture is nearly impossible for most domains. But it does show, more clearly than actual ethnography, where the context is more likely to be taken for granted because it is there; that questions have to be related to larger contexts.

Apart from the distortion of frames into probes, there are certain technical difficulties with the notion of a "question." An inquiry for information (a query) is a kind of speech act that must be distinguished from a question, a grammatical interrogative. An interrogative can, and perhaps most often does, represent such speech acts as summons and greetings, which are not queries. The ethnographer of American disease who goes around our society asking "How are you?" is not likely to elicit a very large inventory of disease terms. In Yakan (a Philippine language), a frequent question is "Who is your companion there?," an ideal question, one might think, for eliciting terms of social identity. Yet, the question is most appropriately posed to someone who is alone. The only appropriate answer is "nobody." This question is, in most contexts, a greeting. The Yakan question "What are you carrying there?" is typically a greeting if what is being carried is easily visible, a query if it is not (Frake, 1975). The status of a question as a query is dependent on the context in which it was uttered. Formal eliciting – so-called white-room ethnography – is an attempt to circumvent this problem by removing all previously relevant context, training the informant to see the white room as an interrogation chamber. This is an excellent methodological strategy, if what we want to know is how people behave in white rooms.

Even when we have a context in which we know that a given question is a query, we still can't be certain what query the question represents. A single question (a given surface-structure form) can represent a variety of queries for different kinds of information. The form of the question constrains the grammatical form of the response, but it does not, in itself, necessarily constrain the semantic domain of information. In Yakan, the common question "X is Y's what?" represents any query, the answer to which can be given in the genitive (surface) case: X is Y's grandfather; X is Y's rice field; X is Y's roof; X is Y's fate; etc. The answer to this kind of problem is not to search for more specific and necessarily highly artificial questions that, it is hoped, will sort out these different semantic relations, but to attend to the wider contexts of questioning that accomplish this sorting for the Yakan.

If one takes seriously the admonition to go out into the real world and look for queries, to seek "query-rich settings," as I once put it, one finds that people talk all the time and ask each other a lot of questions, but disappointingly few of the questions represent queries about the overt topics of the questions. Even children, the champion questioners, use this grammatical form in subtle ways. The child's stock question, "Mommy, you know what?" is not a request for information, but a clever use of sociolinguistic rules to acquire speaking rights (Sacks, 1972).

Perhaps instead of trying to devise provocative questions and other instruments to persuade people to talk about things they do not ordinarily talk about in that way, we should take as a serious topic of investigation what people in fact talk about, or, better, what they are in fact doing when they talk. When we look at talk, we find that people do not so much ask and answer inquiries; they propose, defend, and negotiate interpretations of what is happening. Because what is happening is what we are interested in explicating, these interpretations provide the key to understanding. Viewing informants not just as question-answerers, but also as interpreters of their lives, provides not only a sounder perspective for handling problems of informant variability and reticence, but also a more realistic notion of the relation of cognitive systems to behavior.

It is not so much that some things are hard to talk about. People can and do talk about anything. But some questions, if taken seriously as inquiries, are hard to answer. What kinds of sounds are there in your language? This is obviously a ridiculous question to pose to an informant if what you want to know are his phonological concepts; yet it can be answered, not by asking it, but by attending to interpretations of sounds made by speakers of the language. The problem with verbalized interpretations is not a difficulty in eliciting them but in locating what cues are being responded to in formulating a particular interpretation. Cues of sound, appearance, expression, body stance, and movement often cannot easily be explicitly identified by those who use them. Careful observation of the behavior, object, or event being interpreted is required. Simply recording what people say about things is not more adequate than simply recording what one sees. The informant's interpretations must be linked with the investigator's observations.

Attending to interpretations will not eliminate variation, but it will help to explicate it. Of course, people vary in behavior because they have different life experiences, different childhood traumas, different mental capacities, different hormonal balances, and so on. But this is only part of the story. Informants vary in what they say and do because interpretation itself is problematic. (It can be especially problematic when an informant is confronted with an ethnographer across a tape recorder.) An interpretation is not an answer to a question automatically produced in the mind by a cultural computer program as a result of proper input. It is a proposal, a theory to be tested, tested not only against the reality it covers, but (like scientific theory) also against its reception by one's fellows (or by the ethnographer).

Construing talk about things (including responses to the investigator's queries and tests) as proposals for interpreting not only what is being talked about, but also what is going on *now*, makes variability in verbal responses much more understandable. Where we must seek underlying cultural constants is not in the content of the talk, but in hate principles for formulating interpretations, for making sense of life. It is when things do not make sense that you know you have wandered off the edge of your cognitive map.

My arguments thus far all point to the necessity of expanding our frames to encompass the wider social context that makes interpretation possible. Calls for considering wider context, for defining behavior in terms of the situations in which it occurs, are certainly not new. Malinowski made them, ethnoscientists and ethnomethodologists have made them, sociolinguists have made them. Even straight linguists have begun to make some moves in this direction. Appeals are made, but it is rarely very clear how one specifies and delimits relevant context. All that is clear is that specification of relevant context is problematic, not only for investigators, but also for natives. It is itself, as ethnomethodologits are fond of telling us, a matter of interpretation. Context is not there to be seen. Its specification is a social accomplishment.

One way to begin a search for the units by which the specification of context is accomplished is to track a bit of meaningful behavior through a variety of native interpretations. Take one of the more secure findings of cognitive anthropology: that the English word for *mother* is "mother" (sometimes pronounced "muh-thuh"). Cognitive anthropologists have learned this by asking a query equivalent to "How are you related to so-and-so?," where the so-and-so's are named individuals in the informant's social world. This frame serves to sort out a domain of "relatives" ("We're not related; we're just friends"), and also to distinguish real "mothers" from such metaphorical mothers as mother superiors, mother tongues, and mother nature – the kinds of mothers who attract symbolic anthropologists.

Componential analysis permits us to define real kinship mothers as female, first ascending generation, lineal ($♀G^{+1}L$). Whenever you encounter a $♀G^{+1}L$, you have found yourself a real mother. But even real $♀G^{+1}L$ kinship mothers can suffer a variety of interpretive fates. Here are some recorded comments on mothers, made by a native – an American-English speaking informant of Irish-Catholic background. The informant begins by describing his home community.

(In the oral presentation of this talk, I play here a few excerpts from a phonograph record by the comedian George Carlin [1973]. He does a routine on his neighborhood, "White Harlem" [Morningside Heights], then one on verbal dueling, "slip-fights," in the parlance of his group. He notes that some groups have a rule for slip-fights: "No mothers, man; no mothers." His group didn't have that rule. They started right in with mothers:

"Hey, where'd yuh go last night?"

"I was out with yuh muh-thuh, man."

He then notes that it is a cause of some embarrassment if the mother of the addressee turns out to be dead:

"I forgot, man."

Carlin goes on to acknowledge the origin of slip-fights in such Black street games as "the dozens." He recites an example of the dozens, in which the reference to what the speaker does with the addressee's mother is rather more graphic than in the white, Irish-Catholic slip-fight example.

The recording includes the laughter of Carlin's audience.)

The slip-fight exchange is ostensibly rather innocent. It is not difficult to imagine contexts in which it could so be taken: if the respondent, for example, were the questioner's father. There could also easily be contexts in which this exchange could be a grievous insult: if, for example, there were good reason to believe that the respondent really had been out with the questioner's mother. But what we have is not a real insult, but a ritual insult as part of a game of verbal dueling. But if the target's mother happens to be dead, then the insult can no longer be taken ritually. An apology is called for. So, even though participants clearly take the depicted event as mythical, it is a real kinship mother, not a mythical or metaphorical mother, who is being referred to.

But, of course, what *you* (the member of the audience) heard was not the mention of "mother" in a slip-fight. Nor did you really hear an informant describing a slip-fight for the enlightenment of an ethnographer. I am sure you quickly saw through that fabrication and realized you were hearing a performance intended to entertain an audience. So you knew you were not being insulted, not even ritually. But you were not being entertained, either. For you are not an audience of a "show" but of a "talk." And, although the audience of a talk is allowed to laugh, too, we would all agree that reference to mothers in this talk would be a failure if it could not somehow be interpreted as a reasonably apt illustration of some serious, scholarly point.

The point here is not so much to characterize varieties of such speech acts as insults and invitations. This is an active enterprise now in several scholarly fields. Nor is the real point even that of Goffmanesque frames (Goffman, 1974): how to distinguish real insults from ritual ones in slip-fights; real slip-fight ritual insults from performances of them in a show; and real show performances of ritual insults from illustrative use of them in a talk. These matters are very relevant. But my focus here is not on the kinds of acts that can be discerned within contextual frames, nor on the human capacity to reframe reality repeatedly, but rather on the shape of the contextual frames themselves, frames within which people organize their conceptions of what, basically, is happening at a given time.

It is easy to argue for the indeterminability of specifying what is really happening at any given here and now. What is the spatial extent of here? What is the time span of now? Which of the multitude of detectable motions and changes surrounding us and within us constitute what is really happening here and now? Are we scratching our heads? Feeling hungry? Worrying about taxes? Watching a fly on the wall? Breathing in our neighbor's cold germs? Being bombarded by cosmic rays? Suffering through a drought? Being watched over by the gods? Traveling around the sun on a whirling ball? Actually, we all know very well what is happening now: this is a talk. That this is a talk structures the time and space of what's happening. Within these boundaries of here and now, whatever transpires is interpreted in relation to our shared awareness of what we are doing. You may not be paying attention to the talk – your thoughts may be far away from this time and place – but what you are doing is not paying attention to the talk. And you know that is what you are doing. You might have these same thoughts at some other time and place, in some other context, in which case what you might be doing could be killing time, meditating, solving the problems of your lie, or not paying attention in faculty meeting. But what you are doing now is not paying attention to the talk. And it is only by knowing that this is a talk that you know what you are doing.

A talk, like a slip-fight and a show, represents the kind of thing we are looking for, a basic unit of interpretive context. At a rather immediate level, the kind of thing a talk is might be termed a social occasion. Social occasions are relatively easy to recognize. They are where ethnographers go for their data: to weddings, parties, ceremonies, legal cases, etc. Typically, investigators intrude upon an occasion, a religious ceremony for example, collect samples of behavior within it, and then go home, examine the samples, and write a monograph on religion. But the nature of the occasion that made the behavior "religious" for the participants is often ignored. Making the nature of occasions themselves an object of study has not been entirely neglected, however. A number of studies in anthropology, sociology, and sociolinguistics could be cited.[1]

Some of my work in this area has been guided by an image of a society as an organization for the production of social occasions, or "scenes," as I have called them, and of a culture as a script for planning, staging, and performing scenes. The major chunks of society, institutions like "religion" and "education," can be discerned and defined with respect to particular social systems – "emicly," if I dare use that word anymore – by viewing them as organizations for the production of scenes of the same type. In our society, "education" can be seen as a complex of buildings, teachers, bureaucrats, procedures, values, etc., which have the purpose of assuring that classes and such related occasions as office hours and academic talks take place.

Of more interest for cognitive studies, however, is that by attending to the way occasions are contrastively defined, classified, distributed among settings, scheduled, and linked by planning sequences, this and related approaches have begun to reveal dimensions of cultural structure that do promise to give overall views of a culture's conceptual landscape, tying together the fragments of cognitive maps left behind by previous studies. These dimensions provide an alternative to the traditional institutional rubrics of religion, education, economics, politics, law, etc., which serve to divide up the academic world and organize monographs, but, perhaps, do not always reflect how people divide up and organize their own cultural worlds.

Such dimensions of cultural structure begin to emerge when one considers what makes a talk a talk and not, say, a class, or a speech, or a show. We can note that what goes on in talks and classes is to be taken as instructive, whereas shows are entertaining and speeches are persuasive. Talks can be distinguished from classes by (among other things) role structure: talks have a "speaker" and an "audience"; classes have a "teacher" and "students." The differences are more than terminological. For one thing, speakers get introduced. And that little difference is a marker of a very important dimension of cultural structure found, I would argue, in all societies: the dimension along which some occasions are marked as more special than others, as requiring more planning, as having explicit signals of beginning and ending, as entailing elaborate and explicit rules of procedure, and as demanding marked behavioral displays – dressing up, sitting straight, and speaking in elevated style. This is the dimension of formality, the dimension that occurs so often as a context for linguistic variation.

This dimension has interesting links with social stratification, in that everywhere displays of formality, like a necktie, erect posture, long sentences, Latin words, titles before names, and, among New Yorkers, postvocalic r's, are also emblems of high status and, at the same time, a display of deference. So my necktie may be taken as a tribute to this occasion, or a badge of my middle-class standing, or a sign that I have just come from the Dean's office. (Then, again, I may have worn a necktie, a very unusual garment for me, simply to illustrate this point.) Cultures differ, of course, in how they range social occasions along the dimension of formality. Classes and talks are probably more formal in France than in California.[2] These differences can have important implications for the investigator's interpretation of what a particular kind of activity, say litigation, does in a given society (cf. Frake, 1972).

Societies also differ in the value they place on formality itself as a symbol of identity and differentiation. Some peoples think of themselves as refined and civilized, rather than crude and vulgar; others, like Americans, and especially like western Americans, pride themselves in being natural and casual, rather than artificial and stuffy. These kinds of differences are not limited to the Western world. The Batak and Javanese of Indonesia provide a classic case (Bruner, 1974). In our own society, we also think of previous eras as being more formal than our own. Things seem to get more informal all the time (I can remember when I wore neckties to classes, as well as to talks). Why does formality become a symbol of ethnic and historical differentiation? I do not intend to pursue such questions here, but wish only to indicate some of the directions in which the study of social occasions in their own right has led.

There are other general dimensions like formality – "risk," for example. Assessment of risk can operate in rather subtle ways, even in relatively nonrisky situations. One way in which talks differ from classes is that, in a talk, the speaker faces some risk, a similar risk to that confronting a performer in a show; whereas the audience, you people, can relax. In a class, on the other hand, it is the students who typically face the risk. Facing risk is a test of character. Colloquial English provides a rich vocabulary for evaluating performance in this test: he kept his cool, he pulled it off, he got by, he blew it. Many societies stage risky social occasions for this purpose, for providing some "action" (Goffman, 1967). Among many groups – Chicago street gangs, for example – the assessment of risk provides the primary dimension for distinguishing social occasions, for differentiating "humbugging," "gang-banging," "wolf-packing," and "hustling" from "gigs," "games," "sets," and "pulling jive" (Keiser, 1969). It is in the former set of risky activities that one earns "rep," displays "heart," and shows he is not "punk."

Now let me move on from dimensions revealed by contrasting types of social occasions to the kind of thing a social occasion is. Consider again this talk. What most of you probably planned to do this evening was to come to a talk rather than, say, to go to a show, watch TV, read a book, kill time, or find some action. You probably did not plan to "do education." Nor, at the other end of this continuum, did you plan to sit in a chair in this lecture hall – although that is what a camera would reveal you are doing. But it is not what's happening. Later, if asked what you did this evening, saying you "went to a talk" is an appropriate account. To say that what you did was to sit in a chair in a lecture hall would sound odd, unless you could propose a context, a happening, within which sitting in a chair becomes eventful. "I was sitting in this chair and suddenly the roof collapsed over my head." What is happening is no longer a talk, but an earthquake.

A talk, then, exemplifies a conceptual unit whereby we organize our strips of experience in formulating accounts of what is happening, our memories of what has happened, and our predictions and plans for what will happen. Let me call such units "events." Note that "events," in this sense, are not occurrences out there in the world capturable by a camera, tape recorder, or behaviorist observer. They are proposed interpretations of what is happening at some time and place.

A talk is a social event, an occasion. But there are other kinds of events. Some things are not planned for and staged; they happen to one: earthquakes, droughts, illnesses, wars, gas crises, flat tires. Of course, in many societies it is a matter for some discussion whether such things just happen or are the deeds of motivated agents, but, in any case, unless one is a malicious god, a witch, or a plotting general, such things are not, for most of us, social occasions that we plan and stage. They are happenings that befall us. Like social occasions, happenings provide interpretive contexts for behavior and units for formulating accounts. Ordinarily, in the polite society of Marin County, California, it would be unthinkably crude for a dinner guest to ask his host if he should flush the toilet. Now, in the context of what's happening, being a severe drought, such a question is a sign of gracious consideration. Toilet-flushing and other ordinarily mundane hydraulic tasks have become eminently reportable topics of conversation and favorite subjects for newspaper columnists.[3]

Every situation in life, as it is experienced, can be defined by reference to one or more events that can be construed to encompass it and to lend meaning to what occurs within it. We account for our lives as sequences of eventful chunks of experience. Of course, not all experience is equally eventful. Sometimes nothing much happens. There are occasions when one is hard put to think of interestingly reportable occurrences to fill in conversations, letters, diaries, and field notes. To assert the occurrence of a particular event is to propose something significant and reportable about the experience it encompasses. As a proposal, it is subject to test not only against the reality it covers, but also against its reception by one's fellows.

The view proposed earlier, of culture as a script for the production of social occasions, should be recast a bit into one that sees it as a set of principles for creating dramas, for writing scripts, and, of course, for recruiting players and audiences. Culture provides principles for framing experience as eventful in particular ways, but it does not provide one with a neat set of event-types to map onto the world. Culture is not simply a cognitive map that people acquire, in whole or in part, more or less accurately, and then learn to read. People are not just map-readers;

they are map-makers. People are cast out into the imperfectly charted, continually shifting seas of everyday life. Mapping them out is a constant process resulting not in an individual cognitive map, but in a whole chart case of rough, improvised, continually revised sketch maps. Culture does not provide a cognitive map, but rather a set of principles for map-making and navigation. Different cultures are like different schools of navigation designed to cope with different terrains and seas. In this school, one must learn not only how to map out everyday life, but also how to fix one's position, determine a destination, and plot a course. And because people do not voyage alone, one must recruit a crew. Maps, positions, and courses must be communicated and sold. The last time – on a real boat in a real sea – I tried to sell a position and course to my crew (which included a distinguished cognitive anthropologist), I won the argument but promptly ran the boat aground. That's the way life is.

Notes

Presented as a talk to the Institute of Human Learning, University of California, Berkeley, April 1977. The talk was a revision and expansion of a presentation made under the same main title to a Conference on Cognitive Anthropology at Duke University, 1974, organized by Naomi Quinn and Ronald Casson. The appearance of this version in print owes much to the prodding and encouragement of Ray McDermott.

1. See especially the works of Erving Goffman and of the ethnomethodological sociologists. Useful recent studies by anthropologists include Agar (1974, 1975) and McDermott (1976).
2. Even French elementary-school classes strike Americans as rather formal; see the classes so remarkably portrayed in Truffaut's movie "Small Change."
3. In the 1974 version of this talk, I used the then ongoing gas crisis to make this point. In the current era, there always seems to be some ambient crisis we can orient to.

References

Agar, M. 1974. Talking about doing: lexicon and event. *Language and Society*, 3: 83–89.
Agar, M. 1975. Cognition and Events. In: M. Sanches and B. Blount (Eds.), *Sociocultural Dimensions of Language Use*. New York: Academic Press, pp. 41–56.
Bruner, E. 1974. The Expression of Ethnicity in Indonesia. In: A. Cohen (Ed.), *Urban Ethnicity*. London: Tavistock, pp. 251–280.
Carlin, G. 1973. Occupation Foole (A phonograph record). New York: Little David Records.

Frake, C. 1972. Struck by Speech: the Yakan Concept of Litigation. In: J. Gumperz and D. Hymes (Eds.), *Directions in Sociolinguistics*. New York: Holt, Rinehart, and Winston, pp. 106–129.

Frake, C. 1975. How to Enter a Yakan House. In: M. Sanches and B. Blount (Eds.), *Sociocultural Dimensions of Language Use*. New York: Academic Press, pp. 25–40.

Goffman, E. 1967. Where the Action Is. In: E. Goffman (Ed.), *Interaction Ritual*. Garden City, New York: Doubleday, pp. 149–270.

—— 1974. *Frame Analysis*. New York: Harper and Row.

Katz, J., and Fodor, J. 1963. The structure of a semantic theory. *Language*, 39:170–210.

Keiser, L. 1969. *The Vice Lords: Warriors of the Streets*. New York: Holt, Rinehart, and Winston.

McDermott, R. 1976. Kids Make Sense: an Ethnographic Account of the Interactional Management of Success and Failure in One First-Grade Classroom. Ph.D. thesis, Stanford University.

Sacks, H. 1972. On the Analyzability of Stories by Children. In: J. Gumperz and D. Hymes (Eds.), *Directions in Sociolinguistics*. New York: Holt, Rinehart, and Winston, pp. 325–345.

Experiments as contexts

4   Concepts of ecological validity: Their differing implications for comparative cognitive research

Michael Cole, Lois Hood, and Raymond P. McDermott

The problem of differing observational techniques (experiments, interviews, natural observation) and the inferences they warrant is of particular concern to comparative, cognitive psychologists who have been concerned with individual and group differences in cognitive performance. Inferences about the source of such differences are generally of two types: (1) differences arising from the past history of the individuals under study, and (2) differences arising from the specifics of the experimental tasks. Because of the difficulty of getting tasks well defined enough to differentiate between the two inferred sources of variability across persons or groups, the use of experimental situations as the sole basis for inferences about cognitive abilities has to be considered suspect. But the alternative, natural observation outside of the laboratory, is just as problematic because it makes it difficult to specify in detail how people process information. Further, the *relations* between laboratory and nonlaboratory behavior are problematic. Here, we pursue one line of discussion bearing on the complex issue of ecological validity and representative design in psychological research.

A useful place to begin our analysis of the notions of ecological validity and representative design is the May, 1943, issue of *Psychological Review*, in which Egon Brunswik and Kurt Lewin, two scholars who figure centrally in the history of these concepts, contributed to a discussion of psychology and scientific method (see also Brunswik, 1957, and Lewin, 1935).

Brunswik's general aim was to develop procedures which would prevent psychology from being restricted to "narrow-spanning problems

49

of artificially isolated proximal or peripheral technicalities . . . which are not representative of the larger patterns of life" (1943, p. 262). In order to avoid this problem, Brunswik suggested two closely related changes in the way psychologists should structure their observations:

1. Situations, or tasks, rather than people, should be considered the basic units of analysis; and
2. ". . . one would, secondly, have to insist on representative sampling of situations or tests. . . . For general adjustment this would mean a randomization of tasks, a sampling of tests carefully drawn from the universe of the requirements a person happens to face in his commerce with the physical and social environment" (p. 263).

As an example of such an approach, Brunswik made repeated observations on size constancy by an individual who was "interrupted frequently during her normal daily activities and asked to estimate the size of the object she just happened to be looking at" (p. 264). This person's size estimates correlated highly with actual measurements of the objects and not with their retinal image size. This result, Brunswik tells us, "possesses a certain generality with regard to normal life conditions" (p. 265).

This idea of sampling widely the environments within which a particular task is embedded to determine their effect on the responses of the organism has come down to us as a central tenet of "ecological psychology."

To make Brunswik's idea concrete, consider the operations which he offers for evaluating the ecological validity of size constancy in an everyday environment. First, he poses a problem for the subject (asks a question) which elicits a circumscribed response based upon limited aspects of the physical environment ("How big is that chair?"). Second, he has available a physical model of the stimulus elements that are critical to his analysis (a model of measurement which allows him to scale size of object, distance from subject, and, hence, physical size of image on retina). Third, he has a strong hypothesis which specifies relations between the physical stimulus and the subject's response – that either physical stimulus size (the "distal" stimulus) or stimulus size projected on the retina ("proximal" stimulus) will govern the subject's size-estimation response. Fourth, he obtains a very clear-cut result: correlation between reported size and physical size is essentially perfect, whereas the correlation with retinal size is poor. Of course, other settings could be investigated, and it might be possible to discover conditions in which the same result would not obtain. However, the logic of the enterprise is clear from the example; only the scope of the generalization is in question.

In our opinion, Brunswik's success was not accidentally related to the fact that the examples he actually worked out came from the area of visual perception, which represented (and represents) one of the most sophisticated areas of psychological theory. This gave him several advantages. First, because he could draw on the theory of physical measurement, he could confidently use a ruler to measure the dimensions of the objects whose sizes were being estimated, the distance from the subject to the object, and the size of the retinal image. In short, he could describe exactly the relevant aspects of the task environment and disregard such irrelevant aspects as the heat in the room, the color of the objects, etc.

Next, it is crucial that Brunswik was confident of the behavior that the subject would engage in when asked "How big is that————?" He had strong reason to believe that the question would focus the subject's attention on exactly those aspects of the environment which *he* thought relevant and which he could measure.

In addition, Brunswik could rely on competing hypotheses, derived from the laboratory, about how the crucial aspects of the environment mapped on to two aspects of the subject's response; he could specify the meaning of correlations with retinal or object size.

Finally, and crucially, he obtained essentially perfect prediction for *one* of the alternative hypotheses. Consider what kind of difficulties Brunswik would have faced had he been forced to proceed without any one of these resources for interpretation.

If he had obtained equivocal results with respect to constancy based on proximal or distal cues, he would have been in a quandary. He might have wanted to conclude that real-life perception depends upon a mix of distal and proximal cues; he might have pleaded that his subject was in some way atypical. He might have begun to worry about the efficacy of his question as a means of inducing the subject in a real-world environment to engage in the task which he had successfully posed in the laboratory.

At this point, it is useful to consider Kurt Lewin's contribution to the 1943 symposium on scientific method. On that occasion, Lewin argued his well-known position that behavior at time t is a function of the situation at time t only, and hence we must find ways to determine the properties of the situation "at a given time." To this statement, Lewin added his second major principle – that by situation, he was referring to the "life space" of the individual, "i.e., the person and the psychological environment as it exists for him" (1943, p. 306).

According to Brunswik, Lewin's approach left Lewin "encapsulated" inside the life space, cut off from observable responses on one side and measurable stimuli on the other. Lewin disagreed, saying that his goal was compatible with Brunswik's. He reformulated the overlap in their enterprises as one of "discovering what part of the physical or social world will determine, during a given period, the 'boundary zone' of the life space" (p. 309). Lewin dubbed this enterprise "psychological ecology." Granting its value, he saw his own work as centered on psychological dynamics *within* the "life space," rather than as an exploration of its boundary determinants.

If Kurt Lewin had been present and the difficulties we imagined for Brunswik's enterprise had arisen, Lewin might have suggested that Brunswik's questions to the woman about object sizes had changed the boundary of her life space, but not in the way Brunswik intended. Brunswik's questions may not have been appropriate to the life space of the person he asked. In effect, Lewin would argue that, under such circumstances, there is a possible crucial mismatch between the geographical and psychological environments, such that Brunswik's physical measurements may not have been measuring the aspects of the environment that were a part of the subject's psychological environment.

Lewin would be almost certain to point out another feature of what Brunswik had done, or not done. Instead of observing the occurrence of someone making a size estimation in a real-life environment, he had made a size-estimation experiment happen in a nonlaboratory environment. He had, in Lewin's terminology, changed the subject's life space to fit the requirements of his predefined set of observation conditions. In light of later discussions of ecological validity in psychology and our own research, this distinction between sampling the occurrence of psychological tasks in different environments and sampling environments within which to engineer psychological tasks is crucial. It is a point which we have been slow to assimilate and one we think our colleagues have understood poorly.

Although there have been several recent discussions of the notions of ecological validity (cf. especially Bronfenbrenner, 1979), Brunswik's and Lewin's early discussion, focused as it was on issues in cognitive psychology, retains special relevance for current efforts to expand the generality of cognitive psychology. Precisely because the issues were formulated so clearly and so early, we are moved to ask what impediments have stood in the way of developing the experimental-theoretical program for a generalized cognitive psychology laid out by these pioneers. *Issues of theoretical fashion aside, we believe that the major difficulty arose because in practice, if not in theory, the requirement for representative sampling of cognitive tasks and the requirement for defining the "life space at a given moment" are in conflict with each other. Only under very narrow circumstances is it possible to accomplish both goals at once. Failure in either aspect of the enterprise can vitiate the other and, in general, psychologists have not been able to come up with procedures which would allow them to overcome the resulting ambiguities.*

Consider some modern versions of the call for ecologically valid psychological research. Neisser (who acknowledges that his use of the term differs from Brunswik's) tells us that the concept of ecological validity is important because it reminds psychologists that the artificiality of laboratory tasks may render the results irrelevant to the phenomena (implicitly, phenomena found outside the laboratory) that we really want to explain. He points to the "spatial, temporal, and intermodal continuities of real objects and events" as important aspects of normal environments which are generally ignored in laboratory research (Neisser, 1976, p. 34). Barker (1968) had made a similar point. "Experimental procedures have revealed something about the laws of behavior, but they have not disclosed, nor can they disclose, how the variables of these laws are distributed across the types and conditions of man . . ." (pp. 1–2).

Bronfenbrenner (1976) has been especially influential in his insistence on the crucial role of ecological validity in modern psychological research, particularly in research on children that is purported to have public-policy relevance. In these discussions, he is even more insistent than Neisser or Barker that, in order to be ecologically valid, research must fulfill three conditions. First, it must maintain the integrity of the real-life situations it is designed to investigate. Second, it must be faithful to the larger social and cultural contexts from which the subjects come. Third, the analysis must be consistent with the participants' definition of the situation, by which he means that the experimental manipulations and outcomes must be shown to be "perceived by the participants in a manner consistent with the conceptual definitions explicit and implicit in the research design" (ibid., p. 35).

In these discussions and a number of others (e.g., Brown and DeLoache, 1978; Cole and Scribner, 1975), the common assumption is that one can first identify some task of interest within a laboratory setting and then discover instances outside of the laboratory (in "real life") where these tasks occur, and thereby discover the extent to which the structure of tasks and behaviors in the laboratory are representative of the tasks and behaviors in other environments.

Note the crucial differences between these interpretations of ecological validity and the procedures proposed by Brunswik. Neisser, Bronfenbrenner, and the others cited do not propose that we carry around our laboratory task and make it happen in a lot of settings. They propose that we *discover* the way it occurs (or doesn't occur) in nonlaboratory settings. Moreover, in Bronfenbrenner's version of this enterprise, we must also discover the equivalent of Lewin's "life space," e.g., how the task and all it involves appear to the subject. These new requirements for establishing ecological validity place an enormous analytical burden on the psychologist who would fulfill them. That burden is perhaps more than psychology can, or psychologists would care to, take on.

Modern ideas about ecological validity place additional difficulties on cognitive psychologists who would practice it. As an illustration, we can point to a recent piece of ecologically valid research, in Brunswik's sense, and try to imagine what would be required to make it ecologically valid in Bronfenbrenner's sense.

In a study of memory, Koriat and Fischhoff (1974) asked a large number of passersby on their university campus, "What day is today?" They measured the reaction time for answers to this simple question and found that it produced a bowed curve anchored by Saturday (the Sabbath day in Israel, where this study was conducted): reaction times were slower the further from Saturday the question was asked.

Except that no effort was made to catch people at many different points in their daily cycle, this study shares the features crucial to Brunswik's perception study. However, it should be clear that these observations do *not* match Neisser's or Bronfenbrenner's notion of eco-logical validity. We did not discover individuals being asked (or asking themselves) what day of the week it was. We did not observe their responses when they encountered the need to answer such a question without having the extra task of confronting a student with a "clearly revealed stop-watch." If we had encountered such a task as it arises *naturally* (e.g., in the course of activities which are not organized for assess-ing speed of memory retrieval), we might have observed the person consulting a friend or glancing at a calendar. It is also likely that we would find it very difficult to know if the question had occurred (e.g., in cir-cumstances where the subject had posed the question to himself or herself in the course of figuring out if the children would come home late after school). These latter examples may appear frivolous, but they make the very important point that in order to "discover" cognitive tasks outside of the laboratory, we need criteria to indicate that they have occurred. In addition, we need to know as much as possible about the subject's responses to the task-as-posed, because this is crucial inform-ation for both Brunswik's and Bronfenbrenner's notions of ecological validity. There are no currently agreed-upon methods for accomplish-ing these goals. While several investigators, including ourselves, are engaged in creating the required methods, claims for the ecological val-idity of cognitive tasks should be treated as programmatic hopes for the future. We have made little progress on this issue since Brunswik's and Lewin's discussion a generation ago.

Note

Preparation of this paper was supported by a grant from The Carnegie Corporation.

References

Barker, R. 1968. *Ecological Psychology*. Stanford: Stanford University Press.
Bronfenbrenner, U. 1976. Ecological Validity in Research on Human Development. Paper presented at the Symposium on "External Validity in the Study of Human Development" at the 1976 Annual Convention of the American Psychological Association, Washington, D.C.

Bronfenbrenner, U. 1979. *The Experimental Ecology of Human Development*. Cambridge: Harvard University Press.

Brown, A. L., and DeLoache, J. S. 1978. Skills, Plans and Self-Regulation. In: R. Siegler (Ed.), *Children's Thinking: What Develops*. Thirteenth Annual Carnegie Symposium on Cognition. Hillsdale, N.J.: Lawrence Erlbaum.

Brunswik, E. 1943. Organismic achievement and environmental probability. *Psychological Review*, 50 (3): 255–272.

Brunswik, E. 1957. Scope and Aspects of the Cognitive Problem. In: Bruner et al. (Eds.), *Contemporary Approaches to Cognition*. Cambridge: Harvard University Press, pp. 5–32.

Cole, M., and Scribner, S. 1975. Theorizing about socialization of cognition. *Ethos*, 3: 250–268.

Koriat, A., and Fischhoff, B. 1974. What day is today? An inquiry into the process of time orientation. *Memory and Cognition*, 2 (2): 201–205.

Lewin, K. 1935. *Dynamic Theory of Personality*. New York: McGraw-Hill.

Lewin, K. 1943. Defining the "field at a given time." *Psychological Review*, 50 (3): 292–310.

Neisser, U. 1976. *Cognition and Reality*. San Francisco: W. H. Freeman.

5 What's special about experiments as contexts for thinking

Jean Lave

I have been asked to write about experiments as special contexts for thinking. Experiments might be viewed as exceptional circumstances for problem solving and as unusual social occasions. A great deal has been said by psychologists about relations between laboratory experimentation and everyday activities. Many of the relevant caveats were presented by Wundt (1916). They have been restated, amplified, and added to by Brunswik (1955), Bartlett (1958), Barker (1968), Neisser (1976), Bronfenbrenner (1979), Cole, McDermott, and Hood (1978), to mention only a few appropriate references. To these discussions, I will add an example and a point of view.

The example I have chosen is from my own research among tribal tailors in Liberia. I gathered data on the tailor's uses of arithmetic in their daily routines in the tailor shop and in experimental situations and found that the problem-solving activities of the tailors look quite different in the two settings.

This example serves to illustrate my point of view. Most psychologists' critiques begin with experiments as the normative basis for describing thinking. They then end up treating everyday life as: (a) less demanding than the laboratory experiment (Bartlett, 1958; Case, 1978; Norman, 1975; etc.); or (b) unorganized and only given order by the organizing activity of the mind (this is Barker's (1968) characterization of "most psychologists' views"); or (c) simply, "the residual term which takes on specific meaning as it contrasts with the laboratory." (Cole, McDermott, and Hood, 1978, comment critically about the existing state of the art.) As an anthropologist I started out with an everyday scene as the primary source of information about how people use their heads, and have treated experiments as exotic and narrowly circumscribed events in the lives of the people studied. This point of view leads to questions about how experiments compare with other new situations that might arise in the tailors' mundane work lives.

To compare experiments with mundane social scenes requires a model of those features of everyday situations in tailor shops which might affect the methods tailors used to solve everyday arithmetic problems. I describe below a model of mundane situations and apply this model in a comparison of experiments and everyday situations in the tailor shops.

Background

The research on which this comparison is based stretched over a period of five years. I began by observing in tribal tailor shops, learning the production processes and other routines of tailoring, and studying how apprentice tailors learn their craft. This was followed by a series of experiments on transfer of training which compared the impact of apprenticeship and schooling on performance of more and less familiar tasks. There were two phases to this work. The first set of tasks incorporated problems taken directly from tailoring or school arithmetic. The circumstances surrounding the solving of these particular problems in experimental settings were similar to those found in the mundane setting: that is, the problems were ones the tailors routinely expected each other to solve without help from others. Such problems were viewed by the tailors as challenging previously acquired knowledge or skill. I then invented other, less familiar problems to contrast in specific ways with the problems known to be routine in the shop or school setting. The data for each tailor were analyzed for changes in performance across increasingly unfamiliar problems.

This analysis raised issues which could not be settled with the data from the first set of experiments. As Ginsburg (1977) has pointed out, it is important to compare data on problem-solving processes to draw conclusions about transfer. So on the second set of tasks protocols were collected. Fortunately, tailors learn one set of arithmetic procedures in the tailor shop and a different set in school. This makes it possible to often identify which method tailors were using on a given problem regardless of the setting in which they are solving the problems. The second round of experimentation also differed from the first in exploring more systematically the formal domain of arithmetic and possible dimensions of transfer of training, including numerical difficulty, mundane/exotic problem content, and ways of presenting problems which required different degrees of decoding work by the problem solver.

The first round of experiments used the tailors' everyday activities as a basis for constructing experimental tasks but did not explore the boundaries of everyday competence. The second round included systematically generated problems, sampled a formally generated problem space, and had the virtues of consistency and representativeness of a formal knowledge domain, but did not grow out of the everyday experiences of the tailors. In the first case it was relatively easy to specify relations between experimental and everyday tasks, but hard to account for relations between my experimental tasks and the tasks of more standard cognitive experiments; in the second round this set of circumstances was reversed.

The results (details in Lave, n.d.) may be summarized as follows: In the experimental situations, those who had learned arithmetic in school as well as in the shop used school-learned problem-solving techniques to proceed through the experimental task. Those who had learned arithmetic in the shop used what could be characterized as a maximum-effort version of shop arithmetic and only a subset of shop arithmetic strategies. Many of the maximum-effort strategies appeared to be invented on the spot.

It appears from these results that the experimental situations were ill-specified ones for the tailors. But they individually filled in the gap between their understanding of the situation and mine. Some did so by reference to their problem-solving experiences in school, some by reference to the shop. Those who used their shop-learned skills as a model felt called upon to produce a version of those procedures which was never seen in the shop. They also omitted many techniques which they would have used in the shop.

After analysis of the experimental work, I was very curious as to how well the experimental data on problem-solving process would generalize to mundane situations. Consequently, in a third round of fieldwork, I observed everyday arithmetic activity in the tailor shops. The results of this work could be summarized as follows: Those who learn arithmetic in the shop use a rich and varied, and a streamlined version of this arithmetic in their work lives in the shop. Those who learn arithmetic in both shop and school (and used school math in the experimental setting) use shop arithmetic in the shop on a day-to-day basis.

Problem

It would certainly be useful to tackle the question of why mundane shop problems and experiments "pulled" such different kinds of behavior from the tailors. What features of everyday life in the tailor shop make it a special context for thinking and account for the special kinds of arithmetic strategies employed there by all of the tailors? Are there differences between critical features of everyday situations and experimental ones which help to account for changes in strategies from one situation to the other?

The model of everyday problem-solving situations

It may be helpful to simply state the main features of the model of everyday arithmetic problem-solving situations. "Situation" as it will be used here includes crucial features of both inner and outer environments of the problem solver, as each shapes the other. Experimental and everyday situations can be compared on these features, using the data on Liberian tailors.

The outer environment: Firstly, in the tailors' lives, certain kinds of arithmetic problems routinely reoccur. Secondly, problem solving often occurs in the context of social interaction or is at least vulnerable to social demands, most of which have higher priority than math. Thirdly, arithmetic problem solving is almost never an end in itself. It is instead an instrumental activity, undertaken in order to arrive at a wide variety of higher-order goals. Finally, it takes place in an environment rich with information for the particular problems which are frequently encountered.

The inner environment: Arithmetic problem solving makes heavy demands on attentional resources; it is effortful. Most arithmetic problems can be solved quickly if all the required information is present, although this condition is not often met.

Comparing mundane and experimental problem-solving circumstances

The outer environment: The first issue is that of routine reoc-currence. Given the repeated occurrence of arithmetic problems in daily life, it should not be surprising that tailors show little difficulty re-presenting problems to themselves. What is problematical in every-day circumstances becomes the input for these problems. Even the information-rich environment of the tailor shop is sometimes not rich enough to permit a tailor to solve a problem at the time he recognizes that it exists. Both the reoccurring nature of problems, and potential dif-ficulties in obtaining new inputs, help to explain why procedures for solving arithmetic problems in the shop very often focus on relations between old and new instances of the same problem.

All of these features of everyday problem solving stand in contrast with the problem-solving tasks presented in an experimental context. One goal in choosing the problems for the experiments was to make at least some of them unfamiliar to all subjects. If the experimenter were successful, any strategy which involved comparing old and new versions of the same problem would be unavailable to the subject. Furthermore, the experiment, as a situation, is a one-of-a-kind occasion. This is not a situation in which it could be said that problems routinely reoccur. Everyday strategies which take advantage of routine reoccurrence will not be effective in the experimental situation. Since there is little time for adaptation of methods during an experiment, experiments are always "learning transfer" situations. Learning transfer is a relatively rare occurrence in everyday life.

Second, the outer environment is peopled; social interaction has very high priority in the tailors' lives. Instrumental activities are lower in a goal hierarchy and require social management in order to compete for resources of attention. Very often in the shop the tailors handle this problem with a fluid, shifting division of labor. A tailor dealing with a customer passes the measuring or other figuring along to some other tailor who solves it and gives him the answer while the first tailor con-tinues to attend to the customer. Checking problem solutions, which in addition to objective results provides reassurance that calculation was properly done, are often social, done in parallel by two or more. (For a similar finding see Kreutzer, Leonard, and Flavell, 1975.) All of this contrasts with experimental circumstances in which problem solving is assumed to be an exclusive engagement between a person and the problem. Social strategies are not permitted.

Third, arithmetic problem-solving, like most of the cognitive procedures which are the target of experimental investigation, is a low-level means employed in everyday life in the service of a wide variety of higher-order goals. In an experimental setting where math problem-solving procedures are the topic of investigation, "solving math problems correctly" is the highest order goal made explicit in the situation. Defining tasks through the practice of "giving instructions" ignores the customarily embedded, instrumental nature of arithmetic activity. More important, it often leads to expectations on the part of the experimenter about what constitutes appropriate (i.e., elaborate, high effort) problem-solving procedures. The same expectations would not be appropriate for problem solving seen merely as an instrumental activity.

The means/end relationship between problem-solving goals and problem-solving procedures has a number of implications. First of all, in the everyday setting in which arithmetic is (only) instrumental, minimizing attention allocated to math makes sense. In experiments, in which solving the problem correctly is a major goal, it makes sense to maximize efforts at problem solving. This is certainly what I observed the tailors doing. Once again the contrast between the two sets of circumstances suggests that procedures appropriate in either one are not appropriate in the other.

Everyday strategies for solving problems include ones which violate many of the usual experimental constraints. In everyday circumstances, standard techniques include simplifying problems, delegating problem-solving work, and rejecting problems. More importantly, it is often useful to compare old and new inputs to a reoccurring problem, note the difference between them, and make a decision vis-à-vis the higher-order goal rather than solve the arithmetic problem (e.g., the eggs are 30 cents higher this week. That's too much. We'll get them somewhere else). This contrasts with the assumption in an experiment that the task must remain fixed; that procedures which involve reframing the task are not permitted.

Higher-order goals in everyday problem solving also vary the precision constraints on the problem solutions. Because of the instrumental nature of arithmetic and other demands on attention, it makes sense to pay attention to precision constraints. In general people solve problems no more precisely than necessary to meet the higher-order goal for which they are calculating. Attending to precision constraints is a skill of everyday arithmetic that does not much come into play in experimental situations, since solving math problems is the goal. Perhaps the tailors have a default position: Under ill-specified precision constraints and minimal other demands for attention, be as precise as possible. This would help to account for the maximum-effort arithmetic procedures used on the experimental math tasks.

One further implication of the instrumental uses of arithmetic in everyday life has been touched on at several earlier points. Usually the higher-order goals are well enough defined in everyday situations to provide adequate information about precision constraints, error cost and so on. In experiments the goal may seem well specified: "I want you to solve some arithmetic problems." But this takes into account only the instrumental level of the problem-solving activity and not the crucial function of higher-order goals in determining appropriate problem-solving procedures. Viewed in comparison with a higher-order everyday goal, e.g., "getting groceries," goals which would provide comparable precision constraints in experiments are not clear. This confusion may be a serious problem with many experimentally defined tasks.

Inner environment: No matter what the circumstances, mental calculation is effortful and requires heavy attentional resources. It is also a rapid process (most often less than a minute) if all needed information is at hand and if there are not competing demands for attention. At the same time calculation is slow enough to disrupt conversation. All of this applies in experimental settings as well as in everyday settings.

In everyday settings, however, it may take days to solve a given arithmetic problem. Problem solving is subject to interruption and also to absence of information. The contrast between customary speed when problem solving is in progress, and the enormously greater time periods which are often encountered creates difficulties in "problem management," (e.g., holding onto whatever inputs are available, and the problem representation, seeking additional inputs, pushing to assemble them all at once, or storing some and waiting, etc.). These problems are not generally addressed in assessing math skills in experimental settings. In experiments inputs are given and it is generally possible to solve difficult problem-representation circumstances and relatively easier input acquisition circumstances than everyday life provides.

I have not previously mentioned the impact on problem-solving strategies of experience over time in some environments. Change in strategy over time arises as a function of interaction between outer and inner environments. It seems likely that methods used in solving problems (e.g., memorization or interpolation or re-calculation, etc.) are chosen partly in response to experience with the frequency of reoccurrence of different problems in the environment along with the simplest possible extrapolation to the future ("what has happened in the past is what I expect in the future"). (Kahneman, 1973, discusses some implications of this point.)

But tasks and problem-solving methods in experiments have unspecified relations to the extensional domain[1] of everyday life. Experimental tasks are typically selected from domains which bear no specified relationship with everyday tasks and problems. Certainly they are not carefully constructed samples of problems with different (known) frequencies in the domain of actually occurring problems.

Discussion

It could be argued that an important measure of peoples' problem-solving skills is what happens when they are asked to solve new problems in new circumstances. In this frame of reference experiments make sense as a tool for investigation, since experiments present new problems in a new situation. But if this argument is taken seriously it changes the appropriate comparison to make to everyday situations. The appropriate comparison might be other *new* problems which arise in mundane settings, rather than *routine* problems in mundane situations.

One example of a new problem in a mundane setting occurred in a tailor shop. A man came into the shop one day and requested that a tailor make a set of burial clothes. None of the tailors in this shop had made burial clothes before. But all present felt the customer had come to the right place to get a solution to his problem. Bargaining, sewing, the setting, different kinds of clothes, are all familiar. Only the specific item to be made was new, and it could be compared to other closely related types of garments. In short, people's experiences with new situations in everyday lives tend to be a good deal more like previous experiences in everyday situations than are experiments. It is possible to suggest several ways in which the circumstances of problem solving in new situations are quite differed when experiments and other new situations are compared.

Experiments gain much of their power as tools for investigating cognition from the fact that they are simpler situations than the typical everyday experiences of most subjects. On the one hand, the non-negotiable definition of tasks, the complete presentation of specific tasks is simpler than the fuzzy, often incomplete, unfolding nature of tasks in everyday situations (Cole, McDermott and Hood, 1978). On the other hand, experiments lack specification of higher-order goals which routinely guide the choice of problem-solving method in everyday situations, including new ones. For instance, the burial clothes were extremely simple and also voluminous. No one measured the "customer" and precision constraints on fit were extremely broad, under the circumstances. Yet the goal was there, "make loose-fitting garment x," at the same level as usual, routinely translatable in its impact on subportions of the task.

Experiments constitute ill-specified new situations in other, more complex ways. For instance, neither the experimenter nor the subject is likely to know how the situation is related to previous situations in which the subject has been routinely involved. Neither is the experimenter likely to investigate differences between previous problem-solving experiences and activities in the experimental setting. And there is unlikely to be a clear understanding of differences between the distribution of problems-to-solve routinely encountered by subjects, and the experimental tasks as samples from that or some other domain of problems. In the example of the burial clothes, the situation was a slight variant on routinely occurring ones. Previous problems and previous experience solving problems were clearly specified. This was not the case in my experiments.

Experimental situations also differ from other new situations, in the timing of performance demands. In everyday life one would rarely be called on to perform immediately in a new, or ill-specified situation, until one understood "what's going on." Thus, no one in the shop thought of asking an inexperienced apprentice to make the burial clothes, even though several were available, and skilled enough. Only highly experienced masters talked it over and decided on one of their number.

A third way in which experiments differ from most other new problem-solving situations is in the degree of consistency of certain major features of the situation over a series of routine reoccurrences. Experiments often arbitrarily change features of the situation in ways that mundane new situations rarely if ever impose. This is especially true for (a) social circumstances of performance, and (b) means/goals status of the problem-solving procedures under study. Some tasks have a strong social component, others do not. But in everyday life the social features of a daily activity are very likely to remain constant across numerous reoccurrences. Arbitrary change in the social and physical matrix of an activity is not common. It does happen from time to time – occasionally we cook in someone else's kitchen or go grocery shopping with a friend – with predictable performance difficulties. Experiments, unfortunately, very often create this arbitrary change in the social conditions of activity. It is also rare in everyday life that a task which was an end in itself in one setting becomes instrumental in relation to some other end in another mundane context. In everyday situations where this does happen there are very likely to be strong signals to the actor, including clear specification of higher-order goals where appropriate. *Most of the cognitive skills typically addressed in experiments move from instrumental to goal status as they move from everyday situations into experimental ones.* The math activities described earlier are a good example. But memory experiments, perception, logic problems, and most other foci of heavy experimentation suffer from the same arbitrary change. This may help to explain why it is difficult to "see" cognitive skills in everyday settings, a problem emphasized in Cole, McDermott, and Hood.

If the propositions above are acceptable (that both social circumstances and means/goal status are often changed when transported into an experimental context), then a point made earlier becomes even more important. In everyday situations where there are newcomers or novices, there are almost certain to be provisions for induction, temporary peripheral participation, or at least dramatic signals to flag shifts in social or means/goals circumstances. There is likely to be social support for identifying the out-of-the-ordinary features of the situation and adapting to them. Experimental situations seem atypical situations in being impoverished in the social circumstances which lead people to make rapid and successful adaptations in new mundane situations.

Conclusion

If conventional experiments do not masquerade well as "new mundane situations," is there any hope for generalizing from experimental to everyday situations? Actually, the question is an experiment-centric one. It may profitably be revised to, "Is there any hope that we may learn from contrasting performances in contrasting situations?" From my own experience working in Liberia, I would answer in the affirmative. I disagree, however, with the argument set forth in Cole, McDermott, and Hood, about the nature of appropriate generalization. It is argued there (p. 15 and elsewhere) that "the experiment should be treated as a simulation of the properties of the scenes to which we want to generalize." But if any critical features of experiments cum situations contrast with basic features of mundane situations, an ecologically valid simulation of everyday situations is not possible. If context and performance interact, there are almost certainly important features of the situation which won't agree between experiment and mundane circumstances.

It is possible, however, to make predictions about expected *differences* in performances across contexts, given a careful description and analysis of the differences in problem-solving circumstances in some specific mundane setting(s) and in an experimental one. By trying to understand an experiment as an actual experience in the lives of subjects, by focusing on how the circumstances it presents *differ* from those of routine situations, and by successfully predicting performance differences in the separate contexts, theories (rather than experimental results) can become general without automatically becoming invalid at the same time.

Secondly, the notion that rigorous proof of particular kinds of cognitive processing can *only* come from experimental manipulation seems too narrow. If you understand the social organization of a commercial dairy and the division of labor within it, you should be able, like Scribner, to predict who will be good at one kind of arithmetic but not another, and who will solve customer order problems in terms of pints and quarts, and who in terms of cases and half cases. De la Rocha (personal communication, 1980) predicts from a three-stage model of Weight Watchers curriculum, who will carry out new calculations about food servings in one way rather than another; Murtaugh (1980)[2] predicts on the basis of the functional role of a particular food in a person's food management system whether the person will calculate before buying that item in the grocery store. Confining theory testing or theory development to experiments is an excessive limitation on sources of knowledge, and grows out of the model which specifies that the goal of experimentation is to produce a literal reproduction of the target behavior under study. But indirect evidence abounds, including data on the social structure, data on what people do *not* do under certain circumstances, data on what kinds of mental effort people avoid through the use of external inventions or social skills. These can shed light on problem-solving processes with reasonable rigor. Producing rigorous indirect evidence, rather than literally reproducing target behavior, is a useful goal for at least some new exploration of cognitive processes.

Notes

This paper was prepared for The Social Science Research Council Workshop on Laboratory and Field Research Studies of Cognitive Processes, La Jolla, California, December 6–7, 1979.

1. The "extensional domain" of arithmetic problems is the set of actually occurring problems in a given situation.
2. Proposed research: A Hierarchical Decision Model of American Grocery Shopping.

References

Barker, R. G. *Ecological psychology: Concepts and methods for studying the environment of human behavior.* Stanford: Stanford University Press, 1968.

Bartlett, F. C. *Thinking: An experimental and social study.* New York: Basic Books, 1958.

Bronfenbrenner, U. *The ecology of human development: Experiments by nature and design.* Cambridge, Mass. & London, England: Harvard University Press, 1979.

Brunswik, E. The conceptual framework of psychology. *International Encyclopedia of Unified Science, Vol. 1, Part 2.* Chicago: University of Chicago Press, 1955.

Case, R. Intellectual development from birth to adulthood: A neo-Piagetian interpretation. In R. Siegler (Ed.), *Children's thinking: What develops?* Hillsdale, N.J.: Erlbaum, 1978.

Cole, M., Hood, L., & McDermott, R. P. *Ecological niche picking: Ecological invalidity as an axiom of experimental cognitive psychology.* Unpublished manuscript, University of California and The Rockefeller University, 1978.

Ginsberg, H. Some problems in the study of schooling and cognition. *ICHD Quarterly Newsletter, 1* (4), 7–10. New York: The Rockefeller University, 1977.

Kahneman, D. *Attention and effort.* Englewood Cliffs, N.J.: Prentice-Hall, 1973.

Kreutzer, M. A., Leonard, C., & Flavell, J. H. An interview study of children's knowledge about memory. *Monographs of the Society for Research in Child Development*, 1975, *40*, (1, Serial No. 159).

Lave, J. *Tailored learning: Education and cognitive skills among tribal craftsmen in West Africa.* Unpublished manuscript.

Neisser, U. *Cognition and reality.* San Francisco: W. H. Freeman, 1976.

Norman, D. A. Cognitive organization and learning. In P. M. A. Rabbitt & S. Dornic (Eds.), *Attention and performance V.* New York: Academic Press, 1975.

Wundt, W. *Elements of folk psychology.* London: Allen & Unwin, 1916.

6 Sociolinguistic structure of word lists and ethnic-group differences in categorized recall

Anderson F. Franklin

Performance in memory organization is commonly used as a signpost for intellectual development. Investigation of conceptual processes has often involved measuring the organization in recall of a verbally presented list of words in functionally and/or conceptually related categories. Free recall studies have frequently been cited by Jensen (1972; Jensen and Frederikson, 1973) in support of his theory of the differential distribution of higher-order conceptual skills among American subpopulations. In such studies, words belonging to distinct conceptual categories are presented in a random order, and subjects are asked to recall as many words as they can. The degree to which subjects reorder their recall to correspond with the predetermined conceptual structure of the list is taken as the measure of their underlying conceptual ability.

Because performance on word recall tasks is known to be a function of such variables as word familiarity, meaningfulness, and category cohesion (Tulving and Donaldson, 1972; Cofer, 1967), any conclusions about differential conceptual abilities of sample populations must rest on the assumption that the stimulus materials are equivalent on these parameters for the different populations studied. The present research questions this assumption. It proceeds from the hypothesis that differential familiarity with words and categories present in a list interferes with list reorganization. By building differential familiarity of structure into the list, it should be possible to manipulate population differences in performance. This hypothesis was tested in studies in which list structure was systematically manipulated both across and within ethnic groups.

70

The first study compared recall performance of Black and White adolescents on a list in which half the categories were derived from standard norms commonly used in recall studies (designated as universal categories), and half were derived from elicitation procedures with Black adolescents (designated as Black categories). One hundred Black adolescents were interviewed in their neighborhoods. The five most frequent responses in the categories *drugs*, *dances*, and *soul food* were selected as members of the Black categories. These were combined with five words from standard norms (Battig and Montague, 1969) for the categories *tools*, *utensils*, and *clothing* resulting in a mixed list of 30 words.[1]

This list was presented for five successive trials in a standard free-recall experiment to 34 tenth- and eleventh-grade students, half of whom were White and half Black. White students attended a private high school in central Manhattan; Black students attended a storefront alternative high school for marginal performers in an impoverished neighborhood in Brooklyn.

Amount recalled by Black adolescents was greater than that by White adolescents, with a statistically significant difference occurring in the later trials (see Figure 6.1). Organization in recall was assessed by using a standardized score applied in previous studies (Jensen and Frederikson, 1973; Frankel and Cole, 1971). From this measure, the difference in ability to cluster the recall is greater for the Black adolescents. The significant Trials X Group Interaction indicates that this was a consistently progressive improvement in organizational ability.

It was hypothesized that the superior memory performance of the Black adolescents occurred because they were familiar with *both* the universal and the Black categories. In contrast, the White adolescents may have been familiar with specific words in the Black categories (smoke, latin) but not with their inclusion in an organized category (drugs, dances). To uncover the source of the Black–White differences, the lists were partitioned into sublists containing either Black or universal categories, which were analyzed by the same methods applied to the list as a whole. Table 6.1 contains the recall and organization scores for the two kinds of categories for Trial 5, on which group differences were most pronounced.

Although the degree of category organization is greater for Black subjects on Black categories than on universal categories, the converse is true for White subjects. However, these differences between category

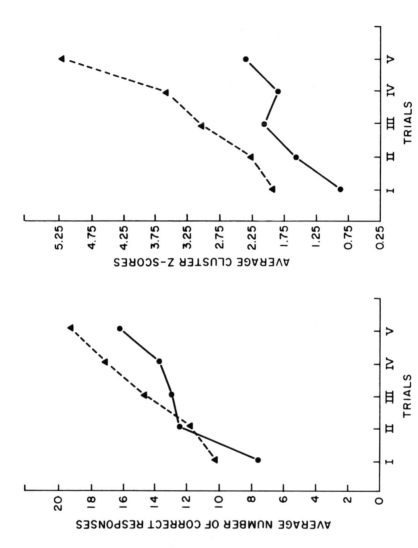

Figure 6.1. Average number recalled and cluster Z-score per trial. ▲ = Black adolescents; • = White adolescents.

Table 6.1. *Recall, clustering, and recall–clustering correlations by subcategory; Trial 5*

	Black adolescents			White adolescents		
	X̄ Recall per category type	Z̄	r_{x,z}	X̄ Recall per category type	Z̄	r_{x,z}
Black categories	9.94	1.93	0.83	8.65	0.29	0.08
Universal categories	9.35	1.50	0.89	7.50	0.57	0.70

types within each population are not statistically significant. Despite small numerical differences, there are no significant within-population differences in the amount recalled in the two kinds of categories. What does vary significantly within populations is the relationship between the amount recalled and the measure of category organization. The recall-organization correlation is high for both kinds of categories for Black students, but is high only for the universal items for White students. These results suggest that differential familiarity with the category membership of some items of a list affects performance on the list as a whole. If this hypothesis is correct, the presence of unfamiliar categories (or items that are perceived as difficult to assign to categories) converts a list that is considered completely organizable into a list which is treated by the subjects as only partially organizable. In effect, a mixed "categorizable-ranoom" list was created, thus presenting an organizational task more difficult for the White subjects than for the Black subjects, for whom all the categories were familiar. Consequently, White subjects must treat segments of the list differently (i.e., as reflected in differing recall-organization correlations).

Another study was designed to test this hypothesis. In this study, part of the list was structured with items distinctly categorizable, and part with items difficult to categorize. Forty White, college-aged subjects were given a standard verbal recall test. Each subject was presented with a 30-item list of words for five trials of free recall, in which the same procedures and instructions as those in the previous study were

Table 6.2. *Recall, clustering, and recall-clustering*
correlations for categorizable items in the
all-clusterable and mixed conditions

Group	$\bar{X}$ Recall for clusterable items	$\bar{Z}$	$r_{x,z}$
All-clusterable	8.6	1.53	0.82
Mixed	7.1	0.64	0.82

employed. The composition of the list differed for the two basic experimental groups. In the "All Clusterable" condition, subjects were read a
list consisting of five items each from the categories *birds, professions,*
spices, weapons, geography, kitchen appliances (Battig and Montague,
1969). In the "Mixed" condition, subjects were read a list consisting of
three of the categories from the All-Clusterable list, and 15 items taken
from the same source, except that each item was from a different conceptual category.

Table 6.2 presents responses to the three categories common to both
the All-Clusterable and Mixed lists. The results show that the difference in list recall of these categories was not significant. Over-all recall
is comparable to that observed in the first study. However, clustering for
the three common categories in the All-Clusterable condition is more
than twice as great as clustering for these categories in the Mixed condition. Finally, the correlation between clustering and recall is high in
both groups, as anticipated from the clustering–recall correlation of the
White adolescents for universal categories in the first study. Although
not shown in the table, recall for the clusterable items in the Mixed list
is slightly, but reliably, greater than recall of the nonclusterable items.
These results were exactly those anticipated on the assumption that the
Black categories in the first study functioned like random items for at
least some of the White adolescents.

A continuing effort to study the effect of sociolinguistic history on
memory organization has supplied additional supportive evidence to that
reported here. One investigation was conducted in a racially hetero-
geneous high school among Black and White students with a common
history of parochial-school training. Five different word lists were prepared from category exemplars provided by Black and White students.

Table 6.3. *Total correct number recalled by common subcategory types and race*

Subcategory types	Black categories		White categories	
	All-Black list	Black-White Mixed list	Black-White Mixed list	All-White list
Black Ss	40.5	37.0	29.5	29.6
White Ss	39.3	29.3	33.3	44.1

On one list, word categories from the Black-student norms were paired with those from the White-student norms, providing a Mixed condition; two homogeneous lists contained either all-Black or all-White exemplars from respective classification norms. Only universal categories were used on a fourth list, and a fifth list mixed universal with White exemplars. There were no over-all ethnic-group differences in performance, but general performance did vary by the type of list content and grade level. A closer examination of performance by individual subcategories was conducted to determine if previous trends were evident at this level of analysis. This required a comparison of subjects whose performance was on the same individual subcategories (e.g., Black singers, food, etc.). This procedure also allowed greater scrutiny of the effects on a single race-category type when the target words were part of either an all-Black list, all-White list, or a mixture of the two (Table 6.3).

The data analysis revealed that when ethnic-group performance is examined at the subcategory level, the trend is supportive of the evidence in the previous studies. In comparing common subcategories, Black subjects recalled more on the Black normative subcategories than they did on the White subcategories. White subjects did just the opposite. Although Blacks recalled more than Whites on Black categories, this difference was not significant. There was a significant difference in the greater recall of Whites on White categories than that of Blacks.

Interpretation of these results, I think, points out the difficulty in deciphering experimental performance in terms of the sociolinguistic development of different ethnic groups, particularly for the adolescent years. To speculate a little: from my observations, the social sharing between the various ethnic groups of this school is reflected in the word composition of some of the respective individual subcategories. When students in each ethnic group were asked to provide a listing of musical stars, they generated lists that differentiated popular Black stars from White ones. Understanding the recall performance in this category requires, in part, a recognition of the prominence of music in the lives of adolescents. Ethnic-group differences in musical preferences are diminishing among contemporary adolescents. Soul music and its stars frequently are featured on both popular-music stations and "all-Black" owned stations. The observed experience (and conversations) is that White adolescents, in their listening and social habits, are more likely to develop musical familiarity and preference within the combined category of soul and popular music than are the Black adolescents. In this instance, we have a highly shared category of experience in the direction of Black to White. This is evident when examining the lists made by White adolescents of musical stars, in which there is a greater incidence of naming prominent Black musical stars. Black adolescents tended to restrict their choices to Black stars. Considering the value of music in the lives of these adolescents, the "associative strength" of this category is probably high for both ethnic groups but the shared-familiarity edge tips more toward White students than Black. If this sharing applies to other categories of experience, it could account for a narrower difference between Black and White performance on Black categories than on White categories. The questions are: How many other conceptual categories have such pluralistic associations, and in what way does "context" mediate their order of priority? In present attempts to account for differential performances between ethnic groups, there is little effort to determine the equivalence of socialization experiences and its specificity and/or (dis)continuity.

Further study is needed to discover the experiential attributes of words and category labels and how daily experiences affect this acquisition process. Heretofore, interest in memory organization paid insufficient attention to how performance is governed by the subject's sociolinguistic history (i.e., how the organization and use of language is affected by past social experiences). It is apparent that the level of an individual's mnemonic performance is directly related to one's experience with the content of the task. Words presented as stimuli in the study of memory vary in their episodic meaning. An identical word may, in the hierarchy of associations, mean something totally different to two groups with diverse sociolinguistic backgrounds. For example, "greens" to a suburban weekend golfer will be perceived in a different associative context than will "greens" to an urban Black family.

This does not mean that either a golfer or a Black cook could not comprehend the semantic contexts of each other. Frequency of word usage in a particular context obviously affects free-recall performances. The task is to discover the domain of associations common to a group. What makes this chore difficult in our society is the cultural pluralism and the pervasive dominance of the media. The sharing of intercultural associations breeds familiarity, but not necessarily dominance, in our storage systems. Therefore, it is easy to assume and expect that subcultural groups in this country have had comparable exposure and, hence, familiarity with the many conceptual contexts of words. Moreover, the acquisition and utilization of mnemonic information is not definitely understood. Consequently variation in performance on recall tasks could be the result of a number of factors; conclusions about ethnic-group differences in mnemonic performance are, therefore, weakened further by lack of knowledge of sociolinguistic history and degree of intergroup assimilation.

Results of these studies are compatible with other current data and theory on recall and organization that emphasize the necessity of matching the subject's verbal organization with that used in the task materials. We can conclude that the relevance of the Jensen studies to the differential distribution of specific types of learning abilities within various American subpopulations is minimal or nonexistent. The assumption that word-frequency counts and category norms taken from the White middle-class population correctly describe the relationship of these same materials to minority-group populations is gratuitous; when materials from such minority-group populations are used in the same way, the common line of inference would lead us to the conclusion that White students lack organizing ability.

Future studies of ethnic and social-class differences on conceptual ability in memory should specify more carefully the relationship between the organization of a group's lexicon and memory as measured in psychological experiments.

Notes

This work was supported in part by grants from the Ford and Carnegie Foundations. Other contributors to this study are Lenora Fulani, Ellie Henkind, and Michael Cole.

1. Black categories and items were: *drugs* (smoke, coke, ups, downs, acid); *dances* (bump, latin, grind, robot, truckin'); *food* (chicken, greens, cornbread, chittlins, ribs). Universal items and categories were: *tools* (drill, axe, saw, file, hammer); *utensils* (spoons, plate, cup, glass, pan); *clothing* (shirt, hat, socks, pants, shoes).

References

Battig, W. F., and Montague, W. E. 1969. Category norms for the verbal items in 56 categories: A replication and extension of the Connecticut category norms. *Journal of Experimental Psychology Monograph*, 80: 3, Pt. 2.

Cofer, C. N. 1967. Does Conceptual Clustering Influence the Amount Retained in Immediate Free Recall? In: B. Kleinmuntz (Ed.), *Concepts and the Structure of Memory*. New York: Wiley.

Frankel, F., and Cole, M. 1971. Measures of category clustering in free recall. *Psychological Bulletin*, 76: 109–123.

Jensen, A. 1972. *Genetics and Education*. New York: Harper & Row.

Jensen, A., and Frederikson, J. 1973. Free recall of categorized and uncategorized lists: A test of the Jensen hypothesis. *Journal of Educational Psychology*, 65: 304–312.

Tulving, E., and Donaldson, W. (Eds.). 1972. *Organization of Memory*. New York: Academic Press.

7 Looking for Big Bird: Studies of memory in very young children

Judy S. DeLoache and Ann L. Brown

The period between one and three years of age is one of the most fascinating eras in human development: in no other comparable span of time do so many revolutionary changes occur. Cognitive processes undergo an extraordinary degree of reorganization as the child acquires language and makes the transition from sensorimotor to symbolic, representational thought. In spite of the importance of this early period, it has been relatively neglected by developmental psychologists until quite recently. One of the main reasons for this neglect has been the fact that young children are notoriously intractable research subjects; it is difficult to enlist their cooperation in the relatively artificial, unfamiliar tasks traditionally favored by psychologists, and even when they do seem to cooperate, their performance tends to be quite low (see, for example, Myers & Perlmutter, 1978). Although most parents recount numerous instances of their toddler remembering personally experienced events over days or even months, we are aware of no memory studies of young children where retention intervals of longer than 30 seconds have been used. It seems reasonable to infer from this discrepancy that the procedures commonly used to study early cognitive development are inadequate.

In this paper we will report an ongoing research project on young children's memory for object location that is aimed at studying the emergence and early refinement of various self-regulatory skills. We have made extensive efforts to avoid artificial experimental formats and to develop naturalistic, meaningful situations. The basic task that we have selected for our current research involves memory for object location (i.e., remembering where something is in space so one can retrieve it later). This is a variant of the delayed response task introduced by Hunter (1917) and used by him to study memory in a variety of species, ranging from rats to his 1-year-old daughter, Thayer. The essential feature of the delayed response problem is that the subject watches while an object is concealed in one of several potential containers. After a specified delay interval, during which the child's attention is typically distracted from the containers, he or she is allowed to find the hidden object.

This general format has been used in several recent studies with children between $1\frac{1}{2}$ and 3 years of age (e.g., Daehler, Bukatko, Benson, & Myers, 1976; Horn & Myers, 1978; Loughlin & Daehler, 1973). In the standard task 2-year-olds, for example, have been found to retrieve the object with no errors on slightly less than 50% of the trials (Daehler et al., 1976; Horn & Myers, 1978). The addition of visual and verbal cues to the spatial cues already present has sometimes increased the level of correct responding, to 66% with labeled pictures (Horn & Myers, 1978) and as high as 69% with containers differing in size (Daehler et al., 1976); but in other studies visual cues have not been helpful (Babska, 1965; Loughlin & Daehler, 1973). Thus, 2-year-old children generally perform above chance (Myers & Ratner, in press) in the standard delayed response task. Getting them to be correct more than half the time, however, requires the addition of carefully engineered cues. Furthermore, we wish to emphasize that in none of the above experiments was the delay interval longer than 25 seconds.

In our research our preliminary goals included devising a task in which we could ask very young children to remember something for more than half a minute. Accordingly, we have attempted to transform the basic delayed response task into a relatively natural situation. It takes the form of a hide-and-seek game that the child plays with a small stuffed animal. Several days before the experiment, each subject is given a toy (Mickey Mouse, Big Bird). Then, following our instructions, the parents teach their child the hide-and-seek game. The children are told that Mickey Mouse is going to hide and that they have to remember where he is hiding so they will be able to find him later. On each trial the child watches while his or her mother (or father) hides the toy in some natural location in their home, with a different location used for each trial. The specific locations obviously depend on the particular home, but include places like behind or under chairs and couches, under pillows, behind curtains, inside desk drawers. A kitchen timer is set for a specified interval and the child is taught to wait for the bell to ring. When it does, the child is allowed to go retrieve the "hiding" toy. The children very readily learn the rules of the hide-and-seek game and show obvious delight and excitement in playing it.

While we hoped that the hide-and-seek task would elicit performance from young children that would more accurately reflect their memorial competence, it was also designed to enable us to study very early forms of self-regulatory skills. These skills are the various processes by which people organize their thoughts and actions (Brown, 1978; Brown & DeLoache, 1978), including activities such as: *planning* ahead, *predicting* the outcome of some action (what will happen if?), *monitoring* ongoing activity (how am I doing?), *checking* on the results of actions (did that work, did it achieve my goal?), *correcting* errors or inadequacies (since what I just did didn't work, what would be a reasonable thing to try now?). These skills are the basic characteristics of efficient thought throughout life, and one of their most important properties is that they are transsituational. They apply to a whole range of problem-solving activities, from artificial experimental settings to everyday life. It is equally important to exercise these skills whether you're reading a text-book or a recipe; whether you're trying to remember who the seventh President of the United States was or where you left your car keys.

What we are referring to here as self-regulatory skills have often been described as a form of metacognition, and they are subsumed under Flavell's (1978) definition of metacognition as "knowledge that takes as its object or regulates any aspect of any cognitive endeavor." However, it is worthwhile noting that this definition comprises two (not necessarily separate) clusters – *knowledge* about cognition and *regulation* of cognition. The first concerns the relatively stable information individuals have about cognitive processes, tasks, strategies, and so forth, in general, as well as the knowledge they have about themselves engaged in those activities and tasks. We would not expect very young children to be capable of this sort of metacognitive activity, i.e., conscious knowledge about cognition. Indeed, Wellman (1977) has demonstrated the very meager extent of such information possessed by 3-year-old children.

It is the second cluster of metacognitive activities included in Flavell's statement, the self-regulatory skills, that we are interested in here. These might be expected to be exhibited by very young children as they attempt to learn or solve problems, However, unlike the activities in the first cluster, whether or not the self-regulatory mechanisms appear depends critically on the nature of the task and the expertise of the child.

One of the prerequisites to observing very early examples of self-regulatory activities is the existence of an appropriate task, one that challenges young children (so that planning, monitoring, and so forth might be helpful), yet that falls within their general competence. Otherwise, even if they have, or are at the point of developing, any rudimentary self-regulatory skills, they may be too overwhelmed by the novelty and difficulty of the task to exercise those skills (Shatz, 1978).

Several features of our hide-and-seek task should increase the likelihood of finding self-regulatory behavior in very young children. The task requires retrieval to be manifested in overt action – finding an object in the environment – rather than the purely internal retrieval of information from memory. In this situation, external cues can be used, and the desired goal state (as well as success or failure in attaining it) is obvious, even to a young child. In addition, the task takes place in the home and with parents, and there is evidence that self-regulation occurs earlier in natural and familiar settings than in artificial, unfamiliar ones (Istomina, 1977). This naturalism of the hide-and-seek task helped us avoid some of the common problems associated with testing children between 1 and 3 years of age. A frequent problem is that one is often not really sure whether the child completely understands the task. The extensive pretraining provided by their parents ensures us that our subjects clearly understand the task before being observed. Also, the children typically enjoy the hide-and-seek game enormously, so they are motivated to participate fully. This is critical, because getting young children to *want* to do whatever it is you want them to do is one of the most difficult aspects of working with them.

We have now completed three studies involving 41 subjects between 18 and 30 months of age.[1] The children participated in a total of four to eight trials of the basic hide-and-seek task for one or two observation days. Except for the first two trials in Study I, the delay intervals were either three or five minutes. (Notice that these are exceptionally long intervals for use with this age group. As stated before, the standard delayed response studies with toddlers have used intervals of less than 30 seconds.)

In all three studies the children's baseline performance was excellent. They went directly (with no errors of any kind) to the hidden toy from 71 to 84% of the trials. For purposes of comparison the subjects in each study were divided into older (25–30 months, mean age = approximately 27 months) and younger (18–24 months, mean age = approximately 20 months) groups. The older children generally did somewhat better (with between 83 and 96% errorless retrievals) than the younger ones (58 to 71% correct).[2]

Although the three- and five-minute intervals we used were much longer than any in the developmental literature, they did not appear to give our subjects much difficulty. In order to examine their performance at much longer intervals, we recruited most of the mothers of subjects in Study I to serve as surrogate experimenters. Each mother made five observations of her own child in the hide-and-seek game – two with 30-minute intervals, two at 60 minutes, and one overnight. They were cautioned to put the toy somewhere the child would not happen upon it by chance. Since the mothers had been given extensive instructions about how to conduct the game with their children, and since we had observed all of them playing with the children, we were fairly confident of their ability to make objective and accurate observations for us. However, as a partial check on their data, one of the regular experimenters was present for one of the 30- or 60-minute observations for each child.

The children did surprisingly well at these longer intervals. They found their toy (with no errors) 88% of the time after a 30-minute wait, and 69% after an hour. After the overnight interval, they scored 77% errorless retrievals. (Several children, after the overnight hiding, retrieved their toy before their parents got up in the morning. One long-suffering mother informed us that her child woke her at 5 A.M. wanting to go downstairs and get Big Bird.) On the occasions we formally observed, the children *always* found their toy, so it seems reasonable to assume that the mothers' reports were not exaggerated.

Most of the children were also given a more complex task on later observation days in Study I. The same basic procedure was followed, except that on each trial three toys were hidden, each one in a different place. After an interval of either three or five minutes, the child was instructed which of the three toys to retrieve (with each serial position during hiding tested equally often). The child was then encouraged to find the other two toys as well. This multiple hiding procedure might be expected to produce a great deal of interference, since each trial involved three different toys hidden in three different locations, and sometimes a location was used more than once over trials. However, performance was again surprisingly good. On 67% of the trials the subjects retrieved the specific toy requested. Overall, they found 70% of the hidden toys, with a mean of 2.1 toys found per trial. These figures were closely replicated in a similar task in Study II.

The data reported so far argue forcefully that if freed from the artificial constraints and demands of standard laboratory tasks, very young children may be willing to demonstrate more of their cognitive competence than they have heretofore done. Given that our young subjects did so well in the standard hide-and-seek task, it seemed reasonable to think that variations in it might elicit some simple forms of the self-regulatory skills in which we are interested. In fact, we believe that in Studies II and III we have evidence showing the appearance of one such skill, intelligent self-correction, during the age period between 18 and 30 months.

A major goal of these two experiments was to examine what can be considered a rudimentary form of metamemory: we wanted to assess how confident our subjects were of their own memory. Only a few studies have examined metamemory in children as young as three. Wellman (1977) investigated 3- to 5-year-olds' knowledge of the effect of various task variables on memory difficulty, and Wellman, Ritter, and Flavell (1975) observed the use of primitive precursors of deliberate memory strategies by 3-year-olds but not 2-year-olds. No form of metamemory has to date been noted for children under three.

An extremely simple form of metamemory would be the assessment of how well or how certainly one knows something. Since our subjects' performance was generally so high, one would expect that they would be quite confident that they remembered correctly, even if they were incapable of verbalizing that confidence. A standard way of assessing certainty in preverbal infants and young children is to present a surprise trial (Charlesworth, 1969; Gelman, 1972), where the experimenter does something to disconfirm the subject's expectations. The degree of surprise shown is used as an index of how strong the expectation was.

Each subject received two surprise trials on which the toy was hidden as usual, but was surreptitiously moved by the experimenter while the child was out of the room on some pretext. The surprise trials were embedded (as Trials 2 and 5) in a series of six or seven standard hide-and-seek trials (i.e., ones in which the toy was not moved). The surprise trials were administered on a separate day following the standard hide-and-seek testing described earlier.

In Study II two observers independently recorded and coded the subjects' behavior upon looking for and not finding the toy where it had been hidden. To be conservative, we have included only behaviors noted by both observers on the surprise trials. In Study III, the subjects were videotaped while participating in the game in their homes, so data from that study have been scored from the tapes. The figures that follow reflect the combined data from the two studies.

The experimenters' subjective impressions were that the children were very surprised indeed not to find their toy on the surprise trials. Several behaviors indicative of surprise were coded and analyzed (including verbalizations and negative emotional reactions), and they substantiate the experimenters' impressions. In this paper we will discuss in detail one of our surprise measures – the patterns of searching other locations after failing to find the toy in the correct place.

We should first mention that in general, the children almost never searched a location that had not been used previously, either on that day of testing or on a previous day. This was true for both age groups, and for both surprise trials and those trials on which subjects happened to make errors. Thus, the children had some general recollection of the set of hiding locations used.

The older and younger groups displayed different patterns of searching after failing to find their toy on surprise trials. The older children generally behaved in an intelligent fashion, much as an older child or an adult would do. After looking in the correct location and not finding the toy, they usually (on 88% of the surprise trials) searched somewhere else for it, and on the majority of the trials (76%) their searches fell into one or more of the following categories: (1) an adjacent location – if the toy had been hidden under one couch cushion, they might look under the next cushion; (2) a nearby or related location – if the toy had been put in a chair, they might look under or behind the chair; (3) an analogous location – if the toy had been hidden under a pillow at one end of the couch, they might look under the pillow at the other end of the couch; and (4) on the second surprise trial only, they sometimes looked in the place to which the experimenter had moved the toy on the first surprise trial.

The younger children were much less likely to conduct additional searches after failing to find their toy. On slightly over half the surprise trials (54%), they did not look in any other location after searching the correct one. They would often wander around in the middle of the room or stand near their mothers, apparently at a loss for what to do next. Some of the younger subjects returned to the correct location and searched there again, sometimes repeatedly. On only 26% of the surprise trials did the younger children search in the kind of related areas favored by the older subjects. They were just as likely, when they searched somewhere, to go to a place where the toy had been hidden on an earlier trial (especially the immediately preceding one). This tendency to search a prior location is reminiscent of the Stage IV error in object permanence (Harris, 1975) and the perseverative errors frequently observed for toddlers in memory and problem solving tasks (Webb, Massar, & Nadolny, 1972).

The older children's tendency to search additional locations on surprise trials reveals a form of certainty of memory in that they concentrated their searching in areas that were nearby or logically related to the correct location. They looked in places where the toy might reasonably be. They seemed to allow for the possibility that they misremembered some detail ("maybe it's under this cushion instead of that one") or that some fairly plausible event intervened ("maybe the toy fell out of the chair"). One subject verbalized exactly this: he looked in the desk drawer in which his toy had been hidden, said "Did Mickey Mouse fall out?", and then proceeded to search behind the desk. The children were also alert to the possibility that the experimenter was tricking them a second time.

To summarize, both the younger and older children seem certain of their memory for the correct location, but they differ in their ability to re-evaluate the situation after failing to find the toy and in their flexibility in initiating alternative measures. The younger children most often do nothing at all. When they do, they are as likely to simply go to a prior hiding place as to search in a related location. The older children are more flexible and logical in their attempt to deal with the disconfirmation of their expectations. They are able to reflect on the situation and consider where the toy *must* be, given it is not where they remembered.

To account for its absence, they appear to consider plausible physical or mental explanations: something happened to the toy, or some detail of their memory must be faulty.

These examples of logical searching on the part of the older children (and a few of the younger ones) represent the exercise of a self-regulatory skill – thoughtful correction of errors. When the children fail to find the toy, they can only assume that they are in error (at least on the first surprise trial). They then try to correct that supposed error by thinking about where the toy is most likely to be. They proceed to conduct the same sort of organized, logical search that an adult might do. If you remembered that you had left your car keys on top of the kitchen counter but then couldn't find them, you would probably look for them behind the cookie jar on the counter and on the floor around the counter.

In conclusion, these very young children performed very competently in our basic hide-and-seek game, which they completely understood and thoroughly enjoyed playing. Even when the game was modified to be presumably more difficult, with multiple hidings and delay intervals extended to as long as an hour, they maintained an excellent level of performance. Furthermore, they showed what is probably the earliest evidence yet observed of self-regulation by the logical search procedures they employed on the surprise trials. The competent and sophisticated behavior of our young subjects suggests that if tasks are made more comprehensible and meaningful to young children, they will be more enthusiastic research participants and provide us with more valid data.

Notes

This research was supported in part by Grants HD 05951 and HD 06864 and Research Career Development Award HD 00111 from the National Institutes of Child Health and Human Development.

1. The number of subjects and their mean ages in the three studies were as follows: Study I – 17 Subjects, mean age = 23 months (Older = 27 months, Younger = 20 months); Study II – 12 Subjects, mean age = 24 months (Older = 27 months, Younger = 22 months); Study III – 22 Subjects, mean age = 24 months (Older = 28 months, Younger = 21 months).
2. The complete data on errorless retrievals in the three studies were as follows: Study I – 76% correct overall (Older = 85%, Younger = 67%); Study II – 84% correct overall (Older = 96%, Younger = 71%); Study III – 71% correct overall (Older = 83%, Younger = 58%).

References

Babska, Z. The formation of the conception of identity of visual characteristics of objects seen successively. In P. H. Mussen (Ed.), European research in cognitive development. *Monographs of the Society for Research in Child Development*, 1965, *30* (2, Serial No. 100), 112–124

Brown, A. L. Knowing when, where, and how to remember: A problem of metacognition. In R. Glaser (Ed.), *Advances in instructional psychology*. Hillsdale, N.J.: Erlbaum, 1978.

Brown, A. L., & DeLoache, J. S. Skills, plans, and self-regulation. In R. Siegler (Ed.), *Children's thinking: What develops*. Hillsdale, N.J.: Erlbaum, 1978.

Charlesworth, W. R. Surprise and cognitive development. In D. Elkind & J. H. Flavell (Eds.), *Studies in cognitive development: Essays in honor of Jean Piaget*. New York: Oxford University Press, 1969.

Daehler, M., Bukatko, D., Benson, K., & Myers, N. The effects of size and color cues on the delayed response of very young children. *Bulletin of the Psychonomic Society*, 1976, *7*, 65–68.

Flavell, J. H. Metacognitive development. In J. M. Scandura & C. J. Brainerd (Eds.), *Structural-process theories of complex human behavior*. Leyden, The Netherlands: Sijthoff, 1978.

Gelman, R. Logical capacity of very young children: Number invariance rules. *Child Development*, 1972, *43*, 75–90.

Harris, P. L. Development of search and object permanence during infancy. *Psychological Bulletin*, 1975, *82*, 332–344.

Horn, H. A., & Myers, N. A. Memory for location and picture cues at ages two and three. *Child Development*, 1978, *49*, 845–856.

Hunter, W. S. The delayed reaction in a child. *Psychological Review*, 1917, *24*, 74–87.

Istomina, Z. M. The development of voluntary memory in preschool-age children. In M. Cole (Ed.), *Soviet developmental psychology: An anthology*. White Plains, N.Y.: Sharpe, 1977.

Loughlin, K. A., & Daehler, M. A. The effects of distraction and added perceptual cues on the delayed reaction of very young children. *Child Development*, 1973, *44*, 348–388.

Myers, N., & Ratner, H. H. Memory of very young children in delayed response tasks. In J. Sidowski (Ed.), *Cognition, conditioning, and methodology: Contemporary issues in experimental psychology*. Hillsdale, N.J.: Erlbaum, in press.

Myers, N. A., & Perlmutter, M. Memory in the years from two to five. In P. A. Ornstein (Ed.), *Memory development in children*. Hillsdale, N.J.: Erlbaum, 1978.

Shatz, M. The relationship between cognitive processes and the development of communication skills. In B. Keasey (Ed.), *Nebraska Symposium on Motivation*. Lincoln: University of Nebraska Press, 1978.

Webb, R. A., Massar, B., & Nadolny, T. Information and strategy in the young child's search for hidden objects. *Child Development*, 1972, *43*, 91–104.

Wellman, M. Preschoolers' understanding of memory-relevant variables, *Child Development*, 1977, *48*, 1720–1723.

Wellman, H. M., Ritter, R., & Flavell, J. H. Deliberate memory behavior in the delayed reactions of very young children. *Developmental Psychology*, 1975, *11*, 780–787.

8   "Body analogy" and the cognition of rotated figures

Yutaka Sayeki

A few years ago, I bought a new moped for daily transportation to my office. For the first couple of weeks that I rode the bike, I could not overcome a particular difficulty in signaling turns: when I was turning, I always found the turn-signal flashing in the opposite direction I intended. The cause of the difficulty was obvious. The turn-signal switch, which was located near the right grip, was set up so that flipping to the right would flash the signal for a left turn and flipping to the left would flash the signal for a right turn. (See Figure 8.1.)

The first thing I tried in order to overcome this difficulty was to flip the switch twice, first to the direction which I naturally *felt* to be correct, then to the opposite side, which I *knew* to be correct. Although this habit ultimately guaranteed the correct signal, it took too long and angry drivers often honked behind my bike.

Fortunately, I found an easy way to make the trouble disappear, and I have never had any trouble in signaling turns since then. The trick was quite simple: I imagined a steering wheel of an ordinary car over the handle bars of the bike. (See Figure 8.1.) In Japanese cars, a steering wheel usually has a *turn-signal* attached to the right side of the steering column. (The driver's seat is located at the right side in Japanese cars.) The right turn-signal flashes if the lever is flipped downward, and the left turn-signal flashes if the lever is flipped upward (See Figure 8.1.) So, when I wanted to signal a turn on the bike, I simply imagined myself manipulating a "turn-signal lever" over the handle, flipping to the direction which was quite natural for turns if I were driving a car.

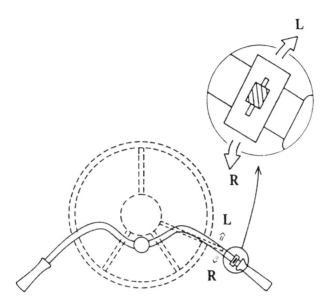

Figure 8.1. Imaginary steering wheel and turn signal lever over the handle-bars of the bike.

Such elaborated imagery of a steering wheel and a turn-signal lever was necessary only at first. The image soon faded away, and after a week or so, it seemed that a faint feeling, or only a small fragment of the "tactile image," or flipping the lever by the thumb was sufficient to elicit a correct response. After a few more weeks of practicing, signaling for turns became completely automatic, and I did not even think of the direction of flipping the switch.

This episode is an example of a very common heuristic, namely, "To see something as if it were something else." This kind of heuristic is well practiced in children's play, poets' metaphors, physicists' models, and equations in mathematicians' theorems. The only thing we know for sure about this heuristic is that it works. Once we discover that object A can be viewed as if it were object B, for the purposes at hand the relevant structural and functional relationships suddenly become apparent.

In viewing A as if it were B, we do not transfer all of the relations or the procedures from B to A. In the above example, when I viewed the

turn switch as if it were the turn-signal lever of a car, I did not grasp
the switch by the right hand, as I would do for the turn-signal lever. I
only pushed a tiny nob in the direction of the "lever" turn with the
thumb. Thus in viewing A as if it were B, most of the schema for A may
remain the same, with modifications at a crucial point. The image of B
seems to prepare the new schema for activation as soon as the old schema
has been "detached" from the environmental constraints. In the present
example, grasping the grip of the handle belongs to the old schema and
is strongly imposed by the environmental constraints: we cannot remove
the right hand from the grip, no matter how vividly we imagine the steering wheel or the turning lever of a car. But the direction of moving the
thumb is a "detachable" part of the schema, although in the old schema
the thumb tends to move in the wrong direction. Thus it is the direction of the movement of the thumb that was replaced by the new schema
which had been prepared for activation by imagining the turn-signal
lever.

From this analysis, we may understand why seeing A as analogous to
B works. It works by opening our eyes to the new *possibilities* which have
been well-practiced with B but which have never been thought of for
A because of the old schema for A. The introduction of B as an analogy
for A replaces those "detachable" parts of the old schema for A by
new possibilities suggested by B, while the "undetachable" parts of the
old schema for A remain the same, because of strong contextual,
environmental constraints.

This interpretation explains the so-called "directionality" of analogy.
The analogy of B for A is not the same as the analogy of A for B. Such
directionality comes from the simple fact that "detachable" parts of the
schema for A are different from "detachable" parts of the schema for B.

The experiments introduced below demonstrate that viewing a configuration of blocks as if it were a *human body* drastically reduced the
reaction time to decide whether the presented shape (rotated through a
variety of degrees) was the same as the standard shape or different (its
mirror image), regardless of the angular disparity. Response time on this
task has been known to be proportional to the amount of physical rotation necessary to align the two shapes spatially, (e.g., Shepard and
Metzler, 1971). In our experiments, however, once a visual cue hinted
at a "body analogy," then even with the "hint" subsequently removed,
subjects could immediately attend to the critical part of the "body"

which distinguishes most effectively different "postures" in the block configurations.

Experiment I compares three conditions: Non-Instruction in which the subject was not given any specific suggestions about strategy, Turn in which the subject was instructed to rotate the standard figure in his mind to align it with the stimulus figure, and Head-at-Normal-Position in which the subject was given a visual "hint" without any verbal comment – a configuration of blocks was shown with a "head" placed in a position which suggested the shape (posture) of a "human body."

Experiment II simply adds two conditions to the instruction; Arrow-Indicator in which an arrow-line was indicated in place of the "head" in the Head-at-Normal-Position, and Head-at-Abnormal-Position in which the position of the "head" was shifted to a position not conducive to interpreting of the block configuration as a "human body." Reaction time was taken separately for "same" judgements and "different" judgements in Experiment II.

Experiment I

Twenty-four male students at Tokyo University of Science participated in the experiment. They were arbitrarily assigned to three groups, Non-Instruction, Turn, Head-at-Normal-Position, each containing eight subjects.

A set of 48 slides were projected on a screen in front of the subject. On each slide, there were two figures displayed horizontally: the figure on the left was always the same, standard figure, a perspective line drawing of a three dimensional configuration of blocks, similar to the figures in Shepard and Metzler (1971). The figure on the right was obtained by rotating on the picture plane either the standard figure or its mirror image. There were twelve different positions of the standard figure, rotated in steps of 30° from 0° to 330°. Twelve positions of the mirror image were similarly obtained. Each of the twenty-four different pairs of figures were presented twice during each experimental run.

The experiment was run for each subject individually. The subjects were informed that there would be 48 trials, with two figures projected on the screen for each trial. The figure on the left was always the same, but the figure on the right was either a rotation of the figure on the left, or a rotation of its mirror image. They were asked to judge whether the two figures were the same, or mirror images, and to respond accordingly as quickly as possible.

The subjects were then shown a slide with a standard figure and a rotated standard figure. The experimenter explained that the two figures were simply different views of the same object. He instructed the subjects to examine the figures and respond when they had confirmed that the figures were the same.

The next slide was of the same standard figure and a rotated mirror image of the standard. The experimenter explained that in these slides the two figures were different views of the mirror images of each other. The subjects were asked to examine the slides and respond when they had confirmed this fact.

After the instruction, subjects under the three conditions were treated differently. The subjects in the Non-Instruction condition were simply shown a slide of the standard figure alone for one minute. The subjects in the Turn condition were shown a slide of the standard figure alone for one minute and instructed to practice mentally rotating it. They were told that rotating the standard figure to align it with the second figure would help them judge identity. In the Head-at-Normal-Position condition, subjects were presented for one minute a slide of the standard figure with a head on it. The head was positioned to suggest correspondence between the block configuration and a specific body posture. This suggested correspondence was not verbally mentioned and no instructions were given concerning strategies for making identity judgements. (See Figure 8.2.)

After the above instructions were given subjects, in all of the three conditions were presented with the same set of 48 slides. The reaction time was recorded to the nearest millisecond by a microcomputer from the time of onset of the projected slide, to the subject's button push.

Results

We computed regression lines for reaction time as a linear function of angular disparity between the two figures in the stimulus display. Angular disparities for more than 180 degrees were transformed into the interval of 0–180 degrees. For example, data for 270 degrees of clockwise rotation, or 90 degrees of counter-clockwise rotation, were both treated as 90 degrees of disparity in the analysis.

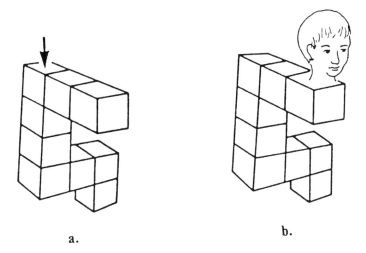

Figure 8.2. (a) Block configuration in standard position. (b) Standard block configuration with head suggesting body position.

The slope of the regression lines for Non-Instruction and Turn were almost identical except for the intercepts (Turn, y = 0.0140X + 2.37; Non-Instruction, y = 0.0147X + 1.81). In other words, the instruction to "Turn" produced almost the same "speed" of mental rotation (68–70 degrees per second) as "No-instruction," but asking subjects to "Turn" their mental images slowed their overall responses 0.6 seconds more than "No-instruction."

On the other hand, the regression line for Head-at-Normal-Position is almost flat (y = 0.0010X + 1.50). This result can hardly be interpreted as the effect of "mental rotation." If we use the Head-at-Normal-Position data to estimate the "speed" of rotation, we would calculate 2.6 revolutions per second! The Head-at-Normal-Position instructions also produced less errors in subjects' judgements: 11.5 percent errors in Non-Instruction, 10.7 percent errors in Turn, and 6.3 percent errors in Head-at-Normal-Position.

In order to see what individual subjects were doing as they became more practiced, we traced the change of the regression coefficients, slope and intercept, for the subject's responses in *moving intervals* of every six trials; that is, the subject's responses from the first trial to the sixth trial were analyzed, and then his responses from the second to the seventh trials were analyzed, and so on. If the subject was really *rotating* his mental image with a fixed speed, then the slope and the intercept in every moving interval should not change. More precisely, if the subject did not learn about the rotation of mental images, but did learn how to respond, then we would expect that the slope would not change much, while the intercept would go down. On the other hand, if the subject learned about the rotation, without learning about responding, then the slopes would become smaller, without much change in the intercepts, and so on.

When we analyzed individual data for the moving intervals, we were surprised to see that in the Non-Instruction and Turn conditions there were large fluctuations of slopes and intercepts like a random walk from one trial to another. On the other hand, responses under Head-at-Normal-Position were, without exception, very stable. All slopes and intercepts were near zero and fluctuated only slightly.

Although the drastic reduction of reaction time and the small effect of figural rotation were observed in the Head-at-Normal-Position group, perhaps those effects simply resulted from the addition of an external cue to the stimulus figure in the instruction period. In order to eliminate such possibilities, Experiment II introduced two additional conditions; Arrow-Indicator in which an arrow line was put at the position where the "head" had been put in the figure for Head-at-Normal-Position, and Head-at-Abnormal-Position in which the "head" was shown in a position that makes it difficult to imagine the configuration of blocks as a "human body." It was expected that neither condition would reduce reaction time and that some "rotation effects" would be observed as in the previous conditions, Non-Instruction and Turn.

Experiment II

Subjects were forty male student volunteers at Tokyo University of Science. They were randomly assigned to two conditions, Arrow-Indicator and Head-at-Abnormal-Position, with equal numbers of subjects. Subjects under each condition were further divided into "SAME" group and "DIFFERENT" groups. Subjects in SAME responded by pushing a button only when the two figures on the display were different views of the same object, and did not respond (simply saying "Pass") when the two figures were views of different objects. Subjects in DIF-

FERENT pushed the button only when the two figures on the display were views of different objects, and said, "Pass" otherwise. The experimental procedure was the same as in Head-at-Normal-Position in Experiment II except for the slide presented during the instruction period. The slides shown in Figure 8.3 were presented in place of the slide shown in the Head-at-Normal-Position condition in the first experiment.

Results

Regression lines were computed for Arrow-Indicator-SAME, Arrow-Indicator-DIFFERENT, Head-at-Abnormal-Position-SAME, and Head-at-Abnormal-Position-DIFFERENT. The two SAME judgements produced essentially the same regression line which has a large slope (0.02) with small intercept (about 1 second). This slope implies about 50 degrees of "rotation" per second. The two DIFFERENT judgements produced similar slopes (0.00786 for Arrow-Indicator, and 0.00109 for Head-at-Abnormal-Position), approximately 100–125 degrees of rotation per second, but with about 1.5 seconds' difference

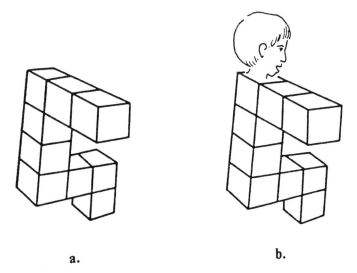

a.   b.

Figure 8.3. (a) Block configuration in standard position. (b) Standard block configuration in Head-at-Abnormal-Position.

of every
six trials. As in the previous analysis of the Non-Instruction and Turn
conditions, the slopes and intercepts fluctuated up and down from one
trial to the next.

Conclusions

The results of the two experiments suggest the following points.

During the ordinary "mental rotation" task, similar to that of Shepard
and Metzler (1971), subjects actually attempted a number of different
strategies to find distinct cues and the ways to match the two figures.
This resulted in great fluctuations of both slopes and intercepts of successive regression lines.

The unstable search for cues seems to be rather unconscious. Even if
the subjects were instructed to "rotate" their mental images (and they
actually reported that they had done so), the fluctuations of the response
data appeared to be even larger than in the no-instruction case.

On the other hand, the suggestion of a "body analogy" for the figures
seems to be very easy for the subjects to use. Without exception, all subjects showed extremely stable responses from the first trial, with almost
zero slopes and extremely small intercepts. The suggestion for the "body
analogy" was not explicitly stated; subjects were shown only a single
slide of a block with a human head placed at a proper position.

Neither placing the human head at an improper position nor putting
an arrow line at the normal "head" position made much difference from
the no-instruction condition, although putting the "head" at the improper position helped slightly for matching the figures with small
angular disparities.

It should be noted that there was a large difference between the SAME and DIFFERENT conditions; with much faster reaction in the SAME condition. This fact may support our conjecture that the so-called "mental rotation" task may not be like a physical process of rotation/matching of a template, but more like a search process of *disproving* the proposition that the two figures were DIFFERENT. The reaction time seemed to be spent for finding what kinds of cues can disprove the proposition most effectively. The reason that the "body analogy" worked may be that it is easy to find cues which trigger entirely different actions (imaginary extensions of the right or left arm), which clearly prove or disprove the proposition that the two figures are the SAME or DIF-FERENT. The distinctiveness of these cues comes from the mental schema which directs the activation of different body movements. The "body analogy" seems to be a rich storehouse of such schemata consisting of a variety of levels and hierarchies of cues triggering different body movements. Moreover, all of the schemata in the body movements have been well practiced, ready to be called upon whenever proper goals and constraints are imposed. Therefore, the schemata are ready to be activated even to a fragment of external stimulus, as long as it is possible to "view the object as if it were (a part of) my own body."

Reference

Shepard, R. N., & Metzler, J. Mental rotation of three-dimensional objects. *Science*, 1971, *171*, 701–703.

9   Paradigms and prejudice

Laboratory of Comparative Human Cognition

The Laboratory of Comparative Human Cognition has always treated research training (supported by a combination of federal and private funds) as a central part of its activities. A constant theme of our research has been the need to bring diverse populations and diverse points of view to bear on the ways in which culturally organized experience shapes the development of human nature. As constant as our basic theme has been the difficulty of convincing the scientific community that highly trained professionals representing the widest possible variety of experiential backgrounds is a scientific necessity in this era of very rapid social and technological change.

In this note we want to address the problem of research and training as they are influenced by the process of funding research grants. We focus on a specific example, brought to our attention by Anna Fay Vaughn-Cooke, a former fellow of LCHC. The particulars of this case are in no way exceptional. But it is timely and exceptionally clear for what it reveals about the ways in which dominant scientific paradigms maintain themselves and the unhealthy convergence between scientific paradigms and patterns of social inequality.

Our discussion is organized in several stages. First, we review the background to Dr. Vaughn-Cooke's research. We then summarize the nature of the objections and support provided by reviewers. We characterize the reviewers' comments in terms of the basic scientific paradigms (linguistic, experimental, quantitative) that are brought to bear in the evaluations. Then we point out an assumption that comes as free baggage with these paradigmatic arguments – the assumption of normativity applied to one ethnic/socio-economic group.

The critiques summarized, we address the problem of institutionally acceptable response. Two categories for questioning the review decision are provided by the granting agency, "prejudice" and "bias." We analyze the way in which these bureaucratic categories translate back into scientific argument, outlining the restricted means available to researchers who would pursue either route.

To quote a long term econometric friend of LCHC, "In variability there is hope." It is our intention here to stimulate discussion of ways to increase the variability of the voices that can whisper to us about human nature.

The particular case

Anna Fay Vaughn-Cooke, and her colleague, Ida Stockman, have asked for reconsideration of a decision by the National Science Foundation (NSF) to refrain from funding a proposal they submitted in the spring of 1983. They have sent copies of their response to the evaluations on which the decision was based along with copies of those evaluations to people throughout the country who are interested in their work. The NSF people to contact for more information are the Acting Assistant Director whose office handles reconsideration requests and the Director of the Linguistics Program, whose office processed the proposal.

The proposed research

The work is a study of children's language acquisition, in particular of locatives. It is basic research, purporting to generalize interest. It describes how children acquire a basic aspect of language competency. Vaughn-Cooke and Stockman identify eight particular locative subtypes of interest, some dynamic (e.g., "They are going away," or "Put it on the table."), and some static (e.g., "They are away," or "It is on the table."). The Investigators are moving beyond the current state of the work which stresses most the acquisition of individual locative words (e.g., "away" or "on"); they designed the project to study ". . . the complex set of factors which affect the use of these words in coding dynamic and static location concepts," and their goal is "to contribute to a more comprehensive account of this area of semantic development."

They point to the importance of having this information available for applied fields that deal with language development. They focus on three specific hypotheses and provide a complex system for describing child utterances that will enable the hypotheses to be examined systematically, and justify this system.

Vaughn-Cooke and Stockman did not have to collect new data. They possessed a video-taped data base of the locative utterances of twelve boys and girls, the sample for each child spanning 18 months. The children ranged in age from a year and a half to six years. All of the children are from working-class Black homes and communities as are the researchers.

There is a deeper background, part of it residing in the biography of the Principal Investigator who was the LCHC fellow. Vaughn-Cooke was a speech therapist who experienced and understood the weakness of the diagnostic and remedial machinery available for dealing with Black children. She entered a new field, receiving a Ph.D. from Georgetown University in sociolinguistics, a field which had a theoretical and practical interest in concerns like those that Vaughn-Cooke expressed. Her dissertation took full advantage of the training provided at Georgetown for quantitative methods useful to study language with respect to its synchronic variation and change in progress. She documented age-graded evidence for lexical change in Southern Black English, going beyond the more common sociolinguistic emphasis on phonetic differences and showing a relationship between phonological change and changes in derivational morphology. While the motivation for her graduate work was practical, her control of the field was extensive and deep and her dissertation reflects her interest in, and ability to handle, theoretical issues of importance to linguistics.

Vaughn-Cooke began her new career in a department which provided an opportunity for her to train students in both of her fields. She taught basic linguistics and sociolinguistics as well as speech therapy diagnosis and remediation. She developed alternative instruments and methods that have proven helpful in dealing with language problems of children from Black homes and communities.

However, there was a major stumbling block to a fully satisfactory approach to the problem – lack of basic research. It is difficult to diagnose and remediate problematic speech development without an adequate research base of ordinary non-problematic development. The gap in the research was two-fold: (1) the available work was, by and large,

limited to studies of children from White middle-class homes in collegiate communities and therefore of unknown character with respect
to generalizability to other children; and (2) much of the available
work omitted interesting, more complex, interactions that would justify
empirical and theoretical links between the studies of language development on the one hand and the concrete circumstances in which
chidren acquired language and displayed their normative or problematic
progress toward full functioning in their native languages on the other
hand.

Subsequently, now working with Stockman, Vaughn-Cooke created a
research program for addressing these problems. Developing the
grounding needed in the methods and theories of child language studies,
they received funding from the National Institute of Education
(NIE) to collect and analyze an extensive corpus. They videotaped
children in various settings and chronicled individual development.
Because of the age stratification in their sample, they have a good base
for considering all of the pre-school years. They began processing
their data; indexing the tapes identifying certain segments to be transcribed in the linguistically appropriate, but complex and time con-
suming way, and beginning analysis of some developing structures. For
the first time, there is some evidence and some argument available to
address the question of those factors in language development studies
in English that appear to be general and those that appear to be specifically related to class and ethnicity. The NIE grant was a provisional
multi-year grant; their application for continuation was viewed as
almost pro-forma. They had made good progress and their initial
work had been presented and praised in various forums. However, NIE
was changing in response to the economy and the new administration.
Just about as soon as they had completed the longitudinal data collection, they were without funds to continue the data processing and
analysis.

Funding from other sources was sought. The proposal to NSF was
a specifically designed and specifically written document that would
support new analysis to continue the research program. The locative
study described above was the result.

The reviews. Five reviews of the proposal are available. An excellent
rating was provided by one reviewer, noting that the proposal was tightly
written and the design exemplary, the literature well searched and

handled with insight. This reviewer notes that the proposal "plugs a hole" in the field, that while the researchers come out of a different tradition, they are "well within the purview of linguistics," and that their work on language development is well supported by their post-doctoral and institutional experiences, including the organization sponsoring the proposal (The Center for Applied Linguistics). A second reviewer rates the proposal very good, pointing to the importance of the Investigators' effort to go beyond the study of individual locative words and the value of the longitudinal data base. Like the first, this reviewer points to "the paucity of research in this particular area" and sees the "research activity of the applicants" as positive.

Now for the bad news. Two reviewers rated the proposal as fair and one rated it as poor. Vaughn-Cooke and Stockman's response concentrates on these reviews.

The response to the evaluation

Vaughn-Cooke and Stockman prepared and submitted a 10 and 1/2 page response, with 2 pages of references, focusing on the two "fair" ratings and the "poor" rating. In lieu of any quantitative evidence from the agency, they examined the reviewers comments for evidence of judgments that are procedurally unfair. They conclude that two reviews "reflect evidence of a deliberate attempt to build a case against our research" because it was conducted with Black children. The other "fair" rating, they conclude, contains unfounded criticisms that should be rejected.

We concur with their statement in the covering letter that the most disturbing aspect of the whole event is the treatment given to studies focusing on Black children subjects. The nature of the reviews and the applicants' responses strike us as yet another indicator of a common, underlying, source of confusion arising from the politics of representation as they are discussed in an earlier issue of this *Newsletter* (see Cole, 1983).

Paradigms give no quarter

One evaluation, with a fair rating, begins positively, "The proposed research addresses an important topic in a creative and provocative manner." The Investigators, in their response, note that the reviewer argues for one small adjustment in their descriptive schema which their analytic procedures are fully capable of accommodating and which they propose to test out.

However, they point out that the reviewer's major criticisms suggest a lack of familiarity with the proposal. First, the evaluation suggests that there are "certain deficiencies of concept and method," but the response shows that in one case, the task the reviewer argued couldn't be done, was not even proposed, and in other cases, that the concept or method the reviewer was looking for was clearly stated on particular pages of the original proposal.

From our reading of the reviewers' comments, it appears that they can best be understood as reflecting what might be termed as paradigm prejudice. In a section of the evaluation called, "*Undue demands on resources*," the reviewer begins, "My final concern is methodological." This turns out not to be quite the non-sequitur that it at first appears, if the reader assumes that the writer is building a case against the proposed research on the basis of a bias, and that the reviewer has prejudged the pertinent issues.

The writer continues, "The appeal of naturalistic data is undeniable, particularly given the ethnographic Zeitgeist. The budget and time line for this project, however, make the costs of this method quite clear: . . . I am not convinced that the putative advantages of this method warrant this expense." The review ends with a suggestion that the data bank is suitable for "general grammatical or discourse schemas [rather] than for the study of a single semantic field."

The reviewer claims that "structured comprehension or expression tasks" are "apparently valid and useful" and "more economical." There is no argumentation, evidence or literature citation offered to back up this claim, although the readership of this *Newsletter* might certainly find it tendentious and wonder if anyone would ever be allowed to question the "apparent" validity and usefulness if this bias prevails. In fact, little attention has been paid to the important issue of what sorts of language structures are best studied with what sorts of data collection methodology.

Most important from our point of view is that the reviewer goes to great lengths to justify claims about small details of the descriptive system (some relevant, some not), but evidently cannot treat the matter of economy/method/Zeitgeist/data with care. Given our own research backgrounds and our understanding of the current research scene, we cannot understand the ease with which phrases such as "naturalistic data" and "ethnographic Zeitgeist" are related to some particular "this method." The descriptive and analytic procedures that Vaughn-Cooke and Stockman propose are the only "this method" referents we could imagine being pertinent. They are in no way the product of a "homogeneous" paradigm of a fictional investigator who undertakes naturalistic data investigations or who participates in an ethnographic Zeitgeist. Only a woeful lack of understanding of the history, breadth and complexities of the work of scientists could produce such a reduction of relevant issues. Those of us whose research paradigm encourages us to read and reflect on the relevant literature are amazed at the diversity in the world outside of quasiexperimental methods (and even within it) and we see no homogeneity of method. The data may have been collected in a way that could fit some definitions of naturalistic, but the agency is not being asked to pay for that; that work was already done. What but paradigm prejudice would lead a reviewer to advise the agency not to pay for something that had already been paid for in the first place?

Another negative reviewer, providing a "poor" rating, reveals a similar tie between paradigm differences and economic resources. The evaluation calls for analysis "using appropriate inferential statistics." Following that, the reviewer worries that the Investigators will not be working enough to merit their salaries.

The reviewer's inability to imagine what the work entails in terms of time and effort, however, seems to arise from a limited understanding of the proper quantitative approach to the data. The data analysis that a linguist or a sociolinguist has to do is quite extensive and requires workers with extensive education. You cannot rely on naive transcribers or coders with a few weeks training, whose inter-coder reliability you then check.

Typically, in work of the type proposed by Vaughn-Cooke and Stockman, when you have progressed to the point in your description of the data that you have any numbers to do statistics on there is no point in doing the statistics because of the prior analytic work. If there are differences to be found, they will be overwhelming. Language is like that. As a conventional communicative system it has to have very staid, very obvious properties – it's not very numerically subtle. Statistical approaches to the sort of data that the proposal is concerned with are cogently discussed within it, and the reviewer provides no argumentation, evidence or literature review to indicate that they are insufficient and that the inferential statistical procedures that are suggested in the review are necessary in addition or are superior as an alternate.

It appears that the reviewer does not know how much work the proposal entails, *assumes* none, and then concludes that the Investigators will be taking a salary illegitimately. There is quite a bit of work involved in handling the language data – which tends to be very subtle in every other way than numerical. The estimate the reviewer makes about the small amount of work to be done makes sense only in the light of paradigm bias about the work proposed.

We don't think it is coincidental that the reviewers who appeared to be outside of the paradigm also made a major issue of spending the agency's money. Consider that one review is arguing for a quasi-experimental paradigm, another for a less well-specified but apparently big N design, and that the proposal is arguing for yet a third approach. To make theoretical headway, supporters of all these approaches should support scholars, attract and provide for new adherents. But there are limited resources. If the "other guys" get resources, your view gets less. We do not believe that reviewers try to limit the resources awarded to approaches that they disagree with; we believe that they simply cannot understand them and hence reach a judgment that they are not worth an expenditure of the limited resources. Readers, including reviewers, bring their understandings to the text; they cannot bring what they do not have and they cannot help but bring what they do have. The motivated misunderstandings are not a product of willfulness, but rather of inadequate enculturation in the *diverse* scientific tradition within which one is working.

Subjects from minority communities in basic research

The assumption of normativity for a particular approach to collecting and analyzing data is often accompanied by an assumption of the normativity of a certain sort of subject. We are familiar with this difficulty as individuals and as a group.

Several years ago, we invited scholars from various parts of the country to participate in a small, relatively informal, conference about development. Several of us were dismayed at one event. A member of our laboratory, Black and not very young looking, who had conducted quite a bit of research, asked one of our invited colleagues about why there was a special point made that the population of the subjects was restricted to white middle-class children and why the restriction had been made in the first place.

The dismay came with the answer. Responding as if to a newcomer in psychological research asking an irrelevant question in a large lecture hall, the researcher said that all basic research must be done first on a normative sample and then later ethnic and racially different children could be studied, with their difference from the mean entered as variables to be considered. In the discussion that followed this lecture, we established that there was no theory or evidence suggesting that the basic research problem being considered specified white middle-class children as normative and others as inappropriate to study. We pointed out that epiphenonema could mask the results because of an unnecessary restriction on the sample and that it was strange that such a criticism would never arise when the restriction was of this type. We also pointed out that the research tradition that supported that sort of bias as at least normal and argued for it as somehow necessary had a bad history, leaving unstudied much of the detail of the ordinary development of children where cultural, linguistic, and economic differences might in fact matter. We also discussed how research of that sort could lead to strange conclusions about children who are not white and middle-class being sub-normal.

It did not do much good. In the end, the researcher who presented the findings said it just didn't matter enough to spend any time on. In the discussion, from both sides in the debate, the preference for publishing and funding was laid out: study white middle-class children as normative or don't get funded and published ... and then you don't get tenure. If you study minorities, study them as minorities. Have a control group of "normals" or evidence from "normals" in the literature for comparison; or else don't do basic research, study the problems the minority subjects have such that they deviate from the "norm." This logic doesn't even rise to separate but equal; it's outright second-class citizenship!

We are not totally surprised, then, to find that two reviewers of the Vaughn-Cooke and Stockman proposal acted strangely about her choice of subjects. Three thought it was all right (that's progress), one citing agreement with the argument they put forth about the nonrelationship of children's race, culture, class or dialect to the basic research issue being addressed.

The other two, however, are just the expectable results of the scientific tradition that the guest at our conference defended. One apparently shares the unfortunate notion that one group is more normative than another. While we cannot say whether or not this reviewer would have required a justification if Vaughn-Cooke and Stockman had worked with a white middle-class sample, we doubt it.

The other reviewer who objected to the study focusing on Black children is in a worse position. This reviewer is worried about "levels" and talks about a major controversy currently existing and implies that the Black English speakers may be at a lower level. Using this line of thinking, people could come to the strange conclusion that children not ordinarily represented in the "normative" samples for basic research were in fact "sub-normal." It is difficult to understand this claim since the reviewer contrasts three entities: Standard English, Black English and some mediating device which measures levels, evidently, called English. The reviewer questions ". . . whether children who speak Black English acquire and use English at the same level as Standard English speakers." Although the reviewer claims that the vita of the Principal Investigators "indicate that they are aware of this controversy," it is hard to imagine what literature is being referred to. Scholars who use the terms Black English and Standard English never propose that there is an entity that can function like a thermometer and exist independent of the other two. The work referenced in the proposal and the work mentioned in the vita certainly do not suggest any such approach. Vaughn-Cooke and Stockman are responsible for some of the evidence and argumentation about where there are points of similarity and difference between the acquisition of the two dialects of English, Standard and Black. Their work and that of other scholars substantiate their claim that dialect differences are not relevant to the basic research issue. In their response they point to the long known fact that the differences between Black and Standard English are documented to exist in certain areas of syntax and phonology, certainly *not in the development of the semantics of locative expressions.* All in all, if the reviewer were not a victim of the research tradition and had access to the literature he or she could be freed from worries about levels and "sub-normals." As we could predict, the reviewer calls for a control sample, although there is no overt reference to such a group as normal.

What to do?

If two Black women living and working in a city where children who aren't Black are pretty hard to find can't use a nicely developed data base to do basic language development research because the children in their sample are Black, what are they supposed to do? Get out of basic research? Join the other Black scholars who have a "low incidence" of applying to Federal Agencies like the NSF? Go along with the state of affairs that says that children in their community are not to be in normative samples? Go along with an idea that children who are members of the community they are members of, children like they were and like their children are, are interesting to study only as problems, as potential deviations from the norm? To join the bias? How can they contribute to basic research, and why should they when it reveals prejudice about their identity? And, if they don't contribute, how does the bias in the research tradition adversely effect the state of our knowledge on basic research? It's not just that two women don't get to do a study or even that they don't get to do any basic research; it is that we have removed from our view any way to find out if or how that barrier has restricted our scientific progress quite systematically ever since the beginning of American scientific research.

Reconsidering the procedures

We called the agency to find out more about the procedure. First we learned that it is a reconsideration request rather than an appeal and that the reconsideration procedure has been in effect for 5 or 6 years. The linguistics program handles between 125 and 150 proposals a year and only about 1 a year is the subject of a request for reconsideration. Each is treated individually and the sample is small, so no odds can be calculated for the success of a reconsideration request; however, there have been no changes in the decisions rendered in the Linguistics Program.

The ground rules for requesting reconsideration are such that merely disagreeing with the outcome is not sufficient; one must base the request on more procedural grounds. The response to an evaluation should make the case that there has not been a fair review; that there has been bias, or that there has been prejudice against a point of view.

We then asked about the availability of evidence for *de facto* bias or prejudice, asking specifically what information was available about the characterization of the range of grant proposals that were successful. There is no such general information available. If a specific question is raised, then a review is undertaken. We were told that, for example, a question was raised about grant proposals submitted by new investigators and one was raised about proposals submitted from small colleges. In both cases the result was that the agency was doing okay; there was no difference in the success ratio of proposals from such sources in comparison to the overall success ratio. The agency person that we spoke with did not know of a similar review of the case of investigators from minority backgrounds. (N.B. The Principal Investigators are known to the reviewers by their name, vita and institutional affiliation, at least. The reviewers' identities are kept anonymous.)

We are interested in the *de facto* evidence about minority principal investigators, but somewhat differently. We would like to know, for instance, about the incidence of success for proposals where minority researchers have attempted to study ordinary, non-problematic development of children from their own communities in order to contribute to the knowledge of ordinary non-problematic development. The agency person to whom we spoke said that he had the impression that there was a low incidence of proposals submitted from Black investigators in the Linguistics Program, at least. We are not sure, then, that a success ratio approach would yield any information of interest, particularly if we raised a question that asked for information on the *de facto* handling of proposals on certain kinds of topics.

In response to our question about whether a third party, like us, could raise a question to get *de facto* information, or if the Investigators or sponsoring institution had to do that, we found that we had the wrong idea on the procedure. A question, like the one about new investigators or small colleges, is raised in the congressional hearing process. Presumably, ordinary citizens like us have access to that information by using a congressional intermediary or by exercising the rights afforded under legislation like the Freedom of Information Act.

In lieu of any quantitative *de facto* evidence, the reconsideration request must be based on issues like the paradigm prejudice and assumptions of normativity that we discuss above. We believe that pre-judging on the basis of good training in a different research tradition and assuming a stance about normativity that the tradition promotes, add up to a bias evidenced in the reviews for this particular proposal. It is very difficult to imagine, however, what would constitute proof positive that would convince people from a variety of research and policy traditions. It is even more difficult to imagine what the funding agency could do to guard against the effect of such bias as they allocate ever-dwindling resources.

What is the decision-making process?   Concern about how to prove something and what to do about the problem, led us to reconsider the whole process. What sort of events are proposing and reviewing?

On the one hand, the notion of "peer review" and the question of whether reviewers are "making a case against" a proposal suggest something like a courtroom. On the other hand, the provision of advice and relevant references by reviewers and the academic affiliations of so many participants suggest something like teaching or testing is going on.

In the present case, good reviews are short and negative ones are long. There may not be a completely consistent relationship between the number of pages and the sort of rating provided, but as we reflect on our experience, we suspect as reviewers and as proposers we've experienced and accomplished this relationship more often than not. Another asymmetry is in who is anonymous and who is known – the reviewer versus the proposer. Both of these contrasts promote the school-like interpretation. An answer that is seen as wrong by the teacher often promotes a greater amount of response from the teacher than a correct one, including a great deal of effort to replace the "incorrect" with a more adequate answer. In testing, each test-taker has to provide a name or some form of identification, and the test-maker remains as anonymous as possible.

The courtroom interpretation is hard to sustain. Peers are usually found on juries, while third and fourth parties present the prosecution and the defense. But in the "peer review" process, the proposer plays the role of both the defendant and the defense counsel, while the reviewers are only in evidence as they become prosecutors or as they join the defense team. Some reviewers, like jurors, have the benefit of face-to-face communication with their fellows. The face-to-face or "panel" review has the additional responsibility of recommending the "sentence" but the agency has a responsibility in this regard, too. And, most important for the American notion of jurisprudence, the accused (the proposer) never gets to face the accusers. The reconsideration process is mediated.

How are we supposed to deal with this? Would defining what different people think they are doing when they participate in such things as proposing and reviewing help us to identify our goal and come closer to approximating it? Sometimes, reading a review one feels privileged to be able to listen in while the writer goes on and on, almost talking to himself and figuring out a knotty problem. The reader likes to trace the problem-solving and get the specific content and maybe thinks about using the experience as a model for future activities, or hopes that it will come out in an article that can be properly cited. Other times, the reader gets impatient with the reviewer's self indulgence, assumes that the reviewer is just showing off or that such improbable arguments or weak evidence would never be presented in a more public forum where the reviewer would be more fully accountable.

If the process is more educational than court-like, it should consider the three-part structure found in instructional/educational exchanges. Why is it a two-part process? Why not have the reviewer suggest or question or criticize and have the proposer respond and then have a decision? Occasionally, large requests go through such a process, "the best and final offer." Some variation on the current procedure might both help us to figure out what it is and might even increase the teaching function – both teaching the reviewers and teaching the proposers.

Conclusion

Our conclusion is simple: the problem with funding and with this particular event is a part of our general problem of how to do science and how to insure that diversity survives in a central enough way that change will represent progress.

We need to know what the propose–review–decide–reconsider process is and what procedures could be experimented with to render it more successful. No one is interested in reducing the amount of cross-talk among scholars working in different research traditions; nor is anyone interested in being insulated from criticism. The current process has some advantages and, we believe, some deep difficulties. The beneficiaries of the funding and of the scholarship that the funding promotes should attend to the problem. We appreciate your thoughtful consideration of these issues of intellectual and practical importance. We invite constructive comment.

Reference

Cole, M. (Ed.). (1983, January). The individual and the social world [Special issue]. *The Quarterly Newsletter of the Laboratory of Comparative Human Cognition, 5* (1).

Exploring cultural historical theories

10 The early history of the Vygotskian school: The relationship between mind and activity

Norris Minick

Only within the past decade have Western scholars begun to appreciate the diversity and breadth of the Vygotskian tradition. Most of us gained our introduction to this tradition through *Thought and Language* (Vygotsky, 1962), an abridged translation of Vygotsky's final attempt to address the problem of the relationship between verbally mediated social interaction and the development of thinking in ontogenesis. With this as a point of departure, the interest of Western scholars moved first to other efforts by Vygotsky and his colleagues to address the relationship between social interaction and cognitive development (e.g., Vygotsky, 1978) and then to the broader range of problems, theory, and research addressed by modern activity theory (Leont'ev, 1978, 1981; Minick, 1985; Wertsch, 1981, 1985).

For those interested in applying and extending this paradigm, the discovery of its diversity has raised several important questions. What is the connection between Vygotsky's work, much of which focused on the role of social interaction in cognitive development, and activity theory, where the inclusion of the individual in socially organized goal-oriented actions provides the foundation for explanations of the development of cognition as well as personality, affect, and motor skills? Is there something more than a general conviction that social and cultural factors play an important role in psychological development that links Vygotsky's work on the development of inner speech and word meaning (Vygotsky, 1962, in press) to Leont'ev's work on personality and affect (e.g., Leont'ev, 1978); is there something that links either of these to the work of Zaporozhets and V. P. Zinchenko on the development of perception,

117

movement, and motor skills (Zaporozhets, Venger, Zinchenko, & Ruzskaia, 1967; Zaporozhets & Zinchenko, 1966; Zinchenko, 1981) or to the work of P. I. Zinchenko and Istomina on the development of memory (Istomina, 1977; Zinchenko, 1981, 1984)? In more general terms, are there principles that simultaneously unite these various middle level theories and differentiate them from their counterparts generated within other theoretical paradigms, principles that might provide some direction to our efforts to extend the theories of the Vygotskian tradition to new problem domains?

Scholars working within this tradition have generally assumed that these various theories are indeed united by a common conceptual framework. In recent years, there have been several attempts to identify the principles which define it (e.g., Davydov & Radzikhovskii, 1985; Zinchenko, 1985; Wertsch, 1981, 1985). In my view, there is a consistency in perspective and problem which unites these diverse middle level theories and explanatory frameworks (Minick, 1985, in press). In fact, it could be argued that it is the general conceptual foundations of the Vygotskian paradigm rather than any particular middle level theory or explanatory framework that will ultimately make the most valuable contribution to our own efforts to develop theory and research on the relationships between mind and society.

Elsewhere, I have argued that one factor which unifies this research tradition is a unique perspective on the relationship between mind and activity (Minick, 1985). In this paper, I would like to take a brief look at the early history of the Vygotskian school in order to provide some of the historical background for this general line of argumentation.[1]

I will begin with a paper published by Vygotsky in 1925, a paper that played a pivotal role in the formation of the Vygotskian school (Vygotsky, 1982). It was the arguments that Vygotsky developed in this paper that initially brought him to the attention of Luria and Leont'ev. This led to a position for Vygotsky at the institute with which Luria and Leont'ev were affiliated in Moscow and to the initiation of their collaborative work. More significantly in the present context, it was also in this paper that Vygotsky first outlined several problems which were extremely important to the subsequent history of the Vygotskian tradition. In fact, I would argue that much of the subsequent development of theory and research within this tradition can best be understood as a series of efforts to resolve the problems that Vygotsky outlined in this paper.

In the present context, I will consider only one of these problems, the problem of the relationship of mind and behavior. Entitled "Consciousness as a problem of behavioral psychology," Vygotsky's 1925 paper represented a critique of the behaviorist theories of Pavlov, Bechterev, and others that dominated Soviet psychology in the 1920s (Vygotsky, 1982). Vygotsky applauded the behaviorists for making it clear that behavior is an important aspect of the object of psychological research. In his view, the more traditional psychology of consciousness had made a fundamental error in abstracting mind from behavior, in trying to investigate the flow of ideas, perceptions, and associations in conceptual isolation from the individual's activity or behavior. On the other hand, Vygotsky was convinced that the behaviorist psychologies had simply reinstantiated the dualism inherent in the subjective psychologies they criticized. He argued that the attempt to study behavior without reference to mind or consciousness was:

Simply the dualism of subjective psychology – the attempt to study a purely abstracted mind – turned inside out. It is the other half of the same dualism. There, there was mind without behavior; here, behavior without mind. And both there and here "mind" and "behavior" understood as two different phenomena. (Vygotsky, 1982, p. 81)

For our present purposes, perhaps the most important aspect of this argument is reflected somewhat cryptically in the final sentence of the preceding statement. As Davydov and Radzikhovskii (1985, pp. 40–41) have pointed out, Vygotsky rejected not only the perspectives of the subjectivists and behaviorists but those of a third group of Soviet psychologists who were attempting to create a unified theoretical system based on a fusion of these traditions. What Vygotsky rejected in these efforts was not the goal of developing a unified science of mind and behavior, but the assumption that this could be accomplished by utilizing the systems of theoretical constructs that had been developed by the subjectivists and behaviorists. In Vygotsky's view, these attempts to study mind and behavior in conceptual isolation from one another had produced systems of scientific constructs which fundamentally misrepresented the nature of both. He was convinced that the problem of developing a unified science of mind and behavior could not be solved by combining these inadequate systems of constructs in the formulation of a unified psychological theory. What was required was an effort to reconceptualize mind and behavior such that they could be understood as aspects of an integrated object of psychological research.

In the remainder of this paper, I will try to outline three "stages" in the early development of the Vygotskian school which can be understood at least in part as attempts to resolve this problem.

The first of these stages is reflected in the work carried out by Vygotsky and his colleagues between 1925 and 1930. During this period, their research focused on what were called the higher mental functions, cognitive processes such as voluntary memory, voluntary attention, and rational thought. As his point of departure, Vygotsky began with the notion that the stimulus–response unit provides the common foundation for psychological functioning in both animals and humans. He defined his immediate task as that of explaining how the higher or *voluntary* mental functions develop in humans on the foundation provided by the S-R unit.

Vygotsky's solution to this problem included two components. First, he argued that the higher mental functions are based on the mediation of behavior by sign systems, especially speech. Signs were represented as a special form of stimuli which function as "psychological tools," tools that are directed toward the mastery or control of *behavioral* processes in the same sense that ordinary tools are directed toward the control of nature (Vygotsky, 1981, p. 137). Vygotsky argued that it is by controlling these sign-stimuli that human beings gain voluntary control over their own behavior and that it is this that leads to the development of the "volitional" mental processes that he called the higher mental functions.

Second, to explain the emergence of these verbally mediated forms of behavior in both history and ontogenesis, Vygotsky looked to the initial function of speech as a mediator of social interaction. It is in behavior carried out cooperatively by two or more individuals and mediated by speech that signs first function as psychological tools in the mediation of human behavior. Following Janet, Vygotsky argued that the individual first participates in social activity where signs are used by one individual to influence the behavior of another and that it is only later that he or she begins to use these signs as a means of influencing his or her own behavior. Vygotsky believed that both the organization and the mediational means that allow dyads or larger groups to carry out cooperative social activities are taken over by the individual, and that it is this internalization or individuation of the means of activity involved in social interaction that leads to the development of mediated, voluntary, and historically developed mental functions.

It was with this general conceptual framework that Vygotsky first established the kinds of conceptual links between mind and behavior which he had called for in his 1925 paper. Here, social behavior was not represented as a system of conditions to which the mind adapts nor as one source of experience that combines with others to push cognitive development forward. Still less was social behavior portrayed as the manifestation of the individual's cognitive characteristics. To the contrary, rather than two variables with characteristics that interact or influence one another like balls on a billiard table, it becomes impossible within this framework to separate the organization and content of the higher mental functions from the organization and content of social behavior. Though primitive, this conceptual framework allowed Vygotsky to begin the analysis of the development of certain aspects of mind in connection with the analysis of the organization of social behavior.

By 1930, Vygotsky had abandoned the notion that the stimulus–response unit is the basic building block of mind and behavior. This move allowed him to begin to incorporate his extensive knowledge of semiotic theory into his thinking about the relationships between speech and thinking. Perhaps even more importantly, it allowed him to expand his work beyond the domains of memory, attention, and thinking to deal with problems of personality, affect, perception, and imagination; it allowed him to begin to work toward a general theory of the history of mind, consciousness, and human behavior.

In his initial efforts (1930–1932) to deal with this broader and more complex range of psychological problems, however, Vygotsky failed to establish meaningful conceptual links between mind and behavior. Even in his work on the relationship between the development of speech and thought, Vygotsky was unable to link the development of semiotic means to the development of social behavior or social activity in a meaningful way.

What I would call the second stage in the effort of the Vygotskian school to create a conceptual bridge between mind and activity is reflected most clearly in the work Vygotsky carried out in the two years preceding his death in 1934. During this period, Vygotsky made several important conceptual moves that allowed him to reestablish links between mind and activity compatible with the more cognitivist framework that he was now working with. These moves were made in two overlapping phases. The first of these phases was associated with his efforts to reestablish the relationship between social interaction and cognitive development that had been so important in his earlier work. The second involved the extension of the ideas that he developed in this first phase to a broader range of problems and issues.

Two of the moves Vygotsky made during the first of these phases are of particular significance in the present context. First, Vygotsky outlined what he perceived as a new approach to the definition of constructs in psychological theory. As developed in his classic work on the relationships between thinking and speech in verbal thinking (Vygotsky, 1962, in press), Vygotsky argued that units of analysis in psychological theory must be defined such that they are at one and the same time units of mind and units of social interaction. Vygotsky rejected the use of scientific constructs such as "concept" or "language" in this context, arguing that they are derived by abstracting the semantic and grammatical aspects of speech from their concrete embodiment in social interaction. In contrast, Vygotsky insisted constructs such as "word meaning" are the proper units of analysis for this research, since "word meaning" is at one and the same time a unit of abstraction or thinking (i.e., a unit of mind) and a unit of communication or social interaction (i.e., a unit of behavior) (Vygotsky, in press, p. 11).

Second, Vygotsky insisted that any genetic analysis in psychology (whether focused on the historical or ontogenetic plane) must begin with the analysis of the development of these kinds of analytic units in connection with the development of social interaction. Just as the physical or technical tool evolves in connection with the systems of productive activity it mediates, Vygotsky argued that psychological tools develop in connection with the development of social interaction. In his words, it is

only when we learn to see the unity of abstraction and social interaction [that] we begin to understand the actual connection that exists between the child's congnitive development and his social development (in press, p. 11).

These two moves allowed Vygotsky to reestablish the kinds of conceptual links between mind and social interaction that had characterized his earlier theory, though within a much more sophisticated conceptual framework. As developed in this work, however, the implications of these

ideas were limited primarily to the problem of the development of thinking in the context of social interaction. They did not begin to provide
the foundation for the construction of a general theory of psychological
development, for the development of the new framework for research on
the development of mind, consciousness, and behavior that Vygotsky
had called for in 1925. The next phase in the development of Vygotsky's
theoretical perspectives represented his attempt to extend these conceptual moves to a broader domain of theoretical problems.

First, in several works completed just prior to his death in 1934,
Vygotsky expanded the scope of his explanatory framework by shifting
his focus from social interaction to the broader domain of socially or culturally organized activity. In this work, Vygotsky emphasized the fact
that the activities which constitute the individual's life are socially constituted and argued that the individual's involvement in these activities
plays a central role in ontogenetic development.

In a paper on the relationship between the development of imagination and play that was written during this period, for example, Vygotsky
did not even mention the role of the child's interaction with adults or
peers (Vygotsky, 1978, ch. 7). Rather, he argued that "like all functions
of consciousness, [imagination] emerges initially from action," that
imagination develops in connection with the development of the form
of socially defined activity that we call play (see: Vygotsky, 1978, p. 93).
Recapitulating his earlier attempts to trace the development of word
meaning in connection with the development of social interaction,
Vygotsky attempted in this paper to trace the development of imagination in connection with the development of the socially and culturally
constituted activity of play.

The central assumption reflected in this paper on imagination and
play was outlined in a more general form in a series of lectures on child
development that Vygotsky delivered in 1933 and 1934 (Vygotsky, 1984).
Here, he argued: (1) that each stage in the child's development is characterized by modes of social activity that are of particular significance
to that stage; and (2) that the central task of developmental psychology
is to clarify how the new psychological formations characteristic of the
child at each stage arise and develop in connection with the way the
child's life is organized by these modes of social activity.

Second, in this same series of lectures, Vygotsky attempted to extend
his ideas concerning the proper approach to the definition of scientific

constructs in psychology to this broader explanatory framework. For example, Vygotsky criticized traditional approaches to the study of the relationship between the child and the environment in psychological theory, noting that the two are generally represented as interacting forces with characteristics that can be defined in conceptual isolation from one another (1984, p. 380). In contrast, Vygotsky argued that for the purpose of constructing psychological theory the environment must be conceptualized in terms of "the child's relationship to the various aspects of his [objective] environment" (1984, p. 381). Implicit in the examples he used to illustrate this point was the notion that this relationship is defined not by the child's inner psychological state but by the child's developing activity. Thus, when the infant begins to crawl or talk, or when the child is introduced into the system of activities that constitute formal schooling, Vygotsky argued that there is a corresponding change in the child's relationship to the environment, a change in the environment as it exists psychologically for the child.

The development of activity theory by Vygotsky's students and colleagues in the late 1930s and early 1940s represents the third stage in the efforts of the Vygotskian school to create a unified science of mind and behavior. In important respects, the development of activity theory – as well as subsequent efforts to extend and refine it – reflects the effort of Vygotsky's students and colleagues to realize the implications of the conceptual moves that Vygotsky made in the last few years of his life.

There is a great deal that could be said in this connection, but in the present context I will limit myself to three points. First, the idea that psychological characteristics develop in connection with the systems of social actions and activities that constitute the individual's life provided the basic explanatory framework for activity theory. Second, Vygotsky's concern with identifying an analytic object that is simultaneously a unit of mind and a unit of social activity led to the identification of the goal-oriented action as the focus of psychological analysis in activity theory (Davydov & Radzikhovskii, 1985; Zinchenko, 1985). As a unit both of the systems of actions which constitute the individual's life and of those which constitute society, the goal-oriented action has provided those working within the framework of activity theory with a key conceptual link in the analysis of the relationships between the development of mind and the development of social behavior, or stated more broadly, in the analysis of the relationships between the individual's psychological development and the development of social systems. Finally, Vygotsky's approach to the definition of psychological constructs, as reflected in the 1933–1934 lectures, was extended to whole systems of theoretical constructs designed to maintain conceptual links between not only mind and activity, but between mind, activity, and the external object world in which human activity occurs.

I am convinced that the efforts of the Vygotskian school to reconceptualize the relationship between mind and activity have profound and wide ranging implications for the psychological and social sciences, implications which even those trained within this paradigm are only beginning to appreciate fully. For the readers of this *Newsletter*, however, among the most important implications of this work is the foundation it provides for a reconceptualization of the relationship between the individual and the social system in which he or she lives and develops. In my view, the theoretical framework provided by these theories allows us to avoid:

1. The conceptual isolation of systems of social activity and psychological characteristics that is reflected in their treatment as independent and dependent variables in a great deal of contemporary research in developmental psychology, cross-cultural psychology, and psychological anthropology.
2. The reductionism inherent in the tendency of some cultural theorists to represent certain aspects of psychological development as the consequence of a simple transfer of cultural values and knowledge from one generation to the next.
3. The tendency of what I would call the "social behaviorists" to characterize the organization and the development of human social activities without reference to the mental processes of the individuals whose activities they are.

The theoretical framework provided by the Vygotskian school provides the rudiments of a research paradigm in which the historical evolution of social and cultural systems are intimately bound together with the development of human psychological characteristics. In my view, it provides the rudiments of the kind of research paradigm that is needed for the creation of a unified science of the systems of activity that constitute socio-cultural systems and of the mind that mediates these activities.

126   *Norris Minick*

Notes

An earlier draft of this paper was presented at the 84th Annual Meeting of the American Anthropological Association, Invited Session of the Society for Psychological Anthropology: Soviet Psychology and the Social Construction of Cognition, Washington, D.C. December, 1985.

1. For a more detailed outline of the early history of the Vygotskian school, see Minick, in press.

References

Davydov, V. V., & Radzikhovskii, L. A. (1985). Vygotsky's theory and the activity-oriented approach in psychology. In J. V. Wertsch (Ed.), *Culture, communication, and cognition: Vygotskian perspectives* (pp. 35–65). New York: Cambridge University Press.

Istomina, Z. M. (1977). The development of voluntary memory in preschool-age children. In M. Cole (Ed.), *Soviet developmental psychology*. White Plains, NY: M. E. Sharpe. (Originally published in 1948)

Leont'ev, A. N. (1978). *Activity, consciousness, and personality*. Englewood Cliffs, NJ: Prentice-Hall. (Originally published in 1975)

Leont'ev, A. N. (1981). *Problems of the development of mind*. Moscow: Progress Publishers. (Originally published 1959)

Minick, N. (1985). *L. S. Vygotsky and Soviet activity theory: New perspectives on the relationship between mind and society*. Unpublished doctoral dissertation. Northwestern University.

Minick, N. (in press). The development of Vygotsky's thought: An introduction. In L. S. Vygotsky, *Collected works: Problems of general psychology* (Vol. 2). (N. Minick, Trans.). New York: Plenum.

Vygotsky, L. S. (1962). *Thought and language*. Boston: MIT Press.

Vygotsky, L. S. (1978). *Mind in society*. Cambridge, MA: Harvard University Press.

Vygotsky, L. S. (1981). The instrumental method in psychology. In J. V. Wertsch (Ed.), *The concept of activity in Soviety psychology* (pp. 134–143). Armonk, NY: M. E. Sharpe.

Vygotsky, L. S. (1982). Soznanie kak problema psikhologii povedeniia [Consciousness as a problem of behavioral psychology]. In A. R. Luria & M. G. Iaroshevskii (Eds.), *L. S. Vygotskii. Sobranie sochinenie: Voprosy teorii i istorii psikhologii (Tom 1)* [L. S. Vygotsky. *Collected works: Problems of the theory and history of psychology* (Vol. 1)]. Moscow: Pedagogika.

Vygotsky, L. S. (1984). *Sobranie sochinenie: Detskaia psikhologiia (Tom 4)*. [*Collected works: Child psychology* (Vol. 4)]. Moscow: Pedagogika.

Vygotsky, L. S. (in press). Thinking and speech. In L. S. Vygotsky, *Collected works: Problems of general psychology* (Vol. 2). (N. Minick, Trans.). New York: Plenum.

Wertsch, J. V. (Ed.). (1981). *The concept of activity in Soviet psychology.* Armonk, NY: M. E. Sharpe.

Wertsch, J. V. (1985). *Vygotsky and the social formation of mind.* Cambridge, MA: Harvard University Press.

Zaporozhets, A. V., Venger, L. A., Zinchenko, V. P., & Ruzskaia, A. G. (1967). *Vospriiatie i deistvie [Perception and action].* Moscow: Pedagogika.

Zaporozhets, A. V., & Zinchenko, V. P. (1966). Development of perceptual activity and formation of a sensory image in the child. In A. N. Leont'ev, A. R. Luria, & A. A. Smirnov (Eds.), *Psychological research in the USSR* (Vol. 1, pp. 393–421). Moscow: Progress Publishers.

Zinchenko, P. I. (1981). Involuntary memory and the goal-directed nature of activity. In J. V. Wertsch (Ed.), *The concept of activity in Soviet psychology.* Armonk, NY: M. E. Sharpe.

Zinchenko, P. I. (1984). The problem of involuntary memory. *Soviet Psychology, 22,* 55–111. (Originally published 1939)

Zinchenko, V. P. (1981). Criteria for evaluating executive activity. In J. V. Wertsch (Ed.), *The concept of activity in Soviet psychology.* Armonk, NY: M. E. Sharpe.

Zinchenko, V. P. (1985). Vygotsky's ideas about units for the analysis of mind. In J. V. Wertsch (Ed.), *Culture, communication, and cognition: Vygotskian perspectives* (pp. 94–118). New York: Cambridge University Press.

11 One developmental line in European Activity Theories

Erik Axel

Background

A forthcoming book on Critical Psychology (Tolman & Maiers, 1991) is the occasion of this article. The paper will relate Critical Psychology to the two theories which constitute the origin of the Cultural Historical School and its activity theory.

The most central aim of the article is to demonstrate that activity theory is fundamentally reversed compared to other explanations of the social creation of mind.

In other theories, the social creation of mind is often taken to mean that general abilities of the brain are realized through social interaction. Social interaction is a mere trigger, which starts up the general ability to perceive, remember and think. These mental abilities are characterized by some properties – like their structure, form, abstract process. They are taken to be independent of concrete socio-historical forms of inter-action, and common to all humanity. One could characterize this approach as an essentialistic functionalism in which form takes prece-dence over content.

Activity theory reverses the relation between form and content. Fundamentally, this reversal is seen in the reinterpretation of the concept of human nature, which takes on the meaning of human poten-tials. The unique, historical content and organization of this conscious-

128

ness is seen as a result of this human being realizing its human nature on the basis of earlier human experience as accumulated in society. You can then state that human beings perceive, think, and remember, but these are open ended statements about human potentials. The real concrete organization of these functions and ultimately of consciousness can only be determined by identifying the life histories of these human beings in particular socio-cultural forms of living. One could characterize this approach as a functional materialism, in which content takes precedence over form.

The article will explore the reasons for and the consequences of the reversed relation between form and content mainly by tracing a developmental line in European Activity Theories. A line will be drawn from Vygotsky via Leont'ev to Critical Psychology, demonstrating the unfolding of a praxis paradigm which responds to still more demands on paradigmatic consistency.

Some of the underlying issues which need reworking in order to obtain paradigmatic consistency are the following:

• In essentialistic functionalism even local and culturally specific activities and their mental functioning are derived from the universal structures of mind. The development of concepts is mostly explained by how and when they are triggered. Their generality, relevancy, and validity are matters for scientific investigation, but not central for their evolution. But in functional materialism one must be able to comprehend how human beings develop from groping with the immediate surroundings to a mastery and penetration of the socially organized activities. It is a constant task to identify how general concepts in consciousness develop out of specific activities. This entails a determination of the relationship between the general and the specific, and the relationship has to be grasped as a part of the way individuals relate to their social positions. It becomes essential to determine how the individual evaluates what is relevant and what is not. This has to be seen in the broader context of how human beings in activity transform the world according to their needs and their needs according to the world. Out of this dialectic the social determination of emotions, interests, and relevancy must be unfolded.

- As a consequence of these deliberations scientists must see their own general theories as developing within social activity of particular social positions. They must understand the theories with which they work as part of their way of relating to the social interests in the positions they and their subjects occupy. New theories can only be developed from these positions through a dialectic between changing social practices and critical social reflection. Praxis is in itself the basis of theoretical change, and at the same time the researcher's grasp of praxis is the basis for the critical analysis by providing criteria of generality, specificity and relevancy. The researcher reviews the theories which have evolved from related social positions – among these also the researcher's own position. In this critical review researchers investigate the relations of the general theories to their specific social positions. Through inner inconsistencies, limits of explanatory power, transcendences and interplay between such aspects of the theories, researchers strive for a precise grasp of the matter, which will allow a more conscious development of praxis.

These issues make it necessary to state the following, which is sometimes overlooked in the study of activity theory. The researchers' reflection of their being in and investigation of praxis is based on a set of fundamental categories, of which any theory must have some. It is characteristic of activity theory that its fundamental categories are set up not arbitrarily for the occasion, but developed systematically within the philosophy of historical materialism.

We shall pursue how these issues have unfolded in one developmental line in European activity theories. A proper presentation of this developmental line should be prospective, all possible directions for development at each stage ought to be presented, and reasons be given for why the next stage will react to only some of the problems of the earlier stage. However, the length of the article confines us to reconstructing development: solely those problems of a previous stage will be mentioned which have had a fundamental significance for the unfolding of the next stage. This also means that the earlier stages will be viewed from the perspective of the later ones of the developmental line with which we are concerned.

Vygotsky

Vygotsky is a transitional figure in Russian psychology, an upcoming scientist from the first years of the Soviet Union. He wrote on the basis of profound knowledge of his contemporary psychology. In his works, therefore, one can find elements of all psychological theories from his time – intellectualistic psychology, i.e., a psychology which describes consciousness in formal terms such as hierarchical concept structures; Piagetian structural psychology, where mind is described in terms of operations outbalancing each other; gestalt psychology; etc. The reception of Vygotsky in the USA has been influenced by these diverse elements. In the context of an eclectic tradition of science, Vygotsky's diversity may be especially advantageous. The psychological concepts from his texts may be selected as tools: "I want to investigate this problem, and would like this concept from Vygotsky, that from Piaget, and why not this interesting concept from gestalt psychology." Also, Vygotsky's varied attempts at theoretical integration, which are mirrored in his works, make it easier to take one's personal pick.

However, one can only get a proper understanding of the inner coherence of Vygotsky's project by seeing it as a radical historical development out of the first two decades of the Soviet Union. There and at that time it was a declared policy to establish a psychology on a Marxist basis. This meant conceiving of consciousness as historically created through praxis (cf. Norris Minick's excellent overview of Vygotsky's theoretical development in Vygotsky, 1987).

Vygotsky was moving away from a psychology which sees thinking as based on universal structures – like formal, hierarchical relations between concepts. He was on his way to a psychology where consciousness is seen as a psychic organization, historically realized through activity based upon a dialectics between instruction and development. He understood instruction as any directive which elicits new activity, and development as the reorganization of consciousness through this activity. Between the organization of instruction and development he saw an internal relationship, which took shape according to the developmental stage of the child or human being. An illustration of this can be found in *Thinking and Speech* (Vygotsky, 1987, p. 202f), where Vygotsky argues that instructions to write – whatever their method – develop a new activity, which according to the kind of instruction and stage of development sets up new abstractions and relations to language in the consciousness of the child. In order to write the child must learn how to disregard the sounds of language and identify the correspondences between sounds and letters. The child must disregard a specific and concrete interlocutor and address an imaginary and general one. The motives for immediate communication in a situation are no longer valid in written speech; the child must grasp a broader motivational span. The interaction of dialogue is gone; the child must apprehend what the general speaker will reply or think about the written content.

It is easy to react to this example by saying: "So what, if you speak before you learn to write many of the elements in your talking performance have to be abstracted and this seems to demand a certain maturity in the competence of the child." This is, however, to miss the whole point. Vygotsky refutes the idea that some more or less specific mental powers have to mature before instructions of, say, writing can be applied. He argues that the activity of writing, by expanding the communicative activity of the child, makes it reorganize the elements of its consciousness on a more complex level. This argument can be put more precisely: The abstractions performed in order to develop the conception of an imaginary and general interlocutor are the result of specific necessities in the writing activity developing on the basis of talking activity. There is no general abstraction ability, but this specific mode of abstraction and generalization is developed by necessity within this particular activity. Here content takes precedence over form.

This idea of a specific mode of abstraction and generalization determined by particular conditions has general implications. It must also have governed the way Vygotsky arrived at his own understanding of a specific mode of abstraction and generalization. Vygotsky was well aware of this implication. That is why he presented his theoretical position as a dialectical transcendence of related paradigms. In a critical review of contemporary positions, Vygotsky (1987, pp. 194–201) identifies two main groupings of the relation between instruction and development. The first grouping gives precedence to development. Some abstract faculty has to mature before instructions in a particular domain will have effects. In this grouping there have been few empirical results, and this has been explained away on the basis of methodological inadequacies, which have been compensated through theoretical abstraction. In the second grouping development and instruction become the same; Vygotsky talks about the predecessor of behaviorism, associanism, and points out that this conception of learning is simply an accumulation of performed instructions. This quantitative approach is not able to demonstrate any transfer of knowledge from one domain to another, and this is an absurd result compared with everyday experience. Neither of the groupings is thus able to grasp development, understood as the continuous unfolding of more and more complex activities, covering still greater fields of action. In this way Vygotsky founded his own theoretical abstractions and generalizations on the necessities within a particular pedagogical field of activity, and his abstractions and generalizations evolved from conceptual inadequacies in theoretical positions related to that pedagogical field of activity.

Thus the conceptual development of children and of scientists has been tied up through the cultural-historical relation between development and specific fields of activity. To talk in this way in general terms about specific fields of activity also involves considering the more general problems of learning, of psychic, personal, and social development involved in each field. In so doing, one embarks upon a foundation of psychology on a theory of praxis. Such a project entails a complete revision of one's understanding of the relation between the world and human beings.

Vygotsky was only able to get this revision started. Within a Marxist tradition he was mainly interested in the objective elements of knowledge and their stability. We must consider his example on the development of writing activity as historical, because it ties up development with specific circumstances. All the same, Vygotsky did not explicitly emphasize the historical character of knowledge and activity. More broadly stated, he did not arrive at a clear distinction between general principles and specific historical realizations of human development on a Marxist base.

He merely plotted out the course for such a project, and also set up an apparently arbitrary end point. In his last writings one can find statements about the necessity of deriving the meanings in language from the emotions and motives governing activity. However, he was not given time to incorporate systematically this perspective of the relation between the world and human beings into his subject: Thinking and speech.

Leont'ev

The premature death of Vygotsky left his project unfinished. It became the task of A. N. Leont'ev and a group of colleagues in Khar'kov to rework the elements until they could make a coherent presentation of it in the late 1950s, after the death of Stalin. A comparison of the text of Vygotsky's *Thinking and Speech* and Leon'tev's *Problems of the Development of the Mind* (1981) will indicate the problems Leont'ev and his group faced: While the references of Vygotsky are up to date, most of the references of Leont'ev date back to the same period. Vygotsky set up his presentations as a dialectic dialogue between opposed positions. Critical dialogue has a peripheral function in the text of Leont'ev; the presentation of his psychology is mainly organized as the phylogenetic evolution and socio-historical development of mind. An advanced psychological theory is developed on outdated references.

However, there are also several reasons for the evolutionary and historical presentation, inherent to the project:

Working within a psychological theory of specific conscious organization developed under specific and particular circumstances entails that circumstances and consciousness both are a concrete unity of many processes. Therefore, at a particular point in time one will find remnants from past epochs, seeds for the future, as well as be able to identify the main organizational principles for the present.

With such a conception of human consciousness we face the problem that the general principles for the development of consciousness cannot be derived directly from empirical research, because each human being is only an instance of all the possibilities to be realized, and we will never be able to see all instances. On the other hand, we cannot stop at what we meet empirically and do nothing but describe it concretely and specifically in its own right. In this way we would get lost in the historical process, and would not be able to achieve an autonomous individual and social development.

Therefore, we do need some conception of general principles – human nature – governing human development under specific circumstances. But the actual organization of the object of investigation can neither be derived nor understood on an isolated synchronic base. One cannot identify a structure of universal elements in consciousness, which has inner coherence, and is independent of and at the same time governs the present field of processes. We must develop a basic notion of human potentials, which in social history are able to realize the observed, multiple specific organizations of consciousness under particular conditions. Such a notion of human potentials must itself be a concrete unity of many possible processes. Therefore, our search for understanding specific human development doubles up. The potentials must themselves be conceived of as a specific answer to specific conditions, in other words, they must be founded on their *historical development* – as a product of evolution.

This is the background for the double task Leont'ev set out for himself. On the one side, triggered by problems in empirical research he set out to develop a general conception about human nature based on its specific evolutionary development. Thus he founded basic categories for human activity. On the other side, this conceptual frame must encompass an understanding of how individual consciousness is organized through specific and particular activity, so that the relations between these elements guide empirical research of particular phenomena. The remainder of the article will mainly focus on this double task. First we will focus on how to found the categories; then we will discuss whether they grasp the individual organization of consciousness.

To determine human potentials through evolution becomes the same as identifying the specific characteristics of the human being as a species, and this identification has to be consistent with the double task outlined above.

Human potentials must be conceived of as a general relation between human beings and the world, and as having evolved in evolutionary processes. Evolutionary processes before humankind can be characterized as an accumulation of genetic information in a species population resulting from the activity of population members in the population specific world. The primacy of biological evolution stops at the threshold of humanity; human activity and consciousness are neither instinctually nor genetically driven. As an answer to specific evolutionary problems (a problem which Leont'ev addresses but we will not discuss here), society has become the pool of accumulated human experience; it has substituted the accumulation of phylogenetic information by genes. Human beings are social beings. Human consciousness itself is socially created. The human being unfolds its individuality through its social activity under social conditions that imply the motives and goals of their activity, their means and modes. The human being is not a tabula rasa; it has a potential direction towards the appropriation of motives and goals and unfolding of the emotions and needs based on activities and tools evolving in the history of society.

The category of *human nature* has thus been reorganized to make room for identifying general principles for specific human development. Given this, Leont'ev could attack the main task hinted at in the example from Vygotsky: The realization of human potentials in individuals must be conceived of as a form which has been created by the content of the social processes in which individuals actively partake and which they develop. Already in the Vygotsky example of learning to write human social activity can be considered the central notion. But now we are in a better position to distinguish between general categorical relations and historical ones. With this distinction Leont'ev now set out to establish categories for human activity to make possible the investigation of how the specific and particular organization of consciousness evolves in specific and particular social activity.

The level of generality of these categories can be determined more precisely in the following way. As they characterize human nature, they must possess validity for the time period, where human nature has not changed. They must be understood as more or less easily realized possibilities in all societies, and – if feasible – they must be founded on their development in the most early human life forms, when the genes were still changing. Thus determined, they can be considered fundamental concepts of a general psychology.

The framework must set up the general relation between activity, society, and consciousness, and it must do so in a nonspecific way with regard to the elements which work in these processes. We will first look upon activity as the focus of the general relation and thereafter upon some of the elements.

Human *activity* is always social and cooperative and occurs within the social division of labour. This is also the case when it is performed in solitude. Human activity is a social net of processes, which comes about as a result of the actions of one or more individuals. The interrelations of necessities in activity – if realized by individuals – insures corresponding relations among them. In this way activity mediates between the cultural and the social on the one hand and the individual on the other.

Leont'ev considers *society* as a unity of actual interlacing patterns of particular activities – as a result of and condition for human praxis. In his writings Leont'ev never treats the characteristics of this unity separately. That is a task for sociology, and we shall not touch upon this aspect in this article any further.

The uniqueness of each human being is to be explained on the basis of social activity. In his later writings Leont'ev stresses that uniqueness is not based on biological individuality as such, like animal individuality. Human individuality is based on social activity. Furthermore, in order to specify how the particular and specific organization of consciousness comes about Leont'ev realized that it was not sufficient to determine the relation between a specific activity and consciousness, as Vygotsky did in his analysis of how writing activity could develop a specific and particular organization of consciousness. It is necessary to identify the particular "knots" or unities of activities, which constitute an "ensemble" in individuals' *personalities*, because it is on the basis of their personalities that they relate to and develop particular activities. Personality is thus the key to determine the species specific uniqueness of each human being.

Having thus established the general relations of activity, society, and personality, we can determine the elements of activity. We shall introduce them by using Leont'ev's example of the primeval collective hunt, which is, at the same time, an instance of cooperative interaction in activity. Collective hunting is the activity, the prey is its *object*, and hunger for the prey is its *motive*. When beaters make noise to frighten the game, the clapping of their hands is an *operation*, and the beating as a whole is an *action* within the hunting activity, motivated by the hunger to be fulfilled by the realization of the activity. This noise making action has as its *goal* the frightening of the game. However, the goal contradicts the object and motive of activity, which is to catch the animal and distribute and consume the food. The beaters' action is part of the activity on the basis of their conscious knowledge that they frighten the game so that it can be caught. This implies that human *consciousness* has an engaging and a mediating representational aspect. The beaters' action is only possible on condition that they represent the link between the goal of their action and the motive of the cooperative activity. They must be able to represent relations between objects, irrespective of their actual needs, or else they would simply go for it themselves and therefore in many instances fail to obtain the object. Their specific and particular consciousness is constituted through its content, which has meanings as elements. Through the *meanings* they are able to represent the connection between the motive and the goal of action; in this way they are engaged in the activity; it makes *sense* to beaters.

One activity is mainly distinguished from another by its object or motive. This can become a key to accounting for the development of activity in the following way. If, for example, a beater discovers it is fun beating, if he starts beating for its own sake, he is motivated by the beating; the beating is an appropriated object; he has produced a new activity from the old action. An action can thus develop into an activity by acquiring a motive, and the new activity might itself become subdivided into a set of actions. On the other hand, an activity can become an action if its motive wanes, and can become integrated into another activity. Likewise, an action can evolve into an operation, capable of accomplishing various actions.

Having thus determined the elements of activity, it is important to stress that they must be understood as potentials which constitute a unity of social, personal, and organismic aspects, and the actualization of the potentials must be conceived of as a specific developmental process, which is beyond their determination as potentials.

The motive of activity is thus an individually constituted unity of an originally nonspecific biological "push" and previously socially produced objectified "pull." Biological functions, which express the arousal of the body, cannot themselves direct activity. Only when desires meet a socially produced object meant for human satisfaction do they become objectified, get their specific direction. Likewise the goal of an action is an individually produced unity of what the objective social circumstances have made possible and the process of actions actualized. Furthermore, meanings are the unity of what appears to the subject on the one hand as relations of the world unveiled through activity, independent of its consciousness, and on the other hand as an instrument to become conscious of objective relations. Lastly, sense is established as a unity when the social meanings unveil the relation between goal and motive to the subject and thus release the engagement or commitment of consciousness.

Such elements constitute each kind of activity, and the recognizable unity of the ever changing activities of the subject constitutes the personality. Personality is the transformations of the subject, which comes about as a result of the development of its activities in the system of social relations. The emotions are seen as a constituent of personality; they reflect the relations between the motives of the personality and the possibility for their positive realization in the social world through activity. With the concepts of meaning, sense, and emotion we recognize a movement in the theoretical constructions of Leont'ev towards a localization of the individual in the knots of the system of activities.

The advantages of Leont'ev's position are evident even from this summary sketch:

Human nature does not determine specific activities, but it does determine the set of possible activities which can be realized. This is because human beings are active social agents who produce objects for the satisfaction of their needs and thereby develop the elements of their psyche and internal relationships.

It is in accordance with this line of thought to state that the system of activity as presented is to be understood as a material as well as theoretical seminal core. It is common to all kinds of actualized historical activities, be they cultural, producing, or reproducing. Each particular activity, then, has a history which has developed through contradictions in different sets of concrete realizations of the elements emotional, conscious, operational, musical, instrumental, etc.

Finally, social and individual reproduction and development are conceived of as constituents of the same process. Society, on the one side, is conceived of as produced and reproduced through the subjects and their social systems of activity. The individual, on the other side, is conceived of as developing through personal appropriation of the accumulated experience of human beings as found in society. So social reproduction and development are more or less intended and cooperatively controlled products of human activity, and individual reproduction and development are based on and a part of social reproduction and development.

Leont'ev's theory unfolds the notion of precedence of content over form: It is actual history which has led to this human being and which is studied when analyzing individual human activity.

However, there are also several problems with Leont'ev's position:

His "babushka" system of activity, action and operation is not straightforward to work with. There are two conspicuous reasons for

this. First, Leont'ev sometimes writes as if activity, action, and operation constitute three independent levels. This allows for a hierarchical
structural conception of activity, which can be identified in some of his
followers. Second, it is difficult to set up guidelines for the categorization of activity in a particular study. The unequivocal determination of
individual motives is decisive in order to differentiate between an action
and activity and between activities, but it is not possible. Leont'ev's aim
is to describe objective activity, but his conception of activity thus easily
becomes subjective and relativistic: Activity is what the researcher
perceives as motivated.

Leont'ev merely talks about an activity system, not about social
organizations and formations. His combination of social theory and
psychology remains too abstract and is only rudimentarily and incon-
sistently developed.

The final problem we shall look into is also the one with which we will
draw a line of development produced by Critical Psychology. Leont'ev's
theory of activity is – as already stated – meant to grasp individual development as socially produced, and thereby as an attempt to realize a not
yet fulfilled promise within Marxist tradition. A central assumption with
which to accomplish this is the conception of how needs and interests
have a determining and indispensable function in producing knowledge
through practice. Objective knowledge can be realized not by abstracting from, but by taking into account the contradictory class interests in
which one is embedded. However, although Leont'ev presents the first
elements to locate the subject and thus to demonstrate the unity among
needs, interests, and knowledge, the picture presented is not totally
coherent. As argued, there are tendencies toward structuralism, ahis-
toricism, etc., and it therefore becomes difficult to go beyond the demonstration of how a certain social position will typically produce a specific
consciousness. In order to understand the specific and particular personal development we must systematically formulate a historical science
of the subject. Critical Psychology set itself this task.

Critical Psychology

According to Critical Psychology the main task of a psychology
is to demonstrate how any particular and specific subject develops as a
product of its own social action, from a life lived in specific social posi-

tions. To do this, one must develop concepts for how human beings relate to social positions, how they maintain their interests in the positions, whether they fight for them, or give in, or adopt any kind of strategy within these limits. Critical Psychology has developed a set of categories to grasp these problems, and we will look into a few of them: subjectivity, action potence, emotions, and restrictive and comprehensive mode of action.

Critical Psychology has been produced collectively by a group of scholars at the Free University in Berlin as their main base. They started out within the wave of radicalization in the late 1960s and participated in the critique of psychology. They argued that the effect of the widespread application of psychology was control over people and assimilation of human beings to society, and they demonstrated how the use of psychological concepts made political and antagonistic social conflicts appear as individual problems. Only a psychology based on Marxist principles would be able to unveil these implications of psychology and develop an alternative understanding of the relationship between individuals and society. In Leont'ev they found a systematic position, which they took as a starting point. They have published a series of books on the transition from animal to humans, on perception, on motivation, on problem solving, etc. Their results have been reorganized in one large volume, and they have published a periodical for 11 years. Their work is more comprehensive and has more implications than can be seen from this article.

Critical Psychology sees its distinctive contribution to psychology as the systematic setting up of *categories* for the psyche. Inspired by Leont'ev the categories are developed according to their function in evolution. We will discuss categories crucial to the constitution of the species specific relationship between human beings and their world. These categories were originally developed through the critique of psychological theories and studies of the transition from animal to humans.

Like Leont'ev, Critical Psychology shifts the theoretical focus from the satisfaction of primary basic needs to the social production of the means of satisfaction because this is the central feature of the species specific relationship. Critical Psychology departs from Leont'ev by stressing that there is always a *break* between the productive actions and satisfactions of primary needs of human beings; what I produce is for general use, and what I use was produced for general use. To overlook this is to mix up human with animal psychology. The break presupposes cooperation through division of labour, and it is crucial to conceive the action of human beings as positioned within an objectively given whole.

Most importantly, focussing on the social production makes it possible to found psychology on the dialectics of consumption and production: by producing the means of satisfactions the human beings produce their *conditions* of existence, which have *meaning* for their actions as *action possibilities*. This proposition can also be illustrated with Leont'ev's example on the primeval hunt: it provides the hunters with the conditions for distribution, e.g., of meat, skin, etc., and thereby has meaning for their actions. There are many possible ways of distributing the meat, not only determined through all the life conditions including the hunt, but also through productive subjective action under these conditions.

Productive human action is determined stepwise in the systematic unfolding of categories, which we will pursue within the species specific relationship.

The social conditions of human existence need human beings to produce them, but not necessarily a specific human being. Therefore social conditions do not necessarily present themselves as an imperative for the individual, but mostly as meanings offering sets of possible actions, which the human being at least can realize or not.

The relation between an individual and his or her set of possible social actions in a social positio... opens up the possibility of a reflective distance to the social conditions. This is the material base for the conscious relation of a human being to his or her social world. Each human being is a source of cognition, of emotion, of conscious relation, and of action, all of which constitute the central characteristics of *subjectivity*. Relations between human beings thus become intersubjective. Each "I" has to acknowledge this in its actions. I must always acknowledge that whatever passes through the psyche of another subject is worked upon, related to, and transformed according to how the subject relates to its social position and its possible set of actions. This is what makes mutual understanding possible and the subjective reasons of others reconstructable. Critical Psychology considers subjectivity as the defining characteristic of psychology, which any method and any investigation must take into account in order to be adequate to the subject matter of psychology. At the same time scientific theories, including psychology, are products of subjectivity. Thus, subjectivity is the reason behind the systematic theoretical criticism outlined by Critical Psychology. Each psychological theory is a result of the way a scientist or a group of scientists relates to their social position. Through the dialectic critique one uncovers these relations and thereby becomes able to reorganize the theories in a more comprehensive way.

On the basis of the categories we have developed up to now, it is feasible to state a core notion for human freedom: Individuals which develop through the social conditions will have the social conditions at their disposal by participating in the collective disposition over the social process. The category of *action potence* is set up to grasp this relationship, signifying that individuals have the conditions for the possible set of actions at their disposal. An implication of the categorical constitution is that any individual in any society will have some kind of action potence; the specific characteristics of action potence will vary according to the organization of society and the way the individual relates to the social positions of his or her life situation.

Of the elements of subjectivity – cognition, emotion, conscious relation, and action – emotions are the most crucial for a social conception of the individual. Most often emotions are considered our very private domain – as well as a sort of coloring of our experiences or actions, which it is impossible to communicate to others – as our last resort of resistance, when society crushes our natural instincts with cultural demands. A critical test of a social conception of the individual is whether it is able to demonstrate the function of emotions. In addition to serving a part of the constantly ongoing social creation of the individual human nature they serve as a source of values in situations of social repression.

Critical Psychology has expanded the theory of emotion hinted at by Leont'ev. *Emotions* function as an evaluation of the environmental conditions based on the meanings for action as they appear to the individual. The emotional evaluations are performed immediately and not consciously. They give direction to the actions of the individual.

Emotions are an integral part of the total species-specific relation of the individual to the environment. This means that the actions of the individual are normally not only determined individually by the immediate pressure of the needs. They are determined socially, on the basis of the general state of needs, meanings, action possibilities, and action potence. This general state appears as an overall emotional tone, a *complex-quality*, which makes it possible to identify a unitary direction of actual actions in a complex setting, where many meanings offer many relevant actions. As human beings are creating the conditions for the satisfaction of their needs, the collective meaning of the current satisfaction on long-term interests and goals is incorporated in the emotional evaluation of the social meanings as well as explored in the conscious reflection on the emotional ease or unease. This is part of the human potential for an overall relation to one's own needs. To drink in order to satisfy one's thirst is consequently not an action determined solely by the psychic equivalent of the physiological state of the body. Let us suppose I am thirsty and sit in a classroom and teach, while there is a jar of water and a mug in front of me. While somebody else says something, I might reach out and drink without giving it much thought. If on the other hand an earthquake just occurred, and we are all confined in the room with the water, my action potence and all it contains have changed – among other things thirst might become a common problem for all of us. My emotions will direct my action accordingly, even if my body's need for water is the same in both situations.

In this way emotions attune human beings to the problems in the species-specific world of meanings. If we discover that something is out of order, the anticipation of the loss of control generates unease and anxiety, and the need for coping is actualized. If we cannot anticipate getting control of the situation, anxiety takes over and may make us turn away. Otherwise the need for coping activates search activities, and we move towards areas where we feel a solution can be found. An ambivalent situation will let us change between the need for coping and anxiety according to our grasp of the ambiguities in the situation. If we stay in an ambiguous situation and do not find an unambiguous direction for action, everything becomes a problem. At some point, however, on the basis of our search we may become able to develop a goal and thereby establish a direction for our action. We can resume our complex of everyday actions directed by our emotions, and by and by everything will work smoothly again. Thus, whenever something has been learned, the new way of doing old tasks creates new social conditions and meanings, new possible sets of action, a new action potence; and it has thereby become a new realization of our human nature or human potentials.

However, the emotional action guidance is only effective under certain conditions. To discuss the varied influence of social conditions marks the beginning of one way to leave categorical development and to enter theoretical construction of actual social history.

The subject must find assurance that after conflict resolution its needs will be satisfied according to the interests of its positions. This assurance might be missing. For some possible real social reasons the subject might feel threatened when it confronts the need for altering relevant conditions of life in its own interest, even though this interest might sometimes be an expression of a common interest. In such a social conflict, the subject might refrain from expanding the possible set of actions, give up its own interests, and comply with interests alien to its own social positions. The subject then has to act according to the interest of other people. This is called a *restrictive mode of action*. But now the emotions of the subject will become a problem. As stated earlier their complex quality is a constant evaluation of all individual needs and all meanings pertinent to their satisfaction. By refraining from its own interests, the subject has to disregard the complex quality of its emotional evaluation and even to deny this denial. The emotional evaluation becomes detached from cognition through defense mechanism. However, they make themselves felt as uneasiness, unrest, a disturbed inner life with odd inclinations; they appear as the phenomena of the "unconscious." Only when the possibility of a better life is apprehended as realistic can my emotions and I locate myself in a readiness for struggle, which opens up the possibilities of a more *comprehensive mode of action*.

In Critical Psychology the categories of the species specific relationship between human beings and their world is taken as the starting point for the development of a categorical body of the subject, only hinted at here.

This body constitutes the foundation with which to address social historical problems, both of personal development, and of a theoretical nature, e.g., in education and therapy. That is, it provides a frame of reference within which I can both interpret what my emotions tell me and guide my research. As a natural consequence of the categories, the focus of research performed within education is resistance to learning, and within therapy it is handling conflict from the subjective perspective of the therapist as well as that of the client.

Conclusion

In this article one line of development in European Activity Theory has been reviewed. It was demonstrated that Vygotsky's conception of the specific and particular development of consciousness necessitated a complete reorganization of the notion of human nature as one of human potentials. This entails that basic categories are to be determined in quite another dimension of generality than is normally found in psychological and sociological theories. Developing this level was the task performed by Leont'ev.

It was also demonstrated that unclarities in Leont'ev's categories inhibit the conception of the specific and particular development of concrete individuals. It was demonstrated how categories developed by Critical Psychology on the basis of Leont'ev's Activity Theory are able to deal with problems such as how individuals relate to their social position, and how individuals act on an inner urge whose social origin need not be clear to them. By working on how to systematically found a science of the subject, Critical Psychology has started to pull psychology back on the track and to expand the realm of subject matters reachable by an activity theoretical historical approach within psychology. Psychology is on its way to being reestablished as a science of the subject, a science of how human beings relate to their circumstances and sometimes are able to struggle to get the conditions of their actions changed.

Note

This article owes its existence to the chaotic and bubbling discussions of a class of graduate students attending an introductory course on activity theory at UC Berkeley given by Professor Jean Lave and the author of this article, Erik Axel.

References

Leont'ev, A. N. (1978). *Activity, consciousness and personality.* Englewood Cliffs, NJ: Prentice Hall.

Leont'ev, A. N. (1981). *Problems of the development of the mind.* Moscow: Progress Publishers.

Tolman, C. W., & Maiers, W. (1991). *Critical Psychology. Contributions to an historical science of the subject.* New York: Cambridge University Press.

Vygotsky, L. S. (1987). *Collected works of Vygotsky. Volume 1. Problems of general psychology, including the volume Thinking and Speech.* New York and London: Plenum Press. (Translated by N. Minick).

12 Activity, consciousness, and communication

David Bakhurst

"Soviet communitarianism" and the socially constituted individual

One of the most pervasive beliefs encountered in the human sciences is the idea that each individual owes his or her existence to society, that our personalities, needs and wants are nurtured and sustained by the communities in which we live. This idea, however, is as elusive as it is ubiquitous. It is hard to make sense of the social nature of our being without appearing either to be labouring something so obvious and incontrovertible as to be empty of methodological significance, or to be advancing a thesis so radical as to threaten the very possibility of human individuality and self-determination. The great achievement of the Soviet intellectual tradition of which Evald Ilyenkov is part is that it offers a powerful account of exactly in what sense man is a social being. I'll begin by characterising the central ideas of this Soviet tradition, and raising a powerful objection aimed at one of the tradition's most attractive features: its theory of the mind. Then, by drawing on Ilyenkov's ideas, I hope to show how this theory can be defended from this objection, and defended in a way which leaves us with a compelling theory of man as a socially constituted being.

Ilyenkov is a member of a school of Soviet Marxism which first emerged in the fertile years of the 1920s and 1930s, particularly in the seminal work of Vygotsky, and also Voloshinov (and/or Bakhtin). It was preserved through the tumult of the Stalin period, principally by psychologists of the so-called "Vygotsky school." In the rejuvenation of the

147

Soviet intellectual life after Stalin it acquired some impressive new exponents, of whom Ilyenkov is the most distinguished philosopher. In the latter half of his career, Ilyenkov was adopted by the psychologists of the Vygotsky school as their philosophical mentor. There is no satisfactory name for this tradition, so I'll refer to it here as the "communitarian tradition" in Soviet thought. The term "communitarian" at least marks the resolute anti-individualism of the tradition, its recognition that we, in some strong sense, owe our very humanity to the communities in which we live our lives.

Although it's difficult to generalise across the tradition as a whole, I think we can isolate four interrelated theoretical insights which all Soviet communitarians endorse (at least under some interpretation):

1. The mental life of the human individual exists in the forms of its expression. That is, the higher mental functions which constitute human consciousness are essentially embodied in, or mediated by, language (in the broadest possible sense of the term). By "higher mental functions" Soviet communitarians mean mental capacities like thinking, believing, remembering, wishing, desiring, hoping, imagining, and so on. These capacities, in their most highly developed form, constitute an interrelated system of mental functions which only humans exhibit.

2. Language is an essentially social phenomenon, in at least this sense, that the possibility of language presupposes the existence of a socially-forged communicative medium: a set of shared social meanings against which alone any communicative act has its reality.

3. This set of "shared social meanings" represents a culture. Cultures are real phenomena which are constituted by socially significant forms of activity of a community: cultures objectively exist in the form of social practices.

4. It is only through the appropriation of such socially significant forms of activity that the human child becomes capable of the higher mental functions. The child's mind is formed through his/her inauguration into a culture.

These four insights already appear to offer the basis of an argument that we are socially constituted beings. For if language is the living actuality of thought, and language presupposes a socially constructed phenomenon – a culture – then it must in some sense be true that the mental life of the individual has its being only in a social context. However, the insights themselves are only the bare bones of this argument: its premises and conclusion remain horribly vague. As I've presented them, the insights tell us that consciousness, culture and language are interrelated, but they don't tell us exactly how. For example, the term "essentially" in (1) and (2) is unclear. When we say that consciousness is "essentially embodied in language" do we mean that the mind necessarily exists in the forms of its expression, that is, that it could not exist otherwise? Or do we mean something weaker – that, say, as a matter of psychological fact, our mental states are always, or almost always, formed in language? So, (1)–(4) need to be developed, if they are to be turned into a theory of the socially constituted individual.

Someone might wonder whether these insights are not insightful enough as they stand without subjecting them to rigorous conceptual clarification. However, one reason why we should care about exactly what these insights amount to is that they appear to offer a potentially innovative and distinctive model for the study of communication as an interdiscipline. For if our mental lives are lived only in society through their expression in socially-mediated communicative practices, then the domains of psychology, sociology and language studies (in all their multidimensionality) will become intrinsically interwoven. But just how these disciplines are interwoven will depend on exactly how mind, culture and language are interrelated. So, the more precise our understanding of (1)–(4), the clearer we shall be about the conceptual framework Soviet communitarianism offers the interdiscipline "communication."

The best way to assess insights (1)–(4) is to look at what the Soviet communitarian tradition has made of them. And in the present context, it makes sense to concentrate on the theory of the mind which Soviet communitarians have developed in the light of (1)–(4), for it's in the philosophical psychology of Soviet communitarianism we find the most radical statement of the social constitution of the individual. This theory of the mind is based on three theses:

A. Activity – that is, social forms of *material* activity explains (or is the "key concept" in the explanation of) the nature and origin of human consciousness. Since consciousness is the mark of our

humanity, "we become human through labour" (as Leont'ev
put it);

B. The higher mental functions are social in nature and origin. The
individual mind lives its life in a social medium: mind is (to
adopt a coinage of Michael Cole's) "in society";

C. The higher mental functions are internalised forms of social
activity (Vygotsky's "General Genetic Law of Cultural
Development").

According to Soviet communitarians, to understand these theses
correctly is to arrive at an understanding of the essence of the human
individual as (in Marx's words) "the ensemble of social relations."

Our task, then, is to find the right way of reading theses (A)–(C).
I want to approach by considering an objection which purports to
show that, since there *can be no* theoretically satisfactory way of interpreting (A)–(C), the basis of the communitarian theory of the mind
is completely misconceived. As this objection might come from a
number of different philosophers, I'll refer to the objector simply as "the
enemy."

The enemy argues that there are two, and only two, ways of reading
theses (A)–(C). While first reading makes these theses so weak that they
become philosophically insignificant; the second makes them so strong
that they are false to the point of unintelligibility. Take, for example, (A)
and (B). On the weak reading, says the enemy, (A) and (B) claim that
material activity and social interaction are empirical preconditions of our
mental lives. That is, explanations of how we acquire mental states and
of how our intellectual capacities and personalities develop must make
reference to our active engagement with our surroundings and with
other individuals. But, says the enemy, this is an utterly uncontroversial
claim! Of course, to acquire mental states and to develop our minds we
have to interact with the world and with others, but no one, whatever
their philosophical colours, ever denied this. And something which
no philosopher ever denied can scarcely be of vast methodological
significance for philosophy!

Okay, the enemy continues, since this weak reading of (A) and (B) is
so hopeless, how else might Soviet communitarians intend these theses
to be understood? Well, in the case of (A), Soviet communitarians some-

times appear to be advancing the strong thesis that material activity is literally *constitutive* of the mental. This *is* a philosophically interesting thesis which, if true, *would* make it the case that talk about activity was essential to the explanation of the mental. However, says the enemy, such a thesis could not possibly be true for the following reason. The mental has all kinds of interesting properties: mental phenomena are capable of having a certain *phenomenology* (experiences "feel" or "seem" a certain way); some mental states have "intentionality," that is, they are directed toward a certain *content or meaning*; we each have a special acquaintance with the contents of our minds which others do not share, and so on. Once we reflect on these qualities of the mental it is obvious that no amount of talk about *material doings*, about transforming nature, could ever explain the possibility of mental phenomena: *We can't get phenomenology out of labour.*

Likewise, in the case of (B), Soviet communitarians could be taken to be making the strong claim that the higher mental functions are literally "not in the head," that the mind is, in some radical sense, constituted in public space. Once again, however, the enemy will say that this thesis is at best only metaphorically true. If we take it literally, in so far as it is comprehensible at all, it is false.

So the objection to (A) and (B) appears as a dilemma. They are either true, but (philosophically) trivial, or false. Either way they're theoretically bankrupt.

It might be thought that Soviet communitarians can rescue both (A) and (B) by appeal to the idea of "internalisation" in thesis (C). Can't they respond like this? When we say the mind is a social phenomenon and is explained by activity, what we mean is that the higher mental functions must be understood as internalised forms of social activity. On such a view, the process of appropriation of socially significant forms of activity in which the child's mind is formed is a process in which these social activities are translated from the *inter*psychological plane onto the *intra*psychological plane, where they reemerge, in restructured form, as the child's higher mental functions. Thus, (A) and (B) need not be taken as implying that mental functions are literally located in society, or actually constituted by material activity. Rather, what we're claiming is only that, in the explanation of the nature and origin of consciousness the direction of the explanation runs from the social to the individual: we explain *intra*psychological phenomena in terms of *inter*psychological phenomena, and not vice versa.

However, the problem with this response is that it invites the same attack as (A) and (B). The enemy will argue that, as a theory of the origin of the mental, the internalisation thesis is ambiguous between two readings. Soviet communitarians may be claiming that the child's intellect only *develops* if he or she engages in certain forms of activity (the child only, say, will learn to count if drilled in certain practices). This, however, is true but trivial: of course the child's mind doesn't somehow develop spontaneously! Alternatively, communitarians may be saying that the child's mind is somehow *created* by the process of internalisation. (They do claim just this incidentally.) But that surely cannot be true! For, the child could not even begin to internalise anything if it were not already conscious: you can't explain the very possibility of the *intra*psychological by appeal to the *inter*psychological because there can be no *inter*psychological relations unless the *intra*psychological already exists.

Thus, all three theses seem open to the objection that they are either trivially true, or false. Either way, it's a disaster for communitarianism. To answer the objection, then, we must find some way of understanding the communitarian's position which restores its theoretical credibility.

Lest it be thought that I'm discussing Soviet communitarianism in a historical vacuum, let me say that the objection I've raised from this unspecified "enemy" has considerable historical actuality. It might be put, not only by some of my colleagues in Oxford, but also by contemporary Soviet thinkers who are suspicious of the communitarian tradition. For, while the Marxist pedigree of insights (1)–(4) and theses (A)–(C) makes it almost mandatory for Soviet theorists to accept them under *some* interpretation, many will endorse them only under the weakest possible interpretation. Consequently, there is a rift in the Soviet philosophy and psychology between those who commit themselves only to the weak reading of (A)–(C), and those who argue for something stronger and who vehemently resent the reduction of what they take to be the central theses of Marxist psychology to a collection of truisms. So, our dilemma reflects a real division in the world of Soviet theory.

In what follows I want to try to defend Soviet communitarianism from this objection. I want to show that a theoretically intense interpretation of its doctrines is the correct one. In so doing, I'll be drawing in particular on Ilyenkov's ideas, though in many places I'll be reconstructing and extrapolating from Ilyenkov's position rather than simply reporting it.

The influence of the Cartesian conception of the self

Ilyenkov would have insisted that we first diagnose the source of the problem. Why is it someone might feel that, at best, (A)–(C) express only trivial truths of no concern to philosophy? I believe – and I think Ilyenkov would agree – that this feeling is caused by the dominance in our philosophical culture of a particular conception of the self. This conception, which was introduced principally by Descartes, has had an enduring and pervasive influence on philosophy. It dominates the thought of the Enlightenment (especially the empiricism of Locke and Hume, and the rationalism of Kant) and still continues to hypnotize the Anglo-American tradition of "analytic" philosophy.

At the heart of Cartesianism is an idea we encountered in the attack on the thesis that activity explains consciousness. The Cartesian stresses that the mental has properties fundamentally different from the kinds of properties physical things can have. Examples of such properties are: meaning or content, phenomenological properties (feelings, seemings, pains), subjectivity, undubitability . . . Descartes himself introduces the idea of a special kind of "mind stuff," a non-extended substance, which is the substratum of all these properties. But the idea of the mind as a special substance is *not*, I believe, the determining characteristic of Cartesianism.

The basic image at the heart of the Cartesian conception is (to use Rorty's favourite metaphor) the picture of the mind as a great *mirror* containing various representations. Onto the glass of the mind images of the external world are cast. In the Cartesian tradition these images are called *ideas*. The self, or the "subject" of consciousness is presented as located, as it were, behind the mirror, surveying the representations which it presents to him. (Imagine that the images appear somehow on the *back* of the mirror.)

The Cartesian position is a form of dualism. The dualism has two dimensions. The first is the dualism of mind and body, the dualism which generates the meta-physical problem of the correlation of mental and physical states and the question of how there can be interaction between the two. The second is the dualism of image and object, which creates the epistemological problems of how our ideas can be like the objects they supposedly represent and whether we can know reality as it is.

The dualism is not so much a dualism of two *parts* of a person, his mind and his body, but a dualism of two *worlds*. The first is the "object world" of material bodies in space, the external world "out there." The second is the "inner" world of the subject, or self, surveying his ideas from behind the mirror. For our purposes, what is crucial is the way in which Cartesianism portrays the world of the subject. The Cartesian self has three principal characteristics: it is *self-contained*, *self-sufficient*, and *ready-made*.

The idea that the self is *self-contained* follows from the Cartesian's allegiance to two tenets. First, the Cartesian holds that the self is incapable of direct contact with material things. The self can only be aware of objects indirectly, in so far as those objects are presented to it in ideas. Objects in their brute physicality are "indigestible" to minds. This is because the Cartesian represents the external world in itself as devoid of meaning, and minds are only capable of dealing directly with meaningful entities. *Mental* objects, according to the Cartesian, are intrinsically *representational* phenomena – they present the world as being a certain way – and are thus fit to play the role of the immediate objects of thought. So, for the Cartesian, an object can be present to the self only if it is translated into an idea. Second, the Cartesian holds that ideas are *private*, each self's ideas are revealed directly only to it. It follows from these two tenets (which are both based on plausible intuitions) that the Cartesian self is acquainted with the material world only via its ideas and only *it* is directly acquainted with those ideas. Thus, each Cartesian self lives in an entirely self-contained world. It is as if we each inhabit our own private picture show.

In its self-contained mental world the Cartesian self is entirely *self-sufficient*: each self is essentially independent of all others. For, since nothing (including no other self) can affect the Cartesian self except by becoming an object of its thought, its capacity to think must be something it possesses prior to and independently of its interaction with other selves. Its self-sufficiency encourages us to think that the Cartesian self comes *ready-made* to think. The capacity to think is, for the Cartesian, something which a being either has or lacks; it is not a capacity a being may develop.

We are now in a position to see how the Cartesian's extremely individualistic picture reduces theses (A)–(C) to banalities. First, the self-containment of the Cartesian self grants the concept of material activity no place in the explanation of the nature and origin of consciousness. The Cartesian self inhabits a world in which material activity is impossible, for thought is construed as a relation between the self and mental entities, ideas, which are not possible objects of material activity. The Cartesian self is a contemplating rather than an acting being. And in so far as it does act, it acts mentally, for material activity is confined to a space beyond the frontiers of the mind. Second, the combined properties of self-containment and self-sufficiency accord no role to other people, or to the social world in general, in the explanation of either the capacity to think or the constitution of our thoughts. On the Cartesian picture, there can be no substantive sense in which our minds are located in a public space, or in which our mental functions are derived from interaction with others. And third, if we must think of the self as an entity ready-made to think, then internalisation cannot be the process of the *genesis* of consciousness, as the coming-into-being of the mind. The Cartesian conception thus rules out the possibility of strong readings of the claims of Soviet communitarianism. By so doing, the Cartesian relegates material activity and social interaction to the status of mere "external conditions" of consciousness, and, as such, they play a role of little interest to the philosopher. Of course, the Cartesian will say, human beings do, as a matter of fact, acquire mental states in activity and social relations, but this is a fact about the historical antecedents of our thoughts, rather than about the nature of the thoughts themselves.

Thus, the Cartesian picture strongly reinforces the objection we've been considering. If it's correct, there will indeed be no way of understanding theses (A)–(C) which renders them both true and philosophically interesting. Cartesianism, then, is the enemy.

We now know that to give a philosophically substantial interpretation of Soviet communitarianism we must jettison the Cartesian conception of the self. On the basis of my sketch of Cartesianism you might feel that to reject it would be not difficult. This is not so. When I said earlier that Cartesianism dominates Anglo–American philosophy, I did not mean simply that the majority of analytic philosophers are Cartesians. Rather, Cartesianism dominates our philosophical culture in that it dictates the very terms of philosophical discourse. The Cartesian framework determines the questions philosophers ask, the methods with which they address them, and (to a large degree) the answers they give.

To substantiate this bold claim would require a lot of argument. Here however, is an illustration germane to the present discussion. It would seem at first sight that the obvious alternative to Cartesianism is a form of psychological reductionism. Simplifying, we can say that reductionist theories come in two varieties. First, those which attempt to analyse mental states in terms of brain states, arguing that the mind is just the working brain. Call this strategy "physicalism." Second, those which analyse mental states in terms of the overt behaviour of the subject. Call this strategy "behaviourism." Are either of these approaches attractive to the Soviet communitarian? The short answer is "No." Soviet communitarians notoriously dismiss both forms of reductionism as a failure. But what is especially interesting about Ilyenkov, Mikhailov and Vygotsky is that they argue that reductionism fails even to be an alternative to Cartesianism! They maintain that though physicalism and behaviourism reject the Cartesian's "substantialism" (that is, the idea of the mind as a special non-material substance), both endorse other malignant aspects of the Cartesian framework. They argue that physicalism, on the one hand, continues to endorse the Cartesian conception of the self: it accepts the idea of the self as a self-contained, self-sufficient and ready-made thinker of thoughts and tries to interpret these properties of that self as properties of a physical system. Behaviourism, on the other hand, accepts the Cartesian's mechanical conception of nature, i.e., of the other half of the Cartesian's dualism, and tries to explain mental processes by principles analogous to those which govern the physical interaction of material objects. What is interesting here is not so much the claim that reductionist strategies won't work, but the idea that reductionism is in fact defined by the position to which it is supposed to be an alternative. Reductionism, as Ilyenkov might have said, is dictated by the "logic" of Cartesianism.

So, where are we? First, we know we're looking for an alternative to the Cartesian conception of the self, and that the standard reductionist alternatives won't do. Second, we know that the rejection of Cartesianism is a very radical project. If Cartesianism does fix the terms of discourse in our philosophical tradition, then its rejection may require us to redefine philosophy as a discipline. Furthermore, the consequences of its rejection may not be confined to philosophy alone. For example, it might be argued that the Cartesian conception of the self exerts a powerful influence on Western political and moral thought, that the self-constituting, "atomistic" individual of Western liberalism is just the Cartesian self under another guise. So dismantling Cartesianism may demand that we rethink the nature of moral and political agency.

So, with a due sense of the magnitude of our task, let's turn to the Ilyenkovian alternative to Descartes.

Ilyenkov, the "ideal," and the socially constituted subject

While the Soviet communitarians often voice hostility to Cartesianism, it is rare to find in their writings a fully fledged *argument* against it. Such an argument can, however, be extracted from Ilyenkov's works. For Ilyenkov, the Achilles heel of Cartesianism is its account of how it is possible for the world to be an object of thought. This is a very esoteric question. To put it another way: How is it possible for us to experience and to think about a world which exists independently of our thought and experience? The Cartesian's answer, as we have seen, is that the objects of the "external" world are given to the mind only via mental entities, ideas, which represent them to the mind. The reason is that minds can only deal directly with objects which are intrinsically meaningful and, for the Cartesian, material objects are devoid of meaning. Thus, the world may be only a possible object of thought if it is translated into a representational mental medium, ideas.

Ilyenkov would argue that this Cartesian theory of how the world gets to be an object of thought is a disaster. For as soon as one argues that the mind is only indirectly aware of external objects in virtue of its direct awareness of internal objects (ideas), one cannot avoid a catastrophic form of scepticism. This scepticism is *not* the traditional form of scepticism about the external world, i.e., "If we are only acquainted with the external world via ideas, then we can never know whether the world is really the way our ideas present it as being." It is an altogether more venomous form of scepticism. The Cartesian picture leaves us unable even to form a conception of what a mind-independent object might be like. Consequently, we can't even ask the traditional sceptical question of whether we can know that our ideas represent the world correctly, because we cannot even know what it would be for there to exist a mind-independent world for our ideas to represent. I shall not pursue the details of this argument; the crucial point is that what's wrong with Cartesianism is its theory of how it is possible for the world to be present to the mind.

Thus, the onus is on Ilyenkov to provide an alternative account of how the world becomes a possible object of thought. And it is in developing this account in his "theory of the ideal" that Ilyenkov's distinctive contribution to Soviet philosophy consists. What, then, for Ilyenkov, makes the world a possible object of thought? Interestingly, Ilyenkov agrees with his Cartesian opponent that there is a problem about how an object with only physical properties can be the kind of thing which interacts with a mind. And he also agrees that this problem derives from the fact that for a mind to experience, or think about, an object, that object must have a certain meaning, or representational significance, i.e., it must be, as it were, present itself to the subject *as* an object of a certain kind. However, unlike the Cartesians, Ilyenkov denies that the only objects that can have representational properties are mental objects, or ideas. He believes that material objects themselves can objectively possess the properties necessary to make them directly accessible to minds. These properties are themselves not material in nature. Ilyenkov calls nonmaterial properties "ideal" properties (ideal properties include, for example, as well as meaning, the various species of value). Ilyenkov's idea is that if material objects objectively possess, as well as their natural (physical) properties, *ideal* properties too, then they *would* be the kinds of things which would be directly present to the mind.

How do material objects acquire the ideal properties which make them suitable objects of thought and experience? For Ilyenkov, it is this question to which activity is the answer:

It is precisely production (in the broadest sense of the term) which transforms the object of nature into an object of contemplation and thought. (Ilyenkov, 1974, p. 187)

Thus, on Ilyenkov's picture, objects acquire ideal properties in virtue of human activity, through their incorporation into social practices. He writes:

"Ideality" is rather like a stamp impressed on the substance of nature by social human life activity; it is the form of the functioning of a physical thing in the process of social human life activity. Therefore, all things which are included in the social process acquire a new "form of existence" which is in no way part of their physical nature (from which it differs completely); an ideal form. (Ilyenkov, 1977, p. 86)

And it is to this "ideal form," impressed upon nature by human activity, to which the objects of the natural world owe their status as possible objects of thought.

How can we begin to make sense of this? Well, Ilyenkov invites us to consider the nature of an artifact or created object, say, a pen. The pen is certainly a material thing. But how do we distinguish this thing's being a *pen* from its being a lump of material stuff? To put the question another way: What would an account of this object in purely physical terms fail to capture? Ilyenkov would say that the object exists as an artifact in virtue of a certain social significance or meaning with which its physical form has been endowed, and it is this fact which would be lost in any purely physical description. It is this significance which constitutes the object's "ideal form." Where does it get this significance? In the case of a pen the answer seems clear: the fact that it has been created for specific purposes and ends and that, having been so created, it is put to a certain use, or, more generally, that it figures in human life-activity in a certain way. One might say, with Ilyenkov, that social forms of activity have become objectified in the form of a thing and have thus elevated a lump of brute nature into an object with a special sort of meaning.

Having grasped Ilyenkov's basic idea in the case of artifacts, the next step is to generalise his insight. Ilyenkov, like many Marxists, stresses that man transforms nature in activity. But, for him, this transformation must be seen, not just as an alteration in the physical form of the natural world, but as the wholesale *idealisation* of it: man transforms nature into a qualitatively different kind of environment. Through social forms of human activity man endows his natural environment with an enduring significance and value, thus creating a realm of ideal properties and relations. Ilyenkov presents this realm as the entire edifice of the institutions of social life, created and sustained by the activities of the communities whose lives those institutions direct. Ilyenkov calls this edifice "man's spiritual culture," and he means it to include the total structure of normative demands on activity which objectively confront each individual in the community defined by these institutions (including the demands of logic, language and morality). It is only against the backdrop of such a structurally organised realm of ideal relations that particular objects – any objects, and not just the ones we create – become endowed with the significance which is their ideal form.

So, for Ilyenkov, man transforms his natural habitat into one replete with social meanings: man creates an idealised environment. And it is in this process of idealisation that the material world becomes a possible object of thought and experience.

Ilyenkov's account of what the world must be like to be a possible object of thought becomes less obscure when it is complemented by his corresponding conception of what it is to be a thinking thing. To be a creature capable of thought is to be able to relate to the world *as* to an object of thought. Thus, for Ilyenkov, to be a thinking thing is just to be able to inhabit an idealised environment, to be able to orientate oneself in a habitat which contains, not just physical pushes and pulls, but meanings, values, reasons. And to have this capacity is, in turn, to be able to reproduce the forms of activity which endow the world with ideality, to mold one's movements to the dictates of the norms which constitute man's spiritual culture.

The picture then is this. The idealisation of nature by human practice transforms the natural world into an object of thought, and by participating in those practices, the human individual is brought into contact with reality as an object of thought. Each child enters the world with the forms of movement constitutive of thought embodied in the environment surrounding him or her, and as he or she is led to reproduce those practices so he or she becomes a thinking being, a person.

If Ilyenkov's theory of the ideal is sound, it immediately justifies a strong interpretation of theses (A)–(C). Take (A). On Ilyenkov's account, activity – the material transformation of nature by man – is not a mere empirical precondition of consciousness, but a necessary condition for its very possibility. For activity explains both how the world can be a possible object of thought, and how there can be a creature capable of thinking about it. And further, on Ilyenkov's position, activity becomes literally constitutive of thought, for (1) he construes the capacity to think as the capacity to act in accordance with the dictates of an enculturised environment, and (2) he identifies thinking itself (in its primary sense) as a species of activity. "Thinking," he writes in *Dialectical Logic*, "is not the product of an action but the action itself" (Ilyenkov, 1974, p. 25). Thus the concept of activity becomes, for Ilyenkov, the basic "unit" of analysis of consciousness – the key concept in the explanation of its nature and possibility.

Once we conceive of thought, as Ilyenkov suggests, as "a mode of action of the thinking body." then it becomes possible to see thought, not as an event in a private, inner world of consciousness, but as something essentially "on the surface," as something located, as Volosinov (1973, p. 26) says, "on the borderline between the organism and the outside world." For thought, on Ilyenkov's picture, has a life only in an environment of socially constituted meanings and its content is determined by its place within them. Thus Ilyenkov leads us to a strong reading of thesis (B): the higher mental functions are constituted in social space. Thought literally is "not in the head."

Further, Ilyenkov's position accords the idea of internalisation a very strong role. For Ilyenkov, the capacity to inhabit an idealised environment is not something the human individual possesses "by nature." We enter the world incapable of the activities which constitute thought, and learn to reproduce those activities only in so far as we are socialised into the practices of the community. As we appropriate, or "internalise," those practices so we are transformed from an epistemically blind mass of brute matter into a thinking being. Thus, on Ilyenkov's picture, inauguration into the community's mode of life must indeed be seen as the process in which the individual mind is *created*.

Ilyenkov offers us a way to resolve the supposed ambiguity of claims (A), (B) and (C) in favour of the stronger interpretation of all three. And this he achieves by ousting the Cartesian's individualistic picture of the self for a theory which represents the individual as socially constituted in a very strong sense. For this is an individual who acquires the very capacity to think only through inauguration by a community into the social practices which constitute "man's spiritual culture," the setting which represents the sole environment in which a being can express itself in thought. On Ilyenkov's theory, the human essence indeed becomes the "ensemble of social relations." We have arrived, then, at the Soviet communitarians' picture of the socially constituted individual.

Conclusion

What are the consequences of taking Ilyenkov seriously? First, the consequences for *philosophy*. If it is correct that the organising principle of our philosophical culture is a conception of the self which is fatally flawed, then philosophy faces the awesome task of completely rethinking its purposes and methods, the questions it asks and the answers it gives. Whether or not one is attracted to the Ilyenkovian alternative to Cartesianism, he, and the other Soviet communitarians, do at least give us an idea of what a non-Cartesian theory of the mind might be like. The communitarians' suggestions for such a theory must be seen not as a definitive account of consciousness, but as the opening move in a debate. And this debate will proceed, I hope, not just within and between Soviet traditions of thought, but between Soviet communitarians and those elements within our philosophical culture which, largely under the influence of Hegel and Wittgenstein, have recently begun to articulate deep dissatisfaction with the prevailing Cartesian orthodoxy. The time is ripe for new and productive dialogue between Soviet and Western philosophers, so long estranged from one another, but now intriguingly sharing a community of concerns.

Second, Ilyenkov's work has important consequences for the tradition of *Soviet communitarianism* itself. It sets an agenda for future theoretical research. For example, if Ilyenkov is right that the communitarian conceptual framework demands that we conceive of thought primarily as a species of activity, then phenomena the Cartesian finds easy to explain suddenly become problematic. For instance, the Cartesian can make excellent sense of the phenomenology of consciousness, and of the privileged access we each have to our own mental states. How can Ilyenkov, with his insistence on the "externality" of thought, account for such "subjective" phenomena? Ilyenkov's work itself, I think, offers no direct answer. However, the communitarian tradition clearly possesses the resources to address this question. It will be the Vygotskian idea of internalisation which will bear the explanatory burden in any communitarian account of the inner dimension of our mental lives. So, Ilyenkov's work puts the development of a thoroughly non-Cartesian conception of internalisation at the top of the theoretical agenda.

Finally, we come to the consequences of all this for the study of *communication*. Clearly, Ilyenkov's work deals with some of the central concepts of communication theory. His account of the ideal is really a theory of the origin of *meaning*, and of how our mental lives are *mediated* by the presence in the world of socially significant ideal properties. Further, his notion of an "idealised environment" may cast light on the idea of a *culture*. So Ilyenkov's work provides a framework in which to reexamine the concepts of meaning, mediation and culture. But much more dramatically, if what Ilyenkov tries to do with these concepts succeeds, then his work establishes that the conceptual framework of Soviet communitarianism is indeed available as an "innovative and distinctive model" for the study of communication. Significantly, this framework does not just make the development of a new interdiscipline attractive, it makes it unavoidable. I've spelled out how Ilyenkov's position justifies a strong interpretation of theses (A)–(C). It should be obvious, however, that it does the same for the theoretical insights (1)–(4) with which I introduced Soviet communitarianism. For Ilyenkov, thought *necessarily* exists in the form of its expression, that expression *necessarily* presupposes a socially constructed culture (i.e., an idealised environment), and entrance into the culture is a *necessary* condition of consciousness. And it follows from this that the study of mind, of culture, and of language (in all its diversity) are internally related: that is, it will be *impossible* to render any one of these domains intelligible without essential reference to the others. But if this is so, then it won't just be a good idea to combine the study of psychology, sociology and language, it will be absolutely imperative to do so. The development of an interdiscipline which seeks to grasp mind, culture and language in their internal relations will be essential if we are to understand the human condition.

References

Ilyenkov, E. V. (1974). *Dialekticheskaya Logika*. Moscow: Politizdat.
Ilyenkov, E. V. (1977). The concept of the ideal. In *Philosophy in the USSR: Problems of dialectical materialism*. Moscow: Progress.
Leont'ev, A. N. (1978). *Activity, consciousness, and personality*. Englewood, NJ: Prentice-Hall.
Volosinov, V. N. (1973). *Marxism and the philosophy of language*. New York: Seminar Press.

13   The sound of the violin

Ernest E. Boesch

Let me start with the obvious: the sound of the violin is the result of an *action*. Thus, producing the sound must be somebody's *goal*. Yet, the musical sound is indeed an ephemeral, intangible goal of no practical use, and we would therefore have to face the problem of apparently gratuitous actions. Indeed, what kind of an action is "contemplating a flower" or "admiring a landscape"? What is the function of actions like skiing, reading a poem, collecting stamps or paintings – or of playing music? Such useless actions may confront us with the very general reasons for which we act.

I propose to start by considering the violin's evolution as a "species," or what I would choose to call here its "phylogenesis." I shall then look at its "ontogenesis," that is, how, from being a mere object, it becomes, for an individual, an instrument to be played. Third, I propose to focus for some time on the strange goal of producing the *beautiful sound*, and, by extension, the beautiful melody. These considerations will, I hope, make this particular object an example of man's relationship with the objects surrounding him and, thus, with the culture in which he lives.

The "phylogenesis" of the violin

According to historians, the first instruments with strings were plucked, like the zither or primitive harps. The bow would have been a later addition. The actual origins of these instruments remain unknown, but they certainly required complex inventions. A primitive hunter

164

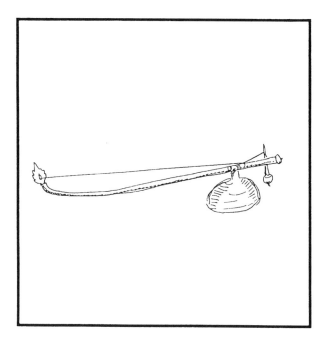

Figure 13.1.

might easily have noticed the peculiar sound of the bow string upon
shooting, but it probably needed a moment of relaxed playing with the
bow to make him discover the *aesthetic* quality of the plucked string. To
observe the different pitches, strings of different length and tension were
needed next, but it was only after discovering, finally, that sounds could
be amplified by connecting the strings with a hollow object, that the
plucking string instrument would have been invented. Such simple
instruments still can be found: The Thai *phin* basically consists of a bow
with a single string to which half a bottle gourd is attached as a sound
chamber (Figure 13.1). Inventing the violin, however, needed an additional, and crucial, step: somebody had to notice that by rubbing the
string with a lengthy object it became possible to prolong the sound considerably. The creation of the violin, thus, required three discoveries:
the sound differences of varying string tensions and lengths, the effect
of a resonance body, and the stroking bow. As with every invention, these
discoveries required a reorientation of attention and perception, a

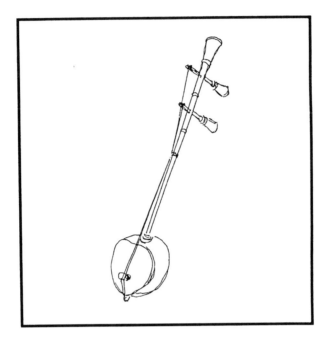

Figure 13.2.

restructuring of actions, and thereby opened to man a new dimension
of action, the *aesthetic* one.

The first violins were crude instruments, but their like are still played
in many parts of Asia. Thus, the Siamese *soo uu* (Figure 13.2), similar
to some Chinese instruments, consists only of half a coconut shell
covered by a piece of skin to which a simple stick of hardwood with two
strings is attached. Interestingly, in these instruments all the essential
elements of our violins are already present: the strings are supported by
a *bridge*, tightened by *tuning pegs*, the *sound box* (coconut shell) is pierced
by *holes*, the function of which is said to be similar to our f-holes (which,
though erroneously, are often believed to "free" the sound). Such
similarities, certainly not copied from Western models, indicate that
producing and controlling the sound led to analogous technical
solutions.

Historians say that the two types of bow-string instruments known in
early Europe were imported from the Near East in the 11th century or

before; the first was Arab, called *Rabab*, which engendered the European *Rebec*. It consisted of an elongated piece of wood, the larger end of which was hollowed out and covered with parchment for forming a sound box, while the narrower end constituted the neck. It was fitted with one or two strings played with a short bow. The second instrument is said to have been a *fiddle* from Turkistan, consisting of a spade-shaped sound box with added neck, fitted with two to three strings and played with a longer bow. The Far Eastern "violins" already referred to have similarities with both the rebec and the fiddle, but while those have been abandoned in Europe, the Chinese and Thai *soo* are still in use.

From these two initial forms derived a range of instruments bewildering in their variety. For our purpose let us simply keep in mind that the original crude instruments led to a search for improvements, lasting over several centuries, experimenting with changes of the sound box, the shaft or neck including the kind and number of strings and their tuning, and the bow, these three elements becoming variously combined "across species."

In this progressive transformation of the instrument, of course, much *bricolage* took place, empirical testing of different woods and shapes; of size, place and form of the sound-holes; of kind and location of the inner stabilizers (bass bar and sound post); of glues and lacquers; of the strings and the bow; similarly, various positions for playing the instrument were tried out. By the 17/18th century this experimentation had apparently about exhausted the available options and became limited to variations in details; from now on the typical violin as we know it, with four strings tuned in fifths (g-d-a-e) remained constant, while the competing forms, mainly the fiddle and the gamba, were abandoned. Of course, this *bricolage* often led to individual solutions – the formulas for glues or lacquers for instance – which the violin-builder tried to keep secret.

The progressive construction of the violin, of course, was guided by the available materials, but no less by the human possibilities of handling. Both, however, were not *a priori* determining; a modern violin is certainly more difficult to play than an ancient viola held on the thigh and fitted with frets, and the typical shape of violins is due to beauty as much as to functionality of handling. Somehow it appears that the old violin-builders felt quality of sound and beauty of shape to be closely related – only a beautiful instrument can sound beautifully.

This is, in short outline, the genesis of a truly cultural object, invented and led to perfection by man. What were the reasons for this development? Indeed, we may understand easily the continuous improvement of a loom from its primitive forms in an African village to a mechanized contraption: it serves ease of handling and, thereby, higher output. What output, however, would the development of violins have served? *Sound*, or to be more specific: *more beautiful sound* – unsubstantial, not measurable like lengths of cloth, and even undefinable. That such an elusive goal should have determined such a prolonged and complex development of an object is indeed a vexing problem.

Let me add another consideration. The pursued sound was, of course, *unknown*. A violin-maker might have changed some aspect of the instrument, but on trying it out, the player could remark: "It sounds better, *but that's not yet it*." What would have been this "it"? An intuition, an intangible anticipation, and although such an image became transformed over and again during the centuries long processes of improvement, it would have remained a *should-value* both inducing change and also controlling it.

This "sound-goal image" not only varied over historical periods, but differs also between cultures. Thus the Siamese *soo* and the Chinese *hu* also underwent modifications, but they were beautifications with only little impact on the sound. Similar beautifications by material or inlay, with mere decorative purpose, were also applied to European instruments, but those, again, differed fundamentally from other transformations. Look at one among many examples, the *bridge*, an inconspicuous element: it underwent multiple variations in form, size and position whose effect on the quality of sound – quite substantial – was tried out over centuries. However, to understand our long-lasting search for a more beautiful sound, somehow contrasting with other cultures, we have to look not at the instrument alone but also at its player.

The "ontogenesis" of the violin

"Ontogenesis," of course, is not used here as in developmental psychology, meaning the unfolding of a being from its conception to maturity; I would rather understand it in its original sense, "the coming into being." Indeed, a violin becomes really a violin only on being played.

Mastering the violin is a long and frustrating endeavor. The optimum age for starting to learn is likely to vary between 5 and 7 years, when the most gross difficulties of sensorimotor coordination have been overcome. The child will of course first be given a small violin, and will probably be eager to start learning. He or she may see mother or father playing and, as all children do, longs to imitate them. Such initial enthusiasm, however, would soon be supplanted by a rather ambivalent attitude, and in most cases it requires much parental coaxing and dragging in order to keep the child from abandoning the instrument. Indeed, practicing the violin provides at first only little intrinsic reward. It is probably fortunate that the ear of the young child lacks fineness of discrimination and that, while it acquires it, the skill of playing improves, too.

To start learning early is, of course, required in order to shape the child's motor skills and perception during the forming years. This is precisely of interest to the developmental cultural psychologist: that *learning to master an object implies shaping the development of the individual;* while, as we saw, the object was formed "phylogenetically," the individual is led to "fit" the object in its ontogenesis. This, of course, implies motor and sensorial adaptations – even transformations – of the learner. Let us consider them more closely.

Since about the end of the 18th century the violin is held between chin and collar bone. This position, more difficult but also more proficient than earlier ones, demands not only strengthening of the neck muscles, but also precise coordination of their innervations with movements of the left arm for position shifts – requiring an optimal balance between muscular tension and relaxation, between flexibility and precision of movements taking years to learn.

A second difficulty the learner has to master is the technique of the left hand. The child's fingers, particularly at an early age, need to gain strength and independence of movement, a precise "feel" for distances and pitches i.e., sensorial discrimination – particularly difficult since the space separating tone intervals diminishes the more the hand moves upwards. Finally, the left hand has to master the vibrato, important for giving volume and warmth to the sound.

All this will be compounded by the even more exacting bow work. The player holds the bow at one end, the "nut," and glides it in an apparently easy movement over the strings. Yet, how this is done will principally determine the quality of sound, and is therefore of major importance. The bow touches the strings in the space between the bridge and the fingerboard. To produce an even sound, the bow should move in a steady straight line – less easy than one might believe, because the "natural" horizontal movement of the hand traces an arc. Particularly important for the quality of sound are the speed of the bow movement on the one hand, the pressure of the bow on the other. For an even sound, both speed and pressure need to remain constant. Since the weight with which the bow rests on the string varies along its length, keeping pressure constant requires compensatory regulations by the bow holding hand, and this, of course, at all speeds. Further, the sound quality is influenced by the number of hairs which stroke the strings. For this reason the player will hold the bow at a sideward inclination, which, thus, must be kept constant or varied according to the sound desired. Of course, the bow movements must be coordinated precisely with the fingerwork of the left hand. Add that straining the muscles of neck, shoulders and arms will be an impediment; accordingly, a delicate balance between relaxation and activation will have to be achieved. Any psychologist who has ever tested motor coordination of children will agree that such a complex interplay of movements is very difficult to learn; even advanced students will often have to concentrate on their bow much more than on the left hand.

The sensory and motor learning required, the development of discrimination, rhythm, muscular strength and coordination, is a process which takes years, with daily training hours definitely longer than many a psychology student is willing to spend on his books or experiments. Becoming a violinist allows no short-cuts, no jumping of chapters one doesn't like, no skipping of arguments one does not understand; ignorance cannot be glossed over by empty works. In music every negligence becomes cruelly manifest in the performance, and therefore the learner is bound by an unrelenting discipline – which inevitably will transform his person.

The initial results of learning, thus, would not be very rewarding. The sound remains crude, harsh, often disagreeable, the strings bite the fingertips, the skin of the chin gets irritated, and even social reinforcements, after a while, may become rare – the admonition to "close the door of your room when you practice" is not particularly encouraging. In spite of that, the child will have to practice daily, often at hours when other children play together. We can thus easily understand that the violin will become an ambivalent object, and that many young learners abandon after a while. The discomfort and constraints they experience become reminders of a limited action potential, of object-derived barriers and social constraints, and such an antagonistic object may even represent the «non-I» in general, the external world basically opposed to the «I» [as to this «I»-«non-I»-antagonism, see Boesch, 1983 and 1991].

Yet, some children "catch on." They accept the frustrations of learning because of the positive valence of some future goal. This future goal may be to conquer an adversity, to extend and confirm the individual action potential; it may also be social – to become a famous violinist, or at least to be able to play quartets like father. However, such explanations do not suffice to understand the child's motivation; they only displace the problem. Indeed, the reinforcement of an action potential would still have to explain why the child strives to achieve this *particular* mastery, and the explanation by social models would have to understand both the valence of the model for the child, and the motivation of the violinist he or she wants to emulate. And if playing the violin would earn social rewards, what then would make the public appreciate music? Explanations by social modeling or some unspecified mastery seem indeed inadequate for explaining the frustration tolerance and the perseverance of a learner.

In the terms I use, learning to play the violin is a *dominant* or *superordinate* goal. Superordinate goals are distant in time but command actions in the present, which – as with violin exercises – may not be pleasant in themselves. It is true that distant goals will usually be reached in steps, so that intermediate rewards may strengthen the motivation. Yet, the applause experienced on the way may provide encouragements to go on playing, but they will not suffice. The more the player advances, the more an additional audience will have to be satisfied: *he himself.* He will be critical of finger accuracy and speed, but as critically – if not more – he will watch and evaluate *his sound.* "*His*," it is here, and not the violin's. In fact, he may be hurt when a listener tells him "You must have an excellent violin, it sounds marvelous!" He wants to feel that it is *his* mastery which forces the violin to sound well. However if, his level of expectation rising, he feels disappointed with the sound, he may start haunting the violin-shops to have his instrument controlled, improved, or changed for a "better" one, and on doing so he will compare the "sound *of violins.*" But then he will again spend hours a day only to improve *his* sound with the new instrument to reach that elusive quality of tone which he feels to be moving, "going to the heart," undefinable and yet inducing a reaction of content and fulfillment in the happy moments where he feels to have reached it.

Sound and noise

What then is it which makes beautiful sound become such a dominating goal? In fact, sound is a very important quality of our perception. Sound says what words don't say. Words remain restricted to consensual taxonomies and are largely unable to express subjective states. Saying that I am angry does not necessarily mean that I *feel* angry – but the tone of my speech shows it. Tones betray our moods, convey love or anger, acceptance or rejection, joy or fear in a way which "grips" immediately – the tone of *our voice is the direct external trace of inner qualities.*

What, however, of the sound of the *violin?* Let us distinguish two aspects. The first is the action of *making objects produce sound,* the second is the *search for perfection of sound.* As a boy I used to tighten a blade of grass between my thumbs and, by blowing into the gap formed in this way, produced a sharp, oboe-like sound. In spring I cut fresh branches from hazel or ash trees and made them into recorder-type flutes. Each time, doing so, I transformed nature into "culture," shaping natural raw materials into forms apt at producing sounds which did not occur in "pure" nature. Yet, the pleasure was immense and can be understood only by the extension of my childish action potential; it made me a creator, albeit in a tiny area. Making objects sound, thus, is a bit like taming animals: *it transforms a resistant non-I into a compliant extension of the I.*

Such sounds, however, although exciting and pleasing, only rarely – and by accident – fulfill any standards of beauty. The *beautiful* sound is moving, it touches our feelings with a particular intensity. Myths and fairy tales illustrate the miraculous power of the beautiful sound: it tames wild animals and ghosts, heals the sick and appeals directly to the angels; Orpheus' voice even opened the doors to the underworld. Somehow we feel that producing a pure, immaculate sound provides the experience of an optimal action potential, able to realize perfection – although only for the fleeting moment of the sound's duration. The experience I mean is very pointedly expressed – although in the realm of color – by the British artist Ben Nicholson who writes on seeing a painting by Picasso:

And in the centre there was an absolutely miraculous *green* – very deep, very potent and absolutely real. In fact, none of the actual events in one's life have been more real than that, and it still remains a standard by which I judge any reality of my own work ... (Summerson, 1948, p. 7).

And Gauguin, to express the strangely real–unreal quality of such experience, wrote: "The sound of my wooden clogs on the cobblestones, deep, hollow and powerful, is the note I seek in my painting" (Hughes, 1988, p. 77). The statements are surprisingly similar – a certain tone of color or sound, experienced as *potent and powerful*, become standards, should-values, goals of aspiration.

We sometimes imagine a world entirely in harmony with our fantasms, entirely in tune with inner experience; we call it *utopia*, and reaching it is a topic of dreams and fairytales. Utopia, we might formulate, abolishes the «I»–«non-I» antagonism. The beautiful sound we aspire to would have to correspond to – or even to surpass – our ideal standards, conferring on them at the same time a reality external to us. Would it not then prove our potential to create utopia, even though in a very limited way? Being nothing but sound, a transient, vanishing trace of our skill, it still would symbolize the existence of perfection and our potential to attain it. This is, of course, not true for the beautiful sound alone, but for any creation of beauty; beauty bridges the chasm between I and non-I. Unlike other forms of art, however, the beautiful sound, by its very ephemeral nature, remains unreal and intangible and hence commands connotations and imaginations of a particular quality.

Beauty, however, is neither the same for everybody, nor in each culture or historical period. A Thai will appreciate other sounds than a European, and the sound of violins at the time of Bach differed from ours. Today we might say that a beautiful sound has, above all, to be *pure*, meaning, on the one hand, free of noise frequencies, on the other, accurately in tune. The first sounds a beginner tries to elicit from a violin will be noisy, scratchy, raw, and tend to be out of tune; in learning to play a main effort consists in eliminating these impurities. In addition, the sound must have *volume*, extended evenly over its duration. An uneven bow movement produces an unpleasingly vacillating tone, which, however, should not be confounded with the vibrato, an intended, rhythmic, although minimal variation not of volume, but of pitch. Sound, furthermore, should be *appropriate* both to the *"spirit"* of *the time and of the particular music* played. Thus, the tone of a jazz clarinet or of a Gypsy violin would not be appropriate to Mozart's concertos, but neither would a Mozart clarinet fit into a Swiss yodel band. Of course, beautiful sound will always be defined also according to *subjective standards* – whatever they be. The ideal a player pursues may veer towards more warmth, or towards more strength and clarity, the one will accentuate the vibrato more than the other – there will be subtle differences between players which sometimes only the initiate, or the player himself, will be aware of.

Purity of sound has obviously been of long lasting importance in European musical culture. Thus, the violin is tuned in quints which are the purest intervals, neither consonant nor dissonant. Until after the romantic period, European music favored consonant chords; dissonances, of course, occurred (as in Bach's polyphony), but were transitional, not "standing" chords, having to be resolved in harmony. It is only in the music of our century that dissonance has acquired an independent, more than transitional, value. In contrast, in Thai music consonant chords are of no importance; Thai music is linear, not harmonic, it coordinates melodies. Consequently perhaps, the purity of tuning appears to be of lesser importance; Morton speaks of a "'rough and ready' approach to precise tuning" (1976, p. 28). We might add another reason: It may be the *symbolism of* pure sound which is important – consider for instance that in Thailand, in contrast to Europe, religion played no significant role in the practice and development of music.

In *modern* Europe, however, we meet musical styles which not only do *not* aspire at a pure sound, but on purpose introduce *noise*. Louis Armstrong cultivated a hoarse voice in singing, and similarly the shrieking of saxophones and clarinets in modern pop music are intended by their players, and may even also require long training. They would not sound beautiful in every ear, but they are, in their own ways, congenially expressive.

Such examples might throw additional light on the meaning of sound. In modern rock concerts the hard jangling of metal guitars is combined with the hoarse shouting, screaming, screeching of singers – they seem to enjoy noise, and their public does so visibly and audibly. But also so-called "serious" modern music frequently makes use of various kinds of noise: purity of sound tends, in whole or in part, to be abandoned. Noise is "sound dirt," and it seems no coincidence that rock musicians have also tended to cultivate a dirty look: unkempt, unshaven, ragged – or at least to affect "out of place" clothing, from torn jeans to Madonna's bras and girdles (*"Dirt,"* says Mary Douglas, *"is matter out of place"* [1966, p. 35]). However, noise and dirt are normal occurrences of everyday life; to keep them away demands discipline, effort, and is related to much social constraint. Cleanliness is required in "good society," and purity, of body and mind, is needed in approaching sacred things and places – otherwise the approach might even be dangerous. Hence, dirt can become a threat, and so can noise – to oneself as well as to others.

In fact, the meaning of noise can differ widely. It accompanies bodily discharges and thus is directly related to dirt and disease; it marks catastrophes, accidents, disaster, war, aggression; it signals a threat from dangerous animals, and nowadays belongs as well to powerful engines roaring through our settlements. But noise can also herald happy events, the convivial feasting, the exuberant joy, the triumphant success, the exhibition of power – easily, however, degenerating into the noises of drunkenness. Noise (in the sense of not purified sound) can even possess aesthetic qualities: the rustling of leaves in a breeze, the murmur of water in a creek, the lapping of waves on the shore. [The German distinction between *Geräusch* and *Lärm* does not exist in English.] Altogether we might say that noise tends to belong to earthly, natural events, but also to out of ordinary occasions. Pure sound, on the contrary, rarely occurs in nature – with the exception of singing birds. The pursuit of beautiful sound, thus, is a truly cultural endeavor, and the long history of creating instruments able to produce pure sound, as much as the individual efforts at mastering them, prove the importance we attach to it. Pure sound is a *mytheme*, corresponding to a *myth of purity* which relates the individual to a social as well as spiritual order – and which, by the same token, opposes the anti-order symbolized by noise.

European music, often and for a long time, was a means for approaching God. *Soli Deo Gloria*, wrote Bach over his compositions, and even recently Sir George Solti, the famous conductor, confessed that Mozart had convinced him of the existence of God. Introducing noise in music, hence, implies rejecting the cultural mytheme representing purity, including both its social and its spiritual contents. In other words, it means shedding constraints and becomes the symbolic realization of unhampered freedom – somehow, it too represents utopia, but of a Dionysian kind (as opposed to the Apollinian – to borrow Nietzsche's dichotomy). The ecstasy such music can produce in many young and less young people relies on this symbolism which is reinforced by sensorial excitement. Sound ideals, thus, can cover a wide spectrum. Noise can be pursued as obsessionally as purity of sound, but they express different myths and fantasms.

Let us come back to the violin which, as we have seen, is the result of a culturally persistent quest for beautiful sound. It belongs to the ideational realm of purity. Hence, the young learner will from the very outset be caught between the cultural goal of purity and the natural propensity (not only of children) for noise and dirt. The violin, thus, may begin to symbolize not only the resistance of the object world, but also the conflict between natural penchants and cultural requirements.

It will then follow almost necessarily that becoming involved in learning the violin must have an impact on the definition of the learner's *self*. Somehow, to some extent, the child will have to side with purity, he or she will veer towards the Apollinian side of utopia. This, of course, implies renouncing those sides of the "natural self" which prefer noise, dirt, disorder, so that mastering the violin then may symbolize this fight against the "darker side" of one's self. However, the violin, representing the – perhaps only anticipated, perhaps already experienced – potential of producing beautiful sound, will also symbolize the "aspired self." Thus, over and beyond simple mastery of a recalcitrant object, learning the violin would mean both overcoming the rejected sides of one's self and approaching one's self-ideal.

All this would also influence the learner's *view of his world*. He would tend to see it divided into a "we-world" and a "they-world." The "we-world" includes all those who embrace the same values, the same quest for the pure sound. They are the ones who support the individual's views and actions, and among whom he would choose the "alters" relevant for his self definition. The "they-world," of course, would be the others who either do not care for, or might even loathe the pure sound and what it represents. In this more or less dichotomized world the violin becomes instrumental – not only in the sense of producing sound, but somehow also for propagating its message.

Sound, indeed, is a signal: it carries a *message*, but it also *is* the message. In this sense, using Raymond Firth's taxonomy (going back to Peirce), the pure sound is more than a signal, it is an *icon*, i.e., "a sign that represents its object by resembling it" (1973, p. 61). The musician, thus, both is a messenger and represents the message. If I remember correctly, both Henryk Szeryng and Yehudi Menuhin carried diplomatic passports, and were considered "ambassadors" spreading a cultural message. Of course, such an ambassadorial role cannot simply consist in playing the violin, however fine that might be; it is perceived more or less consciously as "spreading the gospel of purity" – whatever values the individual may relate to it. Somehow this "messenger" quality is ritually enacted in every concert: The musicians, in an elevated position, dispensing their message to the public, whose reactions are carefully ritualized. In church concerts, by the way, even applause is forbidden: noise definitely does not belong to sacred places. But even in the concert hall, the applause is distinctly different from the one in rock concerts where noisy music and noisy manifestations of the public somehow create a bond of similarity between the two sides. The message differs, and so then do the rituals.

Sound is more than a message: it may also *carry power*. In *"L'histoire du soldat"* by Stravinsky and Ramuz the violin not only symbolizes the antipode of material wealth and might, but it conveys to the player the power of a different kind: To heal, to exorcise, to protect from evil forces. This belief in power related to the realm of purity and order is widespread. A magician has to beware of defilements in order to conserve his powers, and the ubiquitous fear of impurity – although differently defined according to culture (see Mary Douglas' analysis of pollution [1966]) – is a telling expression of this belief. The power of the sound derives, of course, from its spiritual symbolism, but it too requires purity of the player: Stravinsky's soldier had to renounce his worldly wealth and subdue the devil before being able to use the power of his violin. Purity of sound, purity of heart, purity of body, thus, all belong to the same myth – although with different connotations.

In this vein, the beautiful sound *is* pure, yet never as pure as the idea it expresses. Hence, the pursuit of the beautiful sound aims at a goal which will always remain "a step ahead": not the beautiful sound experienced, but the *more* beautiful sound is the real goal. It is a sound model, a should-value, never present and yet intuited. Nicholson, of course, did not intend to reproduce Picasso's green: his experience of it implied the intuition of a transcending perfection, yet pursued without knowing it. Such quest for the "still more perfect," the "still more satisfying" object or action corresponds to a widely shared myth; it expresses an intuitive anticipation of "realities beyond" the present, but also the anxiety of missing fulfillment, of losing power.

The sound of the violin, thus, is deeply embedded in cultural myths, and the individual becoming a violinist will, intuitively rather than consciously, be drawn into the orbit of these myths; but she or he will construct their personal meanings by merging them with subjective experiences and aspirations. Every musician will relate the "mytheme of the pure sound" to different kinds of purity and order, and the pursuit of the beautiful sound will for each carry his own private, and often unconscious, connotations. In this way myths, constituting cultural cadres of orientation, will be given personal relevance by the individual's fantasmic aspirations.

We can now understand the person-violin dyad as a kind of focus within an individual's total «I»–«non-I» relationship, polyvalent and interrelated with various areas of meaning. One aspect, however, appears to me to be of basic importance in the player's pursuit of beautiful sound: to be able, *by himself, to overcome the antagonism of objects.* The violin, we have seen, is a recalcitrant object, and to master it requires profound transformations of the individual. Yet, this accommodation of the player for assimilating the object promises, in the long run, particularly rewarding returns. Indeed, the sound felt to be perfect can be produced only by a perfect fit between instrument and player. Assimilation and accommodation cannot be separated anymore: artist and violin form a symbiotic whole, the I, so to say, blending into the object, and the object melting into the I. As long as it remains imperfect, the sound is experienced as antagonism, but when perfect it becomes the symbolic proof of unity, of a cleavage overcome – or in the words I already used, it symbolically confirms our very personal potential to reach utopia.

The sound trace

All these considerations, somehow, leave a feeling of incompleteness. *Beautiful* sound is certainly more than *pure* sound. But what is it that makes it beautiful? Let me recall here a paradigm I resorted to in several earlier publications: the one of the *trace*. Traces are, in the sense used here, the material imprints of our actions in the external world. We leave, of course, thousands of traces, but some of them possess particular qualities: they faithfully mirror the movement which produced them. I liked to use the example of a skier's track on a slope of fresh snow. We know that every change of movement in our legs, hips, shoulders or even arms would change the nature of the trace. Similarly, the violinist feels that the inclination of his wrists, the weight of his hand, the contraction of his shoulders would express themselves in the quality of the sound: the sonority of his violin mirrors faithfully, sometimes cruelly, the perfection, or even grace, of the movements – and thereby the person – of the musician. In the same way as our voice, manner of walking, or even the look of our face, the sound is indeed felt to be symptomatic of "our self."

Such symptoms, however, may express various aspects of our self, excitement or calm, anger or tenderness, serenity or worry, which, although being momentary affects, often signify permanent qualities as well. Thus, the musician might tend to substitute the word *expressiveness* for "beauty" of sound, thereby allowing himself to vary his sound from soft to harsh, from cool to warm; in a moment of wrath he may even abandon the ideal of purity and violently scratch his strings instead of stroking or caressing them. Aiming at expressing himself, the musician's sound turns into an idiosyncratic trace.

The quality of the sound being a faithful trace of the individual's movements, and those being felt to express his or her person, there thus will start a subtle process of self-regulation which reaches far beyond the mere efforts at improving one's sound. The so-called "technique," the acquisition of the correct movements, will be complemented, even guided, by a search for inner qualities. In our high-school orchestra, having difficulties in creating a high pitch, all of the sudden the conductor advised: "You have to *think* the note before playing it!" – and, to my surprise, it worked. The *inner* performance had to guide the actual one. Motor skill is not sufficient, but requires support by a mental discipline. Mastery of the instrument, then, turns into mastery of oneself.

A single sound may resemble a straight line, but traces result from movements in progression. Sounds tend to follow a course – they cannot just rest on a single note; any note somehow "searches" its completion, it "pulls" the player ahead. Thus, beauty of sound becomes, necessarily, the beauty of a melody; it includes flow, transitions, relations – in short, it resides in the quality of the trace. The trace of the skilled skier becomes aesthetically pleasing by an effortless elegance of its curves, and similarly the beauty of sound consists in a smooth flowing through the meanders of the melody.

Thus, sound becomes truly beautiful only by being extended, sustained throughout a melody. A single sound may be touching, like a soft word, but a soft word is not yet soft speech – the word would hint at, but not yet demonstrate softness. Only when purity of sound spreads over musical phrases and ranges can it symbolize the permanence and pervasiveness of inner qualities. Real mastery proves itself in the form and quality of a trace, but hints at a perfection beyond music.

However, a violinist may master a beautiful sound over long sequences, and yet may not move the listener. Beauty also requires "style," interrelated qualities such as rhythm with its hesitations and accelerations, volume with its crescendos and diminuendos, variations between softness and vigor. Style, by its elasticity and versatility, expresses inner freedom – to play a melody beautifully demonstrates the potential to *create* beauty. By his "interpretation" the artist shows his ability to transform the dead matter of musical scores into a living, somehow "catching" experience – for himself no less than for a listener.

To do this, he needs the musical phrase which gives the sound its course and duration. But he also needs *contrast*. In fact, music *is* contrast – as we already found in comparing sound to noise. Imagine a Matakam youngster promenading in his village with the simple hand-harp shown in Figure 13.3; he nonchalantly strums the instrument while parading among the girls whom he knows are peeping out of their homesteads. The soft, almost timid sounds of the instrument strangely contrast with the laughter, shouting, or the loud discussion of arguing men. Similarly, the sound of a violin would contrast with the blaring of trumpets or the bangs of a gong. It is certainly no accident that drums, trumpets, and fifes were instruments for martial music, while harps, flutes, lutes, or violins became instruments of relaxation, meditation, poetic imagination or courtship. Contrasting with the noise and clamour of everyday life, the invention of string instruments was significant for the development of those sides of man and culture which relate to inwardness, contemplation and spirituality.

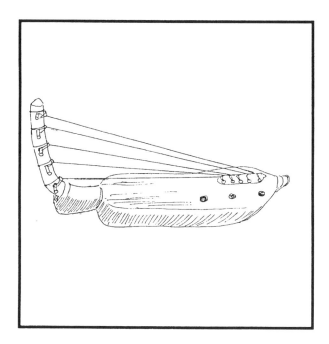

Figure 13.3.

Contrast, of course, also occurs within a melody: it belongs to the versatility required for expression. But contrast also occurs whenever a piece of music reaches its end. The trace not only evolves, but it strives toward what musicians call its *conclusion*. Musical phrases always come somewhere to rest: they necessarily end in silence.

In this, now, the melody differs from the ski-trace which, as an external reality, can last as long as no other skier obliterates it. The sound, however, although real, even measurable like an object, has no permanence. Menuhin lowers the violin, the conductor halts the orchestra – and the sudden silence throws the listener back into his ordinary existence. Applause may offer a means for softening the transition, but we all have experienced the strange, unnameable uneasiness after a church concert where, lacking the release of applause, one has to steer oneself back into "reality."

The silence in which music ends has profound importance. It emphasizes that musical sound results from an intimate symbiosis of man and object which never can be more than a renewed attempt at over-coming the chasm which separates I from non-I, a reaching for a perfection which cannot last. But in the silence will also emerge the wish not only for repeating the experience, but for surpassing it. The pursuit of the *more beautiful* sound is born from the experience of beauty *and* the anxiety of losing it. Music, thus, continuously needs to be *re-created*.

Conclusions

We have now gone a long way, from the mere construction of a material object through its various stages of development to cultural myths and, finally, to object–subject relationships. Thus, the violin *as an object* is first, in Lang's (1992) terms, an "external memory," reminding man of potential uses, their requirements and rewards. Yet, the same object, by the same token, symbolizes myths and the values of the cultural group they entail: learning to master it, therefore is an action of taking sides. But the apprenticeship also implies a *promise*, the anticipation of a not yet realized potential of action. In this sense, the actual object is just the momentary focus in a continuous process of «I»–«non-I» interaction, implying transformations of the object in the attempt at improving it, as well as transformations of the subject in acquiring mastery.

We have, in these pages, mainly concentrated on the isolated action of playing the violin; we neither looked at the more complex performances of music, nor did we consider the extended social fabric within which the pursuit of a beautiful sound takes place. Indeed, much more would have to be examined should we like to make an encompassing study of the actions of building, learning, and playing the violin.

Yet, "the sound of the violin" was a paradigm for more general problems; it exemplifies the cultural as well as individual construction of objects; it demonstrates the extent to which these processes do not simply produce some isolated mastery, but systems of meaning. Mastery is not independent of goals, and goals are polyvalent and anchored in networks of coordinated action, of thought, belief, rules and values. More than that, objects are in movement, they change with the flow of culture on the one hand, with the nature and progress of individual actions on the other.

Action and object, thus, concur to form combined structures; mastering the violin, we saw, will ultimately unite man and object in that
intimate symbiosis resulting in the beautiful sound, and we are likely to
find comparable interactions in man's use of other objects. Already the
invention of an object implies *objectivation*: the subject transforms an
idea into external reality. In mastering the object, the player will in turn
assimilate, and thereby *subjectivize* it, while he or she will simultaneously
be objectivized by accommodation. In addition, the creation of an object
implies its *socialization* – it will be integrated in common frameworks of
action and ideation, and hence the mastery of the object entails an *enculturation* of the user, but also, by the individual variations in style or ways
of handling the object, an *individualization* of culture. The interaction
circle <object–user–object> is at the same time an interaction circle
<culture–individual–culture> and implies progressive transformations
at all levels. Piaget's model of object construction turns out to be valid
not only for physical, but also for cultural objects; the construction
processes involved, however, will become more complex, both with
respect to subject–object extensions and to layers of meaning, and the
interaction subject–object will have to include both proactive (subject
→ object → culture) and retro-active (culture → object → subject)
influences.

All this, I believe, will lead to much more adequate models of reality
than traditional psychology could ever achieve. Cultural psychology, in
this vein (and following Jerome Bruner's claim), would necessarily have
to precede all other psychological investigations not because cultural
psychology would tend to claim more importance, but because any psychological research would have to be localized within the total networks
which action creates. We may, indeed, study the sound of the violin as
a limited phenomenon, yet, only by being able to make evident its multiple implications would such a study become meaningful. Paracelsus
coined the maxim "*nihil humanum mihi alienum esse potest*," and it could
fittingly be a maxim for cultural *psychologists*; the *humanum*, however, the
human ways of being and acting, constitute complex systems, and should
we neglect these, human reality will indeed remain alien to us. "Human
reality"? Does not the incessant pursuit of a more beautiful sound reveal
paradigmatically that a main trait of human reality is to transcend itself?
Then, our example would have uncovered the very essence of culture
formation.

References

Boesch, E. E. (1983). *Das Magische und das Schöne*. Stuttgart: Frommann-Holzboog.

Boesch, E. E. (1991). *Symbolic action theory and cultural psychology*. Heidelberg/New York: Springer.

Bruner, J. (1990). *Acts of meaning*. Cambridge, MA: Harvard University Press.

Douglas, M. (1966). *Purity and danger*. London: ARK.

Firth, R. (1973). *Symbols. Public and danger*. London: Allen & Unwin.

Hughes, R. (1988). Seeing Gauguin whole at last. *Time*, May 9, p. 77.

Lang, A. (1992). Kultur als "externe Seele": eine semiotischökologische Perspektive. In C. Allesch, E. Billmann-Mahecha, & A. Lang (Eds.), *Psychologische Aspekte des kulturellen Wandels*. Wien, Verlag d. Verb. d. wissensch. Gesellsch. Oesterreichs.

Morton, D. (1976). *The traditional music of Thailand*. Berkeley: University of California Press.

14 Non-Cartesian artifacts in dwelling activities: Steps towards a semiotic ecology

Alfred Lang

Common sense and science tend to presuppose human subjects separate from and opposed to an objective world. Questions are raised as to the adequacy of this view for understanding open and developing systems such as humans in their cultural environment. In response, a conceptual methodology is proposed. It explicates *structure formation processes* within persons and in their environment as of basically equivalent function. Throughout their ontogenetic development, not only are individuals building up and modifying structures in the form of dynamic memory in their mind-brains, but they also contribute to the formation and change of cultural artifacts in the physical and social space of their group. Both kinds of structures, internal and external, including their constitution of an ecological super-system and its development, are essential conditions of what a personal and social system can do. Humans are creators as well as they are creatures of their environment. Conceptual tools elaborated from the triadic semiotic of Charles S. Peirce appear appropriate to reconceptualize the relationship between humans and their cultural environment in a framework of semiotic ecology.

Dwelling activities in Cartesian perspective

The present conceptual framework has evolved from attempts to understand human activities designated by such verbs as "to dwell," "to abide," "to reside," "to live in," "being at home" or, in French, "habiter" and, in German, "wohnen." These phenomena withstand

185

clear definition or delimitation (see Lang, in prep.). They can roughly be characterized as involving people and settings in relative continuity, usually small groups and houses, or parts and contents and surroundings thereof. In most cultures these phenomena bear a more private or intimate character to be distinguished from the more public settings and events of the group at large. In addition, in modern civilization they show some opposition to the institution of work and labour. *Dwelling activities*, as a rule, manifest themselves in a rather large variety and loose connection of social or solitary actions interwoven with a similarly large diversity and slowly changing compound of smaller and larger *artifacts* such as buildings, furniture and household contrivances or pieces of craft and trade. Possession or some other form of disposability of space and objects by the people involved often are of serious importance.

Psychologists have, until recently, given little attention to activities in and around homes in spite of the fact that they tend to take, on the average, roughly a third of a person's lifetime in Western societies, not counting sleep time (for reviews of research see Altman & Werner, 1985; Flade, 1987; Lawrence, 1987). As a rule, we believe – be it a prescientific belief or one rooted in various provinces of social science – that artifacts are somehow instrumental for the persons involved. Settings, houses, objects, and arrangements, it is said, are to fulfill an individual's basic *or secondary needs*, such as shelter, storage, sociality, privacy, etc., or they are to serve their *planned purpose* of better comfort and higher prestige.

Unfortunately, such instrumental explanations are quite arbitrary and also circular in their logic (Lang, 1990). First, they explain *nothing*, because neither those needs nor goals can be pointed out independently of their explananda. These terms only mirror the observable in more abstract and collective terms. Second, they explain *everything*, in that anything could eventually become a reinforcer of secondary needs and anything can in principle become a target of human planning. Both the emergence of the supposed secondary needs and the causative path from the supposed needs or goals to the observable facts are obscure.

Indeed, these theories "explain" that anything in matters of building and contriving dwellings is admissible. "Anything goes" appears to be typical of 20th century environmental design in the industrialized countries, whereas in traditional cultures building and arranging things follow constraints within the social and individual life of the people involved.

In fact, dwelling activities in modern civilization, as witnessed by local, regional and national variation, are also quite highly conventionalized; deviations can meet painful disapproval. This contrasts with the widespread belief that we could do as we like. Insofar as the *limitless production of material commodities* in modern societies definitely consumes long-term resources and rapidly pollutes the planet's biosphere, suspicion arises that our instrumental understanding of space and objects in the interest of people is superficial and should be complemented.

Need- and goal-oriented theorizing is anthropocentric and, in addition, highly individuocentric. It obviously discounts our present knowledge of the human species' delicate place in the biosphere. Its background is what is often called the *Cartesian view of the world* and, in particular, of the human being. In a Cartesian view of the world, human subjects or cognitive systems (*res cogitantes*), are thought to be completely different from objects, i.e., material givens or artifacts. The latter are considered just another form of *res extensae*, although they are systematically formed by humans rather than having arisen just by themselves or by "nature." In its essence this dualistic world view opposes active subjects to passive objects, the latter being conceived as material and absolutely lawful in their behavior, the former being, in addition, imbued with a free mind.

This is not the place to discuss the manifold problems of dualism and its disguised offspring, nominalistic materialism, and their repercussions in psychology (for a comprehensive critique see Rorty, 1979). However, a growing number of scientists from different fields have recently begun investing in viable alternatives. Since Cartesian thinking and its idealistic or materialistic ramifications predispose a biased human–environment relationship, attempts at *redefining artifacts in relation to persons* are particularly desirable. The poorly understood dwelling processes offer an exemplary working place.

The present effort tries to dissolve some of the problems of dualism on a very basic level. The reader should keep this in mind when, in the following text, we pass from concrete examples to an abstract conceptual framework. Another point to emphasize is our use of a general methodological approach that has been called *conditional-genetic* and contrasted with the more common investigation of classes of substantive objects ("subjects") and their traits or behavior (Lewin, 1931; Lang, 1992b). The goal of scientific understanding cannot lie in translating into special terms how parts of the world act upon us, their observers. Rather, it is our goal to find and formulate how parts of the world that we can discern act upon each other.

Therefore, as a second *caveat* we should remind the reader habituated to either an objectivistic or a subjectivistic approach that our non-Cartesian perspective is to open a third avenue. If it is true that materialistic reductionism cannot, by its very definition, grasp what is essential in culture, then it is equally inappropriate to consider the world, including culture, exclusively through the looking glass of mental systems, because both approaches are partial and prepossessed.

If we want to free ourselves from these opposed world views, an advisable focus for our interest might be on the processes by which persons, groups, and cultures constitute each other. The task is then to extricate from what we can observe those *genetic series* established by the interplay of structures and processes that have brought about particular dwelling settings and activities or, in other words, to conceptualize what turns human-environment-relations into person-culture-systems of any specific kind. Following Peirce's implicit advice that "this act" of making "reference to a correlate," in other words, of creating or using a sign, "*has not been sufficiently studied by the psychologists*" (W2:53/1867 = CP 1.553, emphasis added), and judging his statement still correct today, I take the liberty of re-interpreting 20th century Cartesian psychological knowledge to fit my purpose.

A young couple's dirty clothes' chest

Let me start with excerpts from transcripts of an interview with a young married woman, called S., asked to talk "about some important things in their apartment" (Translation by A. L. from Slongo, 1991, p. 104):

The *Dirty Clothes' Chest* chosen by S. is one of several items S. reluctantly had to buy from her sister as the sister emigrated.

S.: The interesting thing, now, with the chest that stands in the sleeping room, is that it pleases me highly, it's in fact almost like a sea trunk, that's what it is to me, you can stow away something like the used clothes of 3 weeks or so. I don't really like to do the laundry, and if I have to, I like to have the machine full; and this is the only thing [from the sister] which I have considered, I wouldn't like to give it back to her. Because this chest stands for comfort, on the one hand (laughs!), that is, there is an awful lot of clothes going in, I can hide the things inside, I can make them disappear, and then, on the other side, its decorative, too. And then, the chest in addition takes charge of R. [the husband]. When he has no shirts left, you don't notice, because everything is inside the chest, he only sees it in the cupboard. Earlier, we had a smaller basket, it was overflowing already after one week, so you had to do something, you just had to go somewhere with the dirty clothes. And then, since we live here and have this large chest, it is R. who does the laundry most of the time, not me (laughs!).

. . .

S.: I believe, it has something to do with the capacity of the chest, of what goes in there, there is a connection, that we did the laundry less often since then, and that we did not participate in the wash-day schedule that reigns in the house. In this house, people do their laundry every week, each party has one fixed day, and when the people in this apartment left, then everybody in the house assumed we would take over their fixed day, but we didn't. And that's for me a kind of sign that I do not participate in the Swiss wash-day philosophy.

. . .

S.: Well, this chest, I would not like to give it back, it's a kind of freedom for me, well, a kind of revolt.

People with their things in their rooms

I cannot give here a full account of our psychological theory of dwelling activity and even less of our methodological approach designed to reconstruct formative transactions and their traces from interview and observational data (see Lang, Bühlmann, & Oberli, 1987; Slongo, 1991; Studer, 1993). The reader should peruse the above example as standing for a myriad of interlocking processes that form or modify structures within and around the persons living together.

One of our basic assumptions is that we should not consider the environmental givens as objects and spaces having an elemental and independent existence and fully specifiable character in physical terms. For, in their pertinence to humans, those are *things and places* or entities of relational quality incorporating in some way some disposition of their originators and at the same time presenting all along some capacity to determine people within their range or persons making use of them (see Lang, 1992a). Therefore, in our view, things and places are neither objective facts nor simply subjective constructions. Rather, they are *realities spanning across people and their environment.*

Conversely, this corresponds to persons being found both, or more than, subjects and objects (Lang, in press a). And while the researcher can observe "transactions" between individuals and parts of their environment, there is no necessity to comply with that particular articulation of the world also in his or her conceptualizations of what is going on. If real is what can have effects, then the first task of science is to find those entities in the world that can have effects in a consistent manner. If individuals *per se* show different effects than persons together with their things, then persons-and-their-things or *ecological units* are real. Similarly, if objects alone compared to objects-with-their-people behave differently, the latter are realities to be understood.

It is true, our immediate apprehension seems to articulate ourselves as coherent and self-active individuals and self-contained elementary objects around us upon which we act. We seem to have some intuitive knowledge about this. But can we trust our impressions? It is obvious that many of those objects also determine people's behavior in various ways, while the freedom and power of the subjects, though evident, is rather constrained.

We do not immediately perceive groups and culture in a comprehensive and unitary way in the same way that we "see" individuals. But then, what are "individuals" and where exactly are their boundaries? It is hardly deniable that individuals as well as groups and cultures are to some degree coherent and at the same time divided into fluctuating and interacting parts. While some of the parts may appear more essential and others more accidental, in fact, any change of any part may change the whole in its potential to have effects. Thus, Peirce – in a then-premature philosophy of science statement of utmost actuality today – compares the individual *person* to "a cluster of stars which appears to be one star when viewed with the naked eye, but which scanned with the telescope of scientific psychology is found . . . to be multiple within itself, and on the other hand to have no absolute demarcation from a neighboring condensation" (1893, Ms. 403; see Pierce, 1896, p. 82).

No doubt, groups are themselves like clusters of stars and capable of consistent acting and developing, be it an informal or ritualized manner or through representatives or some other forms. Some degree of coherence and direction is what characterizes social systems and cultures as well as individuals. By direction I mean simply that events tend to form ecosystemic series, of which the later segments depend on the earlier ones in such a way that future steps are as much accidental as they are predictable (Lewin, 1934; Lang, 1992b). In addition, we can infer from observation that organs and even smaller divisions within individuals act upon each other in similar ways. Finally, we must conclude that it is seldom clear in what way the whole or parts of an individual and what parts of her surroundings are really involved in what we perceive as an action of a subject.

Intuitions about coherence and differentiation of individuals and groups vary widely across cultures and change over time. So, our habitual articulation of ourselves and of object-things should be taken as one of several possible inferences rather than an undeniable intuition (see Peirce, 1868 W2:193–211 = CP 5.213-317 or 1905 CP 5.462). Briefly, let us then refrain from any presupposition we are capable of avoiding about the entities involved in, for example, residential transactions, and let us try to describe these processes, using the "chest" example, as they might appear to happen in a non-Cartesian view.

It has been demonstrated that our young couple and their relationship was changed in the course of a few weeks by the simple addition of the large chest to their dwelling. A considerable field of their actions towards each other and, in addition, another set of their everyday behaviors towards third parties is reported to be different than before. The couple in no way appears to have intentionally arranged any of these developments. Though S. is aware of the role of the chest, we have reason to suspect that her talking to the investigator about it has contributed to a deepening of her understanding. We can also assume that R. behaves differently than before, whether he has insight into all aspects or not. On the other hand, it would be risky to ascribe this change to any kind of "stimulation" or other direct causation going from the chest or the clothes stored therein toward S. and R. The chest, like so many other discernible items or places in the household, takes a gradually transmuting role in the series of hundreds or thousands of transactive events in the ecosystem formed by the two persons and their dwelling. It is true that in contrast to our couple, the chest as an object, if we neglect its new placement, has not significantly changed as a result of its new role with the couple. However, our task is to explain the chest's potential to influence the relationship of our couple including their footing in the wider social system.

We propose to consider the system formed by the pair and their dwelling and analyze it in terms of its emergence and change over time. The chest, or for that matter any reasonable sample of things and places, serves the investigator as a focusing method or as a device to bring the functioning of the ecological system into the open. Considering the chest separately would similarly lead us astray as would considering humans in isolation. Taking the chest as a singular collection and arrangement of a multitude of molecules existing at a given place over a certain period of time and specifying it in terms of physical and chemical measures is just one of many possible descriptions. Equally valid are everyday verbal descriptions pointing to its functions as a vessel for all kinds of things or to its shape and ornamentation in terms of style or impressiveness. In principle many more kinds of description can be evoked and combinations thereof might be feasible.

The point is that all such descriptions are selective or abstractive and therefore approximative only. A full description is simply not possible. This should become clear when we ask to what extent any trait of the chest can really be a character of the chest itself. If it would not be in a certain respect or potential effect, it would not matter at all. A trait is necessarily attributed by an observer in a certain respect, notwithstanding the fact that the trait can and should for practical purposes be grounded in reality. On the other hand, to include all attributable characters or potential effects that might, appropriately or fictitiously, ever be found in connection with this or that chest would be a nuisance. So we have to refrain from characterizing things as such or to glorify one particular ("objective") description above all others and, instead, explicate the context of their having effects we are factually interested in. This means to conceptualize people and things in places of inter-activity as evolving ecosystems.

Semiotics appears to be a suitable tool for this task because of its potential to overcome the Cartesian split between the supposed objective and subjective worlds. In Peircean semiotics, both cognitive systems and artifacts are similar in many respects, because they can be seen as sign-types. Signs are neither *material nor mental*, yet belong in a way to both of these realms (for a comprehensive reference to modern semiotics see Nöth, 1990). Indeed, Peirce considered "thought" (CP 5.594/1903), "human beings themselves" (CP 5.314/1868 = W2:241), and perhaps "the entire universe," including artifacts, to be composed of signs (CP 5.448/1906; Peirce exaggerates a bit). "But a sign is not a sign unless it translates itself into another sign in which it is more fully developed" (CP 5.594/1903). The question, to be asked of cognitive systems as well as of artifacts, is how they can be translated into other signs. In other words: how do signs come about and how do signs have effects? Obviously, in many cases, people are involved.

The semiotic function circle

It might be advisable, then, for psychology to combine forces with semiotics (Lang, 1993). A diagrammatic approach is perhaps helpful (a) for introducing semiotic tools and (b) in applying them to the human-environment-in-development constellation (see also Lang, 1992c and in press b).

Let us represent *Semiosis* or the *process of triadic structure formation by the semiosic arrow*, i.e., the directed symbol composed of a circle for the origin or source, a rhombus for the resultant anaform and a band mediating between the two, i.e., interpreting the source into its anaform (Figure 14.1, top). Origin (semiotically: *referent*), mediator (*interpretant*), and resultant anaform (*presentant*) are matter-energy-formations or structures; all three are entities that can in principle be empirically pointed out in their structure or process manifestations. By *anaform* I mean any discernible formation that is semiosically related to two other structures, be it by structural similarity or complementarity (iconically), by genuine causation, contingency or antagonism (indexically) and/or simply by habit or tradition (symbolically). The anaform may be seen as the sign carrier.

Any one of the three parts of the triad are naturally matter-energy-formations (or formations for short) with their respective characteristic binding and effect potential. However, only the three together as a unit is a triadic sign, i.e., a relative implying "meaning." This difference is of utmost importance and often neglected even in semiotics. Any formation can accept and produce effects *by its proper disposition*. Such are dyadic relations and are studied primarily by the physical sciences.

On the other hand, many formations can also induce effects under suitable circumstances that imply a triadic relative which is the proper topic of semiotics. In an encounter with certain other formations the effects of some formations can go beyond their proper dispositions and actually bring about a third formation, called their anaform. Semiosis is thus the process of interpretation of a referent into a (re)presentant. In their sign-character, formations have effects *based on their embeddedness*

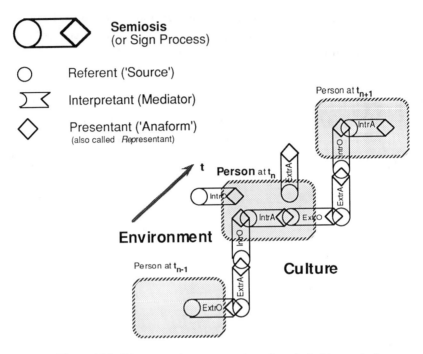

Figure 14.1. Diagrammatic representation of semiosis (the semiosic arrow and its parts) and its application to exchanges between persons and the world in time.

in a contextual history. We can only understand these effects when we can explicate their semiosic embeddedness. While the physical effects of formations have a necessary or chance character, the semiosic effects based on their contextual embeddedness are unique. They could as well be quite different, had their history taken another course. However, due exactly to their semiosic embeddedness, they demonstrate some degree of regularity between necessity and chance or, in other words, a kind of lawfulness-with-freedom. In our intuition we therefore perceive the latter as carriers of "meaning," while the former must just be taken as they are.

Common semiotic parlance would define the anaform as a sign standing for or replacing in some respect its referent. In contrast, I prefer in line with Peirce to say that the anaform (his "representamen") presents the triad, i.e., it proffers the quintessence of the encounter between ref-

erent and interpretant for further semiosic occasions and is thus found-
ing chains of mediated effects or history. The triadic character of this
concept of semiosis is to be emphasized and it should be clear that this
conception requires no split of the world in a material and a mental fraction. The essential point appears simple enough: to represent an entity,
a medium is vital if the entity is to have effects through something other
than itself.[1]

As a physical entity the young couple's chest weighs on the floor with
its mass in the gravity field, or it actually prevents other formations to
pass through its location. As a sign-type the chest is interpreted by an
animal as potentially preventing it from passing or as (im)possible to
move around. This presumes a suitable perceptual-cognitive system in
the encountering animal, i.e., an appropriate interpretant. For a suitably
experienced human seeing the chest a wealth of general and idiosyncratic potentialities are stirred, consciously or not: sumptuous, container,
to be opened from top, antique, richly ornamented, bought from sister,
original property of aunt Clara, no need to do the laundry, "a kind of
revolt."

The triad can be dealt with as a structure or as a process. From the
process perspective, one of several equivalent descriptions would emphasize the encounter of two preexisting structures, the referent and the
interpretant, giving rise to a third, the anaform presentant. It is of no
import whether the parts of the triad are physically transient or lasting.
So, a sentence printed on paper would be a referent formation available
over time for a reading capacity interpretant to understand its meaning,
while the spoken sentence would serve a similar referent role with a
listening interpretant in just one fugitive moment. Physically, both formations are nothing but spatio-temporal matter-energy-distributions.
Together with befitting interpretant structures they develop a thoroughly distinct potential. I tend to speak of formations as structures
when they have a distinguished character in being stable or repeatable
or reproducible. We come back to the structural perspective below.

The illustrative diagram (Figure 14.1, bottom) applies these semiotic
concepts at the process level to the ecological situation. The schema represents the world as the white surface of the paper with entities in the
world rendered as inscribed formations. The world changes over time
from left bottom to right top. The individual *person* we are interested in
is depicted at three successive points in time by the filled-in rectangle.

Exchange processes – one might think of them as "metabolism" on the information level – between the person and the world are indicated by semiosic arrows. In those aspects the person can relate to it, receptively or effectively, the world becomes the person's *environment*.

There are semiosic processes spanning from the environment into the individual (IntrO) and from the individual into the environment (ExtrO). In addition semioses occur within the person (IntrA) and also totally outside the person (ExtrA), the latter usually involving other individuals (see below). A cardinal feature of our approach is the thesis that all of these four classes of processes are of *essentially the same nature*, in that they can be conceived as triadic semiosic processes resulting in an anaform implying an interpreted referent. On the other hand, the four types of semiosic processes can be distinguished on the basis of the location of the involved referent and presentant structures. See Lang (1992c; in press b) for a more elaborate presentation of this semiotic conception inspired by and elaborating on Peirce. The reader should be warned again that the present approach to semiotics is not of the "something-stands-for-or-signifies-something(-to-somebody)" kind but conceives of semiosis as a general form of causation and a device for creating memory and history (see Lang, in press b).

In Figure 14.1 we have indicated IntrO- and ExtrA-processes as coming from and going to the environment in general. Evidently these refer, quite generally, to perceptive and actionable processes, i.e., the taking into account by the individual of her environment and of having effects into that environment. In addition, we have diagrammed IntrO- and ExtrO-processes that, together with IntrA- and ExtrA-processes tend to form genetic series (see above and Lang, 1992b). While the first two are ecological processes relating the individual to her environment, the latter two correspond to psychological processes proper and to social and cultural processes respectively.

In Figure 14.2 these processes are diagrammed schematically abstracting from time and relating them cyclically. This conception elaborates on the idea of the *Function Circle* of Jakob von Uexküll and Kriszat (orignally 1906, see 1934/1991) reformulating it semiotically and adding the IntrA- and ExtrA-phases. If we conceive the four phases in the framework of semiotic ecology as triadic structure formation processes, it is easy to see that the circle in fact goes in a spiral through time and implies the ecological basis of co-development of a living

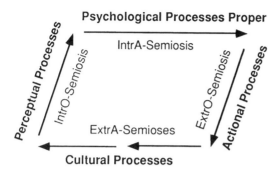

Figure 14.2. Four-phased function circle (spiral) with the processes relating living systems to their environment in common and semiotic terminology.

system within its environment. This is so because each of the four phases has the potential to create *self-referent dynamic memory structures* (an anaform presentant of itself) which can enter in later phases in the same or later cycles either in the form of referents or of interpretants to contribute to the emergence of an ongoing sequence (process) or network (structure) of semioses.

Let's consider acts of an individual that leave traces, i.e., some anaform of her condition, in her environment (*ExtrO-semiosis*, Figure 14.3). These presentants can be taken up, immediately or later on, IntrO-semiosically by the same or by some other person or agency within the social system. In other words, ExtrO-semioses proffer *some concrete embodiment of the actor*. These externalizations "store" some condition of the actor and keep them potentially effective as long as the anaform exists (Fuhrer, 1993). Some aspects of the actor can thus be profused everywhere and everytime the anaform can be brought up without the person herself being present. Presentants of ExtrO-semiosis, thus are a form of external or social memory (see Lang, 1992a and in press a), provided there is some suitable interpretant to make use of it as a referent in one or several ExtrA-semioses.

If this is indeed the case, the minimal condition for *communication* is given (Slongo, 1992). And if eventually the original actor becomes a member of the semiosic chain anew, the function circle is closed, no matter how many intermediate semioses intervene. To the extent that all interpretants involved in the chain or net of ExtrA-semioses are affili-

198   *Alfred Lang*

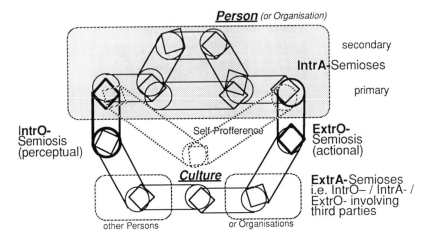

Figure 14.3. The semiotic function circle and the role of IntrO-, IntrA-, ExtrO-, and ExtrA-semiosis in constituting persons and culture.

ated among each other, a system of co-existing and co-constituting entities – semiosic referents, interpretants and presentants – is established
which can rightly be equated with the *culture*, our target person is
dwelling in (Fuhrer, 1993). One advantage of the semiotic conception
lies in its dealing with processes and structure on the same terms.

IntrO-semiosis is the process of building *internal dynamic memory structures*. Take seriously the idea that any semiosic process results in a concrete formation and is unthinkable without equally concrete referent and
interpretant structures. Indeed, if perception is to have effects on behavior, on problem solving, on emotional states, etc., it must leave something upon these that other, further processing can be based. Most
probably, IntrO-semioses can be thought of leaving altered states, tran-
siently or enduring, of the brain-mind, anaforms of the stimulus, if you
like. This corresponds well with Peirce's idea that percepts, feelings,
thoughts, etc. and, indeed, persons themselves, are nothing but signs (see
above). The presentants of IntrO-semioses, like any other semiosic
resultants, need not necessarily stand in an iconic relation to some stimulus, as perception psychologists appear to assume. Indexical and symbolic relations are as well possible. In fact, a semiotic conception of
perceptual processes is an excellent starting point for justifying the

indigenous and autochthonous nature of psychological processes in general while at the same time assuring the adequate relatedness of the living system to the character of its environment (Uexküll and Kriszat, 1934).

Finally, *IntrA-semioses* are fully closing the function circle. They conceptualize semiotically structures and events in the proper domain of psychological and physiological approaches to human functioning. In Figure 14.3 some hints are made as to levels of primary and secondary connections between ingoing and outgoing semioses. While instincts and other routine processing would be seen as semiosic paths on the relatively direct primary level, so-called higher processes would also construct and recruit secondary semiosic structures such as consciousness, imagery, language, and the self. Evidently, the mind-brain is an extremely complex structure and process about which there is a plethora of speculation and knowledge. An important methodological point is the lack of direct access to IntrA-referents, -interpretants and -presentants; we have to infer everything based on covariation of ExtrO-semiosic presentants with IntrO-semiosic referent. In a sense, the person is semiotically one multifaceted interpretant. It is also opportune to mention, as a general heuristic that intra-personal and extra-personal structures of a given individual are unthinkable if not in a peculiar correspondence which is due to the high degree of their phylogenetic and ontogenetic and culture-genetic codevelopment (Boesch, 1991).

Readers should now be able to further unfold our *example of the dwelling activities* with the dirty clothes' chest for themselves. The quotation in section 2 above describes all sorts of events that can be conceptually reconstructed as IntrO-, ExtrO- and ExtrA-semioses in relation to S. Also some conjectures as to her IntrA-semioses might be feasible. In addition, semioses of all phases involving R., as conjectured by S., can be used to complement the circumstances. Important ExtrOs, naturally in conjunction with all kinds of IntrOs and IntrAs, are preparing the course of events in connection with the purchase, placement, and dedication of the chest. Once in use, changes in perception of and actions with underwear and shirts are evident in her and him. But, correspondingly, the chest mediated through the people also changes the factual situation in the dwelling in terms of distribution of the clothes. Most dramatic, perhaps, are the changes in the time intervals for doing the laundry induced by the chest's capacity and the subsequent shift from internal to external control in the laundry schedule. The fact of parallel shifts in responsibility sharing for the laundry among the couple is only understandable on the basis of affiliated but different internal structures that manifest themselves in changes of perception and action patterns. The extended effects of the chest hatching and strengthening certain types of social relations in the house and beyond are quite unexpected. Naturally, the chest is only one of an ensemble of external structures that carry a coordinated semiosic exchange of cultivation processes among the couple and their dwelling.

Changes on many levels and in many directions within this dwelling ecosystem have been induced by the simple addition of the chest to the household. Of course, as Ernst Boesch (see 1991) has repeatedly shown, much of this could be brought to insightful interpretation by means of careful phenomenology based on controlled observation and interview. Valuable insights into transactions between people and their cultural environment can also be gained by traditional methods (Fuhrer, 1990). What we are lacking so far, however, is the conceptual possibility of explicating the genetic series carrying the manifest changes from the chest into the people and back to the things and places or the social system. The present sketch of some conceptual problems and tools for establishing a psychologically appropriate conception of causation can be no more than a first set of stepping stones into the larger domain of semiotic ecology.

Note

1. Readers knowledgeable of Peirce will be aware of some divergence. I emphasize the mediating role of the interpretant in line with some of his statements (e.g., CP 1.554, 1867; 8.177, late). In addition, with the present concept of an elementary semiosis I hope to surmount some of the problems related to his subcategories of "Objects" and "Interpretants."

References

Altman, I., & Werner, C. M. (Eds.). (1985). *Home environments.* Human behavior and environment: advances in theory and research. Vol. 8. New York: Plenum.

Boesch, E. E. (1991). *Symbolic action theory and cultural psychology.* Berlin: Springer.

Flade, A. (1987). *Wohnen psychologisch betrachtet* Bern: Huber.

Fuhrer, U. (1990). *Handeln Lernen im Alltag.* Bern: Huber.

Fuhrer, U. (1993). Living in our own footprints – and in those of others: cultivation as transaction. *Schweizerische Zeitschrift für Psychologie 52.*

Lang, A. (1990). Bauen und Wohnen psychologisch zu verstehen: drei theoretische Perspektiven. In D. Frey (Ed.), *Bericht über den 37. Kongress der Deutschen Gesellschaft für Psychologie in Kiel.* Vol. 1 (pp. 401–402). Göttingen: Hogrefe.

Lang, A. (1992a). On the knowledge in things and places. In M. von Cranach, W. Doise, & G. Mugny (Eds.), *Social representations and the social basis of knowledge* (pp. 76–83). Swiss Monographs in Psychology, Vol. 1. Bern: Huber.

Lang, A. (1992b). Die Frage nach den psychologischen Genesereihen – Kurt Lewins grosse Herausforderung. In W. Schönpflug (Ed.), *Kurt Lewin – Person, Werk, Umfeld: historische Rekonstruktion und Interpretation aus Anlass seines hundersten Geburtstages* (pp. 39–68). Frankfurt a.M.: Peter Lang.

Lang, A. (1992c). Kultur als "externe Seele" – eine semiotischökologische Perspektive. In C. Allesch, E. Billmann-Mahecha, & A. Lang (Eds.), *Psychologische Aspekte des kulturellen Wandels* (pp. 9–30). Wien, Verlag des Verbandes der wissenschaftlichen Gesellschaften Österreichs.

Lang, A. (1993). Toward a mutual interplay between psychology and semiotics. *Journal of the Society for Accelerated Learning and Teaching, 18* (3).

Lang, A. (in press a). The "concrete mind" heuristic – human identity and social compound from things and buildings. In C. Jaeger, M. Nauser, & D. Steiner (Eds.), *Human ecology: an integrative approach to environmental problems.* London: Routledge.

Lang, A. (in press b). Zeichen nach innen, Zeichen nach aussen – eine semiotischökologische Psychologie als Kulturwissenschaft. In P. Rusterholz, & M. Svilar (Eds.), *Welt der Zeichen – Welt der Wirklichkeit.* Bern: Paul Haupt.

Lang, A. (in prep.) Dwelling. In R. Posner, T. A. Sebeok, & K. Robering (Eds.), *Semiotics: A handbook on the sign-theoretic foundations of nature and culture.* Vol. 2. Berlin: DeGruyter.

Lang, A., Bühlmann, K., & Oberli, E. (1987). Gemeinschaft und Vereinsamung im strukturierten Raum: psychologische Architekturkritik am Beispiel Altersheim. *Schweizerische Zeitschrift für Psychologie, 46* (3/4), 277–289.

Lawrence, R. J. (1987). *Housing, dwellings and home: design theory, research and practice.* New York: Wiley.

Lewin, K. (1931). Der Übergang von der Aristotelischen zur Galileischen Denkweise in Biologie und Psychologie. (The conflict between the Aristotelian and Galileian modes of thought in contemporary psychology.) Reprinted in *Kurt-Lewin-Werkausgabe,* Vol. 1 (pp. 233–278). Bern: Huber, 1981.

Lewin, K. (1934). Der Richtungsbegriff in der Psychologie: Der spezielle und allgemeine hodologische Raum. *Psychologische Forschung, 19,* 249–299. (To be reprinted in Kurt-Lewin-Werkausgabe, Vol. 3).

Nöth, W. (1990). *Handbook of semiotics.* Bloomington, IN: Indiana University. Press. (Enlarged translation of (1985) Handbuch der Semiotik. Stuttgart: Metzler).

202 *Alfred Lang*

Peirce, C. S. (1931–35/1958). *Collected papers of Charles Sanders Peirce*. 8 Vols. Cambridge MA: Harvard University Press. Cited as CP x.y-y (=volume.paragraph).

Peirce, C. S. (1982ff.). *Writings of Charles S. Peirce*. 30 vols. Bloomington, IN: Indiana University Press. Cited as Wx: z-z (=volume:pages).

Peirce, C. S. (1986ff.). *Semiotische Schriften*. 3 Bände. Kloesel, Christian & Pape, Helmut (Übers. u. Hersg.) Frankfurt a.M., Suhrkamp.

Rorty, R. (1979). *Philosophy and the mirror of nature*. Princeton University Press. Deutsch (1987) Der Spiegel der Natur: eine Kritik der Philosophie. Frankfurt a.M., Suhrkamp.

Slongo, D. (1991). Zeige mir, wie du wohnst, . . . eine Begrifflichkeit über externe psychologische Strukturen anhand von Gesprächen über Dinge im Wohnbereich. Diplomarbeit, Institut für Psychologie der Universität Bern.

Slongo, D. (1992). Dinge kultiviren: ein Verständnis von Kommunikation. In C. G. Allesch, E. Billmann-Mahecha, & A. Lang, (Eds.), *Psychologische Aspekte des kulturellen Wandels* (pp. 123–134). Wien, Verlag des Verbandes der wissenschaftlichen Gesellschaften Österreichs.

Studer, H. (1993). Individuelle und kollektive Wohnformen – eine explorative Untersuchung ihrer sozialer Implikationen. Diplomarbeit, Institut für Psychologie der Universität Bern.

Uexküll, J. von, & Kriszat, G. (1934). *Streifzüge durch die Umwelten von Tieren und Menschen*. Hamburg, Rowohlt. (Engl. translation 1991 in *Semiotica*).

Historical analysis

15 The invention of writing and the development of numerical concepts in Sumeria: Some implications for developmental psychology

Ageliki Nicolopoulou

Introduction

In this article I will examine in some detail the work of the German psychologist Peter Damerow on the use of historical materials to address psychological questions concerning the development of the concept of number. This work, so far still little known, is a significant example of the recently emerging interest in the systematic analysis of the relation between individual psychological development and the socio-cultural context within which the individual develops, including consideration of the historical and evolutionary processes by which that social context itself develops.

While the effort to situate individual development more self-consciously in a socio-historical framework has a number of sources, one major intellectual impetus has been a renewed awareness and appreciation of the work of L. S. Vygotsky and the socio-historical school of which he was a pioneer. Vygotsky proposes to understand the formation of human nature – which is, after all, the central mission of psychology – through studies of the origin and development of higher psychological functions as such. This development is, for him, a social as well as an individual process – more specifically, it can be understood only by grasping the systematic interpenetration of social and individual processes (Vygotsky, 1978, 1981; see also Bakhurst, 1988 and Wertsch, 1985). As Scribner puts it in an illuminating analysis of Vygotsky's theoretical project (1985), Vygotsky "takes as his conceptual object [the development of] 'higher psychological systems' and separates it from the natural object, [the development of] the 'child'" (Scribner, 1985, p. 133). Furthermore, Vygotsky argues that these "psychological systems" are embodied not only in the individual mind but also in culture; in fact, the cognitive structures which make up the "higher psychological systems" are culturally shaped and develop historically (Vygotsky, 1978, 1981).

As Scribner logically reconstructs Vygotsky's steps in building a method for studying the formation of cognitive structures, Vygotsky would begin with observations of "primitive" adults documented in ethnopsychological records and then, by way of experiment, move to observations of children of his own time. In other words, cultural history was used to generate hypotheses about the origins and transformations of higher psychological systems. But despite Vygotsky's early insight, cultural history did not become a domain of psychology proper. There have been few psychological studies that have examined systematically the historical development of "higher psychological systems" *per se* and then returned to address questions raised by psychological theories of development. There are various reasons why this has been the case, but a practical one is that such work requires the thorough mastery of (at least) two disciplines, which Damerow and associates are able to achieve through their collaborative effort. Hans Nissen and Robert Englund, principal associates in the work I'll be discussing, are both archaeologists at the Free University of Berlin, while Peter Damerow is a developmental psychologist at the Max Planck Institute for Human Development and Education in Berlin. Their work appears to stand in close intellectual connection to Vygotsky's efforts; at all events, it embodies in a fruitful way the sort of method envisioned by Vygotsky for psychological research. The lack of any mention of Vygotsky, or of the socio-historical school he represents, makes it unclear whether there is any direct filiation between their work and his. The significant point, however, is that their work addresses some of the issues which Vygotsky suggested were of crucial importance for developmental psychology.

The theoretical significance of the research

The research headed by Damerow examines the historical development of numerical concepts in Babylonian culture through the systematic study of ancient texts. This study forms the nucleus of a set of investigations which pursue the question of the cultural mediation of fundamental cognitive structures. In particular, they address the question of whether there are certain basic structures of thought which are independent of specific cultural influences – or whether even the most basic structures are dependent on available systems of symbolic representation or on the content of experience so that, despite their universality, they must be viewed as culturally mediated.

Specifically, this historical study takes issue with Piaget's epigenetic[1] conception of structural constructivism in explaining the development of the number concept in children. This development, according to Piaget, is the result of the construction of a cognitive structure based on experience and abstraction. Thus, it is neither an inherited intellectual schema (performed or innately given) nor a property directly abstracted from real objects; rather, it is the result of "reflective abstraction" from the actions carried out with the objects. In particular, Piaget explains the concept of number as the result of the coordination of actions such as the construction of one-to-one correspondence between sets of objects or between qualitative relations, the adding or taking away of objects or groups of objects, etc. In the fully developed cognitive structures, these actions are mentally represented by reversible operations constituting a closed system of possible inferences. But the arithmetically structured substratum of the number concept is an ideal substratum. Numbers are ideal objects of thought whose existence is not bound to the existence of material objects to which they are applied. They are independent of their particular representations by the various systems of numerical signs which might differ from one culture to another (Piaget & Szeminska, 1965).

In short, according to Piaget, the concept of number – though not inherited but acquired through the experience of objects – is in its substance not influenced by the content of these experiences. He interprets the coordination of actions as resulting from an endogenous unfolding of *biologically predetermined possibilities* in interaction with the environment, and hence sees the basic structures of cognition as a special form of biological adaptation. Its endogenous development is nonetheless an epigenetic process governed by inner necessity (Piaget, 1971, 1972).

This view, however, excludes the possibility that the structural transformations of cognitive structures are influenced by the material representations of those structures – in actions, pictures, or symbols – or by the forms of social interaction mediated by these representations. In contrast, Damerow advances the view that the particular representations of cognitive structures have the function of marking off *the horizon of possibilities* for the ontogenetic realization of cognitive structures (Damerow, 1988). Thus, conceptual change might not only be endogenous to a cognitive system; the initial qualitative changes might be exogenous to it and historically as well as culturally determined. Part of individual development would then consist of the effort to appropriate culturally developed cognitive structures.

In the following sections, I will first present the historical findings from the study, which will require reconstructing the socio-historical context in some detail; then I will discuss the significance of these results for theoretical issues in developmental psychology.

The historical study

The archaic texts from Uruk.   The subjects of the study is the systems of number signs in the Archaic texts from Uruk, a Sumerian city-state in the ancient civilization of Mesopotamia, located in the southern part of today's Iraq. This group of texts consists of some 4000 clay tablets and fragments of tablets, most of which have not yet been analyzed. With very few exceptions, these tablets were found in the district of Eanna, which from early times was a (perhaps *the*) central district of the city. Later this district housed the large cultural installations for Inanna, the city-goddess of Uruk.

These tablets were written around the end of the 4th and the beginning of the 3rd millennium B.C., and are the oldest surviving written documents from this part of the ancient Near East, if not the oldest in the history of mankind. By about 3100 B.C., the officials of such administrative centers as Uruk had developed a system of recording numerals, pictographs, and ideographs on specially prepared clay tablets. These texts are of great importance for the study of the relation of culture and cognition because they document the change brought about by writing in the existing number system.

The majority (85%) of these texts are economic records, while 15% constitute the so-called "lexical lists." Lexical lists were presumably used for the training of scribes and consist of lists of semantically related words whose order of enumeration has not yet been deciphered (Nissen, 1985, 1986). The "economic texts," on the other hand, were part of a bookkeeping system which recorded such matters as business transactions. For example, they seem to be receipts and lists of expenses, of animals, of all kinds of goods, or of raw materials. Given the overwhelming preponderance of economic texts, the invention of writing has been attributed to the creation of administrative city centers – themselves the result of urbanization – and the need to coordinate an expanding economic unit. This set of conditions prompted the introduction of coordinating economic devices better suited to manage larger quantities of information than had previously been available.

Record-keeping systems in Mesopotamia: Origins of the economic texts. Archaeologists have identified an even older record-keeping system used in the ancient Near East which was based on using pebbles or clay bits ("tokens"), accumulated in heaps or containers, as a temporary record of numbers (Goody, 1986; Schmandt-Besserat, 1978, 1983). This system is of particular interest as a more or less direct precursor of writing since many of the written signs (numerals and ideographs) seem to be two-dimensional representations of the clay tokens themselves. The clay tokens of the preliterate period are small, geometrically shaped objects (e.g., spheres, pellets, cones, tetrahedrons, cylinders, ovoids) which in their later forms are further specified by incised markings. These tokens appear widely in the Near East around 8500 B.C., roughly contemporary with a profound change in human society. An early subsistence pattern based on hunting and gathering was transformed by the impact of plant and animal domestication and the development of a farming way of life. This new agricultural economy, although it increased the production of food, probably introduced new problems which provided the impetus for the creation of record-keeping devices (e.g., storage and distribution of foods and textiles).

The clay tokens stood for particular natural objects such as different goods, animals, or produce. The tokens used in a particular context express in their form the kind, and in their number the quantity, of the goods represented. In animal accounting, for example, one token of each particular kind represents each of the animals of the herds. When new animals were born, the appropriate number of tokens would be added; when they were lost or slaughtered, the appropriate number of tokens would be taken away. Also, the tokens were probably moved from one shelf to another to signal other changes such as animals moved from one herdsman to another, etc.

Early in the Bronze Age, between 3500 and 3100 B.C., there were significant changes in the recording system. At some point between 3900 and 3400 B.C. – in what archaeologists refer to as the Early to Middle Uruk period – there had been a shift in population patterns. According to Adams (1981), about half of the people in southern Mesopotamia now lived in settlements of at least 10 hectares with a population of about a thousand more. These new developments resulted in the emergence of cities with an urban economy, rooted in trade. Subsequently, the new economy must have multiplied the demands on the traditional recording system. Not only production but also inventories, shipments, and wage payments had to be noted, and merchants needed to preserve records of their transactions.

About 3500 B.C., the tokens themselves underwent a radical change indicated by the proliferation of markings on their surfaces. About 3500 to 3200 B.C., we also find the first clay envelopes, round hollow objects about the size of tennis balls, which were used as containers for the tokens. Previously, the tokens were kept in insecure places, either in heaps or in open containers. This period begins to mark the users' desire to segregate the tokens representing one or another transaction. Those tokens were enclosed in a lump of clay on whose surface one or two cylinder seals were rolled to seal the document and safeguard the contexts for transportation. As discussed by Schmandt-Besserat (1978), Amiet suggested that these clay bullae might have served as bills of lading, for example, accompanying shipments of merchandise from centers of production in the country to the administrative centers in the town.

In case of dispute, the envelope could be broken, but being broken it was of no further use because it could no longer validate the transaction. So a new phase consisted of marking the contents of the envelope on its surface either by imprinting the shape of the tokens themselves in the clay or by some inscribed copy. It was no longer necessary to open the envelope. Indeed the tokens themselves, being a part of a double record-keeping device, became superfluous in this context; they were dispensed with, and what had been the envelopes were flattened out (though still slightly curved), becoming what archaeologists call the "economic texts." It is of theoretical importance to note, though, that in another context the tokens were not totally replaced, so that even to this day shepherds in Iraq use pebbles to account for the animals in their flocks (Schmandt-Besserat, 1978, 1982).

The numerical signs of the economic texts. The economic texts were marked with both ideographic characters and numerical signs. These were impressed in the clay with three different types of stylus. For the ideographic characters, a sharp-edged stylus was used. In the older texts, the characters were inscribed with a pointed stylus; this was later replaced with an oblique stylus that impressed the "heads" of the lines more deeply than the "tails," leaving impressions in the shape of wedges (=cunei; thus, cuneiform script). In contrast, drawing the numerical signs involved the use of the whole range of different types of stylus. The numerical signs were usually pressed into the clay with rounded styluses which came in a smaller and a larger size. In general, smaller quantities or smaller units of a particular system were impressed with the smaller rounded stylus, while larger quantities or units were impressed with the larger rounded one. In addition, the scribes used a sharp-edged stylus (the same used for the characters) to draw horizontal or vertical strokes, or even dots that some number signs required.

As opposed to the numerical information in the economic texts, which is always given in full, the non-numerical information is extremely brief. Writing was not used in its full capacity but rather as a means of producing catchwords for someone who was more or less familiar with the context and only needed to be reminded of the particular details. So there is neither a trace of a verbal system in the texts nor even a hint of syntactic relations. This situation means that at present the interpretation of the numerical information is still tentative and incomplete; in particular, the archaeologists' suggestions about which objects are being counted, and about the context in which different numerical expressions are applied, are restricted to rough categories based on the most prominent characters on the tablets.

The overall system of the numerical signs and their use is very complex. At present, a total of 60 separate number signs have been identified. Like the tokens of the preliterate period, these signs are both counting and measuring units. With small quantities, the number of objects is indicated straightforwardly by repeating the appropriate sign the same number of times as the number of natural objects to be represented. As opposed to the clay tokens, however, the signs are systematically subsumed under higher-valued signs whenever a particular quantity is reached; even here, however, the pattern is not uniform, as I will go on to explain.

This set of signs is used more or less interchangeably in a total of (at least) ten number sign systems which are organized very differently from each other; the archaeologists have identified five basic systems and five derived ones. Each of these systems is context-dependent in that each one is used to measure different *kinds* of objects; for example, one measures discrete objects, another objects of mass consumption, another grain, etc. In addition, each of the basic systems is organized differently in the sense that each works with a different base value. This latter feature makes the different systems not readily commensurable to each other.

Of the 60 identified number signs, at least 52 were used in more than one of the five basic (and the further five derived) number systems. As a consequence, the number signs do not carry a context-independent meaning; the value of each sign and the size relation between them differs depending on which system they are being used in. For instance, the meaning of the two most frequently used signs, which are often incorrectly interpreted as 1 and 10, is dependent on the subject matter to which they are applied. They stand in relation 1 to 10 when measuring discrete objects, but in relation 1 to 6 when measuring grain, and 1 to 10 when measuring surface areas of land.

To make matters more complex, within each basic sign system there is not necessarily the same fixed base value between *any* of two consecutive number signs for that system. In some systems, however, the size relation between consecutive signs – although not uniform – can be easily described by a rule; in some of the other sign systems, however, it is difficult to abstract such a rule. (For more details of these numerical systems, see Damerow, 1988; Damerow & Englund, 1986; Englund, in press.)

In brief, the five basic numerical systems identified in the texts are: the sexagesimal, the bisexagesimal, the SE, the GAN_2, and the EN system.

The sexagesimal system was used for discrete objects of various kinds. The system corresponds to the series of number words of the Sumerian language, which is believed to have been the language of the people of southern Mesopotamia at the time of the invention of writing. However, the exact relationship between the numerical system and the number words and, in particular, the direction of interpenetration, is difficult to decipher.

The bisexagesimal system is a second system of numerical signs for discrete objects and agrees with the sexagesimal system up to the sign with the value of 60. The two systems were used completely separately and, after a few hundred years, the bisexagesimal system disappeared completely from the economic texts in favor of the sexagesimal system. It is believed that this system was used to measure particular discrete objects, such as foodstuffs for mass consumption: bread, (possibly) cheese, and a certain kind of fish.

The SE system designates measures of grain. The smaller units of this system are formed as fractions and indicate the types of bread according to the amount of grain contained in them. This system is found only in the older texts; in the newer ones, it is replaced with another system with very similar function – whose arithmetical structure changed, though, with every reform of the measure of grain.

The GAN_2 system designates field measures. Like the sexagesimal system, this system remained in use for a long time without any change in its arithmetical structure. The EN system, finally, is the least well known of the systems, and so far the meaning of the character designating its context of application has not been deciphered.

Implications for psychological theory: Individual and cultural development

Damerow's interpretation of the data. This historical study has, it appears, brought to light two distinct stages in the cultural development of the Babylonian number concept: the first encompasses the arithmetical operations of the preliterate period as demonstrated by the clay tokens; and the second encompasses the arithmetical operations revealed through deciphering of the archaic economic texts. It is of theoretical interest to try to compare these stages to the ones discovered so far in the development of number in other cultures or in children, and also to highlight the factors which might have brought about this conceptual change.

As Damerow observes, the preliterate representation of quantities by a corresponding number of tokens manifests characteristics associated with the concept of number in contemporary "primitive" cultures. "[It] displays the same ties to particular, concrete contexts of application and action . . . , especially through the simultaneous representation of quality and quantity" (Damerow, 1988, p. 148). In particular, it is tied to the concrete use of clay tokens as auxiliary means, and all arithmetical operations are conducted exclusively through them. The result is that they can apply only to limited quantities as well as to a restricted part of human life, as is apparent from the set of clay tokens available.

In accord with Piaget's epigenetic constructivist theory, Damerow argues that the genesis of the representation of quantities by one-to-one correspondence does not require as a prerequisite any cognitive skills of a specifically arithmetical nature. It requires only the appropriate handling of the symbol function (i.e., the ability to ascribe to an object like a clay token a symbolic meaning, such as having it stand for "sheep"), which develops in the early years of life in the child and is found as well in the earliest cultures. He argues further that the essential prerequisites for the concept of number must have arisen in the process of the extensive use of the one-to-one correspondence technique. In his own words, "one can scarcely avoid the compelling conclusion that such a technique of the intellectual construction of correspondence must have brought forth as a result of reflection an equivalent to the conservation of quantity defined ontogenetically by Piaget" (Damerow, 1988, p. 149).

However, his agreement with Piaget's theory stops here. For Piaget, the achievement of this abstraction (the understanding of conservation of quantity) carries with it the more or less simultaneous achievement of the whole range of other structural elements which are necessarily associated with an abstract concept of number. Damerow contends that, even after this initial abstraction has been carried out, there is no reason to assume the presence of all the other structural elements which, in sum, would constitute a fully developed number concept. He puts forth as evidence the fact that the second stage in the cultural evolution being examined, which stabilizes with the use of the archaic economic texts, seems to be intermediate between the absence and the full presence of the number concept.

As discussed above, the numerical signs of the archaic texts are organized in highly complex systems which can be used to measure large quantities. These signs, however, do not possess any context-independent meaning. The concrete context of application determines how the signs are to be interpreted, and also determines the number of arithmetic operations that can be applied to them before changing to a higher- or lower-value sign. Thus, on the one hand, the arithmetical system revealed through the texts seems to have advanced beyond the level of a primitive number system. On the other hand, it does not yet possess an abstract concept of number, without which one cannot speak of a fully developed number concept in the Piagetian sense. This system, Damerow argues, stands at a stage somewhere between the two, and it "represents a missing link in the cultural evolution from proto-arithmetic to the number concept providing [evidence] that this process does not display the synchronous character of the emergence of the various structural elements of the number concept, which we can ascertain in ontogenetic development and on which Piaget based his epigenetic conception" (Damerow, 1988, p. 150).

Furthermore, Damerow asserts that the real impetus for the transition to a *semi*-abstract system of numerical signs in the archaic texts was the change in the medium of representation. This new medium, consisting of inscriptions on the surfaces of partially-flattened clay tablets, was a by-product of the invention of writing. This led to (relatively) rapid and substantial changes in the earlier record-keeping system, which had remained unchanged for several millennia. There is no reason to think, then, that this transition was preceded by a change in cognitive structure or an expanded arithmetical technique. Rather, it was induced – or, at least, facilitated – by the emergence of a richer and more flexible representational medium; and this cultural change was, in turn, set against a comprehensive change in social organization, particularly socio-economic organization, that marked a shift from an agricultural to an urban way of life. This change in the medium of representation, then, cannot be seen as a secondary or derivative one, nor as merely reflecting an expansion of cognitive capacities; rather, it triggered long-lasting cognitive effects which are reflected in the complexities of the systems of numerical signs it helped to generate.

Some critical reflections. I find Damerow's broad characterization of the transition from the use of clay tokens to the archaic texts as culturally mediated very convincing; however, I find his more detailed characterization of the cognitive significance of each stage much less so. An important underlying tension in Damerow's article stems from the fact that he is using a culturally-informed approach to make a *partial* break with certain arguments of Piaget's; however, he is unwilling to make as complete a break with the Piagetian framework as the logic of his own position should have led him to do. Damerow, following Piaget, argues that the emergence of the use of clay tokens could take place without the existence of any specifically numerical concepts, requiring instead only a "symbolic" capacity. Furthermore, he suggests that the key development within the first stage – the stage marked by the use of clay tokens – is the development of the concept of conservation of quantity (or "an equivalent to the concept of quantity"). Both these assertions – assumptions, really – seem to me gratuitous and unconvincing.

It seems to me more plausible on theoretical grounds – and at least as well supported by the empirical evidence – to assume that the use of the clay tokens required from the very beginning the presence of at least amorphous numerical concepts, and that these were then refined and crystallized in the course of further development. Furthermore, the use of the clay tokens in itself seems to suggest the presence, at least in limited form, of a concept of conservation of quantity.[2] Here one has to proceed cautiously, since Damerow does not make it precisely clear to what he is referring when he speaks of "an equivalent to the conservation of quantity." The overall structure of his argument, however, implies a somewhat less demanding way of conceiving this concept than the standard Piagetian definition, which requires that children have attained an invariant abstract notion of number as manifested by the fact that they have grasped the irrelevancy of perceptual-spatial transformations (e.g., length, density). What Damerow seems to have in mind by "an equivalent to the [concept of] conservation of quantity" – at least, this is the only interpretation intelligible to me – is a grasp of the rudimentary elements of the concept of quantity itself, including a recognition of the stability of quantities over time, or when individual items are moved or transferred.

Assuming this is the case, we can follow Damerow on this point somewhat farther than he himself wishes to go. I would suggest that the earliest use of the clay tokens must have involved the presence of a limited concept of quantity and, in the weak sense implied by Damerow, of "the conservation of quantity." Indeed, the use of the clay token scheme by adults in connection with their concrete everyday concerns is incomprehensible otherwise. Granted, this would be what I have called a limited version of the concept of quantity; and what makes it limited (or, one might say, primitive or undeveloped) is indeed that it is so intimately related to the symbolic function. Thus, a clay token stands in a stable way not only for a kind of object but, in particular, for a *single* object of that kind. Hence, it would appear that the unit of quantity that a token represents stands for the (smallest) "natural" unit in which that object exists in the world. The notion of quantity I hypothesize for this stage would therefore involve accepting a natural object as a quantitative "given." (If this is correct, incidentally, it would probably follow that, at least at the beginning of this stage, the clay tokens would represent only discrete but not continuous objects.) But the use of the tokens allows the representation of *collections* of "natural" objects; that seems to be their main point. Representing a multitude of objects is accomplished by accumulating as many symbolic objects as there are "natural" objects to be accounted for; the tokens can retain their value independently of the movement or transferral of the "natural" objects. The fixity of heaps of tokens despite the quantitatively irrelevant changes in the items they represent, and the ability to transfer tokens readily from one heap to another, would indicate the earliest stages of a concept of conservation of quantity.

We can now take another aspect of Damerow's argument one step further. Having stressed the significance for cognitive development of available media of representation, Damerow might have pushed the implications of this view further than he does. For example, I would advance the view that what lies behind the emergence of the first stage, like that of the second, is the discovery of a richer and more powerful medium of representation. In the case of the clay tokens, the crucial impetus is likely to have been the discovery of the possibility of using a symbolic one-to-one correspondence between a miniature object and a "natural" object; on this basis one could create a *set* of miniature objects which could be acted upon to enactively symbolize different arithmetic operations and, in particular, to deal with practical problems concerning quantity. As I have argued above, this does not require assuming that a notion of quantity was only later abstracted out from the repeated applications of the one-to-one correspondence technique. Rather, it seems probable that the appearance of the clay tokens, which marks the beginning of this cultural stage, must have been intended as a solution to practical problems concerning quantity that had already been dimly grasped. The availability of the new medium, however, would have allowed the number concept and the arithmetical operations it can support to become crystallized to an extent that was previously impossible; it would open up a whole new realm of possibilities.

I would like to mention, though, that Piaget's characterization of the development of conservation of quantity in children from repeated applications of one-to-one correspondence might still be an appropriate way to describe *individual* development in, for example, contemporary western culture. I would hasten to add, however, that this pattern of development probably attests to the shaping of the child's thought toward an adult abstract concept of number. Unfortunately, Piaget ignores the mediating concepts drawn from the adult culture – transmitted by parents, teachers, even experimenters – and erroneously interprets all development as epigenetic. But the individual child is not in the position of creating a conceptual world from scratch; the child is not only interacting with its physical environment but is also, in part, attempting to appropriate the conceptual resources of a pre-existing cultural world. In cultural evolution, though, the change one is trying to account for is one of creation and not appropriation of a concept. (See Scribner, 1985 for some discussion of this distinction.) Thus, perhaps paradoxically, in some ways the process of cognitive development emerges in a "purer" form in the context of historical development than in the case of individual development.

Further possible directions. Finally, I would like to suggest – somewhat speculatively – some further directions in which the lines of argument opened up by Damerow might be carried. To return to one of Damerow's central contentions, one phenomenon which consideration of historical development brings out with particular clarity is the impact of different media of representation on cognitive structures. Let me assume for the moment that the reinterpretation of the first stage I have suggested is correct. Building on this, I will now briefly consider how the media utilized in the different stages of numerical representation might have offered different sets of possibilities, and imposed different sets of constraints, on the cognitive structures they helped generate and shape.

In characterizing these stages, Damerow adapts Aebli's distinction between primary and secondary representation (Damerow, 1988, pp. 129–130). The use of clay tokens to represent number and carry out arithmetic operations involves the use of primary representations, which coordinate action and cognition directly. The symbols used accentuate the quantitative aspect of the objects but also retain some minimal qualitative characteristics, since they stand for specific objects in the concrete world. We might say that this schematization of objects helps produce a miniature world, a microcosm, which creates its own space of operation by allowing concrete actions with arithmetic meaning to be performed directly on the symbolic objects. Handling the symbols is easier than handling the natural objects, and its main purpose is to keep track in the microcosm of the changes taking place in the macrocosm (i.e., the "real world").

The fact that this system of representation is tied so closely to the direct symbolic reproduction of "natural" objects has one implication whose potential importance in limiting the development of abstraction is worth considering: namely, that any changes carried out in the distribution or arrangement of the clay tokens would eliminate all record of the previous state. That is, the medium in which these changes were recorded would not promote abstraction from the fleeting and changeable character of concrete quantities, since previous states do not receive the sort of stable representation which would allow for simultaneous reflection on previous states and end-states. Now, addition and subtraction are operations which can potentially be grasped on a relatively concrete level, and which this medium can thus represent tolerably well. Grasping multiplication and division, however, requires to a greater degree the conscious juxtaposition of two temporally separated states, which is made difficult by the limitations of the enactive medium. For this reason, I would expect that the use of the clay tokens enhanced the psychological reality of the operations of addition and subtraction, but did not promote a grasp of multiplication and division beyond a rudimentary level. This possibility is worth looking into.

It is also worth mentioning that the feature of this mode of representation which I have been emphasizing – its weakness in "fixing" or stabilizing different states so that they can be conveniently and precisely compared – is also a crucial feature which distinguishes an oral from a written mode of communication. I suspect that it would be useful to bring Damerow's investigations into connection with the body of work which has examined the cognitive implications of oral cultures and the transforming impact of literacy (e.g., Goody, 1977, 1987).

Some of Goody's suggestions, incidentally, might shed light on the matter of the impressive historical continuity of each of these systems of representation, especially of the one based on the clay tokens. The clay-token system, it will be remembered, remained essentially unchanged for at least five millennia and possibly even longer (see Schmandt-Besserat, 1978, pp. 6–9). Once the system of the archaic texts had emerged, it probably remained relatively stable for about a millennium (this is what I gather from Damerow, 1988, p. 151). The available evidence does not allow us to be very definite about dates, but it does bring out that: (1) the longevity of the archaic-texts system was impressive; but (2) it displayed considerably less stability than the clay-token system; and (3) while the basic system of the archaic texts remained stable over a long period, it did display more internal development in its details than the clay-token system. Goody argues that there is a systematic tendency in oral cultures toward homeostasis (Goody, 1977); if so, then the structural similarity between the clay-token system of representation and oral communication might make its tendency toward continuity part of this more general tendency. At least, this parallelism might suggest some clues toward an explanation. At the same time, of course, this factor would at most be one among many. We would also need to reconstruct, for example, the socio-political role that the practices involving the use of each medium might have had, and the position and interests of the strata who used and controlled it (considerations which, by the way, are also stressed by Goody, 1986, and which would in addition lead us back to more fundamental arguments such as those of Weber, 1978). But at the moment these speculations suggest primarily what we don't know – and need to investigate – more than they outline the specific lines our inquiries ought to follow.

Despite the rather glacial pace of change, however, the historical story remains one of development as well as stability, and the key issues raised by Damerow concern how we should understand this process of development. Here, as the whole line of discussion in this article has implied, the challenge is to grasp the connection between two different but, presumably, interconnected phenomena: the cognitive changes generated by a *change* in the medium of representation; and the cognitive changes we might expect to emerge over time from the *use* of a given medium. Let us begin with the second issue.

I argued above against Damerow's suggestion that the key cognitive advance produced by the use of the clay tokens would have been the emergence of a concept "equivalent" to that of conservation of quantity. In doing so, however, I did not mean to call into question the most general point, that the use of the medium over a long period of time might well have generated some pressure for cognitive advance, particularly advance in capacity for abstraction. This strikes me as plausible. The question is what *kind* of cognitive advance was involved. Aside from the specific objections I raised against Damerow's formulation, I proposed – and would like to stress again here – a more general interpretive guideline: The kind of cognitive change I would expect us to discover within this stage is likely to involve, not the attainment of genuinely new concepts, but rather the refinement and crystallization of concept already present in an amorphous state. Or, to restate this point in more general terms, within a larger framework: Each numerical "stage," as we have seen, is defined by its specific system of numerical representation, which in turn is tied to a specific medium of representation. I would propose that, once a given stage is initiated by the invention of a new medium of representation, the development of cognitive structures *within* that stage is likely to be largely "continuous"; it would involve, to a considerable degree, bringing out the structural possibilities already inherent in the medium. However, *dis*continuity in cognitive structures, involving for example the attainment of genuinely new concepts, would require the impact of an external disruption, most crucially a change in the medium of representation (see Luria, 1977, for an analogous discussion at the individual level).

At the same time, the more "continuous" developments within a given stage would be required to prepare the way for the more dicontinuous breaks associated with the emergence of a new medium of representation. Let me suggest one way in which this might be the case with the Babylonian numerical systems.

In my tentative characterization of the clay-token stage, I concluded that it probably involved a gradual refinement and crystallization of the amorphous concept of quantity which was originally present. This tendency would go along, in a mutually-reinforcing way, with an effort to encompass a greater variety of situations under the different arithmetic operations. This effort seems to have included the extension of the token-representation technique to more objects of economic life (e.g., Schmandt-Besserat, 1978). Thus far, what seems to be involved is largely the quantitative extension of an existing technique; however, there is some reason to think that it could have involved qualitative differentiation as well. I say this on the basis of the situation reported by Goody (1977) among the LoDagaa in northern Ghana. They used different procedures for counting different kinds of objects; in particular, they grouped different objects into sets of different sizes, and found it amusing when he attempted to count them laboriously one by one. Thus, it is possible that extensive use of the one-to-one correspondence technique in ancient Sumeria could also have given rise to a tendency to go beyond the "natural" unit of a given object and to group objects into multiple units. Nevertheless, such a movement would mean only a limited degree of abstraction, since grouping operations of this sort are not context- and content-independent. And a new medium of representation was required before these operations could be expressed in the representational system.

The emergence of the archaic texts involved an enormous advance in the complexity and flexibility of the system of numerical representation. One important change was the appearance of higher-order signs, which were, of course, absent from the clay-token system. The bases of the different higher-valued signs appear arbitrary to us at this stage of research. It is possible, however, that they express the different counting procedures which had begun to develop during the clay-token stage for dealing with different kinds of objects. This might explain the complicated base variations that we encounter between and within the different number sign systems. If so, this would accord with the general approach I outlined above for interpreting the cognitive structure of the first stage. If the notion of quantity was originally tied directly to concrete natural objects, so that the "natural" unit was the original "base" for the system, then the next level of generality would involve grouping the objects in ways which were still closely tied to contexts of practical activity. What would develop during the first stage would be an increasing cognitive need, so to speak, for a representational system which could embody such groupings. (This might, of course, involve not only a "learning" process induced by the use of the numerical system itself but also new requirements generated by changes in the economy and social structure, etc.) However, a change in the medium of representation was required for the breakthrough to the new system. The new system was thus at an intermediate level of generality: more abstracted from the "natural" unit than the clay-token system; but not *entirely* free from it since it was still closely tied to the concrete objects and their use, though at a more inclusive level.

The new system was, however, not only more cognitively powerful but also potentially more dynamic – remembering, of course, that we are still talking in relative terms. In part, this was due to the shift, in the terminology of Aebli and Damerow, to a system of secondary representations, which coordinate action and cognition indirectly, thus allowing a considerable increase in abstraction. In addition, another crucial implication of the introduction of writing, and of the archaic-text system in particular, was that it was now possible to stabilize the records of quantities at different times and to represent the physical and economic events affecting them. I have already indicated why changes of this sort should have had an impact on arithmetic understanding. Furthermore, the possibility of representing and comparing the sequential end-states produced by quantitative changes should have made the *processes* involved in arithmetic operations more visible; and this, in turn, would at least have facilitated the effort to reflect on these operations as recurrent processes, and to formalize the rules implicit in them. The ability to formalize transformation rules and to consider them explicitly is, of course, the first step toward thinking about deliberately changing them. At the moment, however, arguments about the tendencies of cognitive development during the archaic-texts stage are necessarily speculative; the refinement of our own questions will depend on the information produced by the further examination of the texts themselves.

In closing, it is worth underlining Damerow's assertion that historical studies of cognitive structures are necessary for developmental psychology to evaluate its different theories. This is the case because developmental psychology attempts to explain change, which requires a perspective that embraces both individual and historical development. If we limit ourselves to studying individual development, we can never convincingly capture the way in which the endpoints of individual development are not universal but culturally shaped, a fact that historical studies bring immediately into proper focus. In this respect, Damerow's work extends Vygotsky's use of ethnopsychological studies and quite

224   *Ageliki Nicolopoulou*

successfully makes the development of cognitive structures its proper object of study. This framework highlights, by contrast, the limitations of work which restricts itself to studying only individual development. Arguments that focus on the individual's cognitive development need to be effectively integrated with those that deal with issues arising at the level of historical change. Damerow and his associates have made a noble effort to expand the horizons of psychological research and to demonstrate the indispensability of a comparative and historical approach in conducting psychological inquires.

Notes

1. Piaget borrows this term from biology, where it indicates the emergence of structure from the interaction between the organism and its environment, as opposed to the notion of an entirely preformed inherited structure.
2. My suggestions here grow out of a larger argument which is too complex to pursue in detail in this article. Theories of cognitive development often tend to assume, explicitly or implicitly, that the development of cognition follows a sort of building-block model, in which each block is added on to the one before. Thus, development seems to involve the gradual *accumulation* of different cognitive capacities. This theoretical imagery seems to me quite misleading; among other things, it obscures the fact that, as Piaget has consistently emphasized, a cognitive structure always involves an integrated *system* of cognitive relations. This suggests that, rather than emerging out of nowhere, a cognitive capacity is initially present in amorphous form and then has to be crystallized and refined through (learning and) development. But, though the logic of Piaget's position points beyond the building-block approach, he himself has not always or entirely shaken it off (and this holds even more true for many of his followers). This is, in part, because he stresses the necessarily systemic nature of a cognitive capacity once it has been *attained*; but he does not always treat the process of its attainment as involving a developing systemic structure. In this context, we should be more consistently Piagetian than Piaget. (I have been trying to work out this argument in a more comprehensive way, beginning with my dissertation; see, e.g., Nicolopoulou, 1984.) In dealing with the problem of cultural mediation, on the other hand, we need to go beyond Piaget.

References

Adams, R. McC. (1981). *Heartland of cities*. Chicago: University of Chicago Press.
Bakhurst, D. (1988). *E. V. Ilyenkov and contemporary Soviet philosophy*. Unpublished doctoral dissertation, Oxford University.
Damerow, P. (1988). Individual development and cultural evolution of arithmetical thinking. In S. Strauss (Ed.), *Ontogeny, phylogeny, and historical development* (pp. 125–152). Norwood, NJ: Ablex.

Damerow, P., & Englund, R. K. (1986). Die Zahlzeichensysteme der Archaischen Texte aus Uruk. In M. W. Green & H. J. Nissen (Eds.), *Zeichenliste der Archaische Texte aus Uruk* (pp. 117–170). Berlin: Mann.

Englund, R. K. (in press). Administrative timekeeping in ancient Mesopotamia. *Journal of Economic and Social History of the Orient.*

Goody, J. (1977). *The domestication of the savage mind.* Cambridge: Cambridge University Press.

Goody, J. (1986). *The logic of writing and the organization of society.* Cambridge: Cambridge University Press.

Goody, J. (1987). *The interface between the written and the oral.* Cambridge: Cambridge University Press.

Luria, A. R. (1977). The development of writing in the child. *Soviet Psychology, 16,* 65–114.

Nicolopoulou, A. (1984). *Young children's development of similarity and difference relations and their implications for the origins of negation.* Unpublished doctoral dissertation, University of California, Berkeley.

Nissen, H. J. (1985). The emergence of writing in the ancient Near East. *Interdisciplinary Science Reviews, 10,* 349–361.

Nissen, H. J. (1986). The archaic texts from Uruk. *World Archaeology, 17*(3), 317–334.

Piaget, J. (1971). *Biology and knowledge: An essay on the relations between organic regulations and cognitive processes.* Chicago: University of Chicago Press.

Piaget, J. (1972). *The principles of genetic epistemology.* New York: Basic Books.

Piaget, J., & Szeminska, A. (1965). *The child's conception of number.* New York: Norton.

Schmandt-Besserat, D. (1978). The earliest precursor of writing. *Scientific American, 238,* 38–47.

Schmandt-Besserat, D. (1982). How writing came about. *Zeitschrift für Papyrologie und Epigraphik, 47,* 1–5.

Schmandt-Besserat, D. (1983). Tokens and counting. *Biblical Archaeologist, 46,* 117–120.

Scribner, S. (1985). Vygotsky's uses of history. In J. V. Wertsch (Ed.), *Culture, communication, and cognition: Vygotskian perspectives* (pp. 119–145). Cambridge: Cambridge University Press.

Vygotsky, L. S. (1978). *Mind in society: The development of higher mental processes.* Cambridge, MA: Harvard University Press.

Vygotsky, L. S. (1981). The genesis of higher mental functions. In J. V. Wertsch (Ed.), *The concept of activity in Soviet psychology* (pp. 144–188). Armonk, NY: M. E. Sharpe.

Weber, M. (1978). *Economy and society: An outline of interpretive sociology.* Berkeley, CA: University of California Press.

Wertsch, J. V. (1985). *Vygotsky and the social formation of mind.* Cambridge, MA: Harvard University Press.

16   Collective memory: Issues from a sociohistorical perspective

James Wertsch

When we speak of collective memory, the term "collective" often indexes the notion that two or more people are involved. For psychologists, this typically means that the concern is with how groups function as integrated memory systems. Examining this type of social or collective activity (what I shall term here "interpsychological" functioning) has produced a variety of interesting insights such as those outlined in this issue of the *Newsletter* [vol. 9, No. 1], and it has motivated much of my own writing (cf. Wertsch, 1985). However, I have recently become increasingly concerned with another sense in which mental functions such as memory can be collective or social. This sense of collectivity has to do with the fact that these mental functions are mediated by sociohistorically evolved (i.e., collective) tools or instruments.

As is the case with my research on interpsychological functioning, my concern here is rooted in the ideas developed by Vygotsky, Luria, Leont'ev, and other figures of what has been termed the sociohistorical perspective (cf. Smirnov, 1975) in the USSR. From this perspective, the two types of collectivity that I have outlined are by no means separate. This is reflected in Leont'ev's 1981 summary of Vygotsky's ideas on the relationship between mediational means or instruments that are collectively generated and maintained and the interpsychological plane of functioning.

Vygotsky identified two main, interconnected features (of activity) that are necessarily fundamental for psychology; its tool-like ["instrumental"] structure, and its inclusion in a system of interrelations with other people. It is these features that define the nature of human psychological processes. The tool mediates activity and thus connects humans

226

not only with the world of objects but also with other people. Because of this, humans' activity *assimilates the experience of humankind*. This means that humans' mental processes [their "higher psychological functions"] acquire a structure necessarily tied to the sociohistorically formed means and methods transmitted to them by others in the process of cooperative labor and social interaction. But it is impossible to transmit the means and methods needed to carry out a process in any way other than in external form – in the form of an action or external speech. In other words, higher psychological processes unique to humans can be acquired only through interaction with others, that is, through *interpsychological* processes that only later will begin to be carried out independently by the individual. (p. 56)

This review of Vygotsky's ideas is somewhat biased, reflecting Leont'ev's ideas about what a sociohistorical approach to mind should be. For example, instead of focusing on the concrete dynamics of interpsychological functioning as Vygotsky did (e.g., in the latter's account of the zone of proximal development), Leont'ev tended to view interpsychological functioning almost as an accidental fact about the way that it is possible to transmit "means and methods" needed to carry out a process. And when considering these means, especially language, he tended to overlook the ingenious semiotic analyses that were central to Vygotsky's approach. Instead, he approached these means primarily from the perspective of the more general problem of how it is possible to "assimilate the experience of humankind." This treatment of these issues reflects Leont'ev's general concern with formulating the foundations for a theory of activity in Soviet psychology, a formulation that was grounded in Marx's ideas about subject–object interaction as laid out in the *Theses on Feuerbach*.

The debate over whether Leont'ev's work represents a legitimate extension or a misappropriation of Vygotsky's work has been going on for several years now (cf. Davydov & Radzikhovkii, 1985; Kozulin, 1984; Minick, 1986). It is my opinion that Leont'ev did not understand, or at least did not incorporate into his own approach, many of Vygotsky's most powerful insights about semiotic mediation and interpsychological functioning. However, as I have argued elsewhere (Wertsch, 1985, ch. 7), I also believe that Vygotsky's approach can be extended in important respects by incorporating some of Leont'ev's ideas into it. In particular, I think that Leont'ev's account of activity can provide a mechanism for extending Vygotsky's account of the social beyond the interpsychological plane. It seems that Vygotsky was beginning to recognize the need to do this late in his life (cf. Minick, in press), but he did not produce a complete account of how individual ("intrapsychological") and interpsychological planes of functioning are tied to social institutional processes. It is only by developing such an account that the Vygotskian approach can become a full-fledged analysis of mind in society instead of mind as it relates to microsociological, interpsychological functioning.

One way to deal with these issues in a concrete way is to focus on the mediational means involved. In his analysis of the tools that mediate human activity, Vygotsky touched on a variety of items, ranging from the relatively simple external artifacts (e.g., tying a knot in a handkerchief to remind oneself of something) to complex aesthetic patterns of inner speech. The tools that I want to consider here fall nearer the inner speech end of the continuum. These tools are in the form of complex verbal texts, in particular, sociohistorically evolved descriptions and explanations of events. For example, a police report of an event would be a text, as would an account provided by the news media.

An essential fact about such texts is that various genres have strict prescriptions for what counts as a good description or explanation. Furthermore, genres typically differ in their prescriptions. Thus certain facts that must appear in police reports of a crime are typically left out of news accounts and vice versa. Many of these differences cannot be accounted for in terms of accuracy or truthfulness; instead, they are differences in what it is appropriate to represent and how it is appropriate to do so. For this reason, the selection of a particular text genre places a variety of constraints on what can be said and how it can be expressed.

The issue of how these and other mediational means are selected is something that Vygotsky did not deal with in any great detail. A first step in any attempt to do so would be to extend his tool analogy to a tool *kit* analogy. By talking about tool kits rather than tools, we are making an important statement about the relationship between psychological processes on the one hand and sociohistorical and cultural forces on the other. The modification in the metaphor means that instead of viewing mediational means as ironclad determiners of these processes, they are seen as providing a set of options that at least in principle allow some choice and some possibility of emancipation from established patterns. Schudson (1986) has dealt with these issues in connection with what he terms an "optimistic" view of culture in which individuals or groups are seen as having some degree of conscious choice in the mediational means they employ when approaching tasks. In contrast, a pessimistic view of culture sees culture as constraining us in fixed, deterministic ways, the consequences of which are that we are not aware of them and hence have little hope of bringing them under our control.

In accordance with the tool kit analogy an individual or group is viewed as approaching a task setting that requires a mental function (e.g., memory) in such a way that several different options are at least in principle available for dealing with it. The existence of a range of choices, however, does not mean the task is represented and solved. It is in connection with the evolution of these instruments as well as in connection with the forces that shape their use that we need to go beyond the individual or small group and examine sociohistorical and cultural forces.

The example I shall use to illustrate this point is usually considered to involve some type of reasoning or self-reflection rather than memory, but as I hope to demonstrate, in the end it can also tell us something important about collective memory, in at least one of its senses. My argument is generally concerned with a finding that has emerged repeatedly over the past few decades in psychology and other social sciences. This finding is that subjects in fact often have access to more than one tool or mediational means (e.g., strategy) for responding to a task, but they tend to have a very strong tendency to approach the task as if only one of the tools is relevant. Instead of focusing on whether or not subjects "have" capacities, concepts, or abilities of some sort, this finding has led researchers to focus on the notion that factors of context, habit, or some other type encourage subjects to privilege the use of one tool over others. Findings from research as diverse as that of Bellah, Madsen, Sullivan, Swidler, and Tipton (1985); Cole, Gay, Glick, and Sharp (1971); Gilligan (1982); and Luria (1976) are consistent with this general observation. In all cases these results have led investigators to note that people privilege the use of one mediational means over others and ask how this process shapes the way these subjects can represent and solve a task.

The particular example of privileging mediational means that I shall examine here comes from the research of Bellah et al. (1985). These authors have examined various ways in which contemporary Americans think and talk about individualism and commitment. A fundamental construct that they employ to make their case is that of "language." In this connection they state:

We do not use *language* in this book to mean primarily what the linguist studies. We use the term to refer to modes of moral discourse that include distinct vocabularies and characteristic patterns of moral reasoning. We use *first language* to refer to the individualistic mode that is the dominant American form of discourse about moral, social, and political matters. We use the term *second language* to refer to other forms, primarily biblical and republican, that provide at least part of the moral discourse of most Americans. (p. 334)

What Bellah et al. call language is what I have above called text, and the various languages to which we have access may be thought of as tools in a kit of mediational means. Hence Americans generally have access to more than one language when they describe and explain their own and others' patterns of thought and behavior.

Although Bellah et al. do not go into detail in the mediational role of languages, they assume that when a speaker begins to speak in one language as opposed to another there are powerful constraints on what that speaker can think and say. This is reflected in statements such as, "Given this individualistic moral framework, the self becomes a crucial site for the comparative examination and probing of feelings that result from ultilitarian acts and inspire expressive ones" (p. 78). Thus, implicit in their view is the claim that speakers shape the situation by choosing a language, but they are in turn shaped in what they can say by this choice. Of course this does not mean that a speaker is permanently frozen into a particular text or "mode of moral discourse" – after all, he or she has access to other languages and hence other patterns of thought and speech.

Without even touching on the vast majority of issues raised by Bellah et al. I would like to outline a few general implications that their arguments have for collectively organized mediational means in general and for collective memory in particular. The first of these is that the languages they mention are part and parcel of a sociohistorical and cultural system; there is no sense in which they are appropriate, powerful, useful, and so forth in an absolute, universal, or ahistorical way. In different societies today and during different periods of American history the languages, or at least what serves as a first language, could be quite different. Hence, what is available in particular people's tool kits depends in a central way on their sociohistorical and cultural situation.

Furthermore, Bellah et al. do not really address this issue; there are probably important differences in when and where members of a particular culture choose to use one as opposed to another of the languages to which they have access. That is, given that contemporary Americans have access to several different languages, how do they know which one to use on particular occasions? To say that one of these languages serves as a first language implies that there is a predisposition within the individual in all situations to use one language over others. However, there are obviously powerful contextual constraints that these and other authors have not yet explored which influence the choice of language. Just as sociohistorical and cultural background shape the languages available to someone, they presumably influence the nature of the situations that call for their use.

With regard to memory, the languages that groups speak can be expected to have a profound impact on how they go about remembering something and hence what it is that they remember. Bellah et al. deal with this issue in their account of "communities of memory." They point out that because a community of the sort that interests them is in an important sense constituted by the history it shares, it must constantly retell its story, "its constitutive narrative" (p. 153). But as should be clear by now, the way in which this story is told is shaped by the language the members of the community speak. Furthermore, this story will be shaped on particular occasions by speakers' selection from among the various languages available to them. For example, instead of recounting a community's history by using the language of individualism, a speaker may use a language of communal commitment to create a nostalgic version of better times. Again, choice of mediational means to a great extent shapes what can and cannot be thought and said, or in this case, remembered.

In the end, we need to combine the analysis of collectively organized mediational means with the analysis of interpsychological functioning. In this connection, several issues arise. For example, if choice of mediational means is a major determinant of how thinking and speaking can proceed, then processes whereby groups make decisions (either implicitly or explicitly) about these means should become a focus of our research. In many instances, the negotiation or imposition of this decision may have more to do with group performance than anything else.

Making statements and suggestions such as these means above all that the study of memory or any other mental function must begin to incor-

232 *James Wertsch*

porate findings and methods from a variety of approaches and disciplines. If we are to take the study of memory, thinking, attention, or any other aspect of human consciousness seriously, we must begin by recognizing the sociohistorical and cultural embeddedness of the subjects as well as investigators involved.

References

Bellah, R. N., Madsen, R., Sullivan, W. M., Swidler, A., & Tipton, S. M. (1985). *Habits of the heart: Individualism and commitment in American life.* New York: Harper & Row.

Cole, M., Gay, J., Glick, J. A., & Sharp, D. A. (1971). *The cultural context of learning and thinking.* New York: Basic Books.

Davydov, V. V., & Radzikhovaskii, L. A. (1985). Vygotsky's theory and the activity-oriented approach to psychology. In J. V. Wertsch (Ed.), *Culture, communication, and cognition: Vygotskian perspectives.* New York: Cambridge University Press.

Gilligan, C. (1982). *In a different voice: Psychological theory and women's development.* Cambridge, MA: Harvard University Press.

Kozulin, A. (1984). *Psychology in Utopia: Toward a social history of Soviet psychology.* Cambridge, MA: MIT Press.

Leont'ev, A. N. (1981). The problem of activity in psychology. In J. V. Wertsch (Ed.), *The concept of activity in Soviet psychology.* Armonk, NY: M. E. Sharpe.

Luria, A. R. (1976). *Cognitive development: Its cultural and social foundations.* Cambridge, MA: Harvard University Press.

Minick, N. (1986, October). *Mind and activity in the theories of the Vygotskian tradition.* Paper presented at the First International Congress on the Theory of Activity, West Berlin.

Minick, N. (in press). Introduction to L. S. Vygotsky. *Thinking and speech.* (N. Minick, Trans.) New York: Plenum Press.

Schudson, M. (1986). *How culture works: Information and reminder in social life.* Unpublished paper, Department of Communication, University of California, San Diego.

Smirnov, A. N. (1975). *Razvitie i sovrememmoe sostoyanie psikhologicheskoi nauki v SSSR* [The development and present status of psychology in the USSR]. Moscow: Izdatel'stvo Pedagogika.

Wertsch, J. V. (1985). *Vygotsky and the social formation of mind.* Cambridge, MA: Harvard University Press.

Classroom settings

17 Students' interactional competence in the classroom

Hugh Mehan

Courtney B. Cazden, a noted authority on child language and education (see, for example, Cazden, Brown, and Bellugi, 1969; Cazden, 1972), took leave from the Harvard Graduate School of Education to spend the 1974–75 academic year in her previous career as an elementary school teacher. She taught in a cross-age, ethnically mixed classroom at the Emerson School of the San Diego Unified School District. There was an equal number of Black and Mexican American students in her combined first-second-third grade classroom. Cazden assumed full teaching responsibilities. She designed curricula, conducted lessons, evaluated students, met with parents, and attended faculty meetings. In January, 1975, she was joined by LaDonna Coles as a team teacher.

Cazden's decision to experience once again the "real world of teaching" provided her with invaluable personal insight (Cazden, 1976). It also provided us with the opportunity to use her classroom as a field laboratory to examine the structure of classroom interaction and the social organization of classroom instruction.

Database and topics for analysis

We are using videotape as a data-gathering device in our study of classroom interaction. Two different batches of data lend themselves to different topics of analysis. One set of tapes, gathered in the Fall and Winter, focuses on teacher-centered classroom activities. The other set, gathered in the Spring of the year, concentrates on student-centered activities.

235

Teacher-centered activities

We videotaped the first hour of classroom activities each day of the first week of school and that same hour approximately every third week thereafter. That data-collection schedule produced a corpus of nine teacher-directed academic lessons.

We are comparing teacher–student interaction across these nine tapes to examine a number of topics, including: (1) the interactional activities of teachers and students that assemble classroom lessons as sequentially organized events; (2) the often-unstated normative procedures which sustain interaction during lessons; and (3) the skills and abilities that students must use in order to be competent participants in classroom lessons.

1. The sequential organization of lessons.   We have described classroom lessons as a series of "topically relevant sets of instructional sequences" (Mehan et al., 1976a). The teacher elicits information from the students, provides them with information, and directs them to take procedural action in a series of sequences that are topically related.

Co-occurrence relationships govern the organization of classroom lessons such that particular replies are demanded by particular Initiation acts. Once a speech act has been initiated, interaction continues until a symmetry between Initiation and Reply acts is obtained. If the presuppositions of the Initiation act are realized in the next turn of talk, the result is a three-part, teacher–student "exchange." The first part of the exchange is the Initiation act, the second part is the Reply act, and the third part is an Evaluation act, which comments on the completion of the Initiation act. If the presuppositions of the Initiation act are not immediately realized, the teacher employs one of a number of interactional strategies (including prompting incorrect or incomplete replies, repeating or simplifying the initial Initiation act) until the presuppositions are realized. The result is an "extended sequence" of interaction, the end of which is marked by the positive evaluation of the appropriate reply. Teachers and students progress through these ordered sets of sequences from the beginnings of lessons to their conclusions.

2. The normative order of classroom lessons.   We have found it heuristic to treat the classroom as a small society or community. As in other communities, preferred patterns of activities prescribed for members of the classroom community are guided by rules or norms.

The normative order to classroom lessons includes a set of procedures for allocating turns and gaining access to the floor. Each speech act initiated by the teacher during classroom lessons not only specifies the kind of action to be taken; it also specifies who is to take the action. The "Individual Nomination" procedure prescribes that the speaker identified by name is the next speaker. The "Invitation to Bid" procedure also indicates that one speaker speaks at a time, but requires that speakers first bid for and be awarded the floor. The "Invitation to Reply" procedure allows many speakers to reply without first bidding for the floor.

Thus, while access to the floor is governed by rules, the rules prescribe different behavior. There are occasions when pupils can reply directly and others when they must first receive permission to reply. There are occasions when one rule rather than another operates. This variation occurs from exchange to exchange within a lesson, between phases of a lesson, and across lessons.

3. Students' competence in teacher-directed lessons. Our research, like other research on the social organization of the classroom (Shultz, 1976; Hall, 1974; Shuy and Griffin, 1975), is showing that the academic dimensions of classroom instruction are embedded in an interactional nexus. To be competent members of the classroom community, students must not only master academic subject matter; they must also learn the normative demands of classrooms.

Although the teacher's practical concern is for classroom order, the rules governing this normative order are not communicated directly to students. Because the rules governing turn-taking are tacit, students must infer the appropriate way to engage in classroom interaction from contextually provided information. To be competent members of the classroom community, students must be able to interpret implicit classroom rules and provide the proper action on the right occasion. They must know which classroom rule is in effect at a given time, and know which behavior is demanded by each rule.

The students' primary responsibility in these lessons was to reply correctly and appropriately when called upon, although as the year progressed the students found seams in the fabric of this predominantly teacher-directed activity. As the teacher turned to write on the chalk-board, pin information to a map, or consult learning materials in her lap, the students inserted their own information into the conversation, and then ceased talking as the teacher turned toward the class again. Although the Individual Nomination and Invitation to Bid turn-taking procedures specified that only speakers identified by name were to reply in the next turn of talk, the students found other conversational "slots" for their replies on certain occasions. Students who were not specifically allocated the floor inserted replies when the teacher had difficulty obtaining correct information from a series of nominated students. They also began to insert information after a nominated student replied, but before the teacher reclaimed the floor to evaluate a reply, or to begin a new sequence of initiations.

The ability of these students to find appropriate ways to contribute their interests to teacher-directed activities developed over the year. It demonstrates an aspect of the interactional competence required to negotiate the normative aspects of the classroom. Being a competent member of the classroom involves learning when and with whom and in what ways to talk, and knowing the right times and places to act in certain ways.

Student-centered activities

The competent student.   Our interest in students' interactional compe-tence suggested that we examine students in a variety of classroom sit-uations. Therefore, when we obtained a wireless microphone in the spring of the year, we videotaped a different student for the first hour of each school day. During this time, the students worked alone or in small groups on a classroom activity of their own choice ("choosing time"), as they were involved in whole-class procedural and academic activities ("circle on the rug"), and as they worked in small groups on a classroom activity of the teacher's choice ("lessons"). This data-collection procedure gives us a continuous "hour in the life" of each student in a student-centered academic activity, a teacher-directed aca-demic/procedural activity, and a teacher-directed academic activity.

These hour-in-the-life tapes are enabling us to compare students' displays of interactional competence when they are with peers and when they are with adults. The procedure is revealing the seldom-seen student perspective on classroom activities and contributions to classroom organization.

As we study classroom interaction from the student's perspective, we are finding that the alignment of behavior and situation is a significant skill in the repertoire of the "competent student." It appears that the raw number of appropriate and inappropriate behavior does not vary across students in the classroom. But those students whom the teacher independently rates as "good students" are those who are able to keep their appropriate behavior in the eyes of the teacher, and their inappropriate behavior out of sight. The students who are not rated as "good students" have not made that distinction. They indiscriminantly perform inappropriate action both in the teacher's gaze and out of it.

This phase of our analysis is showing how teachers and students cooperatively accomplish classroom events like a "lesson" or a "circle on the rug." During the course of classroom activities, teachers and students mutually influence one another, and thereby jointly contribute to the social organization of the classroom. Indeed, students are structured and modified by adults in the classroom. But equally importantly, students modify the behavior of adults just as much as they are socially structured and modified by them (Mehan et al., 1976c).

The instruction chain. When Cazden was joined by Coles as a team teacher in January, they set up a number of learning centers. This new classroom arrangement also enabled us to introduce more controlled observational techniques into our study.

We constructed an "instruction chain" between teacher, the student with the microphone for the day, and that student's work group as a natural part of the morning activity. The teacher provided a set of instructions about an academic task to the "target student." After the teacher listened to that student formulate the instructions, the student gave instructions to her/his work group. The students in the group then worked on the assigned task.

This instruction chain enables us to compare the teacher's formulation of instructions to the target student with the target student's formulation of the instructions to the teacher and to the work group. Our analysis of these materials (Mehan et al., 1976b) is revealing important differences between teacher-to-student and student-to-student instructional styles.

The formulation of instructions to work groups by target students appears to be less elaborate than the teacher's. While the teacher relied primarily on words to provide instructions, the target students employed both verbal and nonverbal modalities to accomplish these same instructional functions.

Although the target students did not duplicate adult modes of instruction, the reduction in oral information does not imply a limitation in students' competence. The students provided functionally equivalent instructions when they coded information in other modalities. There is a potential implication for classroom instruction if we continue to find that the use of nonverbal modalities are functional for instruction. Such findings recommend a de-emphasis on predominantly oral modes and an emphasis on "modeled" and "demonstrated" instructions.

References

Cazden, C. B., Brown, R., & Bellugi, U. 1969. The Child's Grammar from I to III. In: J. P. Hill (Ed.), *1967 Symposium on Child Development*, pp. 28–72. Minneapolis: University of Minnesota Press.

Cazden, C. B. 1972. *Child Language and Education*. New York: Holt, Rinehart and Winston.

——— 1976. How Knowledge About Language Helps the Classroom Teacher, Or Does It: A Personal Account. Invited Address, AERA Convention, San Francisco, California.

Hall, W. S. 1974. A Proposal to Study Ethnic Group and Social Class Differences in the Uses and Functions of Language. The Rockefeller University.

Mehan, H., et al. 1976a. The Social Organization of Classroom Lessons. Final Technical Report to The Ford Foundation (Grant 740–0420).

——— 1976b. Students' Formulating Practices and Instructional Strategies. *Annals of The New York Academy of Sciences*. Forthcoming.

——— 1976c. Research Towards a Mutually Constitutive View of Socialization. Paper presented at AERA Convention, San Francisco, California.

Schultz, J. 1976. It's Not Whether You Win or Lose, It's How You Play the Game. Working Paper #2, Newton Classroom Interaction Project, Harvard Graduate School of Education.

Shuy, R., & Griffin, P. 1975. A proposal to study children's functional language and education in the early years. Center for Applied Linguistics, Arlington, Virginia (unpublished).

18   The competence/incompetence paradox in the education of minority culture children

Ronald Gallimore and Kathryn Hu-Pei Au

A paradox is evident in many efforts to improve the educational opportunities available to minority culture children. While the children appear well-adjusted and entirely competent in their home environments, they often exhibit inappropriate behavior in the classroom and are slow to learn academic skills and content. It has occurred to some researchers and educators involved in the development of curricula for these children that their performance in school could be greatly improved if the abilities shown in the home environment could somehow be transferred to the classroom. In practice, this effort has proved more difficult than might be supposed.

The purpose of this paper is to address the problem of the home competence/school incompetence paradox as it applies to minority culture children. While this discussion will be based on our experiences in working with Hawaiian children at the Kamehameha Early Education Program (KEEP) in urban and rural Oahu, we believe this research suggests ways in which the educational achievement of other minority culture groups might also be improved.

The KEEP reading program

KEEP was begun in 1971 to solve through research and development the problem of teaching Hawaiian children who are educationally at risk to read at or above average levels (Tharp & Gallimore, in press). The conditions under which this effort was conducted must be considered nearly optimal: funding was stable, researchers had full

241

control over the operations of a research and demonstration school, and professionals and scientists from a variety of disciplines (psychology, education, anthropology, and linguistics) participated. Still, the initial outcome was discouraging; during the first $2^1/_2$ years, students in the KEEP research school read no better at the end of first grade than public school counterparts who generally score at the second stanine on standardized tests.

Beginning in 1976 and continuing through Spring 1978, a new reading program was employed; in its current form this curriculum is known as the Kamehameha Reading Objective System (KROS; Crowell, 1978; Tharp, in preparation).

Administrations of standardized reading tests indicated improved performance for the KEEP children taught with KROS while there was essentially no change in the scores of comparable public school controls during the same period. Indeed, the KEEP students on average read near the national norm for their respective grade levels (Gallimore, Tharp, & Sloat, in preparation [a]).

Quite naturally, a number of different explanations for the success of the KEEP reading program have been suggested. We will argue that the KEEP reading program or KROS is successful, in part, because it resolves the competence/incompetence paradox by encouraging the more consistent application of cognitive strategies already in the children's repertoire.

Cognitive strategies and the school performance of minority culture children

Brown suggests it is well established that early in their school careers, disadvantaged children have "difficulty generating aids, mnemonics, research strategies, etc., to enhance deliberate learning" (in press, ms. p. 92). Without these cognitive strategies a child is greatly handicapped in the ordinary classroom where tasks are presented in the absence of a meaningful framework; this is sometimes called a decontextualized instructional style. If children are accustomed in the home environment to using cognitive strategies for which there are external cues, they may not be prepared to generate and selectively apply internally mediated aids. There are numerous examples of external aids. but for young children many are likely to be embedded in situations in which they interact with adult socialization agents (Wertsch, 1978).

There seems to be general agreement that children and adults who employ self-generated cognitive strategies perform better on school-type tasks than those who do not. Presumably because of the greater continuity between home and school, middle-class children are much more likely to use "school-efficient" internally mediated cognitive strategies than culturally and socially disadvantaged children (Brown, in press). The ready use of these strategies allows for more rapid adaptation to the school's learning style in which content is likely to be unrelated to daily life and initially meaningless to the child.

If the failure to use self-generated cognitive strategies accounts for the poor school performance of disadvantaged minority culture children, then it is important to specify exactly how they are involved. Some researchers have assumed that disadvantaged children lack certain school-relevant cognitive strategies. According to this "cognitive deficit" hypothesis, we would expect to find uniformly low performance on all school-type tasks requiring the use of cognitive strategies.

The results obtained at KEEP, however, do not fit the pattern predicted by this assumption. We can summarize the KEEP results by stating that we do not observe uniformly low performance on all school-type tasks; what we see instead is a widespread *inconsistency* in performance across tasks and settings. This finding of inconsistency suggests that the children possess many of the same cognitive strategies as more school-successful middle-class children; the reason their school performance is so much poorer is that they apply the cognitive strategies much less consistently than their middle-class peers.

We further speculate that inconsistent application results from discontinuities between the school and home environments. A middle-class child is more likely to identify correctly the type of cognitive strategy called for in a given school task because of the similarity of elements, e.g., task and process variables, to those in the home. Greater differences between the school and home contexts for disadvantaged children make it much less likely that they will recognize the task as one which calls for the use of a certain cognitive strategy, although that same strategy might be readily used in home situations.

In short, we argue not only that cognitive strategies are implicated in the success of the KROS reading program, but also that the program specifically encourages more consistent use of classroom-useful cognitive strategies. In some cases these strategies may be developed through the KROS program, but the program also appears to function to make explicit to the children which cognitive strategies are required in particular situations.

Our argument is supported by data from (1) standardized testing, (2) experiments, and (3) formal and informal observations.

Standardized testing.   During the time that a phonics-emphasis reading program was in effect at KEEP, the children did not learn to read any better than public school comparison groups. Yet during the years of phonics-instruction their scores on general cognitive and verbal ability tests such as the WPPSI and WISC-R were average or better (Gallimore, Tharp, & Sloat, in preparation [b]). After the KROS curriculum was installed, the children achieved rapid and impressive gains on standardized reading tests, relative to controls.

Two points relevant to our thesis will be emphasized here. First, it is evident that the KEEP students do not exhibit uniformly low performance on all school-type tasks; rather, after first grade they perform, as a group, at average levels on standard IQ tests, which incorporate many school-type tasks. Second, the relatively short time – kindergarten and first grade – required for the children to obtain average IQ scores would not allow for the development of basic cognitive strategies, if such capacities were entirely absent to begin with. The new reading program did not remediate deficits in fundamental processes; rather its effects appear to be on variables not tapped by the general ability tests.

Experimental evidence.   Experimental data indicate that adults can easily elicit use of cognitive strategies by KEEP students. In one study, KEEP kindergarteners showed significantly better long term recall of shape names when they were prompted by an experimenter to associate the shape name with a common-place object, e.g., circle-plate; octagon-stop sign, etc. (Gallimore, Lam, Speidel, & Tharp, 1977). Other students learned a labeling strategy which they did not generalize to similar stimuli until given an augmented explicit prompt (Speidel, Hao, & Gallimore, 1976). Finally, a receptive adult can elicit impressive linguistic performances from primary-grade children, performances which reflect substantial cognitive complexity (Watson-Gegeo & Boggs, 1977).

Observational evidence.   Informal observations at the KEEP research school point to the involvement of cognitive strategies in the improved reading performances. These observations suggest that before the KROS curriculum was introduced, KEEP students generally used inefficient and lower-level learning strategies, in particular when faced with the type of episodic tasks which predominated in the previous phonics-oriented reading program. Among the observations were these: (1) when given a slightly new or altered task, KEEP students often failed to use skills/knowledge they had been observed to use on similar tasks; (2) unless directly prompted they usually did not relate personal knowledge and experiences to school tasks; (3) they were likely to adopt a passive rather than active learning role; (4) guessing and other rote learning strategies were frequently observed; and (5) each problem was typically approached as a new and different task rather than as an instance of a class to which an already mastered solution might be applied.

After the new KROS reading curriculum was installed, the learning efficiency of the children appeared much improved. Observations suggest that the children made more use of deliberate strategies for learning; they became active and involved; answers were altered and changed. A child might make a response which was not accepted, and minutes later reintroduce the topic and offer an alternative response. Taken together, these observations suggest that Hawaiian children can be taught more efficient learning or cognitive strategies, an achievement which seems unlikely if generalized deficits were the main problem. In this respect the observations are consistent with previous ethnographic and behavioral studies which indicated that Hawaiian children are competent learners in the home environment (Gallimore, Boggs, & Jordan, 1974; Gallimore & Howard, 1968). Evidently KROS provided a bridging experience which encouraged and taught the children to perform at school at a level consistent with their home performance.

KEEP reading lessons and cognitive training

The KROS differs from the previous phonics program in its curricular emphasis. At present, more attention is given to direct instruction of the understanding of what is read, while previously the focus was on the learning of phoneme-grapheme correspondences, or phonics. The KROS attempts to strike a balance, by directly teaching phonics *and* comprehension simultaneously, an approach which has been recently described as urgently needing a thorough evaluation if progress is to be made in reading theory and practice (Resnick, in press).

What are these small group lessons like? Each KEEP class of 25–30 is divided into from 4 to 6 groups for reading instruction on the basis of criterion-referenced test scores. Within these more or less homogeneous groups of 3 to 8 children, the teacher is able to interact with each child more frequently and to informally assess his or her progress more accurately. Each group meets with the teacher for 20 minutes per day; a fixed amount of daily instruction is thus guaranteed for each child, although additional individual help may be given as time permits. At other work stations, sight vocabulary, language awareness, listening skills, and word attack skills are taught through individualized activities.

The teacher-led lessons are almost always based on a story from the children's basal text and consist primarily of interchanges in which the teacher asks questions which the children are expected to answer, interspersed with segments of silent reading. On first inspection the most impressive feature of these lessons is the constant give and take between teacher and child; the teacher continually asks questions to which the children respond. The types of questions asked by the teacher are intended to develop the children's proficiency in the hierarchy of comprehension skills specified in the reading curriculum (see Crowell, 1978). Upon closer inspection these reading lessons are shown to have a consistent structure. This conclusion is based at present on only a small sample of teachers whose lessons were thought to exemplify the type of instruction desired in the KEEP reading program. The analysis was developed through the study of videotapes of three reading lessons, each taught by a different teacher, one lesson in a first-grade class at KEEP, and two with KEEP second graders (Au, in press).

On the basis of transcripts it was found that each lesson could be divided into topically defined interchanges. For example, the key questions marking the interchanges at the beginning of the first-grade lesson were:

1. Why does this story seem familiar?
2. What does "make music" mean?
3. What do you think Jasper will do to make music?

The topical interchanges fell into three categories: E or experience, T or task, and R or relationship. An E or experience interchange is one in which the teacher has the children discuss experiences or knowledge they have which are related in some way to the story. For example, at the beginning of the first-grade lesson the teacher has the children talk about what the phrase "make music" means to them. After this first section of the lesson, the teacher then has the children read silently short parts of the story, usually a page or two, asking them questions about the content of the story after each section read; these are the *T* sequences. In the final category of interchanges, the *R* interchanges, the teacher attempts to draw relationships for the children between the content of the story discussed in the *T* interchanges and their outside experience and knowledge. Thus the *R* interchanges provide for the integration of information contained in the *E* and *T* interchanges. Examples of *E*, *T*, and *R* interchanges are presented in Au (in press).

The three types of interchanges appear to differ in terms of what is needed to produce an acceptable response; the sources of information and task requirements related to each are different. In *E* interchanges the underlying form of question is, "What information obtained prior to this lesson do you have about the subject of the story?" In *T* interchanges it is, "What is the information given by the text?", whereas in *R* interchanges it is, "What interpretation can be given to this story as a result of combining these two types of information?"

The *E*, *T*, and *R* categories and the set of structural rules for the lessons seem to reflect the teachers' efforts to give the children systematic practice in the application of the cognitive strategies related to understanding a written story. The three teachers are skillful questioners, particularly adept at leading children to the correct answers, rather than telling them the answers directly! This tactic seems to be an important aspect of the lessons. First, answering gives a child practice in producing the right kind of information at the right time. Second, after hearing a child's response, the teacher can determine which steps in the process are easy for each individual and which are more difficult, so that ensuing questions can be adjusted to the proper level.

As children gain more experience, it seems reasonable to expect that they will begin to apply consistently on their own the same cognitive strategies that the teacher encouraged in the reading lessons. It could thus be hypothesized that a child who has interacted frequently with a teacher in these consistently structured lessons would show better reading comprehension than a child who has not had the same experience. In fact, this is what the KEEP reading test results indicate may have happened (Gallimore, Tharp, & Sloat, in preparation [a]; Tharp, in preparation).

For Hawaiian children, who often do not succeed in school, E interchanges may be of particular importance in learning to read, because they can serve as links between the home and school environments. The teacher's use of E interchanges thus signals to children that certain cognitive strategies already in their possession may be relevant in an otherwise unfamiliar school situation, the reading lesson. By beginning the lesson at level of the child's own experiences (E interchanges), the teacher increases the probability that existing cognitive strategies will be applied. When unfamiliar story content is introduced (T interchanges), it is presented within the context of content familiar to the child. Finally, by making explicit to children the relationships between their own knowledge and information in the text (R interchanges), the continued steady application of cognitive strategies throughout the lesson is encouraged.

What strategies does the program affect?

Why did KEEP fail to teach reading to the Hawaiian children before the new program was introduced? Why did motivated, well trained, and dedicated teachers using a solid, dependable curriculum not teach these competent children to read? After all, most children learn to read, and are taught to do so with a wide variety of approaches. It seems safe to assume that one of the commonalities among these highly varied sets of circumstances is that they do not prevent children from learning to read. This notion, it will be seen, is analogous to Scarr-Salapatek's (1976) idea that development is supported by a wide variety of seemingly very different environments; another way to think of the problem is to consider those few circumstances under which it does not proceed apace (Flavell, 1977). This point of view may seem somewhat implausible until we consider the following fact: two long-term research projects obtained convincing evidence that Hawaiian children should learn how to read (Gallimore, Boggs, & Jordan, 1974; Tharp & Gallimore, in press), including experimental, observational, psychometric, and ethnographic data. It may be that we have, in our failure, made an important discovery – we have succeeded in identifying one of the ways to *prevent* Hawaiian children from learning to read. How does the process of prevention work? We might hypothesize, in the case of reading, that it operates by interfering with the naturally developing strategies of the child.

Now we are able to turn to the long-deferred issue of defining more precisely what these strategies are. We hypothesize that the original phonics curriculum interfered with the application and natural development of *top-down processing strategies* through an overemphasis on *bottom-up processing strategies*. Top-down processing begins with already existing language and knowledge; bottom-up processing begins with recognition of letters and words and proceeds to comprehension; sometimes this distinction has been described as episodic versus semantic learning or processing.

In the mind of the competent reader, bottom-up and top-down processing occur simultaneously. Information continually flows from top to bottom and from bottom to top so that the results of analysis at any level may serve to facilitate further analysis at every other level (Adams, in press; Rumelhart, 1976). Too heavy reliance on top-down processing will mean existing knowledge and understanding may obscure the content of the text so the reader fails to comprehend the author's message and ignores visual information necessary for the accurate recognition of words. Conversely, use of strict bottom-up processing may lead to the identification of individual words without an understanding of the meaning of the text.

Indirect evidence that the phonics program discouraged use of top-down strategies by KEEP students was provided by a study of oral reading errors (Au, 1976, 1977). Fifteen second-graders were identified as good and poor readers on the basis of standardized reading achievement scores. All children read the same stories; using tapes of the performances, judges categorized errors according to whether they reflected use of context, visual-phonic information, both, or neither. Among the conclusions, Au noted that the KEEP students, who had been taught a bottom-up (phonics) approach, appear to be less proficient in use of context than children who were subjects in similar studies in both the mainland U.S. and New Zealand. It also appears that the phonics-instructed KEEP students did not approach reading as a language task; they did not use their fluency in language to aid them in reading, and did not have the idea that trying to solve a problem in reading can be approached by testing linguistic hypotheses.

Au (1976) does not present data for error patterns with comprehension-emphasis instruction, so it is not certain that the conclusions of her study can be used to support the present argument. However, these findings are consistent with the hypothesis that Hawaiian children, taught with a phonics or bottom-up approach, do not make use of existing skills – e.g., language fluency – to facilitate top-down processing. Instead, the children in Au's study relied on bottom-up strategies, in this case visual-phonic, rather than top-down strategies such as context.

In a strict phonics approach the child may learn to focus exclusively on the phonemic-graphemic and visual-phonic cues while systematically ignoring the semantic ones. This is a major criticism of such programs (Adams, in press), one which may be particularly apt in the case of minority culture children. While other populations of children apparently do learn to read in programs where there is a heavy emphasis on phonics, the KEEP students did not. It is evident that there are interactions between program effects and the characteristics of different groups of young readers; specifically, the top-down processing strategies of the KEEP students may be more sensitive to disruption than those of middle-class children because of the greater discontinuity between home and school, in terms of physical features of the environment, styles of interaction and learning, and types of content. If there is a pre-existing bias for inconsistent application of these strategies due to the nature of the school setting and the child's resulting uncertainty about its demands, a strict bottom-up reading curriculum might well suppress use and development of top-down reading strategies. But if the child's natural impulse is to make sense out of all but the most completely nonsensical situations, comprehension (top-down) strategies will emerge as soon as they are encouraged and taught. We hypothesize the KEEP children readily began to use such strategies once the reading program was altered. Their reading scores then improved dramatically, to a level commensurate with their scores on the general ability tests.

We believe that including top-down approaches in instruction may increase the likelihood of minority children applying existing knowledge, linguistic skills, and strategies to unfamiliar classroom situations. Exclusively bottom-up approaches may cause the children to view culturally unfamiliar tasks as episodic, rote, decontextualized activities unrelated to previous experience. In contrast, majority culture children may find school work more familiar and see more rapidly the relevance of ideas and strategies learned at home, and thus develop and use appropriate top-down strategies even when taught with a phonics curriculum. We do not know whether the progress of majority culture students would also be improved by a better balance between bottom-up and top-down strategies in instruction. However, provision of ETR interchanges increased listening and reading comprehension skills of moderately retarded adolescents (TMRs), a conclusion based on pre- and post-testing, weekly criterion tests, and transcript analysis (Zetlin & Gallimore, 1979). One explanation of these results is application to written text of top-down processing which retarded students are rarely encouraged to use; most special curricula feature low-level tasks and do not promote higher-order cognitive processes on the assumption that TMRs learn best by rote and repetition (Levine, Zetlin, & Langness, 1979; Winschel & Enscher, 1978).

According to Resnick (in press) there are no fully documented accounts of reading programs which simultaneously feature top-down and bottom-up processing, with any populations including middle-class majority culture groups. Research in progress at KEEP is designed to test the hypothesis that simultaneously fostering top-down and bottom-up processing is a key factor in the success of Hawaiian children taught with the KROS program. The outcome of this effort will also bear on the argument that suppression of top-down processing strategies produces the competence/incompetence paradox so often observed in minority culture children.

Note

This research was supported by the Kamehameha Schools and the Estate of Princess Bernice Pauahi Bishop. Assistance was also provided by the Sociobehavioral Research Group, mental Retardation Research Center, University of California, Los Angeles. Requests for reprints should be addressed to Ronald Gallimore, Department of Psychiatry and Biobehavioral Sciences, UCLA, Los Angeles, California 90024. Copies of KEEP Technical Reports and work in preparation may be obtained from Editor, Technical Reports, KEEP, 1850 Makuakane Street, Honolulu, Hawaii 96817.

Our appreciation is due Dr. Roland Tharp and Dr. Andrea Zetlin for critical reading of the manuscript.

References

Adams, M. J. Failures to comprehend and levels of processing in reading. In R. J. Spiro, B. C. Bruce, & W. F. Brewer (Eds.), *Theoretical issues in reading comprehension.* Hillsdale, N.J.: Erlbaum, in press.

Au, K. H. An analysis of oral reading errors and its implications for reading instruction (Tech. Report #50). Honolulu: The Kamehameha Schools. The Kamehameha Early Education Program, 1976.

Au, K. H. Analyzing oral reading errors to improve instruction. *Reading Teacher,* 1977, *31* (1), 46–49.

Au, K. H. The role of the adult in the development of metacognitive processes related to reading. Unpublished manuscript, 1978.

Au, K. H. Using the E-T-R method with minority children. *Reading Teacher,* in press.

Brown, A. L. Knowing when, where and how to remember: A problem of metacognition. In R. Glasser (Ed.), *Advances in instructional psychology.* Hillsdale, N.J.: Erlbaum, in press.

Crowell, D. C. Kamehameha Reading Objective System. Honolulu: Kamehameha Early Education Program, 1978.

Flavell, J. H. *Cognitive development.* Englewood Cliffs, N.J.: Prentice-Hall, 1977.

Gallimore, R., Boggs, J. W., & Jordan, C. *Culture, behavior and education: A study of Hawaiian-Americans.* Beverly Hills: Sage, 1974.

Gallimore, R., & Howard, A. (Eds.) *Studies in a Hawaiian community: Na makamaka O Nanakuli.* Pacific Anthropological Records No. 1, Department of Anthropology, B. P. Bishop Museum, Honolulu, 1968.

Gallimore, R., Lam, D. J., Speidel, G. E., & Tharp, R. G. The effects of elaboration and rehearsal on long-term retention of shape names by kinder-garteners. *American Educational Research Journal,* 1977, *14* (4), 471–483.

Gallimore, R., Tharp, R. G., & Sloat, K. C. M. Analysis of achievement test results for the Kamehameha Early Education Project: (1972–1978). KEEP Technical Report, in preparation (a).

Gallimore, R., Tharp, R., & Sloat, K. C. M. Analysis of WPPSI and WISC-R scores for the Kamehameha Early Education Project: (1972–1978). KEEP Technical Report, in preparation (b).

Levine, H., Zetlin, A., & Langness, L. Everyday memory tasks in a school for the TMR learner. Paper presented at the 103rd Annual Meeting of the American Association on Mental Deficiency, Miami, Florida, May, 1979.

Resnick, L. B. Theory and practice in beginning reading. In L. B. Resnick & P. A. Weaver (Eds.), *Theory and practice of early reading.* Hillsdale, N.J.: Erlbaum, in press.

Rumelhart, D. E. Toward an interactive model of reading (Technical Report #56). Center of Human Information Processing, University of California, San Diego, 1976.

Scarr-Salapatek, S. An evolutionary perspective on infant intelligence: Species patterns and individual variations. In M. Lewis (Ed.), *The origin of intelligence: Infancy and early childhood.* New York: Plenum, 1976.

Speidel, G. E., Hao, R., & Gallimore, R. Production deficiency of labeling skills in a pre-reading letter discrimination task (Technical Report #37). Honolulu: The Kamehameha Schools. The Kamehameha Early Education Program, 1976.

Tharp, R. The direct instruction of comprehension within an integrated reading curriculum: Description and results of the Kamehameha Early Education Program (KEEP). KEEP Technical Report, in preparation.

Tharp, R., & Gallimore, R. The ecology of program research and development: A model of evaluation succession. In L. B. Sechrest (Ed.), *Evaluation Studies Review Annual* (Vol. 4). Beverly Hills: Sage, 1979, in press.

Watson-Gegeo, K. A., & Boggs, S. T. From verbal play to talk story: The role of routines in speech events among Hawaiian children. In S. Ervin-Tripp & C. Mitchell-Kernan (Eds.), *Child discourse*. New York: Academic Press, 1977.

Wertsch, J. V. Adult-child interaction and the roots of metacognition. *The Quarterly Newsletter of the Institute for Comparative Human Development*, 1978, *2* (1), 15–18.

Winschel, J. F., & Ensher, G. L. Curricular implications for the mentally retarded. *Education and training of the mentally retarded*, 1978, *13*, 131–138.

Zetlin, A. G., & Gallimore, R. Can TMR's think? Paper read at Gatlinberg Conference on Research in Mental Retardation. Gulf Shores, Alabama, April, 1979.

19 The organization of bilingual lessons: Implications for schooling

Luis C. Moll, Elette Estrada, Esteban Diaz, and Lawrence M. Lopes

The research reported here attempts to break away from summary measures of classroom performance to see, if possible, how curriculum and instruction are organized in a bilingual program. We videotaped classroom lessons in a school that seemed to provide an excellent case study of children's experiences in such a program. The focus of our attention was the development of reading skills. We sought to specify the variations in the communicative activities that constitute the reading lessons, and to pinpoint sources of interference in the development of second-language skills. The results show that despite their best efforts, teachers are currently structuring lessons in ways that seriously interfere with their curricular objectives.

Research procedures

The setting.   Our study was conducted in a combined 2nd and 3rd grade classroom in a school south of San Diego, bordering Mexico. This school implements a "maintenance" program aimed at promoting academic development in two languages. Two "sister" classrooms were involved in the study – one teaching in Spanish (L1) and one in English (L2). During the course of the day the children received instruction in basic content areas in their native language. The children also went to the other classroom for oral language and reading lessons *in their second language*. Only those children judged sufficiently fluent in English to take part actively in lessons participated in this dual arrangement. Native Spanish and English speakers were mixed for such activities as art,

254

music, and recess, but otherwise "parallel" instruction was conducted in separate languages and in separate classrooms. This instructional arrangement was ideal for our project because it gave us the unique opportunity to observe how the *same* native Spanish speakers participated in reading lessons in two distinctive language and instructional settings.[1]

The participants. After several days of preliminary observations and consultations with the classroom teachers and aides, we videotaped 12 target children that formed part of three teacher-defined ability groups. The children, all 3rd graders, came from Spanish-dominant homes and represented varying levels of English speaking ability. In total, 3 of the children were predominantly Spanish speaking, and, according to our observations, the rest of the target children functioned with relative ease in both languages. The results of a standardized English reading test indicated that 2 of the children were at or above grade level, 2 were one grade below, and the other 8 were substantially below grade level. Whereas there was no one-to-one correspondence in reading levels across language settings for each child, the relative number of children at, near, or substantially below grade level was paralleled in Spanish.

The criteria each teacher employed in determining the composition of the groups varied. The Spanish teacher grouped the children largely on the basis of conversations with the children and by having them read aloud. The English teacher relied more on previous teachers' reports and recommendations. Interestingly, neither teacher paid much attention, if any, to language dominance test scores.

The Spanish teacher was a female, Mexican-American, and a fluent bilingual. Her instructional aide was a female, monolingual Spanish speaker from Mexico. The English teacher was a male, Anglo, English-monolingual speaker. His instructional aide was female, Mexican-American, and English-dominant. The English teacher spoke to the children only in English; his aide, almost exclusively in English. The Spanish teacher spoke almost exclusively Spanish; her aide, only in Spanish.

Design of our observations. Our primary research strategy was to contrast the different contexts of instruction in order to specify important communicative activities as they interact with the characteristics of the participants. Consequently, we videotaped the high-, middle-, and low-ability groups as they participated in their daily reading lessons in Spanish and English.[2] First, we focused our attention on the three different teacher-defined ability groups *within* each classroom setting. These "ability-level" contrasts were extremely important because *ability group (and individual) distinctions are the very foundation on which curriculum implementation is built; they organize the nature of the experiences for the children.*

Second, we contrasted the ability groups *across* the two different language and instructional settings. We quickly formed the impression that the children encountered markedly different instructional environments when they went from Spanish to English. But, as we will make clear, it is not the language of instruction that is the critical difference. Crucial is the general focus of instruction and the organization of lessons that this focus entails. The social organization of communication activities in great part determines what the children do or don't learn in their second-language reading lessons.

The Spanish reading groups: Differential instructional environments

The children are assigned to learning centers and seated separately in distinct groupings in the Spanish classroom. The three lesson environments under study are organized to provide time on learning tasks that familiarize the children with different aspects of the subject of reading. The specific reading behaviors that the children practice in each group become increasingly complex as we move from the lower to the higher ability groups. This simply shows that students tracked into different ability groups are given different curriculum content.

The low group.   The primary objective of the lessons was to provide the children with the necessary teacher or tutor help in learning how to pronounce accurately the words on the page. This instruction was carried out, in many instances, without the children seeming to understand *what* was being read. Secondarily, the lessons were also structured to familiarize the children with the process of examining the content of the story. This is an important skill to develop, since answering comprehension questions becomes a primary activity in the more advanced groups.

In the following example, the teacher questions the student after the student has read a story about decorating a Christmas tree.[3]

1. Teacher (T): Who put the star on the Nativity?
2. Child (C): Fernandito.
3. T: Did they all help?
4. C: Yes.
5. T: Did they like it?
6. C: Yes.
7. T: Why?
8. C: (silence)
9. T: What paper did they use for the star?
10. C: Paper – ummm –.
11. T: What color do you think it was?
12. C: Gold (without looking at illustration).
13. T: Did they mention the Three Kings?
14. C: Yes.
15. T: How?
16. C: (silence)
17. T: What did they compare?
18. C: (Pause) What is that?
19. T: Compare or make a comparison? When they mentioned the Three Kings? Here, look (Reads from book) "We are going to make a star, A star like the Three Kings saw, Big and bright." How did they want to make the star? – Like whom? – Like which?
20. C: (silence)
21. T: Like the Three Kings, right? The ones who followed the star.

The child has no problems with the first three questions (1–6). However, when the teacher asks a question for which the child needs to pull information from the text in order to answer, the child doesn't respond (7–8); the teacher simplifies the questioning (9–14) and again elicits a response. She then again asks a more difficult question, and the child does not respond (15–16). After another question, the child requests clarification (17–18). In line 19 the teacher directs him to the exact place in the book where he can extract the answer, *reads the passage to him*, and asks him questions directly related to the passage. *When the child can't answer (20) she provides the response (21)*, and completes the task for the student. The form of this question–answer exchange is typical of lessons at more advanced stages and the primary vehicle used by the teacher for assessing the student's knowledge and/or level of comprehension. However, the structure of the exchange is not typical of advanced classes, because the teacher often ends up supplying answers. In a manner sometimes called scaffolding (Wood, Bruner, & Ross, 1976), the teacher will ask a question at some level of difficulty and, finding that the group or certain children in the group can't function at that level, moves to less difficult levels until the group's instructional level is met (see also Cole, Dore, Hall, & Dowley, 1978; Mehan, 1979). Thus, the teacher provides several kinds of assistance to help the student answer the questions that the student is unable to answer alone. In the example, the teacher even reads the text for the student as an aid in responding to the comprehension questions. Variations in the systematic organization of this mediating strategy, a kind of organization that fits Vygotsky's (1978) idea that learning occurs in a "zone of proximal development," becomes very significant as we examine the middle- and high-group lessons.

The middle group. In contrast to the low group, the middle group lessons primarily involve teacher guidance in promoting reading *comprehension*, along with instruction about *how* to answer in ways that communicate the knowledge of content. In the following example the teacher has asked each child to read a question to the child next to him using the questions in the book as a script. The response has to be correct in both content and form (in this case, a complete sentence).

1. T: I want you to ask Marcos this question.
2. J: Do you put a letter in the mailbox?
3. M: Yes, I put a letter in the mailbox.
4. T: Very good. You ask Ali question 2.
5. J: Do you place a letter in an envelope?
6. A: Yes, I place a letter in an envelope.
7. T: Very good, Ali. Okay, number 3 – Ali to Jorge.
8. A: Do you have to give stamps to the mailman?
9. J: No, you do not have to give stamps to the mailman.
10. T: Or, I don't give stamps to the mailman. Number 4 to Ali.
11. M: Does the mailman write the letters?
12. A: No.
13. T: In a complete sentence.
14. A: No, the mailman does not write the letters.
15. T: Very good. Number 6.

Although on the surface this activity seems very simple, as in the example provided for the lower group, it provides the students with early and very explicit practice in basic question–answer exchanges (often to known-answer questions), so common in school lessons.

In this example, the children assume a different role in the interaction than the lesson format of the low group requires. They assume (via the use of a script) both the role of questioner and respondent. In comparison with the lower group lessons we studied, the teacher's role clearly changes. The emphasis on content is different and she does not perform as much of the task herself. She also relies more heavily on the reading materials, rather than oral discourse to mediate her interactions with the children. In the above example, the teacher not only has the children use the questions in the book to ask their questions, but also to structure the form of their responses. In the next example, also with the middle group, the teacher is asking the questions, as is most common, but the children are asked to answer *without* looking at their notebooks or at the text book – without material help. Their answers are, consistent with the model she has created, given in "complete sentence" form and faithfully reflect the content of the story. The results of adding *remembered* question–answer formats to the task is reflected in the interaction which is reminiscent of interactions in the lower groups. In at least one instance the teacher provides both the question and the answer for the student.

1. T: What kind of . . . I am going to ask the question and you are going to answer it in complete sentences, without looking at your books because I want to see if you remember what happened in the story. What kind of bird is the penguin?
2. C: The penguin is a very famous kind.
3. T: Let's see, yes, no, what does he do, what does he not do?
4. C: The penguin cannot fly, only . . .
5. T: Very good, that's the kind of bird, the bird that does not fly. Very good. How are his feathers and what color are they, Ali?
6. C: The penguin's feathers are black.
7. T: Are what?
8. C: Black.
9. T: And are they long or short? The penguin's feathers are black and short, right? OK, how are his wings?
10. C: His wings are short.
11. T: Very good, short. Where do they live, Marcos?
12. C: The penguins live in colonies.
13. T: Very good, you have studied. Where do they lay their eggs, Angelica?
14. C: In their nests.
15. T: In their nests, right. Do they (the book) tell us how many eggs they lay?

16. C: Ten.
17. T: Okay, ah, what do penguins eat, Ali? Complete sentence.
18. C: The penguins eat fish.

Although the children are not looking at the materials, they are able to answer the questions correctly. With some reminders, they can also phrase the answers in the teacher's desired complete sentence form. After the lesson terminates, the teacher asks the children to write the answers to questions found in the text. She makes it very clear that they have to incorporate the structure of the questions into their answers.

The high group.   The high group lessons reveal yet other kinds of skill emphasis. The most obvious change is that the children are required to write book reports. But there are also qualitative changes in the way the teacher interacts with the students as a part of reading itself. In the activities the high group shares in common with the two lower groups, the questions are more spontaneous and informal. That is, the questions are less text-bound; they do not come straight from the book. Rather the teacher pursues questions that arise from the exchanges with the students and the topics developed by these exchanges. Furthermore, the emphasis is now on the communication of *generalizations* drawn from the reading and the requests for complete sentence answers are less. Take the following example, in which the teacher starts a combined evaluation/instruction activity after the group reads a popular poem about a cobbler.

1.   T: Sandra, what is this poem about?
2.   C: About a cobbler.
3.   T: What is he doing?
4.   C: Using his hammer.
5.   T: Right. /Tipi tapa/, who is making that sound?
6.   C: The hammer.
7.   T: The hammer, right. Does the poem say that he is a good cobbler or a bad cobbler?
8.   GR: (Group) (mixed responses)
9.   T: Yes or no?
10. GR: He's a good cobbler.
11. T: He is? How do you know?
12. GR: (Several students respond together)
13. T: Where does the poem say that he is a good cobbler?
14. GR: (Several students respond together)

15. T: Sandra, read the part that tells us.
16. C: (Reads) "Ay tus suelas, zapa-zapa-zapatero remendon,
          Ay tus suelas, tipi-tape, duran menos que el carton!"
17. GR: Bad shoemaker.
18. T: Why is he a bad shoemaker?
19. C: "Duran menos que el carton." (They [soles] last less than the cardboard.)
20. T: How long should the soles last?
21. C: A little less than the nails. (The teacher laughs at his response and then the lesson continues.)

It should be mentioned that the poem itself has no direct reference to whether the cobbler is a good or bad shoemaker. This conclusion must be inferred from the information given in the poem. The teacher invites this generalization in line 7. There are some differences of opinion among the group whether the cobber is good (competent) or not (8, 10, 12). The teacher selects a student who has answered that the cobbler is not too good, to specify which lines of the poem she used to reach her conclusion (15). She does (16), and the group confirms her opinion (17). The instructor then requests more information (18), a child quotes the exact part of the line (19) that tells the reader that the shoes do not last long. In this example the teacher controls alternatives by her choice of questions and by directing the children to find the relevant part of the text. However, some overlap does exist between the way that the high-group's and the middle-group's activities include the use of material objects as support to construct responses.

Consider the following brief example from a lesson in which the students are reading about a Native American group and their customs. In the portion of the transcript presented here the teacher is asking questions regarding the content of the story.

1. T: Who can. . . . How can the Navajos be hurt?
2. C: The corn, rain, and wind.
3. T: The corn, rain, and wind, and what else? (She looks around the entire group.)
4. C: The sun.
5. T: The sun and what else?
6. C: (Inaudible response)
7. T: What do they (the book) say could also damage them? The what. . . . What type of thoughts (she points to her head)?
8. C: Bad thoughts.
9. T: Very good, then can you make it into a complete sentence? You (points to a girl who answered previously)? Okay, read the question so you can remember how you are going to construct it.

10. C: (Hesitates in providing answer.) The Navajos can be hurt by the sun, the rain
         . . . (interruption, then the child continues) . . . and bad thoughts.
11. T: Very good. (The lesson continues.)

Note the way that the teacher, in requesting that the answer be given
in a complete sentence (9), points out to the student that she can use the
question in the text to help her organize the response. The result is an
independent construction using the text as a tool of verbal communication. In the next example, another student readily provides an answer to
a question by incorporating the question into his response:

1. T: What do they do with the hogan when a person dies?
2. C: When a person dies in the hogan, they burn the hogan.

In this case, the construction of the answer is independent of teacher
directions or the use of material aids. Note that the student uses the com-
plete-sentence form to respond. This is the same form that the teacher
requires so frequently from the lower groups and occasionally with the
high group. This suggests the possibility that the student now uses the
communication activities previously provided by interaction with the
teacher as a means of organizing a response.

Finally, consider book reports. This activity typifies the most
advanced reading-related activity found in this classroom. The students
have to select books of interest to them, and without teacher help, read
them, analyze the contents, and write reports. Through the process of
writing reports, the children practice reading and at the same time
display their mastery of all the skills we observed in the three lesson
environments. This activity culminates in the children's carrying out
independently the reading behaviors with new materials and creating a
new product (i.e., the book report) in the process (cf. Wertsch, 1979, in
press). Again, the children are observed to successfully assume the medi-
ations that are the responsibility of the teacher during the reading lesson
we have described.

To summarize.   We have briefly sketched out the nature of the three
reading environments found in the Spanish classroom. We have shown
that these environments are organized to provide time on learning tasks
that familiarize the children with different aspects of the subject of
reading. Our basic conclusion is that the specific behaviors the children
practice and learn become increasingly complex and, through modifica-

tions in the teacher's role, independent of adult mediation and regulation as we move from the lower- to the higher-ability groups. These changes in skill-emphasis seem to suggest a progression of behaviors[4] which may reflect the teacher's implicit "theory" of reading.

The English classroom: A contrast in the organization of lesson environments

Once armed with the analysis on the Spanish reading lessons we applied the same procedures to the examination of the English reading lessons for the same children. There was a good correspondence between membership of the high group across classrooms; the target children in the high group in Spanish were the same children in the high group in English. However, this common membership in groupings across classrooms did not hold for the children in the other two groups; some of the children in the Spanish middle group were assigned to the lower English group.

The following four points will be made in this section: (a) The English reading lessons are also organized differentially for each ability group, but at a much *lower level* than the Spanish lessons. (b) The overriding concern of the lessons in English is decoding, pronunciation, and other forms related to the sounds of the second language. (c) This focus is based on the implicit theory that the children need to develop their pronunciation and decoding skills before they engage in more complex reading tasks. (d) Comparing the lessons in the two classrooms, we conclude by arguing that (1) there is an underestimation of the children's level of reading skills in English, and (2) that this misestimation arises from the confounding of phonetic errors and decoding errors. The resulting interaction limits the children's involvement to lessons that are essentially mechanical in nature and at the lower ranges of their abilities.

The low group. The predominant activity for the low group involved providing the children with help and practice in decoding (phonetically) the text. Particular attention was also paid to providing the children with practice in producing *correct word sounds*. In fact, all of the lessons emphasized pronunciation skills. The following example illustrates one such activity. The teacher has written words on the board and is asking the students to identify and cross out the letters that correspond to the sound being made.

1. T: mmuh . . . mmuh . . . Juan (calls on a student) . . . mmuh.
2. S: (student crosses out the correct letter)
3. T: All right, what's the letter?
4. S: "m"
5. T: All right, "m." Angelica, thhuh . . . thuhh . . .
6. S: thhuh (crosses out the correct letters)
7. T: All right, what are the letters?
8. S: thhuh
9. T: No, what are the letters, that's the sound . . . "t" . . .
10. S: "t, n"
11. T: No, that's not an "n" . . . "t" . . .
12. S: "n . . . (hesitates) . . . h"
13. T: "t, h," all right.
    (the lesson continues)

In addition to providing help with phonics, the teachers spend a great deal of time on decoding skills, using a textbook. There is an absence of activities intended to familiarize the student with the procedures involved in reading comprehension (such as those we saw students receiving in Spanish).

The middle group.   Decoding is also the primary activity with the middle group, the same emphasis on pronunciation is prevalent. Thus, the lower and middle group activities are very similar in the degree to which lessons are organized around decoding or phonics, and pronunciation skills. What distinguishes this group is that the teacher also provides help in the identification and construction of words, pluralization, etc. But, as in the lower group lessons, there is an absence of activities related to reading comprehension. Recall that the Spanish middle-group was organized to promote reading comprehension as well as to provide instruction in how to answer in ways that communicate the student's knowledge of the content of the story.

The high group.   Even in the high group the members of which we *know* can read for comprehension, the lessons are primarily organized to provide time on decoding and oral language practice, such as word construction and the identification of sounds. To a small extent the lessons contain reading activities designed to assess comprehension. In the next example the teacher is assessing whether the children have understood some of the passages he is reading to them.

1. T: "Sue played in the playground after lunch." Where did she play?
2. S: (The students bid to answer)
3. T: Julio.
4. S: Playground.
5. T: All right, on the playground. Who was it? Who was doing this?
6. S: Sue.
7. T: All right. When was it? When was it? Eduardo.
8. S: After lunch.
9. T: All right, after lunch. "Joan had dinner at night at their own house." When did she have dinner?
10. S: At night.
   (Lesson continues)

It is clear that when the children shift from one language setting to another, they do not encounter "similar environments." We did not even find some correspondence of environments for the high group, which, after all, has demonstrated the ability to read with comprehension beyond what they show in the above example. The organization of the reading environments in English is such that students are encouraged to focus primarily on the mechanical tasks of practicing decoding skills or word sounds. Practically absent in the middle and high groups are the key activities that promote reading *comprehension* and help the students learn how to *communicate their knowledge* of content. In short, we do not find the types of functional communication activities related to reading that occur in the L1 setting for these groups.

A possible explanation for the organization of lessons in English (and one suggested by the teacher) is that the children are weak in English and they cannot engage in more advanced reading asks. This "English deficiency" explanation makes sense and initially we were inclined to accept it. However, as we gathered more information, we began to realize the social organization of lessons in the English classroom is not solely a matter of the children being limited English speakers. Remember that the children are not allowed to participate in English classrooms until it has been determined (through testing and teacher observations) that they have sufficient fluency to benefit from English instruction. This fact, coupled with our observations of the children in various classroom situations made us conclude that *the children were much more fluent in English than they displayed during the videotaped lessons.* In fact, we had taped several occasions of children interacting *outside* of the general structure of the lessons when even children in the low groups were able to speak English in ways that are more sophisticated than those that occur *within* the lessons.

The analysis of the Spanish lessons clearly shows that most of the children, and especially the high group children, have developed decoding skills in Spanish. The high-group children also display good decoding skills in English. In this limited sense, at the very least, they demonstrate that they know how to read. But if the children are sufficiently fluent in English and possess decoding skills, why aren't they being practiced on higher level skills? How is the difference in the level of instruction/performance across classrooms constructed? If most of the children can already decode in Spanish, why are the English lessons organized to place so much importance on phonics or accurate pronunciation as if they did not know how to decode? A likely source of the problem is that in the English setting pronunciation problems and decoding problems are being mistaken for each other. It is assumed that decoding is a prerequisite to comprehension and that correct pronunciation is the best index of decoding. This assumption is often used to guide instruction in bilingual programs (Goodman, Goodman, & Flores, 1979). Consequently, the teacher organizes the lessons to provide the children with the necessary time on tasks to help them practice pronunciation, phonics, and other aspects of language learning such as word construction. To make an accurate differentiation between a child's inability to decode and inaccurate pronunciation of English words, it seems that the teacher would need to assess reading comprehension. But, as our analysis indicates, activities permitting a display of reading comprehension rarely occur in the English reading lessons.

Further information about the interactional sources of this mismatch between language settings came from "viewing sessions" with the teachers. Owing to the teachers' hectic schedules they had never observed their students perform in each other's classrooms. The Spanish teacher's comments as she saw for the first time the children participating in English lessons is revealing: "Those can't be my kids. Why are they doing such a low-level work? They are much smarter than that." What she indicates, of course, is that the children's behaviors in the English lessons are very different from what she knows they can do on the basis of observations in her own classroom.

One way to talk about the difference in competence levels observed for these children in the two classrooms is to claim that there is little transfer of reading behaviors across language setting. But if we are correct in our descriptions, the problem is not with the children's lack of language or reading skills in English. Instead the problem is in the social organization of the lesson environments. Reading skills cannot be shown to transfer across language settings unless the lesson environments are structured so that the transfer can manifest itself. However, in the classrooms we observed the English-lesson environments are not organized so as to facilitate transfer of reading behaviors from Spanish because the lessons in English presuppose a lack of competence and restrict the children to decoding or phonics work.

Although these different organizations greatly influence what children learn, teachers do not seem to focus on how the structure of the communication activities that make up the lessons in *both* classrooms determine the nature of the experiences of the groups involved in the lessons. As a consequence, the tendency is to attribute characteristics to the children (e.g., language deficits) that are equally attributable to the environments in which the children function.

Notes

Research supported by a grant award from the National Institute of Education – G 790024.

1. We also videotaped English oral language development lessons which are not discussed here.

2. A total of 20 hours of videotaped data were collected during the months of March and June 1979. The goal in each case was to videotape the 12 target children at least twice in each lesson. This narrow focus made it possible to collect data in several related classroom contexts.

3. The examples provided in this section have all been translated from the Spanish.

4. We should emphasize that these general "stages" of development of the lesson environments are not as clearly distinguishable as we have briefly described them; and that there is a considerable overlap of activities between them. This is a point to which we will return later in the paper, since we think it may have important implications for the children's transfer of skills across contexts.

References

Cole, M., Dore, J., Hall, W., & Dowley, G. Situation and task in children's talk. *Discourse Processes*, 1978, *1*, 119–176.

Goodman, K., Goodman, Y., & Flores, B. *Reading in the bilingual classroom: Literacy and biliteracy.* National Clearinghouse for Bilingual Education, 1979.

Mehan, H. *Learning lessons.* Cambridge, Mass.: Harvard University Press, 1979.

Vygotsky, L. S. *Mind in society.* Cambridge, Mass.: Harvard University Press, 1978.

Wertsch, J. V. *A state of the art review of Soviet research in cognitive psychology.* Manuscript, Department of Linguistics, Northwestern University, 1979.

Wertsch, J. V. Adult-child interaction as a source of self-regulation in children. To appear in S. R. Yussen (Ed.), *The growth of insight during childhood.* New York: Academic Press, in press.

Wood, D., Bruner, J. S., & Ross, C. The role of tutoring in problem solving. *Journal of Child Psychology and Psychiatry,* 1976, *17*, 89–100.

20 *Kanji* help readers of Japanese infer the meaning of unfamiliar words

Giyoo Hatano, Keiko Kuhara, and Michael Akiyama

Japanese sentences in newspapers, books, journals and letters are usually written by using "*kanji*," and "*kana*" (more specifically, "hiragana") in combination. *Kanji* is the word for Chinese character(s), about 2000 morphograms which originated in China, while kana are 71 syllables. Since the number of kinds of syllables is limited in the Japanese language because no two consonants appear consecutively, the 71 *kana* are enough to effectively represent any Japanese word. Therefore, one might ask: isn't the use of *kanji* unnecessary? It has often been claimed, by scholars as well as laymen, that we could stop using *kanji*, or at least reduce the number, in order to increase practical efficiency.

As Glushko (1979) aptly pointed out, the desirability of an orthography may be different for writers and readers, and differ according to the extent of their experience. The use of morphograms is apt to be difficult for beginners, and in fact Japanese students spend much time learning how to read and write *kanji*. For experienced writers, the use of *kanji* may not be inconvenient (except for typewriting), but it is not necessarily facilitative either. Therefore, it may benefit experienced readers only. Readers are certainly able to comprehend a text with *kanji* faster than without *kanji*. But what else? Suzuki (1975, 1977) claimed that *kanji* help readers resolve homonymic ambiguity and infer meanings of unfamiliar words.

Before reporting experiments examining this claim, let us briefly explain a unique characteristic of *kanji* in the Japanese language, one not shared by these characters in the Chinese language. Our basic assumptions about *kanji*'s cognitive function are derived from this characteris-

269

tic. *Kanji* are unique in that most of them are given two readings (pro-
nunciations), i.e., Chinese and Japanese readings. Each Japanese reading
historically originated by attaching a native Japanese word representing
the meaning of the character to a Chinese character. Therefore, the
Japanese reading is sometimes called the *semantic reading*, while the
Chinese reading is regarded as the *phonetic reading*. A rough approximation in English is found in "etc.": "et cetera" could be called the Latin
reading, and "and so on" the English reading.

Giving each *kanji* a Japanese reading has strengthened the association
between individual *kanji* and their meanings. This dual reading system
has also served to weaken the association between a *kanji* and either of
its readings, as has the fact that many different *kanji* share the same
Chinese reading. This is not the case for Chinese characters in the
Chinese language, where each character is always given one and the same
reading, shared by few, if any, other characters.

Does this unique characteristic of the dual readings of *kanji* affect the
information-processing of words in the Japanese language? A majority
of the substantive words in Japanese are comprised of several *kanji*,
with or without *kana*. They are given either the Japanese or the
Chinese reading, seldom both. However, because of the increased association of the component *kanji* with meaning (and the decreased association with pronunciation), we assume that the meanings of words
transcribed in *kanji* can readily be retrieved by experienced readers in a
direct manner and need not be mediated by phonetic codes. This notion
of alternative information processing routes is schematically shown
in our model in Figure 20.1. It implies the following three specific
hypotheses:

Hypothesis 1: Meanings of words written in *kanji* can be understood
even when their phonetic codes are not retrieved from the written transcriptions; meanings of the same words transcribed in *kana* can be
understood only through the mediation of the phonetic codes.

Hypothesis 2: Meanings of words transcribed in *kanji* are better
understood than those in kana when the phonetic codes are insufficient
for determining meanings.

Hypothesis 3: In retrieving meanings from unfamiliar words transcribed in *kana* or their phonetic codes, *kanji* codes stored in the long-
term memory (LTM) may be used as mediators.

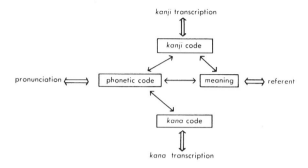

Figure 20.1. Retrievability relationships among various internal codes of a word (in rectangles) with the corresponding observables.

Hypothesis 1 has been fairly well supported. The strongest evidence has come from studies on brain injuries. For example, aphasic patients with apraxia of speech showed much greater difficulty in transcription-to-picture matching for tachistoscopically presented *kana* words than for *kanji* words (Sasanuma & Fujimura, 1971). Alexia patients' reading ability was better preserved for *kanji* words than *kana* words (Yamadori, 1975). But Hypotheses 2 and 3 have not received any direct support, and we have, therefore, tried to investigate these two by experimentation.

Kanji words have high inferability of meaning

Now let us turn to our experiments on the role of *kanji* when a person must infer the meanings of unfamiliar technical terms. Most technical terms in the Japanese language, which are often translations from one of the European languages, are made up of two or more *kanji*. The resulting compound is usually given a Chinese reading which is simply the Chinese reading, in order of the component *kanji*. This is similar to the practice in English in which Greek words or Latin words are combined. In both cases these are compound words consisting of morphemes which are not used in daily conversation and are free from varieties of connotations, but semantically appropriate. Our basic model and Hypothesis 2 imply that, in comparing the inferability of meanings, technical terms transcribed in *kanji* are superior to the corresponding *kana* transcriptions (i.e., in the within-language comparison), and better also than Greek or Latin derived compound words in English (i.e., in the between-language comparison). The latter prediction was initially made by Suzuki (1975). He gave two primary reasons: (a) The component *kanji* are semantically understood far more easily than the component Greek or Latin words, because the former are already imbued with Japanese or semantic readings; (b) The component *kanji* are, unlike Greek/Latin components, not deformed by the influence of modified pronunciation.

An example will help readers recognize the plausibility of these predictions. Suppose that a person is trying to infer the meaning of the unfamiliar technical term *limnology* written in *kanji* (three morphograms), *kana* (six syllables) and English (nine letters). The English speaker can probably infer that the term has something to do with a branch of science from -*logy* but not beyond that, since he or she does not know what *limno* means. Presented with the term in *kana*, the Japanese speaker will list several possible semantic interpretations, but will not be able to narrow them down. With *kanji*, however, the reader of Japanese will be able to identify the meaning of each component character and then infer the meaning of the term.

In our experiment, undergraduates were asked to match 30 unfamiliar, technical terms with their definitions (and/or descriptions). We selected 30 Latin- or Greek-derived English technical terms and their Japanese translations, which are *kanji* compound words with 2–5 component characters from the list given by Suzuki (1978). These were mostly from botany, zoology, medical science, psychology and linguistics.

Let us examine two examples of the technical terms and their definitions. They are: *limnology* – the scientific study of physical, chemical, and biological conditions in lakes and ponds; and *piscivorous* – eating fish as a regular diet.

Three groups of Japanese students were asked to match the words with their definitions. The word lists were presented in *kanji*, *kana* and English, respectively. A group of American students were tested by using the English definitions and word list.

The results are shown in Figure 20.2. The inferability in the *kanji* condition is almost perfect. Why is it so easy to infer meanings from the

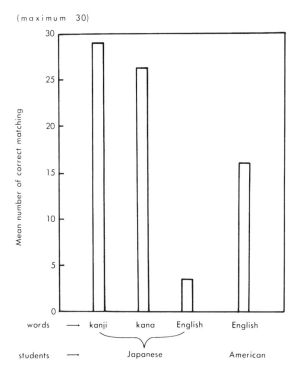

Figure 20.2. Mean number of correct matchings of definitions with words.

kanji expressions? The *kanji* expression for limnology is constructed of three characters, 湖沼学 .

Though it naturally has a phonetic reading, the three characters have semantic readings roughly corresponding to "lake(s)," "pond(s)" and "study (studies)" respectively, and these semantic readings can easily be understood even by children. (In Japanese we use the same character for singular and plural nouns: e.g., 湖 湖 represents "lake" and "lakes.") Similarly, the component *kanji* of the Japanese word corresponding to "piscivorous" are semantically, "fish-eat-nature."

The order of performance of the four conditions was *kanji, kana,* English (Japanese students) and English (American students). It is not surprising that the Japanese students in the English condition performed very poorly, since English is not their first language. The *kanji* condition is superior to any other condition. This is consistent with our prediction that the words in *kanji* have higher inferability than the words in *kana* and English. Another interpretation is possible, however: Japanese students are already more familiar than Americans with the technical terms. To check this, we asked other groups of Japanese and American students to give the words corresponding to 30 definitions. When the students did not know the words, they were encouraged to invent them. The mean correct responses, which included invention, were 7.23 among the Japanese students, and 5.00 amomg American students. The difference in mean correct responses between the two groups was small, and could not explain the large difference found in the matching performance.

The reader may wonder if the meanings of component *kanji* are really sufficient cues for inferring the meaning of most compound words. It is true that the meaning of a compound word cannot be determined solely by the meanings of its component *kanji*. However, there are other constraints by which the range of possible meanings for the word can be limited. First, experienced readers have acquired several compounding schemata by which *kanji* words are constructed. For example, when two nouns are compounded, the new word belongs to a family of the last noun. Thus 乳牛 (milk-cow) means a cow for milking and 牛乳 (cow-milk) means milk of a cow. Secondly, our world knowledge can be used to exclude some possible meanings and also to choose likely ones. This is similar to English speakers' differentiated interpretation of structurally similar phrases, like "horseshoe" and "alligator shoe." Finally, the context of the sentence, passage, or work as a whole can give additional clues to the meaning of the word in question. Therefore, meanings of component *kanji* only increase the inferability, but this increment is often very helpful.

Kanji's latent cognitive functions

Figure 20.2 shows that performance in the *kana* condition is at a fairly high level and only a little lower than that in the *kanji* condition. Hypothesis 3 suggests that this is because students in the *kana* condition often succeed in retrieving mentally the appropriate *kanji*, overcoming the phonetic constraint of the *kana*, by using the definitions as contextual information.

To test this idea, we examined the *kanji* representation of the technical terms chosen by the students in the *kana* condition. After matching the definitions with the words, the students in the *kana* condition were given a *kanji* encoding test. In the test they were given the 30 definitions and corresponding *kana* words correctly combined, then asked to change the *kana* into *kanji*. We examined the proportion of correct matchings as a function of correctness in the *kanji* encoding test. When *kanji* encodings were correct, the mean proportion of correct matching was 0.89, but when *kanji* encoding responses were incorrect or missing, the mean proportion was 0.69.

This difference is statistically significant, but the latter proportion is still fairly high. This is due to the fact that only the "critical" character(s) must be correct in order for the correct matching. For example, the Japanese word corresponding to "laryngeal" consists of three *kanji*, but only the last one meaning "sound" is critical in order to match the word with the definition, "a sound articulated between vocal cords when breathing out."

Thus we conducted an auxiliary experiment to examine the correspondence of inferred meanings and the *kanji* representation of technical terms in a weaker sentential context. Ten technical terms sampled from the main experiment were used. Each of the sentences included one target word written in *kana* and underlined. As shown in the following examples, the target words were not given strong sentence contexts as had been done with the defintions in the main experiment.

He is a specialist in *koshogaku* (limnology) and has studied everywhere in Japan.

This animal lives by the river bank and is *gyoshokusei* (piscivorous).

A group of Japanese undergraduates were asked to write meanings of *kana* target words and to change the target words into *kanji*. Both inferred meanings and *kanji* encodings were classified into three categories: correct response, incorrect response, and no-answer (including incomplete response). The relationships between the meanings and *kanji* encodings were examined. Table 20.1 shows that the correspondence between inferred meanings and *kanji* encodings is very close. When the students make correct *kanji* encodings, they infer correct meanings in most cases. When they retrieve incorrect *kanji*, inferred meanings are

Table 20.1. *Relationships between meaning and kanji representation of target words*

Meaning (lenient criterion)	Kanji Responses		
	Correct	Incorrect	No answer
Correct	51.2%	4.2%	0.8%
Incorrect	2.7	16.9	1.5
No answer	6.5	6.2	10.0

also incorrect. Where the students fail to give *kanji*, they can not infer meanings.

Close correspondence is observed also among the incorrect responses. Three different incorrect responses are given for *koshogaku* (limnology) in the *kanji* encoding test: 古証学 古匠学 古称学 (all pronounced *koshogaku*). The component *kanji* have the meanings of "old-document-study," "old-artist-study" and "old-naming-study," respectively. As expected, the meanings of the words inferred by the students are highly similar to the integration of the meanings of the three component *kanji*. For example, students who gave 古匠学 in the *kanji* encoding test infer that *koshogaku* is a study of great artists in olden days. There were few incorrect responses for *gyoshokusei* (piscivorous). This can be attributed in part to the small number of *kanji* having the pronunciation of "gyo" or "shoku."

Several psycholinguistic studies (e.g., Rubenstein et al., 1971) have tried to demonstrate that a written word is transformed into a phonetic code before its meaning is retrieved. This may be true with the Japanese language as long as the word is written in *kana* and is a familiar one, which can easily be understood by its phonetic code. However, when a phonetic code is insufficient for retrieving its meaning because it is unfamiliar, experienced Japanese readers do quite the opposite: they try to find a combination of *kanji* satisfying the given phonetic code and seemingly appropriate in the context, and then retrieve the meaning. This is what Hypothesis 3 is about. People rely on the same procedure when a pronounced word is ambiguous because of the presence of homonyms.

If this analysis is correct, as suggested by our experiments, it has an important implication. Readers of Japanese can understand unfamiliar words, spoken or written in *kana*, by the help of *kanji* codes stored in

LTM. Therefore, it may well be misleading to claim that the use of *kanji* can be reduced without much sacrifice because readers of Japanese can communicate effectively in a spoken language.

Multiple mental lexicons

From the above findings and those from other experiments on the cognitive functions of *kanji* (e.g., Kuhara & Hatano, 1981), we now think that experienced readers of Japanese have, in addition to the usual mental lexicon of words, a mental lexicon of *kanji* or the corresponding morphemes as building blocks for compound words. The latter lexicon has a complex structure so that the component *kanji* can be retrieved either phonetically or semantically. Suppose Japanese readers fail to find the word in their word-lexicon that matches a given word-like utterance or string of characters. They will recognize that they do not know the word as a word, but still try to figure out its meaning by using the *kanji*-lexicon. Compounding schemata, world knowledge and contextual information may also be relied upon.

The readers can continue reading or oral conversation without break if the inferred meaning of the unknown compound word seems correct. Even when the inferred meaning has proven to be incorrect, they can easily learn the word "meaningfully" by using the *kanji* lexicon. After the inference or learning, they may add the word to their word-lexicon or store the word only temporarily. For the purpose of the efficient processing of linguistic information, the word-lexicon should not be very large, and must be comprised of frequently used words. The *kanji*-lexicon can potentially generate a great number of compound words, though it may not give specified precise meanings, and retrieving word meanings from the *kanji*-lexicon tends to take a longer time. Thus these two lexicons can be used most effectively in combination, producing a flexible, large vocabulary

Because of this multiple mental lexical system, experienced Japanese readers have, in fact, been able to increase and reorganize their vocabulary quite easily. According to a newspaper article by S. Ono (Mainichishinbun, June 17, 1980), about 15000 words were invented in the first 20 years of the Meiji period to represent Western ideas, customs and things, and many of them were incorporated into the vocabulary of ordinary Japanese people. Most of the invented words were, as expected, compound *kanji* words. Thus we may credit *kanji* with playing an important role in the rapid modernization of Japanese society.

Note

This study was partially supported by a grant from the Hoso-Bunka Foundation.

References

Glushko, R. J. Cognitive and pedagogical implications of orthography. *The Quarterly Newsletter of the Laboratory of Comparative Human Cognition*, 1979, *1* (2), 22–26.

Kuhara, K., & Hatano, G. Comprehension and memory of a short oral discourse involving homonymic ambiguity: Effects of headings. Paper presented at the Meeting of the American Education Research Association, 1981.

Rubenstein, H., Lewis, S. S., & Rubenstein, M. A. Evidence for phonemic recoding in visual word recognition. *Journal of Verbal Learning and Verbal Behavior*, 1971, *10*, 647–657.

Sasanuma, S., & Fujimura, O. Selective impairment of phonetic and non-phonetic transcription of words in Japanese aphasic patients: *Kana* vs *Kanji* in visual recognition and writing. *Cortex*, 1971, *7*, 1–18.

Suzuki, T. On the twofold phonetic realization of basic concepts: In defence of Chinese characters in Japanese. In F. C. C. Peng (Ed.), *Language in Japanese society*. Tokyo: Tokyo University Press, 1975.

Suzuki, T. Writing is not language, or is it? *Journal of Pragmatics*, 1977, *1*, 407–420.

Suzuki, T. Are *Kanji* compound words loan words from Chinese? *Gekkan Gengo*, 1978, *7*, 2, 2–8 (in Japanese).

Yamadori, A. Ideogram reading in alexia. *Brain*, 1975, *98*, 231–238.

21 Functional environments for microcomputers in education

Denis Newman

Introduction

For the last several years, researchers at the Center for Children and Technology have been conducting a program of research on the use of computers in education. One of the central themes of this research is that the computer is a tool that can be used for a variety of functions or purposes. Thus, we talk about the computer operating within a "functional learning environment" (FLE). Here, functional means that the learning activities have a function or purpose from the point of view of the child.

In this paper, I discuss three projects undertaken at Bank Street College in which we implemented and studied such environments. These studies raise fundamental questions about the design and implementation of FLEs, particularly the relationship between the children's purposes and those of their teachers. Coordination of divergent purposes within a FLE turns out to be a critical factor in the success of classroom microcomputer activities.

While research on microcomputers is relatively new at Bank Street, concern for FLEs is quite old. Since its beginning in 1916, the college has been at the forefront of the progressive education movement founded by John Dewey. A central theme in Dewey's (1902, 1938) writing on education is the notion that classroom activities must be related to the child's experiences, interests, and goals. This was a radical proposal for an era in which the teacher stood at the front of the class and lectured or conducted drills. Although the general notion has found

279

wide acceptance in United States schools in recent decades, many teachers find it impossible to implement because of limited resources, materials, and training. It is the hope of many people in the field of educational computing, including staff at Bank Street, that the microcomputer can be a resource for engaging children's interest and fostering a more creative learning process.

In this paper I will first describe the notion of FLE in more detail, and will then present observations about three projects that have tried to create FLEs. These projects concern the use of the Logo language in Bank Street classrooms, a project on science and mathematics education, and the creation of a network of microcomputers. In each case, the observations illustrate the importance of coordinating the goals of children and teachers.

Functional learning environments

We start with two assumptions: (1) Children are intrinsically motivated to work on tasks that are meaningful to them; and (2) the most effective educational environment is one that provides meaningful tasks, i.e., tasks that embody some function or purpose that children understand. While some children enjoy learning about a particular topic "for its own sake," in most cases, facts and skills are best learned in connection with larger tasks that give them significance or meaning. In this way, not only are children motivated to master the facts and skills, but they have a framework in which to understand the cultural significance of the facts and their relation to other facts. For example, a science project in which children attempt to answer specific questions about whales and their habitats by constructing a database provides an environment for learning scientific categorization schemes as well as specific facts about whales. It can also demonstrate to the children the variety of resources – such as textbooks, encyclopedias, and films – that are available in our culture for obtaining the facts, and confront them with the need to cull information from several sources.

Our assumption, however, leave two fundamental questions unanswered. First, we must understand where the goals that the children are interested in come from – are they inventions of the children or are they imposed by the teacher? Second, we must understand the relation between the goals that children undertake in the classroom and the tasks they will be confronted with in the real world outside of school. Unless students can apply the knowledge and skills they have acquired in school to tasks outside the classroom, any FLE will have been for naught.

Our approach to the first issue takes a middle position between the idea that the teacher must impose problems and the idea that children must invent their own classroom activities. On the one hand is the traditional view of education, and on the other is a radical version of the child-centered approach to education based on interpretations of the writings of Dewey as well as Piaget (1973).

It is very clear that Dewey felt that the purely child-centered approach was as erroneous as the traditional view that the teacher must impose the classroom tasks. The teacher has very important responsibilities which include suggesting tasks and presenting to the children alternative interpretations of problems. In many respects, Dewey's approach is more consistent with the sociohistorical approach to child development presented in the recently published writings of Vygotsky (1978) and Leont'ev (1981), in which the importance of the teacher–child interaction is emphasized, than with the universalist approach of Piaget, which deemphasizes the cultural context (Laboratory of Comparative Human Cognition, 1984). According to these theorists, the child's initial attempts to solve an arithmetical problem, write a story, or operate a computer program are carried out in interaction with teachers or more experienced children. What the child internalizes is not what the expert says, but a version of the interactions that constituted the joint activity. Thus, without coercion, these interactions guide children toward the cultural interpretation and significance of the tasks in which they are engaged (Newman, Riel, & Martin, 1983).

Meaningful tasks may come from a variety of sources. One source is the spontaneous ideas of the children themselves: most children have some topic which they simply "like." However, for some school topics this source may not be the most important. Teachers can make classroom tasks meaningful by showing children their significance in terms of a variety of uses for the skills involved, or in terms of the adult world they will be entering. The FLE created in this way can be a simulation of a real problem (e.g., role-playing commercial transactions as a context for doing arithmetic calculations), or it can be a real problem (e.g., actually selling food at a school fair to raise money to buy a classroom computer). The FLE can also be of a more abstract nature (e.g., a geometric problem can provide a meaningful context for calculating the size of an angle, providing that geometry itself has meaning within the children's experiences). A teacher can create interesting FLEs by crossing traditional discipline boundaries (e.g., by showing how geometric concepts such as triangulation can be used in geography to solve navigation problems).

Our approach to the second issue – the relationship between classroom and real-world goals – is closely related to the first. We suspect that the usability of school learning in later life is inseparable from the variety of FLEs in which it is embedded. Being able to see the same fact from multiple perspectives (i.e., recognizing the different uses it can have) engenders a flexible approach to acquiring knowledge that would otherwise be absent. This flexibility makes it possible to adapt the knowledge to new functional environments that cannot be specifically anticipated in the classroom.

Microcomputers can play a very useful role in FLEs because of their capacity for stimulation and because they themselves are important tools for the solution to a variety of interesting real-world problems. They also provide fluid and manipulable symbol systems in which many interesting abstract problems can be represented and solved. But they cannot be expected to function on their own. A teacher must build the bridges between the tool, the school task, the thinking skills, and their functional significance for the culture beyond the classroom.

Logo in a classroom

Logo is a programming language popularized by Seymour Papert (1980) and colleagues. According to Papert, Logo is an environment in which children can learn fundamental mathematical concepts and powerful problem-solving methods without the intervention of teachers. Papert takes his inspiration from Piaget, who has argued forcefully that

each time one prematurely teaches a child something he could have discovered for himself, that child is kept from inventing it and consequently from understanding it completely. (1970, p. 175)

One of Piaget's (1965) earliest examples was the game of marbles played by boys from preschool to adolescence. In Switzerland, where

Piaget studied the game, adults were not involved. The children learned from each other. Not only did the children master the complex rules of the game, but they came to understand that the rules were not absolute but a matter of convention and agreement among equals. The same kind of process is at the heart of Papert's claims for Logo: Without the imposition of adult authority and adult ideas, children can come to an understanding of the nature of concepts such as recursion that are as fundamental to programming as cooperative agreement is to games with rules. Of course, the peer play group for marbles included undisputed experts; the same may not be true for programming, which is seldom mastered by young children. This weakness in the analogy might lead us to question peer interaction as a basis for learning programming.

The initial interest in Logo at Bank Street, however, was not in testing its adequacy as a peer group FLE but with quite a different question. Researchers from the Center for Children and Technology set out to see if experience with programming would enhance planning skills in children. It was a reasonable hypothesis since writing a program is like creating a plan for the computer to execute. The question was whether there was any transfer from the activity of programming to other experimental tasks that also required making a plan of action but did not involve computers.

The researchers arranged to do their study in two classrooms at Bank Street's School for Children (SFC). The teachers in the SFC are highly committed to the child-centered approach to education, and were eager to try out Logo and the pedagogy developed by Papert. Neither teacher was an expert programmer, although each had taken a course with Papert prior to the study. The teachers were, however, experts in creating functional learning environments for children and approached the new task with enthusiasm.

For two years, the researchers observed and interviewed the children and teachers in the third and sixth grade classes. Pre- and post-tests were administered using a chore-scheduling task based on the work of Hayes-Roth and Hayes-Roth (1979). The findings concerning the transfer of Logo experience to the experimental planning task were very clear: The researchers found no effects at all (Pea & Kurland, 1984). By the time the researchers compiled their data, however, the negative findings came as little surprise. Observations of the children as they interacted with

Logo and with each other showed that very little planning was involved in their programming practices. Thus, there was little reason to expect programming to make children more planful.

As Pea (1983) observed:

> Much more common was on-line programming, in which children defined their goals, and found means to achieve them as they observed the products of their programs unfolding on the screen. Rather than constructing a plan, then implementing it as a program to achieve a well-defined goal, and afterwards running the implemented plan on the computer, children would evolve a goal while writing lines of Logo programming language, run their program, see if they liked the outcome, explore a new goal, and so on . . . In most cases, children preferred to rewrite a program from scratch rather than to suffer through the attention to detail required in figuring out where a program was going awry. As one child put it when asked why she was typing in commands directly rather than writing a program: "It's easier to do it the hard way."

From the children's point of view, Logo was for the most part an interesting classroom activity, although there were certainly differences among the children in their level of interest and in the amount of programming that they learned. But, despite their enthusiasm, they did not explore the more conceptually challenging aspects of Logo in the course of their discovery learning. They were essentially "playing." In Piaget's (1962) terminology, assimilation was dominating accommodation; that is, the goal was assimilated to the procedures rather than the procedures being accommodated to a set goal. Whatever worked became the goal retrospectively.

From the teacher's point of view, the children were engaged in the Logo activity but were not learning to program. Experiments involving the better Logo programmers showed that few had correct understanding of such central concepts as flow of control, conditionals, or recursion (Kurland and Pea, 1983). As time went on, the teachers began to question the discovery-oriented approach to teaching programming. It became clear to them that Logo could not just "happen," but that they, the teachers, had to have an idea of what they wanted the children to get out of the activity: Goals had to be set, activities had to be formulated, and the teachers had to come up with effective ways of getting their ideas across to the children. The teachers themselves wrote a book (Burns and Cook, in press) based on their efforts to make Logo part of their classrooms. Their experiences while attempting to follow the radical child-centered approach advocated by Papert suggests that, in the case of complex symbol systems, the educational activity must be guided by more mature members of the culture.

When an activity is made functional from the teachers' point of view, the children's activity may change. Those who follow Papert's child-centered approach fear that the activity will lose its intrinsic motivation once teachers decide they want to teach programming. This should not be the case if the teacher's role is to guide rather than impose the activity. However, important changes can result when the activity becomes part of the children's schoolwork. For example, children were often observed to work cooperatively while doing Logo. The children's interviews indicated that the relatively high level of cooperative work was a result of the activity's not being seen as part of the official schoolwork (Hawkins, 1983). There is some concern that, even in Bank Street classrooms where a high value is placed on cooperation, children will be less cooperative when the activity is no longer perceived as play and they have to be accountable to a teacher. FLEs must be functional for both teachers and children for education to happen. The coordination and optimization of these functions, however, remains a difficult issue that demands the attention of educators.

Simulating a function: "the science show"

Another illustration of the importance of the teacher in the structuring of a FLE is found in Bank Street's Project in Mathematics and Science Education. Materials developed by the project include a television series, software simulations, and workbooks, all of which emphasize the process and tools of scientific work. I will focus on one aspect of the project in which a FLE is based on a multimedia simulation of a navigation problem. While the content is more specific than is the case with Logo, the use of the content is still conditioned by the teacher's interpretation of its function.

A television series, "The Voyage of the Mimi," tells the story of an expedition to study whales off the New England coast. A group of scientists and their teenaged research assistants charter a schooner captained by an old sailor. Although the boat is old-fashioned, it is equipped with electronic navigation equipment, as well as computers and other sophisticated scientific gear. Thirteen episodes take the expedition through a series of adventures in which the crew learns a lot about the sea, whales, navigation, survival in the wilderness, and each other. In one episode, a bad electrical connection causes several instruments to malfunction. The captain suspects that they have been moving faster than his knotmeter indicates, so he has one of the assistants use the battery-operated radio direction finder to establish their position. The assistant calls down the compass bearings for two beacons while the captain plots the position of the boat on the chart. He finds they are actually much closer to dangerous shoals than he had thought. This episode illustrates a functional environment for navigational equipment, as well as for geometry-related skills concerned with intersecting lines and measurement of angles.

A simulation created as part of this project engages the same skills in a similar FLE. The game Rescue Mission simulates a navigational problem in which the players must determine their own position using a simulated radio direction finder, locate the position of a ship in distress using chart coordinates, and then plot a course toward the ship. A simulated radar screen, binoculars, and compass are also available to indicate the current location of the ship. Children play in teams, each attempting to be the first to get to the distressed ship.

The episode described above was designed to show how navigational instruments and geometrical concepts function in a real problem. It engaged children's interest both because they could identify with the teenaged characters and because of the emotional and dramatic tension of the narrative. The Rescue Mission game builds on the understanding of navigational instruments, and adds the motivation of peer interaction and the fantasy goal of rescue. Together with the print materials – workbooks and study guides to be used in the classroom – the show and software provide the basis for FLEs for a number of school-relevant subjects. However, as we saw with Logo, the teacher plays an important role in determining the nature of the software experience.

Char (1983; Char, Hawkins, Wootten, Sheingold, & Roberts, 1983) carried out formative research to guide the design of the classroom materials. Working in fourth, fifth, and sixth grade classrooms, she observed the way the teachers used the materials and the children's responses to them. From the children's point of view, the materials were a success. They enjoyed the TV show and were excited by the software simulation.

Interviews with the children showed that, after seeing the show and playing the Rescue Mission game, most of them understood the function of the navigational tools and the concepts of plotting positions at the level needed to win the game.

From the teachers' point of view, the results were mixed. The teachers in the study represented a wide range of expertise in their own science and mathematics training and in their use of classroom microcomputers. These teacher differences in training and computer expertise appeared to lead to differences in their interest in and perceptions of the Rescue Mission simulation. Some considered it limited to the function of teaching about navigation, while others found a variety of uses for it across the whole elementary curriculum. For the latter, the simulation and the navigation unit functioned as a jumping-off place for teaching about geometry, mathematical measurement, estimation, the history of the whaling industry, geography, and literature.

Interestingly, it was the teachers less familiar with computers and the teachers responsible for a wider variety of subjects (i.e., those who taught more than math or science) who found Rescue Mission most useful. In contrast, the science and math specialists, who were also more familiar with computers, were less receptive to the game's long-term use. Char (1983) points out that these teachers used computers primarily for programming instruction and were not accustomed to software that presented specific content. Perhaps as a result, the navigational content seemed to them to comprise the primary educational function of the software. Thus, an important finding from the formative research was the need to make explicit the full educational potential of the simulation to those teachers familiar with computers, as well as to those who are computer-naive.

The formative research on the science show materials clearly indicates the extent to which teachers shape children's exposure to materials through the FLEs they set up. It is not sufficient for software developers to create activities that embed important educational facts and concepts. A computer program per se constitutes a very limited FLE. The program must be interpreted by a user or teacher who understands its significance for a variety of culturally important contexts. Like any tool, a program is most useful in the hands of someone who knows how it can be used.

The functions of networking for children and teachers

The third project that will help to illustrate the coordination of teachers' and children's goals in FLEs is one that has just begun at Bank Street. However, we can draw on the experience of researchers Margaret Riel and James A. Levin of the University of California, San Diego (UCSD) for examples of how networking can function as a FLE. Networking is a general term for communications systems that link up computers. Most microcomputers, when enhanced with a piece of hardware known as a modem, can send and receive messages, text, and even programs to and from other computers over phone lines. Networking is becoming a popular pastime among young computer users who call up computerized bulletin board systems (BBSs) to read messages from other people, leave messages about topics of interest, and exchange software.

We at Bank Street are interested in finding out if networking can be used as a FLE for writing and communication skills. Can we take advantage of children's strong motivation to communicate with their peers to create environments in which children can practice writing and learn to write better? An experimental FLE at UCSD gives reason to be optimistic. The Computer Chronicles (Riel, 1983) operated between schools in San Diego and Alaska, several of which were located in isolated areas. Children wrote news stories using a word processor, which were then sent to the other participating classrooms. In each site, the children, with their teachers' help, composed a monthly newspaper drawing on both local stories and those coming from distant places. In many cases, children edited the stories that came in "over the wire" just as newspaper reporters would do. In fact, the frequency of editing someone else's work for style and meaning using the word processor was much higher than is the case when children write their own stories using the same technology (Quinsaat, Levin, Boruta, & Newman, 1983). Thus, the production of a newspaper became a FLE that not only encouraged children to write, but also provided a context for the editing and revision of their own work as well as the writing of others.

The Computer Chronicles shows the potential for networking as the basis for a FLE. It also illustrates a feature of FLEs that have been suggested as important by our other examples: the coordination of the goals of children and teachers. From the children's point of view, the activity was interesting because they were able to communicate with peers who lived in interesting and exotic places (Alaska and southern California, depending on your point of view). From the teachers' point of view, the activity provided a context in which children could practice writing and were motivated to edit and revise their work. These goals are not identical, but neither are they in conflict. It was because the teachers wanted an activity that would encourage writing and revision that they set up the newswire idea, thus giving the children a chance to communicate with interesting peers. However, without the specific structuring, it is unlikely that the children would have engaged in editing each other's writing.

Conclusion

Three examples of FLEs have illustrated the importance of the teacher in creating and interpreting children's learning environments. While computer software can play an important role in FLEs as a tool, it should not be expected to carry the whole burden of education. Teachers are needed in order to interpret the tools in terms of classroom goals and the larger culture outside of school. Our examples have all been drawn from elementary schools, where the need is especially clear. We suspect that, as children develop, the role of the teacher as interpreter or as someone to present another side of the story is gradually internalized, with the result that the mature college student can be expected to use books and manuals to discover multiple points of view on many subjects. Yet, even mature students require the insights of experts when the subject matter is particularly complex.

Our focus on the teacher is not meant to detract from a concern for the children's point of view. Obviously, a FLE cannot work unless it makes contact with the children's interests and experiences. A well-designed FLE is one that coordinates children's and teachers' points of view so that both the children and the teachers can achieve meaningful goals.

Note

Paper presented at the conference on Microcomputers in Education, Tokyo Institute of Technology, Tokyo, Japan, January 8, 1984.

290 *Denis Newman*

References

Burns, G., & Cook, M. (in press). *Logo: A learner's guide.* Englewood Cliffs, NJ: Prentice-Hall.

Char, C. A. (1983, April). *Research and design issues concerning the development of educational software for children* (Tech. Rep. No. 14). New York: Bank Street College of Education, Center for Children and Technology.

Char, C. A., Hawkins, J., Wootten, J., Sheingold, K., & Roberts, T. (1983). *"The Voyage of the Mimi": Classroom case studies of software, video, and print materials.* Unpublished manuscript. New York: Bank Street College of Education, Center for Children and Technology.

Dewey, J. (1902). *The child and the curriculum.* Chicago: University of Chicago Press.

Dewey, J. (1938). *Experience and education.* New York: Collier Books.

Hawkins, J. (1983, April). *Learning Logo together: The social context* (Tech. Rep. No. 13). New York: Bank Street College of Education, Center for Children and Technology.

Hayes-Roth, B., & Hayes-Roth, F. (1979). A cognitive model of planning. *Cognitive Science, 3,* 275–310.

Kurland, D. M., & Pea, R. D. (1983, February). *Children's mental models of recursive Logo programs* (Tech. Rep. No. 10). New York: Bank Street College of Education, Center for Children and Technology.

Laboratory of Comparative Human Cognition. (1984). Culture and cognitive development. In W. Kessen (Ed.), *History, theory, and methods* (Vol. I), of P. H. Mussen (Ed.), *Handbook of child psychology* (4th ed.). New York: Wiley.

Leont'ev, A. N. (1981). *Problems in the development of the mind.* Moscow: Progress Publishers.

Newman, D., Riel, M. M., & Martin, L. (1983). Cultural practices and Piaget's theory: The impact of a cross-cultural research program. In D. Kuhn & J. A. Meacham (Eds.), *On the development of developmental psychology.* Basel: Karger.

Papert, S. (1980). *Mindstorms: Children, computers, and powerful ideas.* New York: Basic Books.

Pea, R. D. (1983, April). *Logo programming and problem solving* (Tech. Rep. No. 12). New York: Bank Street College of Education, Center for Children and Technology.

Pea, R. D., & Kurland, D. M. (1984, March). *Logo programming and the development of planning skills* (Tech. Rep. No. 16). New York: Bank Street College of Education, Center for Children and Technology.

Piaget, J. (1965). *The moral judgement of the child.* New York: Free Press.

Piaget, J. (1970). Piaget's theory. In P. H. Mussen (Ed.), *Carmichael's manual of child psychology.* New York: Wiley.

Piaget, J. (1962). *Play, dreams and imitation in childhood.* New York: W. W. Norton.

Piaget, J. (1973). *To understand is to invent.* New York: Grossman.

Quinsaat, M. G., Levin, J. A., Boruta, M., & Newman, D. (1983, April). *The effects of microcomputer word processing on elementary school writing.* Paper presented at the annual meetings of the American Educational Research Association, Montreal, Canada.

Riel, M. M. (1983). Education and ecstasy: Computer chronicles of students' writing together. *The Quarterly Newsletter of the Laboratory of Comparative Human Cognition, 5*, 59–67.

Vygotsky, L. S. (1978). *Mind in society: The development of higher psychological processes.* Cambridge, MA: Harvard University Press.

22 "But it's important data!" Making the demands of a cognitive experiment meet the educational imperatives of the classroom

Marilyn G. Quinsaat

As a relative newcomer to research on children, I have noticed a trend in the titling of research papers. Authors have found a creative outlet in using cute phrases from children who are their subjects to exemplify the intent of the paper. I have chosen a cute phrase, but this time the saying is from the classroom researchers: "But it's important data." This paper is intended as a reflection on the difficulties encountered, and how consequent decisions were made, while I was the teacher in a classroom where psychological research was being done. It is also intended as a comment on the difficulties encountered by the practitioner among researchers.

The research described in this paper took place in my 3rd/4th grade classroom. The three-year project (two years in the classroom have been completed, one year of analysis remains), sought to study the cognitive demands children are faced with when learning to deal with the "same task" in different classroom situations. Videotaped data were designed to trace specific cognitive tasks through different settings: large-group lessons, small-group lessons, one-to-one tutorials, children-only school interactions, and after-school clubs. A set of lessons incorporating all of the settings within a curriculum-cognitive task unit was called a "cycle." A more complete description of the project from the researchers' point of view is available in Griffin, Cole, and Newman (in press).

It was extremely important that the teacher work closely with the project to help with the planning of cycle lessons, documentation of decisions which might affect the kind of data collected, and analysis. In many respects the practitioner and observers had much of the same relationship as others who had been involved in classroom research (Florio & Walsh, 1976; Mehan, Cazden, Coles, Fisher, & Maroules, 1976). Florio and Walsh labeled the teacher's role "Observant Participant," giving the impression that researchers and practitioners collaborated in finding and making observations about the classroom. However, while in previous classroom work researchers were primarily observers, in this project, researchers set up and participated in specific tasks in order to systematically explore the ways in which cognitive tasks are influenced by the interactional and curricular variations necessary to run a classroom. Researchers sought to understand the context of cognitive tasks, and the teacher had a more responsible role in the project. The problem of coordinating the needs of cognitive research with the ongoing business of teaching and learning in the classroom had to be confronted continually.

Background

At the beginning of the project, I had two years experience teaching in public schools. Prior to that, I had been a Sociology major and had graduated from the same university and the same teacher-training program with which the research was associated. Much of my upperdivision work emphasized learning about current educational research, considering the teacher as ethnographer, and using video-tape equipment to study classroom interaction. When Bud Mehan contacted me about participating in this research I thought it might give me a chance to build on my undergraduate background, allow me to get a glimpse of what graduate work would be like, and perhaps show me something about my teaching. But I considered self-improvement to be an indirect objective of my involvement in the project, since the project was not directed at changing my teaching.

It is important to note that I had some prior experience which put me at an advantage over many teachers who might find themselves in such a situation. I had been video-taped while teaching as an undergraduate. I knew that video-taping could be an extremely important and beneficial means of gathering data about teaching. Despite the fact that I had this experience, I still felt somewhat uncomfortable about the prospect. At the outset, the researchers assured me that they were not interested in looking at my *teaching* as data. The *students* were the "subjects"; aspects of "how they learned" were the data.

I soon began to understand the design and interests of the project, and realized that, although I was not primary "subject," my role as the teacher, and the way I taught, were extremely important to the analysis. Although the study was not focused on teachers, knowledge about the teacher's role in designing lessons, making decisions about what and how tasks should be learned, and his/her actual implementations of plans would be essential to specifying what the task was and how the children perceived the task. These considerations were central to claims about social organization and cognition. As the teacher, I clearly had privileged sources of knowledge. As I came to understand my role in the project as a mediator between abstract research plans and concrete classroom reality, meeting the demands of both teaching and the process of doing research became more difficult.

Problems in doing classroom research in general

Before proceeding to the specifics of our research, I want to review problems that may arise when teachers become involved in classroom research in their own rooms. Although it is rarely addressed openly, the first hurdle to doing classroom-based research is the difficulty in finding educators willing to participate. In principle, it should be expected that educators would be interested in keeping up with educational research because of its implications on how teaching should go on in the classroom. However, some teachers feel an unwillingness to cooperate in classroom research, afraid of work disruption, and especially of accusations of failure to keep abreast of new trends in their field. Fear of such criticism is, in fact, central to the reluctance of teachers to participate in such work.

Many teachers I know assume that educational researchers end up exposing and criticizing the practitioner and/or the educational system. It is easy to see how teachers might get this impression from the kind of research that is published about teachers and schools. Aside from curriculum research, teachers usually hear about work that shows how teachers are doing it all wrong. *Pygmalion in the Classroom* is a good example. It points out that a teacher can make or ruin a student's academic potential without even knowing how the influence was accomplished.

Why, one might ask naively, should a competent teacher worry? If everything was going all right, there would be nothing to hide. This point of view really *is* naive. I am willing to admit that things go wrong in my classroom more often than I would like, as would any honest professional. And if video-tape equipment recorded what was going on, it would be extremely easy to find cases which could be embarrassing.

When observers are in the classroom, especially observers who are presumed to be experts on the teaching/learning process, teachers experience an unpleasant role reversal. Under ordinary conditions, the classroom teacher is regarded as an agent of benefits for the children. S/he is responsible for helping them acquire the academic skills necessary for success in their everyday lives, a responsibility that extends beyond textbooks to the social organization of the classroom as well. Once an observer/researcher enters the classroom, the teacher begins to feel his/her role change. The researcher is there to improve classroom effectiveness. The researcher is an advocate for the children, even if s/he does not know their names or their academic histories. The researcher's advocacy may result in recommendations for changes in the classroom. Some of the changes may stem from an evaluation of the teacher, viewed as part of "the problem," instead of as a beneficial agent.

Many educators I know are discouraged with their work, and have good reason to be. Complications with the demands of the public, bureaucratic organization, high student–teacher ratios, and other constraints all add to the stress of the teaching profession. Given the opportunity, they would like to talk about the difficulties of teaching in addition to the difficulties that face the children. Yet such conversations rarely happen as a part of the research process because to enter such a conversation is to undermine one's own authority with little hope that the risk will pay off in terms of improved classroom conditions.

Cognitive experiments in the classroom

These very general remarks about classroom research are intended as an introduction to the special problems of the project that I engaged in. I did not simply agree to have someone observe in my classroom over a two-year period while I went about my own business. Instead, I agreed to participate in a project that would, from time to time, involve me in the planning of lessons that were motivated by the researcher's focus on specifying the way that the children processed information at each step in the lesson. Based on my past experience, I had ideas about what kinds of lesson content and structure would work well with my room full of 4th graders. But my ideas didn't always fit the requirements of the research.

The project conducted in my classroom was focused on the ways that the social organization of a learning task influences how well children master the material. Intuitively it seems that some children learn best when left with paper-and-pencil work; others respond well when working with a small group of other children; still others can't seem to understand the material unless the teacher is working with them on a one-to-one basis. These intuitions are a part of classroom folklore, but they are very difficult to pin down because so many aspects of the lesson change from one kind of teacher–student interaction to the next. Our research tried to find a way to evaluate such ideas.

The basic idea was to present the kids with the same basic material in lessons structured in very different ways. We had large-group lessons where I presented material to the whole class at once. We had some lessons where a small group of children worked with the teacher, and others where the same small group worked independently. Finally, we created "tutorials," one-on-one reviews of a whole unit, that were supposed to evaluate what the child had learned – while teaching the child as much as possible by way of a lesson wrap-up.

This systematic variation in the way that lessons were organized was the first source of problems for me. I like to organize my classroom so that I am usually working with a small group, while other groups are working on their own, rotating these groups throughout the day. My classroom was not organized in such a way that large group lessons would be easy to do, so we had to make arrangements to accommodate that need. Whenever the research was in progress, my normal routine occasionally had to be modified to allow for the scheduled kinds of lesson organization.

A second area where I had to modify my usual procedure was in the forming of lesson plans. The research sought to evaluate the influence of different kinds of social organization on the performance of specific cognitive tasks. This meant either finding a ready-made curriculum unit that fit our needs, or developing our own. In many cases we had to work quite hard to find ways to implement research ideas in the classroom. It was in this area that the research team relied most heavily on the teacher. I was regarded as the expert on presenting curriculum to 4th graders, so in the translation between abstract research goals and practical day-to-day activities I had to be the translator or at least arbiter of translations. For example, we decided to teach a cycle on Household Chemicals. The unit had the potential of being a success, especially if the lessons included some "exciting" experiments. It also had the potential of being a disaster, if the content or the cognitive task was too difficult. I had to insure that the materials used were interesting and accessible to 4th graders. Abstract formulations from a college text wouldn't work.

These goals were not completely incompatible. The researchers accepted my goals and I accepted theirs. I, too, wanted the children to master the cognitive skills underlying the curriculum. But implementing these two goals simultaneously turned out to be one of the central difficulties of the project. It didn't take me long to learn that whatever areas the researchers might be experts in, tailoring classroom lessons to the needs of cognitive psychological analysis was not one of them!

A useful example of conflicting goals occurred soon after the begin ning of a cycle on Mapping. The children were given areas to measure and then were instructed to draw an accurate map of the area, given the measurements they collected. As the lesson progressed it became clear to me that many of the students were eager to do something with their measurements, but didn't quite know how to go about doing it. I felt that a lesson on scaling was in order, but that lesson wasn't planned to occur until later. I got together with the research team and negotiated a change in the cycle. Since I was interested in teaching the concept of scaling, I was made responsible for writing up the lesson plan. This aspect of the cycle had previously been guided by the researchers' notions of the structure of the topic. During the course of this replanning, it was also decided that the lesson would be done as a tutorial instead of a small- or large-group lesson. This procedure was different from past tutorials, which occurred at the *ends* of cycles in order to serve as assessments of what a child knew. For the mapping cycle, the tutorial was in the middle of the cycle, and definitely oriented toward teaching.

Implementing this new piece of research/curriculum produced a new kind of conflict. I viewed the tutorial as an opportunity to teach the concept of scale. I believed that this was what the children needed to know in order to get on with the upcoming lessons on mapping. The research team, on the other hand, viewed this tutorial like the others, as an opportune time for the teacher to do some careful assessment of what the children knew, while incorporating good teaching. What constituted "important data" for them was a chance to look carefully at the levels at which children were able to do the scaling task. This conflict led me to believe that even the idea of doing tutorials, or individual evaluations on my students, was a luxury which I couldn't possibly engage in during regular classroom instruction. The researchers needed tutorial situations in which children were taken to the limit of their abilities in order to determine exactly the level at which they could process the information from previous lessons. Given my time constraints, I certainly didn't need that precise an evaluation. More general evaluations of my students would have been enough for me to see how to go about teaching them.

The conflict is in the fact that, as a teacher, it is important for me to find ways in which children can succeed as well as possible in their academic work. Yet this was not necessarily the goal of the researchers since they were also interested in the ways and situations in which children were having *difficulties* with cognitive tasks. Sometimes situations would occur that could only be "negotiated" while I was in the process of teaching. I took it as my responsibility to make certain that lessons went as well as possible once the planning phase was over, no matter what the logic of the research demanded. Sometimes I would modify what I should have said or done in lessons, using my intuitions about the needs of individual students.

My modifications during the lessons complicated life for the researchers. It would have been convenient, from their viewpoint, for my lessons to be uniformly structured. They weren't, of course. But the changes eventually became part of the data since we wanted to know when the requirements of classroom goals would require changes in the cognitive demands placed upon the children. This simply alludes to the idea that research, as well as teaching, often needs to be modified as the process under observation unfolds.

It is important to note that the primary reason I was willing to negotiate changes in the lesson plans was not to improve data collection, but to act as a guardian for the children. This advocacy was carried on simultaneously on several grounds. Research is intended to be a benefit for the children in the long run. But in the immediate circumstances, it is up to the teacher to protect the child from research situations which might violate their rights. For example, it is well-known that classroom research involves possible invasion of the subjects' privacy as well as the potential disruption of classroom activities.

All participants in this project were covered by a Protection of Human Subjects Declaration. The criteria for protecting the rights of the children while collecting data were quite stringent. Yet knowing when a child's rights were violated remained rather ambiguous. For example, one part of the Human Subjects Protection Declaration required that video-tape and camera equipment remain as "unobtrusive as possible" so that regular classroom business could continue. "Unobtrusive as possible" is a difficult phrase to translate into classroom reality. I was left as the agent for the children in deciding what equipment got in the way, and in negotiating how equipment could be set up to obtain proper sound and camera angle for data collection purposes.

Conflicts were minimized by spending energy educating each other. I often felt that I was the student. For example, at the beginning of the project, it was unclear to me why the tutorials for each child were necessary. I welcomed the opportunity to teach one-to-one lessons in the classroom, but the idea of teaching 27 "identical" tutorials per cycle, some lasting an hour, while the rest of the children went about their business, promised a lot of strain on my part, not to mention the effect it might have on classroom management.

The researchers carefully explained the importance of doing tutorials in the way they had in mind. I was given recently published research to read on new methods of mixing evaluation and teaching that the tutorials were designed to model (Brown & French, 1979). I found the ideas interesting and we had several discussions about how we could organize such extensive one-on-one work.

Over the following two years, the research team worked to help me understand all facets of the project. They provided large amounts of background reading, made themselves available for questions and discussion, provided access to helpful consultants, and invited me to participate in Laboratory meetings where our own and other related projects were being discussed. This program of education, centered on the research, provided me with the information needed to make intelligent decisions about what needed to get done in the classroom.

As the project continued, the goals of the research became clearer to me, and to the researchers as well. I began to understand that research is a continually changing process. I was given more responsibility in the planning of the lessons as my interest and understanding of the research grew. One of these areas was in the planning and teaching of a Division cycle.

Division cycle was an ongoing activity throughout the second year of data collection. Since division is a standard part of the 4th grade curriculum, and children were seen to do the calculation in other lessons, it was decided to tape any occurrences where children were trying to solve problems involving division.

At first I thought that this cycle would be much easier for me. There would be no long hours of planning and lesson preparation. However, in a sense, what occurred was even more difficult than the specially planned lesson. It was important to the researchers to have a very detailed specification of what each lesson entailed. This specificity was normally accomplished by the preplanning of each regular cycle. In this case, the information was contained in my notions of what I thought the lesson was and how I thought it should be taught. I found myself being questioned about every aspect of the division process. Why did I choose the algorithm I taught? What were the steps involved? What did the child need to know in order to do each step? How did it help some children and not others? How did I come to learn this algorithm? These are all good questions, but they are not the kind that I ask myself when I teach division. I began to feel defensive about my work, feeling that the researchers might now be investigating me!

Understanding why it's important data

The Division cycle provided another example where the everyday demands of the teacher's job come into conflict with that of the researchers. To a teacher, it is not necessary to be able to specify all aspects of a lesson. It is enough to be able to find or create lessons which serve the purpose, are appropriate to the class, and are manageable. If a teacher were to work on it, s/he could spend the time figuring out the specifics of the lessons in the way that the research team needed it, but it would demand a great deal more time than the competing demands of the curriculum permit.

But, to the researchers, that very specificity of lessons is what enables them to understand what the children are doing. As one of the researchers pointed out, the teacher's specific notions about the lessons were important data, because they shaped the way that the children experienced the curriculum. I began to understand better that everything that happened to shape classroom lessons was important. The students alone were not the subjects. Interaction was the "subject" also. And in the sense that interaction was the subject, the teacher became a subject, too.

I recall several occasions when I made a casual observation. A researcher would stop me and ask me to clarify my statement. At that point, the researcher would mutter, "We've got to remember to write that down." No one could specify ahead of time all that constituted good data, so at any point anything could be important.

In reflecting generally on the past two years of data collection, it is difficult to know exactly how the research has affected the children or their ability to do schoolwork. One hopes the children gained some knowledge from the curriculum areas taught. I know from being with them that they found the cycles to be interesting as well as fun.

However, I feel that *I* probably was affected the most. I spent hours working on the project, to the point where it seemed like a second job. Those hours often included negotiations which were made difficult by the ambiguous, paradoxical conditions of advocacy. Yet I felt that I had emerged after two years from the best teacher-training inservice program I had encountered.

The experience I've gained from having been involved in research continues to have a great impact on my work. Designing curriculum for the cycles and the amount of specificity involved in doing that made me more aware of the quality of materials that I was coming in contact with in my classroom. Getting to understand better the theories behind our research project and learning how to be critical of theory taught me how to analyze the vast number of educational curricula that I encounter. The analysis of my classroom thus far reveals that I do plenty of things I wish

I could do better. But I think in the long run, it also reveals that I am learning how.

Note

I would like to thank Denis Newman, Peg Griffin, Mike Cole, and Bud Mehan for providing comments about the paper, and for helping me get through the first two years.

Research supported by a grant award from the National Institute of Education – G 780159.

References

Brown, A., & French, L. The zone of potential development: Implications for intelligence testing in the year 2000. *Intelligence*, 1979, 3, 255–277.

Florio, S., & Walsh, M. The teacher as collaborator in research. Paper presented at the American Educational Research Association Convention, San Francisco, 1976.

Griffin, P., Cole, M., & Newman, D. Locating tasks in psychology and education. *Discourse Processes*, in press.

Mehan, H., Cazden, C., Coles, L., Fisher, S., & Maroules, N. The social organization of classroom lessons. CHIP report 67. Center for Human Information Processing, University of California, San Diego, December, 1976.

23   Performance before competence: Assistance to child discourse in the zone of proximal development

Courtney B. Cazden

> It is the distance between the actual developmental level as determined by independent problem solving and the level of potential development as determined through problem solving under adult guidance or in collaboration with peers (1978, p. 86).[1]

This is how Vygotsky described what he called the "zone of proximal development." The concept of a zone within which a child can accomplish with help what later can be accomplished alone can be useful in helping us understand the child's acquisition of discourse.

If we substitute "speaking" for "problem-solving" in Vygotsky's definition, then the zone of proximal development for speaking,

> is the distance between the actual developmental level as determined by independent speaking and the level of potential development as determined through speaking under adult guidance or in collaboration with peers. (Mehan, 1979)

What kind of assistance to discourse development through "speaking under adult guidance" do children get in school? It is my impression, from both personal experience as a teacher and from the research literature, that children get help in answering teacher questions, and, more rarely, they get help in participating in the discourse structure typical of classroom lessons. An example of each in turn:

Help with particular questions

It's important to distinguish between help that somehow gets a child to produce the right answer, and help from which the child might

303

learn how to answer similar questions in the future. Only the latter is of educational interest. All teachers sometimes have to get the answer said somehow in order to keep the lesson going for the sake of social order, what Mehan empathetically calls "getting through" (1979, pp. 111–114); but one cannot defend the value of such sequences to the individual child. If, for example, when a child cannot read the word *bus* on a word card, the teacher prompts the answer with the question, "What do you ride to school on?" the child may correctly now say "bus." But that is not a prompt that the child could give to herself the next time, because the prompt depends on the very knowledge of the word that it is supposed to cue. We are looking for assistance that at least has the possibility of helping children learn how to answer, even if we lack evidence that it in fact does.

Here are two examples from reading lessons with first-grade children analyzed by Mehan (1979). From one theoretical perspective, these are excellent examples of "negotiated interactions" or "interactional accomplishments": the children get the teacher to give them the clues they need to find the answer. (I am grateful to Peg Griffin for this observation.) But, speaking for the teacher, I want to suggest another non-contradictory perspective: that the teacher was providing implicit information about how to answer such questions – information that is applicable, and, I hope, eventually transferred, beyond the particular instance.

Examples of question sequences (from Mehan, 1979)

(1) T.   OK, what's the name of this story? (points to title of story)
    Ss.   (no response)
    T.   Who remembers, what's the name, what's the story about?
    Ss.   (no response)
    T.   Is it about taking a bath?
    Ss.   No.
    T.   Is it about the sunshine?
    Ss.   No.
    T.   Edward, what's it about?
    Edward.   The map.
    T.   The map. That's right. This says 'the map.'

(2) T.   What else, what else, Edward, what do you think we could put there that starts with an M?
    Edward.   (No answer)
    T.   Somebody in your family, Edward. . . .

Audrey. I Know. I know.
T.   What?
Audrey. Man.
T.   Man, good for you, Audrey.

In the first example, the implicit message is about the meaning of the question "What's the story about?" The form of simplification here is from the initial wh-question to yes/no alternatives, a sequence common in adult talk to children (J. B. Gleason, personal communication). The specific alternatives are deliberately absurd members of the category of things that could answer that question.[2] In the second example, the general wh-question about "What else to think of a word," a useful heuristic is to narrow the field to a small set you can run through in your mind.

Help with participation in lessons

There are various reasons why help with particular questions may not be enough, why children may need help with known-answer questions, in general, and the lesson structure in which they are embedded. They may be newcomers to school; they may need to get used to particular lesson structures in particular classrooms; they may come from a cultural background that may lead to sociolinguistic interference between the discourse patterns of home and school.

Even in the now growing literature on cultural differences between home and school, there are few descriptions of what can be called "second discourse teaching." More attention has been given by researchers to how the teacher can adapt to children's preferred ways of interacting than to how teachers can help children adapt to the school, even though Philips (1972) presented both alternatives in the concluding section of her influential paper. One important exception is Heath's (in press) work with teachers in a Black community in the southeast U.S., which she calls Trackton. When the teachers complained that children did not participate in lessons, Heath helped them understand what she had learned from five years of ethnographic field work in the Trackton community. For example, the children were not used to known-answer questions about the labels and attributes of objects and events; as one third grade boy complained, "Ain't nobody can talk about things being about theirselves." Heath then worked with the teachers to try out

changes in their classrooms. Because Heath's work is such an imagina-
tive and rare example of assistance to children's discourse development
in school, I quote at some length:

For some portions of the curriculum, teachers adapted some teaching materials and techniques in accordance with what they had learned about questions in Trackton. For
example, in early units on social studies, which taught about "our community," teachers began to use photographs of sections of different local communities, public buildings of the town, and scenes from the nearby countryside. Teachers then asked not for
the identification of specific objects or attributes of the objects in these photographs,
but questions such as:

> *What's happening here?*
> *Have you ever been here?*
> *Tell me what you did when you were there.*
> *What's this like? (pointing to a scene, or item in a scene)*

Responses of children were far different than those given in usual social studies lessons.
Trackton children talked, actively and aggressively became involved in the lesson, and
offered useful information about their past experiences. For specific lessons, responses
of children were taped; after class, teachers then added to the tapes specific questions
and statements identifying objects, attributes, etc. Answers to these questions were pro
vided by children adept at responding to these types of questions. Class members then
used these tapes in learning centers. Trackton students were particularly drawn to these,
presumably because they could hear themselves in responses similar in type to those used
in their own community. In addition, they benefitted from hearing the kinds of questions and answers teachers used when talking about things. On the tapes, they heard
appropriate classroom discourse strategies. Learning these strategies from tapes was less
threatening than acquiring them in actual classroom activities where the facility of other
students with recall questions enabled them to dominate teacher–student interactions.
Gradually, teachers asked specific Trackton students to work with them in preparing
recall questions and answers to add to the tapes. Trackton students then began to hear
themselves in successful classroom responses to questions such as "What it that?" "What
kind of community helper works there?"

   In addition to using the tapes, teachers openly discussed different types of questions
with students, and the class talked about the kinds of answers called for by certain questions. For example, *who, when,* and *what* questions could often be answered orally by
single words; other kinds of questions were often answered with many words which made
up sentences and paragraphs when put into writing. (Heath, in press)

Help with other discourse forms

   In the San Diego classroom described by Mehan, we created
one special speech situation that we called an instructional chain (IC)
(Cazden et al., 1979), and I want to describe it briefly here as an example

of the possible benefits of non-lesson discourse. Briefly, in each IC the teacher taught a lesson to one child who then taught the same lesson to one or more peers. Leola, a Black third grader, was asked to learn and then teach a language arts task. Here are the first three items on her worksheet in completed form.

1. new   1. Y ~~ø~~ ~~ł~~ o ~~đ~~ u   2. t ~~ɏ~~ ~~ɇ~~ o l ~~ɇ~~ d   3. m ~~ø~~ ~~ń~~ e
2. no
3. off   *You*   *told*   *me*

Table 23.1. gives a skeletal version, minus repetitions, corrections, etc., of the teacher's directions as she talked Leola through the first two items on the task, and the full transcript of Leola's subsequent directions first back to the teacher as a rehearsal, and then in actual instruction of her peers. Note in passing that the teacher's questions serve to talk Leola through the task until she can do it herself. That such aid does help Leola work independently is shown by a comparison of the teacher's instructions for the first and second items. The first three parts are repeated, but then a much vaguer and incomplete question "Now what are you going to – " is sufficient, and Leola takes off on her own.

The important aspect of this IC for thinking about discourse development at school is the increased articulateness and precision in Leola's instructions from her first rehearsal to the teacher:

Spell these letters, and then put out that letter, and then have another letter left.

to the most elaborated version in item 3. Here it is without the hesitations and self-repairs:

The opposite of *off* is *on*, so on number 3, you gotta cross *on* off. O-N. And it is *me* left, M-E.

This is a good example of what Wertsch, following the Soviet psychologists, calls microgenesis – that is, development within an observable time period, and it is a kind of development that Leola seemed to need. In the nine lessons analyzed by Mehan, some three hours of talk in all, she spoke four times, and only twice more than one word. This is not to say that she was in any way non-verbal; but it is to suggest that she could benefit from challenges to talk about academic topics, not just in response to questions.

Table 23.1

Teacher's instructions to Leola

ITEM 1

Teacher	*Leola*
OK, now number one here says *new*.	
What's the opposite of *new*?	Old.
Old. How would you spell *old*?	O-L-D
OK, in the letters that are on this paper, cross out the letters you just used for spelling *old*.	(L. does it)
Good. What word is left?	Y-O-U
What does that spell?	You.
OK, and down here you'll write *you*.	

ITEM 2

Teacher	*Leola*
OK, now number 2 here says –	No.
No. What's the opposite of *no*?	Yes.
OK, how do you spell *yes*?	Y-E-S
All right, now what are you going –	(L. crosses out the letters Y-E-S)
	Told.

Leola's versions of the instructions

In rehearsal to the teacher:

L.   Spell these letters, and then put out that letter, and then have another letter left.
    (Later, after T. goes over the instructions again) To do the opposite of this. You got to write old. I'm gonna tell 'em: you gotta write old, cross old out and you have another letter left.

In actual instruction of her peers:

(1)   [Goes to get pencils, then returns to work desk and sits down]
    It is hard. . . . You gotta write – what's the opposite
    So you got – so you gotta cross O-L and D, and you have a letter left, and you – you put the letter left in these words.

(2)   You cross it – you see, you got to do the opposite of "n–no" i – "no" is "yes" on number two. "No" – "no" is "yes", so you gotta write Y-E-S. And you have a "told"

(3)   left, so you write T-O-L-D. See, d–do the op – the op – the opposite of ah – uh – "off" is "on," so you gotta cross, on number three, you gotta cross "on" off. O-N. And you – it is "me" left, M-E.

Discussion

Earlier I pointed out the obvious difference between helping a child somehow get a particular answer, and helping a child gain some conceptual understanding from which answers to similar questions can be generated alone at a future time. We can think about this distinction more generally as different relationships between performance and competence.

Child discourse under adult guidance that is more advanced than what the child can speak alone can be called "performance without competence." Gleason and Weintraub (1976) first pointed out the existence of such performance in early social routines like *bye-bye, thank you,* and *trick-or-treat.* I am generalizing her description to other kinds of adult-assisted talk. In the school examples, the teacher assumes – with Vygotsky – that the assisted performance is not just performance *without* competence, but performance *before* competence – that the assisted performance does indeed contribute to subsequent development. Our task as researchers is to find out if and how that happens.

Notes

This paper is a revised version of the third part of Cazden, 1979.

1. Perhaps because the adjective "proximal" is infrequently used in English, some writers use the term "zone of potential development." But the two are not synonyms. The trouble with *potential* is that it has no boundaries; potentially, any child is capable of learning anything at some future time. By contrast, the zone of *proximal* development is much narrower. Instruction in this zone leads to development by aiming at the "ripening" function; by being just a little ahead, not out of sight.
2. As this article was going to press, I found a relevant analysis by Churchill (1978) of disconfirming answers to yes/no ("specific proposal") questions. His "generalized invitation maxim" says in part: "If you are asked a specific proposal question and . . . your answer is the disconfirming one, either give the disconfirming answer and then give the correct answer or give the correct answer only (p. 48). Presumably the teacher would have welcomed a one-turn answer that followed this maxim:

   > Is it about taking a bath?
   > No, it's about the map.

But that did not happen. Whether for developmental or situational reasons, the children answered only "no"; and a separate teacher turn was necessary to elicit the correct answer.

References

Cazden, C. B. Peekaboo as an instructional model: Discourse development at home and at school. *Papers and Reports on Child Language Development*, No. 17. Stanford University, Department of Linguistics, 1979.

Cazden C. B., et al. "You all gonna hafta listen": Peer teaching in a primary classroom. In W. A. Collins (Ed.), *Children's language and communication*. Hillsdale, N.J.: Erlbaum, 1979.

Churchill, L. *Questioning strategies in sociolinguistics*. Rowley, Mass.: Newbury House, 1978.

Gleason, J. B., & Weintraub, S. The acquisition of routines in child language, *Language in Society*, 1976, *5*, 129–136.

Heath, S. B. Questioning at home and at school. In G. Spindler (Ed.), *The ethnography of schooling: Educational anthropology in action*. In preparation.

Mehan, H. *Learning lessons*. Cambridge: Harvard University Press, 1979.

Philips, S. U. Participant structures and communicative competence: Warm Springs children in community and classroom. In C. B. Cazden, V. P. John, & D. Hymes (Eds.), *Functions of language in the classroom*. New York: Teachers College Press, 1972.

Vygotsky, L. S. *Thought and language*. Cambridge: MIT Press, 1962.

Vygotsky, L. S. *Mind in society: The development of higher psychological processes*. Cambridge: Harvard University Press, 1978.

Cognition in the wild

24 Low-income children's preschool literacy experiences: Some naturalistic observations

Alonzo B. Anderson, William H. Teale, and Elette Estrada

Our current work is aimed at characterizing the preschool literacy experiences of children from low-income families and communities. As several authors have suggested (Forester, 1975; Goodman and Goodman, 1979; Rubin, 1977; Shuy, 1977; Griffin, 1977), literacy may be viewed as an extension of oral language development. From this perspective literacy exists in the domain of communication and social interaction. For young children, then, developing literacy involves adding "new ways" to transmit and receive meaning through social interaction. We assume that the acquisition of these "new ways" is guided in some fashion.

Our approach to understanding the development of literacy begins with a detailed description of the immediate social environment of the child. We are especially interested in how this environment organizes the child's activity and how the child operates within that organization. Our focus for the study is on literacy events that occur in everyday family and community settings.

Our description of the literacy environment includes at least: (a) a detailed description of the print materials available to the child; (b) a description of the people and social activities involving the child where these print materials exist; and (c) a description of how these people use print as a part of their ongoing activity. Literacy events both within and outside of the home are taken into account. We shall discuss what is meant by a literacy event more fully below; however, for now we nominally define it as *any action sequence, involving one or more persons, in which the production and/or comprehension of print plays a role.*

313

The sample for our current study includes twelve low-income youngsters (six whose ages at the outset were 2 years 6 months and six whose ages were 3 years 6 months) and their families. The sample consists of three ethnic groups (Black, Mexican-American, and Anglo) with four families representing each group. At the beginning of the second year of the study twelve new families will be drawn from these same groups.

The twelve families presently participating in the study have the following characteristics: the annual income of each family is estimated to be below $10,000; none of the adults has earned more than a high school degree (the average years of schooling completed is 9.3); both the mother and father are present in all the families; and the size of these families ranges from four to seven people. Seven of our target children have older siblings, four have only younger siblings, and one is an only child.

As mentioned above, the focal point of our data collection is the literacy event. In order to operationalize our earlier definition we must establish at least a minimal definition of reading and writing. For purposes of our observations and analysis we have defined the terms *reading* and *writing* quite specifically. First, in the traditional sense a reading event will be taken to be any occasion upon which an individual comprehends (or attempts to comprehend) a message encoded in graphic signs. In a like manner a writing event will be taken to be any occasion upon which an individual mechanically manipulates appropriate tools to produce (or attempt to produce) graphic signs representative of oral speech which have meaning to the producer and/or to anyone who might be a reader of those graphic signs. Thus, a literacy event is deemed any occasion upon which an individual alone or in interaction attempts to comprehend or produce graphic signs.

None of the 2- to 4-year-old children in our sample is presently capable of reading or writing in a formal sense. We wish to capture those events which are precursors of this capability. Therefore we look for events in which the child interacts with objects as if s/he is reading or writing. That is to say, if the child "reads" a story or sign or whatever (even though what the child says may have little or no relation to the graphic configuration present), we consider this a reading event. In essence we have expanded the notion of reading and writing to include any reading- or writing-like behavior which mimics components of the activities that are generally considered reading and writing.

We are attempting to adapt and create methods which will allow us to collect and analyze relevant data about the acquisition of literacy in three ways: (a) natural observations, (b) self-report (daily diaries produced by primary caretakers), and (c) controlled behavior sampling.

The natural observations provide us with some idea of the family and community contexts within which literacy events occur. We hope to use them to discover cultural factors controlling the context and frequency of literacy experience.

The self-reports tell us how parents define literacy events by providing us with descriptions that are not constrained (in any direct way) by our expectations. We want to find the features of literate events common to all groups as well as those which may be unique to each.

The controlled behavior samplings present a set of literate experiences common to all subjects in the study. The children's behaviors in these situations provide us with information about cultural diversity in response to stimuli that, in the social science literature, are considered central to the development of literacy.

Natural observations

Each family in the study is the subject of four hours of observation per week, and we rotate our observations through all phases of the day and all days of the week. (Such a procedure corresponds to the "spot observations" employed by Whiting, Child, Lambert, et al. (1966) and others (see Rogoff (1978)).

Once a literacy event has been identified we attempt to describe activities which lead up to it, events subsequent to it, and any activities which co-occur or alternate with it. And of course, we seek a detailed description of the event itself. From such a description we hope to be able to draw conclusions about the contexts which give rise to literacy events and to determine if these contexts vary according to cultural groups.

We have found it useful during our first six months of observing to classify the print and print-related activities which our preschoolers are exposed to into several categories so that we can draw some general conclusions about the nature of these events (e.g., the participants, media/materials, and activities involved). For instance, print may be present in the home (books, labels, calendars, etc.) or outside the home (signs, billboards, etc.). Print-related activities may involve the child

Table 24.1. *Total number of reading events and total minutes spent in reading activity for five month time period*

| | Ethnic group | | | | | |
| | Black | | Mex. Amer. | | Anglo | |
Participants	Events	Minutes	Events	Minutes	Events	Minutes
T.C. alone	19	42	21	178	14	110
T.C. & adult	9	70	11	158	28	266
Adult alone	15	148	5	31	18	75
Total minutes observed		6129		10008		7350

Table 24.2. *Total number of writing events and total minutes spent in writing activity for five month time period*

| | Ethnic group | | | | | |
| | Black | | Mex. Amer. | | Anglo | |
Participants	Events	Minutes	Events	Minutes	Events	Minutes
T.C. & adult	9	37	3	7	23	268
T.C. alone	9	34	10	83	17	226
Total minutes observed		6129		10008		7350

alone (writing/scribbling, looking at a book, watching TV) or in interaction with someone else (being read to, mimicking the writing of a parent or older sibling). The child may be an active participant (as in the previous examples) or an observer (watching a letter being written or the mail being read). Tables 24.1 and 24.2 summarize the types and frequency of literacy activities that have gone on in the homes of our research participants during the first five months of observation.

A quick glance at the tables suggests that there is a difference in the pattern of literacy activities as a function of ethnic group. Indeed, χ^2 analysis performed on these frequencies (all <0.005) generated from observations indicates that literacy activity and ethnic group membership are not independent. Closer examination of the proportionate distribution of reading activity suggests that Black parents read to their children less than might be statistically expected, while Anglo parents seem to read to their children more than might be statistically expected. This apparent difference is virtually eliminated when we look only at diary-reported frequencies. Also of interest is the relative low frequency Mexican-American parents were observed to read alone.

The most notable observation regarding writing activity is that Anglo target children and caretakers spend a comparatively large amount of time in "writing" activities, while Mexican-American youngsters spend less time than might be statistically expected working alone in writing activities.

These observed frequencies should be treated with extreme caution. They are preliminary observations organized within an evolving classification system. Several types (categories) of events are not included, e.g., electronically mediated events (watching Sesame Street or the Electric Company on TV) and those which involve participants other than an adult (like an older child). Also excluded is any consideration of the type of material the activity is organized around. Certainly an approach which sacrifices a qualitative analysis for a quantitative analysis raises many more questions than it answers. In fact, its real value in this research has been to generate several alternative explanations for the observed frequencies and thereby suggest additional directions for continued data collection. Some of these alternative explanations include (a) the availability of human resources in the environment (presence or absence of older children or other more skilled members of the environment); (b) variation of more skilled members' conceptions of the instrumentality of literate activities; (c) literacy demands of parent's job (which may or may not carry over into the home); (d) prior literacy training and/or the literacy level of the parents; and (e) a discontinuity between values associated with literacy and the actual daily activities related to literacy. As the work progresses we shall continue to examine how these and other factors affect the frequency of literacy events in each child's life.

In addition to our documentation of print and print-related activities in the environments of our total sample of children we shall eventually look at these factors as they apply to individual children in order to determine if certain forms of print and activities are especially salient or not salient for particular children. Finally, once we have a more thorough documentation of representative events (described as discussed above), we shall look across these to compare, contrast, and better understand the process – as well as gain insight into intervening variables.

Given the number of questions raised by a quantitative analysis, one might doubt that there is any value of this type of analysis. We think, however, that it is the combination of quantity *and* quality of interactions involving print material that guides the acquisition of literacy, and thus we are seeking a systematic description of both.

Literacy event analysis

In addition to noting the types of literacy materials in the children's environment and describing in general terms the situations in which the child and others in the home are involved in reading and writing, we are conducting detailed analyses (micro-analyses) of particular literacy events. These micro-analyses permit us to examine the ways in which the social environment organizes and conducts literacy events for the target child. The analyses are of central importance to the study because they reveal the dynamics of the literacy environment and serve to suggest hypotheses for future investigation and to sharpen the skills of the researchers on the project. The following is a shortened version of one such micro-analysis which shows the way in which these analyses are performed, and the types of information we are obtaining from them.

Literacy event R_1

Researcher arrives at 9:30 a.m., sits on couch in the living room. Present in the house are the father (F), mother (M), a target child (D) aged 3–9, and the target child's 18-month-old sister (K). At approximately 10:20 F "settles" into his chair in the living room after completing a repair of the television. He talks with M who is in the kitchen fixing breakfast and with the researcher. (The actual remarks between F and the researcher were not noted; however, they could be characterized as general chit chat.) Beginning at 10:25 a.m. the following takes place:

(001) F: (to D who is in the kitchen) Did you ever show [researcher] that whole book you can read?
(002) D: What book?
(003) F: *Toys in. Things in My House.*
(004) D: I don't know.
(005) F: You read it except for a couple of words.

(006)   D: Yeah.
(i)   [D comes to living room, F looks around living room for book].
(007)   F: Here it is. (has *Things in My House*)
(008)   D: (takes book from F, goes to couch, sits down) Here it is (to researcher).
(ii)   [F sits on couch to left of D, puts right arm around behind D on couch. F
             holds book with left hand, D with both hands. D opens book to first page
             (title page) then begins to turn to first of text. F stops him].
(009)   F: We have to start reading here. What's this say? (pointing to words of the
             title moving from left to right direction.) Things in . . . ? (waits approxi-
             mately three seconds) Things in My House. (turns to first page of text)
(010)   D: A shoe. (pointing to picture on the bottom of the page)
(011)   F: No, we have to start up here at the top (points to first word of sentence at
             top of page). [in reading prosody] There are all kinds of things in my house.
             A . . .
(012)   D: . . . things . . .
(013)   D: . . . shoe.
(014)   F: No. Have to go from the top of the page to the bottom. So what's this?
             (pointing to the word *hammer* and partially obscuring the picture of the
             hammer) A . . .
(015)   D: Hammer.
(016)   F: A . . . (pointing to the word *shoe*)
(017)   D: Shoe.
(018)   F: (on next page pointing to word) A . . .
(019)   D: Pencil.
(020)   F: A . . . (pointing to word)
(021)   D: Sock.
(022)   F: An . . . (pointing to word)
(023)   D: Apple.

(032)   F: A . . . (pointing to word)
(033)   D: (two second pause) I don't know this one. It's too hard.
(034)   F: Yes, you do. A /li . . . /
(035)   D: —
(036)   F: It's the things on trees. A /li . . . /
(037)   D: Leaf
(046)   F: (points to picture of a pair of glasses)
(047)   D: Glasses.
(048)   F: A . . . (pointing to word)
(049)   D: —
(050)   F: /bl . . . /
(051)   D: Block.
(052)   F: And a . . . (pointing to word)
(053)   D: Cap.
(054)   F: Hat.
(069)   F: A . . .

(070) D: — (looking at book)
(071) F: It's what you measure things with. A . . .
(072) D: —
(073) F: /ru . . . /
(074) D: —
(075) F: (begins to "sound out" word) /ru – lɪr/ (D mimics this sounding out)

(103) F: And a . . .
(104) D: —
(105) F: It's what you put on a letter.
(106) D: I don't know. A square.
(107) F: No, if you don't put it on a letter, they won't send it. A
(108) D: —
(109) F: Stamp.

Turns to final page of book.
(120) D: And the stars and the moon.
(121) F: (points to first word) A . . .
(122) D: —
(123) F: (points to frame around window, outlining it) A window and outside the stars and moon.
(iv)   [At this point D's younger sister (K – 18 months) picks up book and drops it on floor. D goes after it but F's father comes to the door at that point and the event ends. (10:40 a.m.)]

An analysis of this event provides useful information about D's literacy environment and it serves both to suggest research hypotheses and to guide further observations (and interviews). We are especially interested in what messages the environment provides for D about the nature of the reading situation, the conventions of books and of reading, the information which can be found in books, and the purposes of reading and affective factors associated with reading. Also, we are very interested in how F, as one caretaker in D's environment, negotiates the zone of proximal development with him in a literacy event.

This event is a highly structured, rather formalized situation. In it F creates a two-part structure: he calls for the name of an object and provides the lead in ("A . . .", "An . . .") and D is supposed to provide the label for the object. When D provides the correct label, there is no verbal reinforcement; however, when D is incorrect, a tactic (discussed below) is used by F to help D get the right label. We have mentioned the concept of the zone of proximal development – a paradigm for examining the notions about the acts of reading and writing which the child receives from people in her/his environment and which s/he is thus likely to internalize him/herself. In the literacy event noted here, F helps D to complete the task of reading *Things in My House*. By doing so, F provides for D, through his questions and statements, certain "information" about what reading is and how it gets done.

Where D is unable to supply the appropriate label for the object in focus (032–037; 048–051; 069–075; 103–109 are examples included here), F provides information for D to use to obtain the message encoded in the book. On the first occasion that D does not know the appropriate label (033), F supplies a phonic cue (034). This cue proves insufficient (035) so F offers some "world knowledge" about this thing/word and repeats the phonic cue (036). D is then able to provide the label (037). For *block* (048–051) F provides only a phonic cue. With the *stamp* episode (103–109), only "world knowledge" is offered.

In some cases, D is ultimately successful at stating the label (037); in others, he is not (108). However, in all cases, the way in which F attempts to help D negotiate the meaning of the book can serve for D as examples of strategies to be used in reading. For instance, F's "sounding out" of the initial part of a word is one strategy which D may glean from literacy events like this one. Another is the use of world knowledge. This latter factor will be especially interesting to investigate as the adults in D's environment interact with him in reading narratives. Researchers have placed a great deal of emphasis on the importance of the use of background knowledge in reading comprehension; we shall pay close attention in future events to how D's use of such knowledge is fostered (or not fostered) when reading.

In another respect, we can see how F's interactions with D in this literacy event provide information about the conventions of using books and of reading. By his statements and actions in 009, 011, and 014 and by repeatedly pointing to words in the text and moving his finger in a left to right direction under the words, F demonstrates to D (a) that in reading one proceeds in a left to right, top to bottom direction and (b) that the graphic markings on the page are used in reading. These understandings about reading are, of course, crucial for young children.

We are also concerned with affective factors associated with literacy by our target children and their families. Analysis of this literacy event provides us with some clues about affect and reading for the family. F could not be described as excited or enthusiastic during this event. In fact, his demeanor seemed rather like the formal, structured situation itself. As was mentioned, at no time does F verbally praise D for getting a label correct. It would have been interesting to note what F did in this regard at the end of the reading were the event not peremptorily closed by K and by the arrival of F's father. We plan to continue investigating the affective nature of literacy events between D and his parents in the future to determine if the "feel" of this event is typical of book readings in this family.

These aspects of the micro-analysis, then, demonstrate how we are investigating the literacy events we observe in our attempt to characterize the ways in which the children and families in our study interact with written communication. As we continue in these analyses, we feel that an overall picture of each child's literacy environment and of the child's interactions in that environment will become clear.

Another facet of these qualitative analyses is an attempt to describe the contexts which give rise to and sustain literacy events for low-income families. We shall be studying the events which precede, co-occur/ alternate with, and follow all literacy events to see if there are discernible cultural patterns to the practice of literacy for our subjects. This type of analysis, combined with the micro-analyses discussed above, should give us a more complete understanding of the interactional contexts which are literacy.

Self-report

Audio-tape recorders have been placed with each primary caretaker and the following minimal instructions were given: "Please take about five minutes at the end of each day to record all of your child's literacy activities which took place during that day." This constitutes the first phase of "taped diary" data collection. There are two reasons for giving this minimal set of instructions to our primary caretakers. We wanted to determine both what parents would consider literate activities to be and how much information the parents would spontaneously give us about the literacy events. We have found that the diary reports vary a great deal along these two dimensions. All parents mention the occasions upon which their children write/scribble or interact with books. Several, however, mention little beyond these typical, or well-marked, literacy events. A few of our parents go beyond these typical events and cite instances when their children play with mail, read labels or signs, spell their names, listen to stories, and so forth. One parent has even mentioned such things as her daughter's sorting of cards into categories according to the symbols on them. In terms of the amount of information supplied about each literacy event there is also a range in the entries. Some provide very brief entries like these:

> Karen had memorized her Sunday School verse and she was holding the paper saying the words as if she was really reading from the paper.

> Karen is holding her medicine bottle reading the label her way. She is explaining how supposedly she is to take it or not to take it.

Then there is this type of report (for one day):

> Wednesday. This morning, early, Kristin played with some old Medi-Cal stickers. She likes to get some papers and glue them on. Then she pretends she's a lady at the doctor's office that fixes them all on and she tells them what they're for – like this one is for Doreen got a shot or this one is for getting sick and going to the doctor – and different things like that. And I showed her which ones were for who by names on them – we even spelled them out for her so she can see; and pointed out each one started with a certain letter. And later on when the mail came, there was some junk mail from HBO saying, "Buy our service." And I let her have that to play with. She likes it because there's lots of pretty colored pictures. And she particularly asked me, though, when she sat down by me and asked me exactly what each word said, and I had to read the whole thing to her while she pointed to each word. And then afterwards . . . (continues with entry).

Overall from the taped diaries to date we find that parents tend to regard as literacy events only typical situations like book reading or writing and that they tend to give very little information about the literacy events in which their children are involved.

Once we have established for each of our parents a "base line" idea of their unprompted notions of a literacy event, we shall begin giving the parents more detailed instructions for making their taped diaries. Our objective will be to have our parents produce tapes which provide a much more complete description of the literacy event and to have them supply information about the events which precede, co-occur and alternate with, and follow it. We will ask parents to do this within phases of the day. As they become more experienced over time they should generate descriptions which approximate the detail of our naturalistic observations.

Controlled behavior sampling

Our approach to behavior sampling includes two basic techniques: interviews and the staged literacy event. As regards the first technique, the children in our study will go through a variety of interview-like situations in order to determine the extent of their print awareness and conceptions about writing. For assessing print awareness we have generated lists (for each child) of products and logos that are common in the children's environments and that may be familiar to them (e.g., Aim toothpaste, Superman logo, road signs, etc.). Drawing on these lists, we will take our youngsters through a three-phased interview on three separate occasions. First, our children will be presented with the print in a context one step removed from its normal environmental setting. The children will be shown, for example, a cut-out portion of a cereal box which has been pasted on a flat surface rather than retaining the shape of the original. Second, youngsters will be presented with representations of these graphic units without familiar accompanying color or texture of material. (For example, Coca-Cola in its usual script but without its distinctive colors.) Finally, language units presented in phases 1 and 2 will be presented in standard print. Subsequently we will conduct these interviews approximately every 3 months in order to note changes in our youngsters' awareness of print.

Another of the aims of this research is to examine the children in relation to writing. To that end, we are attempting to describe (a) the functions which writing serves for these children, and (b) the children's conception of the writing system at various points in their development. The research of Luria (1929, in Russian; 1977–78 English translation) and Ferreiro (1978) have served both to suggest the aspects of writing which might profitably be studied and to provide a methodology for doing so.

Luria was concerned with charting the development of the child's realization of certain functions and conventions of a writing system. He demonstrated that children passed through developmental stages in understanding that a graphic system can represent meanings and thereby act as a mnemonic device. The actual systems that Luria observed were ones idiosyncratic to the particular children in the study. Thus, his work can be considered an exploration of the precursors to the culturally elaborated system. Ferreiro, on the other hand, examined the child's conceptions of the nature of the culturally elaborated system. She identified six developmental categories of responses which show the children's ideas about what can be found in a written text.

Each of these researchers has focused upon factors in literacy which are important to our research concerns. At the time of this writing we are in the first phase of conducting interview-like situations with our research participants using instruments constructed to tap these factors. Following Luria's model, we are engaging the children in memory tasks that are too difficult for them to accomplish alone and noting the ways in which they use writing to accomplish these tasks. Also, as Ferreiro has done, we are presenting the children with written sentences and attempting to elicit their conception of what is written in those sentences. Subsequently we shall employ the two instruments approximately every three months in order to note change in these aspects of the subjects' interactions with written communication. This procedure will allow us to examine the areas outlined above. Of course, our ongoing naturalistic observation will also be used where appropriate to supplement and/or elucidate findings from the interview situations, especially to tie in what is found about each child's developmental level in writing with the nature of the child's literacy environment (in particular the way in which the zone of proximal development is negotiated in writing activities involving caretakers and/or older siblings with the child).

In environments where literacy interactions do not normally occur, our final behavior sampling technique involves staging such events. On these occasions we ask the primary caretaker (and/or another member of the family) to, for example, read to the child. These staged events contribute to our understanding of the child's literacy environment because they provide an indication of the parents' conceptions of what is involved in such an event and how such an event is organized and carried out. For example, one of the mothers in the study has an extremely low level of literacy. She has never been observed to read herself or to read to her child. We staged a literacy event between this mother and her 3½-year-old son. The interaction was set up by asking the mother if she would mind "looking at" a book or some books with her child and having the event taped. She was compliant and seemingly at ease with the idea.

Three simple and brief books in Spanish were made available: one about a farm, one about fish, and one about baby animals. During the interaction the mother and child faced each other much of the time, the book being oriented to the child and the mother turning it occasionally to get a better view of something. The interaction generally took the form of the mother's leafing through the book, beginning more often in the middle or at the back than at the front and not necessarily proceeding page by page or stopping on each consecutive page. The mother did stop on pages which had pictures that interested the child.

Most often the mother would ask, "What is this?" to which the child would provide an answer. The mother would then approve the response or probe for a different or more differentiated response, either by disagreeing (e.g., "Look closer; this isn't a cow") or providing the answer (e.g., "No, it's a calf"). In addition, the mother would frequently provide related comments (e.g., "The seals are climbing on top" or "There are peaches on *our* tree"). The interaction could generally be described as a question-response-evaluation format which was non-threatening to the child.

When the mother came to the book on fish, she asked the researcher if it were written in English. The researcher replied, "No . . . Spanish." The mother then produced "pes-ca-do" while looking at another word.

There are several things we have noted initially from this staged literacy event. First, there are indications that interaction between mother and child around print is a rare occurrence. The awkward postural configuration arranged by the mother and the mother's unorthodox handling of the books (starting sometimes at the back of the book, sometimes at the middle) and her rather random progress through the pages suggest this to be the case. (By staging another literacy event employing wordless stories which have a conspicuous sequential plot, we plan to determine if this method of proceeding through a book is typical for her.) Moreover, this virtually illiterate mother worked around the print in the books, except for her one attempt to sound out a word.

Also, we find very important the messages about the conventions of literacy which the child is likely to obtain from this type of interaction. The mother does little to arrange for the child to learn about directionality, the fact that the print carries meaning, or book handling knowledge.

As to the affective factors associated with literacy events, it was evident that in spite of the novelty this task presented to both participants, the mother's approach was enthusiastic, and she incorporated the child's comments and responses smoothly and appropriately. He often turned pages himself and occasionally turned back to pictures they had already discussed. Similarly, on occasions when, triggered by a picture, the child referred to personal experiences (e.g., a trip to Disneyland, the peach tree outside), the mother explored these and related them to the picture and their discussion of it.

Thus, we feel that such staged literacy events between caretaker and child are useful for exploring several areas of interest in this study. We shall continue this data gathering technique where appropriate and attempt to infer both the caretaker's theory of how literacy events with children are structured and the ideas about the conventions and techniques of and values associated with literacy which the children may be obtaining from interaction with their environments.

We are aware that our behavior sampling techniques will alter the child's normal literate environment. For example, Hood and Schieffelin (1978) present data which show that elicited imitation (and our procedure is but a variation of that linguistic procedure) represents a complex *new* task for the child which is unlike any event which naturally occurs in the child's environment. It is therefore possible that this type of intervention could provide sufficient contrast to contribute to some degree of vertical elaboration of existing notions about literacy. We shall be very sensitive to this possibility and remain alert to employ procedures in our analysis of data which will inform us about the consequences of our intervention.

Discussion

This investigation was initiated in order to study systematically an area of considerable speculation. It is generally *believed* that the home experiences of low-income and ethnic "minority" children do not prepare them effectively for becoming literate. The home backgrounds of such children are often cited as a source of their school difficulties in reading and writing. It is assumed that insofar as reading and writing are concerned, a mismatch exists between the home and the school.

Large scale studies (e.g., Bulcock, 1977; Grant & Lind, 1975; Thorndike, 1973) are of little help on the issue of a mismatch; they serve only to demonstrate that lower class children in general and Blacks and Mexican-Americans in particular, do not, on the whole, learn to read and write as well as middle- and upper-class children. There is little systematic evidence about the everyday literacy experiences of the children that schools need most to respond to. What evidence there is is collected in ways that force the children's histories to fit the school's expectations and therefore may ignore important parts of the real histories. By investigating the literacy environments of the children in this study in the ways outlined above, we hope to be able to shed light on the children's preschool experiences and thereby provide information which schools and teachers can use to help them respond more effectively to low-income and "minority" children.

Our results are at present only suggestive of what is transpiring in these environments. We hope by the completion of the study to have developed an exhaustive taxonomy of the types and frequencies of literacy events which occur in the lives of these preschoolers. In addition, our approach to the research will facilitate a qualitative analysis of these events. Finally, we hope to describe the social organization of literacy in the homes and communities we are studying and gain insight into the relationship between this organization and the resulting kinds of literacy which particular children develop.

Note

Research supported by a grant award from the National Institute of Education – G 790135.

References

Bulcock, J. W. Evaluating social facts related to school achievement in Sweden and England. *Scandinavian Journal of Educational Research*, 1977, *21*, 4–12.

Ferreiro, E. What is written in a written sentence?: A developmental answer. *Journal of Education*, 1978, *160*, 25–39.

Forester, A. D. *The acquisition of reading*. Unpublished master's thesis, University of Victoria, 1975.

Goodman, K. S., & Goodman, Y. M. Learning to read is natural. In L. B. Resnick & P. Weaver (Eds.), *Theory and practice of early reading* (Vol. 1), Hillsdale, N.J.: Erlbaum, 1979.

Grant, W. V., & Lind, C. G. *Digest of education statistics*. Washington, D.C.: U.S. Department of Health, Education, & Welfare, 1975.

Griffin, P. How and when does reading occur in the classroom? *Theory into Practice*, 1977, *16*, 376–383.

Hood, L., & Schieffelin, B. B. Elicited imitation in two cultural contexts. *The Quarterly Newsletter of the Institute for Comparative Human Development*, 1978, *2*, 4–12.

Luria, A. R. The development of writing in the child. *Soviet Psychology*, 1977–78, *16*, 65–114. (Translated from: Problems of Marxist education, 1929, Vol. I, 143–76).

Rogoff, B. Spot observation: An introduction and examination. *The Quarterly Newsletter of the Institute for Comparative Human Development*, 1978, *2*, 21–26.

Rubin, A. The relation between comprehension processes in oral and written language. In B. C. Bruce & R. J. Spiro (Eds.). *Cognitive processes in learning to read and comprehend* (Vol. III). University of Illinois, Urbana: Center for the Study of Reading, 1977.

Shuy, R. Children's functional language development and reading. Paper presented to the Wisconsin Conference on Reading and Oral Language, 1977.

Thorndike, R. *Reading comprehension education in fifteen countries*. International Studies in Education (Vol. III). New York: Wiley, 1973.

Whiting, J., Child, J., Lambert, W., et al. *Field guide for the study of socialization*. New York: Wiley, 1966.

25 Selling candy: A study of cognition in context

Geoffrey B. Saxe

This paper is concerned with the way children's participation in cultural practices can influence their developing mathematical understandings. My focus is on the practice of street vending, an activity common for unschooled children in developing countries. The vendors I will describe are 10- to 12-year-old boys who sell candy and are from poor urban areas in Brazil's Northeast.

The study is guided by a basic assumption: children construct mathematical understandings in their efforts to achieve mathematical goals, goals that often emerge as an interplay between their own prior understandings and the practices in which they participate (see Saxe, Guberman, & Gearhart, 1987 for an elaboration). This assumption leads to the view that analyses of children's understandings should be coordinated with and in part directed by socio-cultural analyses of the character of their practice-linked goals. In Table 25.1, I have sketched the structure of a two-part study with the candy sellers that follows from this view. On the left side of the table are basic questions I addressed, and on the right, the methods used.

My first concern represented in the table was to understand the form children's mathematical goals take in the candy selling practice. To answer this question, I conducted a series of ethnographic studies of the practice focusing on social processes that influenced the form of sellers' mathematical goals. The second question indicated was to discover the characteristics of candy sellers' mathematics. To address the second question, I conducted interviews with individual children using practice-related mathematical problems and contrasted the understand-

330

Table 25.1

Question	Methods of study
1. How are children's everyday mathematical goals influenced by participation in the candy selling practice?	Observations of sellers conducting their practice
2(a) What are the characteristics of sellers' mathematics?	(a) Interviews with sellers on mathematical tasks
2(b) Is sellers' mathematics influenced by participation in the candy selling practice?	(b) Contrasts between the mathematical understanding of sellers and matched nonsellers

ings of sellers with those of both urban and rural nonsellers. By contrasting sellers with nonsellers, I was able to determine whether practice participation affected the kinds of mathematical understandings children developed (see Saxe, in press a, for a complete presentation of these data). I am going to summarize briefly the results of both types of investigations, focusing first on the ethnographic studies.

Ethnographic analyses of mathematical goals that emerge in the candy selling practice

The sellers that were the target of study are entrepreneurs. Their practice has a four-phase cyclical structure and in each phase they are likely to form particular kinds of mathematical goals. During a *purchase phase*, a seller buys a wholesale box of candy containing from 30 to 100 units from one of the many wholesale stores in a downtown urban center. During a *prepare to sell phase* a seller must translate the wholesale price for the multi-unit box into a retail price for just single units of candy. During a *sell phase*, a seller must sell his goods to customers. Finally, in a *prepare to purchase phase*, a seller must determine which of the many wholesale stores has the best price for the best box. While the basic cyclical structure provides a general context for mathematical goals to emerge, sellers' goals take form in and are thus influenced by a variety of social processes including macro-social processes like *inflation* and micro-social processes specific to the practice like *retail pricing conventions* and *social interactions*.

Inflation

Brazil has had a high inflation rate for many years – during the year of the study the inflation rate was about 25%. As a consequence of inflation, the mathematical goals that sellers construct in the practice involve inflated or very large numerical values, and the tokens of currency for these numerical values continue to shift as prices rise. For instance, the wholesale prices for boxes of candy ranged from about Cr$3600 to Cr$12,000 when the study began and four months later they ranged from Cr$6500 to Cr$20,000. The inflated monetary system has also meant that the government issues new denominations of currency frequently. Just before the study began, the government issued a Cr$50,000 bill – during the study, the government issued new coins in values of Cr$200, and Cr$500, and issued a new bill of Cr$100,000, and, just after the study was completed, the government altered the currency system by eliminating three zeros from the cruzeiro, and calling the new unit the cruzado. Thus, because of the inflated currency, at all phases of the practice, sellers are dealing with very large numerical values as they generate arithmetical goals.

Social processes specific to the practice. Within the four phases of the practice, two types of social processes enter into the emergence of mathematical goals – sellers' mathematical conventions and sellers' typical social interactions.

Sellers' social conventions and their influence on sellers' mathematical goals. Over the history of the selling practice, sellers have developed social conventions that facilitate the conduct of their practice. Some of these conventions affect the nature of the mathematical goals that emerge in the practice. For instance, sellers use a retail price ratio convention in which they offer their candy in the sell phase to customers for multiple units for a single bill denomination, such as three chocolate bars for one thousand cruzeiros (Cr$1000). The convention reduces the complexity of arithmetical problems that would emerge in the sell phase if units were sold for odd numerical values – values that would give rise to time consuming and complex problems involving adding and subtracting bills. In turn, these very conventions give rise to new goals involving ratio comparison – many sellers, particularly the older ones, offer their candy for more than one ratio, such as 2 bars for Cr$500 and 5 for Cr$1000, and in determining these ratios, sellers compare the relative profit gained.

Sellers' social interactions and their influence on sellers' mathematical goals. At each phase of the practice, sellers have transactions with other people and, like the practice-linked conventions, these social interactions often give rise to or lead to an alteration in the mathematical goals of the practice. For instance, in the prepare to sell phase, sellers may negotiate with one another in price setting interactions to minimize local competition, interactions that may entail forming additional ratio comparison goals. In the sell phase, sellers may bargain with customers resulting in renegotiation of the pricing ratios, renegotiations in which sellers may need to form, again, new arithmetical and ratio comparison goals. In the purchase phase, wholesale clerks may help simplify sellers' mathematical goals by telling children box prices so that they do not need to read large numerical values as well as help with the translation of wholesale prices into retail prices.

Studies on sellers' mathematics

So far I have attempted to show that as a part of practice participation, sellers construct three principal goals involving the representation of large numerical values, arithmetic with large numerical values, and ratio comparisons. Now, I am going to address the question of whether sellers' engagement with the candy selling practice influences the character of their mathematical understandings. To address this question, children with little or no schooling from three groups were interviewed on mathematical problems related to the practice. The groups included 10- to 12-year-old candy sellers, 10- to 12-year-old nonsellers from the same urban environment, and 10- to 12-year-old nonsellers from a rural community about 100 miles away from the urban community. All children were presented with problems involving the representation of number, arithmetic, and ratio comparisons.

Expectations about children's performances were based on analyses of differences in the kinds of mathematical goals with which children are engaged in their everyday activities. Children from each of the three population groups engage in some commercial transactions in activities like running errands for their parents to grocery stores. This means that children from all groups are frequently faced with representing large values of currency. However, nonsellers do not often engage with problems involving arithmetic with multiple bill values, and problems involving ratio comparisons are even further removed from the activities of the nonsellers, especially the rural nonsellers. Because of these population group differences in the kinds of goals children structure in their everyday activities, I expected to find related differences in the character of children's mathematics.

Representations of large numerical values

I used two types of tasks to assess children's ability to represent large numerical values in problem solving. In *Standard Orthography* tasks, children were required to read and compared multi-digit numerical values. As an alternative to the use of the standard orthography, I suspected that children might be using currency bills themselves as a basis for number representation. To test this hypothesis, I constructed *Alternative Representation* tasks that consisted of a *Standard Bills* condition in which children had to identify the numerical values of bills that varied in value from Cr$100 to Cr$10,000; a *Number Occluded* condition in which they had to identify the numerical values of identical bills with the printed numbers on the bills covered with tape so the child could not attempt to read them; and a *Numbers Only* condition in which children had to identify copies of the printed number on the bills without the bills' figurative characteristics. If children were identifying bills on the basis of their figurative characteristics, then children should perform better on both the standard bills and Number Occluded conditions than on the Numbers Only condition. This is just what I found. For the Standard Bills and Numbers Occluded conditions, there were no group differences – children from each group performed at or near ceiling; however, for each group, children made significantly fewer correct identifications on the Numbers Only condition. These results then indicate that children across population groups had developed an ability to use bills themselves as signifiers for large values and did not need to rely on their imperfect knowledge of the standard number orthography.

A counter interpretation of these findings is that perhaps children treat the values they use to identify bills as merely linguistic terms and do not order them as a numerical series. To evaluate children's knowledge of the numerical relations between currency values, children were presented with *Currency Comparison* tasks in which they were presented with pairs of bills and coins and asked to determine which was the greater value and then to determine how many of the lesser values was equivalent to the greater value (e.g., Cr$200 bill vs. Cr$1000 bill). An analysis of children's responses to these currency comparison tasks revealed that children across population groups correctly identified the larger of the two valued currency units with great regularity. Children's answers to questions about the numerical relations between currency units revealed that all groups achieved a near ceiling performance on this task. Thus, not only do children identify bills without reference to the standard orthography, they also know both ordinal and cardinal relations between currency values.

Solutions to multi-term arithmetic problems

The second area targeted for study was arithmetic with large currency values, a problem type more exclusively linked to the everyday activities of the candy sellers. To assess arithmetical competence with large bills, I presented children with a variety of tasks – tasks like adding a stack of 12 currency bills to Cr$8600 or subtracting Cr$3800 from Cr$5000. Typical strategies on this task involved "regrouping bills" into convenient values (Carraher, Carraher, & Schliemann, 1985), strategies in which, for example, children would reorganize a series of bills to be added in an order in which they could add in multiples of 500 to 1000 cruzeiros. Unlike the *Alternative Representation System* tasks, children's performance varied across groups. Consistent with expectation, the sellers more frequently solved these problems than did the nonsellers.

Ratio comparisons

The third type of problem targeted for study involved ratio comparisons, problem types that were not at all common in rural nonsellers' everyday activities, more common in the urban nonsellers' activities (who were sometimes the customers of the sellers), and, as we have seen, very common in the candy sellers' activities. To assess children's ability to compare ratios, an interviewer presented children with problems in which the child had to determine in which of two pricing ratios a child would make a larger profit (e.g., selling 1 candy for Cr$200 vs. selling 3 candies for Cr$500). Children were then required to tell which ratio would yield the larger profit and to explain their answers. Children who achieved accurate ratio comparisons typically justified their answers by constructing a common term, a construction that entailed transforming the numerator or denominator of one or both ratios so that it was comparable to the other. As expected, children's solutions varied markedly across population groups: Sellers' typically identified the appropriate pricing ratio and provided appropriate justifications for their answers whereas few nonsellers (especially the rural nonsellers) provided such responses.

Concluding remark

The findings of this study add to our understanding of the processes by which children's participation in cultural practices influence their developing understandings. Mathematical problems are generated as children participate in cultural practices like candy selling. These problems are linked both to more general socio-economic processes like inflation, conventions like pricing ratios that arise in practices, and patterns of social interaction. As children participate in practices, their goals become interwoven with these social processes. In their efforts to achieve practice-related goals, children construct new understandings and solution strategies, new cognitive developments at once linked to their own constructive efforts and to social life.

Note

This paper was presented as part of a symposium at the 1987 Meetings of the International Society for the Study of Behavioral Development in Tokyo, Japan. The paper is based on work supported by the National Science Foundation under Grant No. BNS 8509191 and by a small grant from the Spencer Foundation administered through the Graduate School of Education, UCLA. A more detailed analysis of some of the findings described here is presented in Saxe (in press a), and a more general description of the larger project from which this work is drawn is contained in Saxe (in press b).

References

Carraher, T. N., Carraher, D., & Schliemann, A. D. (1985). Mathematics in the streets and in schools. *British Journal of Developmental Psychology*, *3* (1), 21–29.

Saxe, G. B. (in press a). The mathematics of child street vendor. *Child Development*.

Saxe, G. B. (in press b). *Cognition in context*. Hillsdale, N.J.: Erlbaum.

Saxe, G. B., Guberman, S. R., & Gearhart, M. (1987). Social processes in early number development. *Monographs of the Society for Research in Child Development*. No. 216, *52* (2).

26 Mediation and automatization

Edwin Hutchins

I take *mediation* to refer to a particular mode of organizing behavior with respect to some task by achieving coordination with a mediating structure that is not itself inherent in the domain of the task. That is, in a mediated performance, the actor does not simply coordinate with the task environment; instead, the actor coordinates with something else as well, something that provides structure that can be used to shape the actor's behavior. What this something else is, where it may be located, and how simultaneous coordination with it and some task relevant environment is achieved are central questions in understanding what sorts of creatures we humans are. Skill *automatization* refers to the process presumed to underlie the observation that skilled performance may become effortless or phenomenologically "automatic" after extensive practice. This article discusses some relationships between these two concepts based on the behavioral properties of so called "neurally inspired" models of cognitive processing. The first section attempts to explore the sorts of activities that are involved in the use of a simple mediating artifact. Here I make two assumptions: (1) That all "skilled" performances are initially mediated by some structure, either internal or external, that provides some sort of description of the performance of the skill, and (2) that the descriptions in this mediating structure provide constraints on behavior; constraints that can be used to control behavior. The control may not be direct in the sense of producing behavior; the constraints need only permit the actor to evaluate behavior that has been produced and judge whether or not it is appropriate. In the worst case, the actor might behave randomly until an appropriate behavior is

338

produced. In such a case, learning would be undirected and would surely be very slow, but it could still occur. The second section describes what a Parallel Distributed Processing (PDP) or "connectionist" approach to cognition would lead us to expect as consequences of repeated mediated task performance. In brief, this approach leads us to expect that a neural apparatus will learn the sequence of states that constitute the task, and with sufficient practice may be able to move through them without the application of the constraints provided by the mediating structure. I will argue that this condition of no-longer-mediated performance is precisely what has been seen as automatized performance and that the changes that obviate the need for mediation are the process underlying the development of skill automatization.

The phenomena of mediated performance are absolutely ubiquitous. For the purposes of exposition I have chosen as an example a simple, explicit, external mediation device, a checklist. Many tasks in our culture are mediated by checklists or checklist-like artifacts, but even considering all of them would not scratch the surface of the full range of mediated performance. Language, cultural knowledge, mental models, arithmetic procedures, and rules of logic are all mediating structures too. So are traffic lights, supermarket layouts, and the contexts we arrange for each other's behavior. Mediating structure can be embodied in artifacts, in ideas, in systems of social interaction, or in all of these at once. I have chosen the checklist because it is an artifact that provides a relatively explicit example of mediation for which a relatively simple exposition can be given.

Checklist as mediating structure

Consider an actor using a checklist to organize the performance of a task where it is essential that the actions of the performance be taken in a particular order and that all of the actions be taken before the performance is judged complete. In order to use a checklist as a guide to action, the task performer must coordinate with both the checklist and the environment in which the actions are to be taken. Achieving coordination with the checklist requires the actor to invoke procedures for the use of the checklist. These include reading skills and a strategy of sequential execution which permits the task performer to ensure that the steps will be done in the correct order and that each step will be done

INSIDE	OUTSIDE
Sequential Strategy	Checklist (as a list of steps)
NEXT STEP INDEX	NEXT STEP

Figure 26.1. Finding the next step.

once and only once. The fixed linear structure of the checklist permits the user to accomplish this by simply keeping track of an index that indicates the first unexecuted (or last executed) item. Real checklists often provide additional features to aid in the maintenance of this index: boxes to tick when steps are completed, a window that moves across the checklist, etc. The mediating artifact has been designed with particular structural features that can be exploited by some procedure to produce a useful coordination. Such a procedure can be seen as meta-mediation, a mediating artifact that permits the use of some other mediating artifact. An actor always incurs some cognitive costs in coordinating with a mediating structure. But the savings of the mediated performance over the unmediated performance hopefully outweigh the costs of using it. The reduction of error or increase in efficiency obtained via the use of the checklist may compensate for the effort required to use it. For the unskilled performer, of course, the task may be impossible without the use of the checklist so the economy of mediated performance in that case is clear.

The first stage in the use of the checklist is depicted in Figure 26.1. The left-hand column of the figure contains relevant things inside the actor and the right-hand column contains relevant things in the environment of the actor. All of the things listed are brought into coordination with each other by the actor to achieve the described action. The items in UPPERCASE letters are the things that are meant to be shaped or brought into existence by the action. Figures 26.1 through 26.4 present a pseudo-sequential picture of the actual activities of the user of a checklist. Because the action described by each figure depends in some way on the actions in the previous figures, it is tempting to think of these as sequential stages. However, because of interactions among them in the doing of the task, they are better thought of as concurrent levels of activity than as stages.

In finding the next step to do in the checklist, the actor invokes the sequential execution strategy on the checklist to determine which step is the next one, and possibly to determine an index of the next step that can be remembered. There are two related issues concerning this index: where it is stored and what it contains. The index could be encoded in the memory of the actor, or the actor could take some action on the world, making a mark on the checklist itself, for example, that acts as the index. The content of the index might be simply a mark on paper, a number if the steps are numbered, the lexical or semantic content of the step description itself, or something else. Each of these alternatives requires a different procedure to implement the sequential execution strategy. For example, if the content of the step index is the lexical or semantic content of the step itself, then finding the next step and establishing the step index are the same action. If the content of the step index is a mark on a paper or a number to be recorded or remembered, then some action in addition to finding the next step must be undertaken to establish the step index. Although the primary product of the application of this strategy is the determination of the next step to do, it is important to notice that either the checklist as an object in the environment or the procedure that implements the sequential execution strategy may also be changed as a consequence of the activities involved in finding the next step.

Having generated a step index (in whatever form) the actor can bring that index into coordination with the checklist to focus attention on the current step. Although the goal of the use of the checklist as a mediating artifact is to ensure sequential control for the actions taken in the task domain, it is clear that the task of bringing the checklist into coordination with the domain of action may not itself be linearly sequential. For example, if a user loses track of the step index, in order to determine the next step to be taken, the user may go back to the beginning of the checklist and proceed through each step in the checklist, not executing it, but asking of the task world whether or not the expected consequences of the step's execution are present. When a step is reached

INSIDE	OUTSIDE
Next step index	Checklist (as a list of steps)
Shallow Reading	CURRENT STEP
"WHAT THE STEP SAYS" WORDS	

Figure 26.2. Finding what the step says.

whose consequences are not present in the task world, it may be assumed that it has not yet been executed. This is a simple illustration of the potential complexity of the meta-mediation that may be undertaken in the coordination of a mediating structure with a task world.

Once the current step has been identified, the user may coordinate its printed representation with shallow reading skills in order to produce an internal representation of what the step says in words. This is depicted in Figure 26.2. The shallow reading skills here refer to organized (possibly already automated) internal structures that can create internal representations of words from their external printed counterparts.[1] It is obvious that this may proceed concurrently with the stage of reading what the step means. However, I have separated shallow and deep readings primarily because shallow and deep readings produce different sorts of products that can be shown to exist independently. Thus, a user who does not understand the domain of action may know and be able to recall what a step "says" without having any idea at all of what it "means."

Figuring out what a step means requires the coordination of what the step says with the task world via the mediation of a deeper sort of reading (see Figure 26.3). This deep reading relies on two internal structures, one that can provide semantic mappings from linguistic descriptions provided by the checklist to states in the world and another to provide readings of the task world to see what is there. What the words in the step description are thought to mean may depend upon the state of the task world that has been produced by prior steps. In this process it also becomes clear that the right way to think of this situation is not

```
┌─────────────────────────────────────────┐
│     INSIDE              OUTSIDE           │
├─────────────────────────────────────────┤
│                                           │
│   "What the step says"                    │
│        words                              │
│                                           │
│                                           │
│   Language              Task World        │
│   Deep Reading                            │
│   World Understanding                     │
│                                           │
│                                           │
│   "WHAT THE STEP MEANS"                   │
│    IDEAS/IMAGES                           │
│                                           │
└─────────────────────────────────────────┘
```

Figure 26.3. Discovering what the step means.

that the words and the world are coordinated by language in order to produce the meanings, but that the meanings, the world, and the words are all put in coordination with each other via the mediating structure of language. As we saw in the very first figure, the item in uppercase letters is in some sense the product of the activity, but the other items with which it is brought into coordination may be changed in the process of producing the product. Thus, the structure of language may be changed by its use, and what is thought to be in the world may be changed by describing it in a novel way. All of the structures provide constraints on the others, and all are to some extent malleable. The system composed of task performer, mediating structures, and task world settles into a solution that satisfies as many constraints as is possible.

Finally, having determined what the step means, the user of the checklist may take actions on (and in) the world to carry out the step. This is described in Figure 26.4. Whether the action should be placed inside or outside the actor is difficult to say. This is because actions taken on the environment involve phenomena inside and outside the actor and because for some mental acts the task world itself is inside. In any case, the meaning of the step, the action, and the task world are brought into coordination. Having completed this step, the checklist user may find the next step and continue.

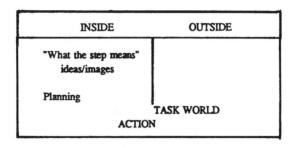

Figure 26.4. Performing the step.

While following the checklist, high level control of task related behavior is given over in part to the structure of the mediating artifact. The interaction with the checklist produces for the actor a sequence of experiences of step descriptions. Each of these experiences may have several components: what the step says, what the step means, and the actions in the task world that carry out the step. Although it might have seemed at first blush that the actor alternates coordinating with the checklist and coordinating with the world, the coordination with the two media is in fact simultaneous to the extent that understanding a step in the description may depend upon understanding the state of the world in which it is to be carried out. The experience of the meanings of the descriptions of the steps embeds experience of the task world, and the doing of the actions embeds the experience of the meaning of the task steps. The importance of this is that in this mediated performance the actor becomes a special sort of medium that can provide continuous coordination among several structured media. Looking across Figures 26.1 through 26.4, we see that many layers of transformed mediating structure may lie between a simple mediating artifact like a checklist and a task performance.

Consequences of mediated task performance

Parallel Distributed Processing (PDP) models of cognition assume an architecture of computation that is inspired by the general organization of neural networks in biological organisms.[2] A PDP system consists of a set of processing units and a set of unidirectional connections between the units. At each point in time, each unit has an activation value. This activation is passed through the connections to other units in the system. Each connection has a *strength* which determines the amount of effect that the unit sending activation has on the recipient. The combined inputs to a unit from other units along with its own activation value determine its new activation value. If we were to force some subset of the units of the system to assume particular activation values, the effects of that input would propagate across the connections and the set of units as a whole would assume a pattern of activation that is determined by the combined effects of the structure of the input we forced upon it and the pattern of the strengths of the connections among the units. Such a pattern of activation across the set of units as a whole can be interpreted as a state of the system. When we are thinking of PDP networks as cognitive systems, a state as a pattern of activation across the units corresponds to a representation. Such a simple system can do pattern matching and can complete patterns from incomplete inputs. Which states the system assumes in response to which inputs is governed by the pattern of connectivity among the units. What the system *knows* is encoded in the connections among the units, rather than in the activation states the units assume. The strengths of the connections among the units are not fixed. Instead, they can be modified on the basis of experience. This means that the state the system assumes in response to an input can change, or, put in other words, the system can learn to respond to an input in a particular way. If the units that are the output of the network are connected back into the network's own input, the network can be trained on a sequence of states and will learn to transition through the sequence automatically. With appropriate training, the occurrence of each state in the network becomes the condition that causes the network to assume the following state. Notice that although the states of the network may be taken as explicit representations, the way the network gets from state to state is not explicitly represented anywhere in the network. It is implicit in the pattern of connectivity among units.

Imagine three such neural networks, a lexical network dedicated to representing what the steps of the checklist say, a semantic network dedicated to representing what the steps mean, and an action network dedicated to effecting the actions taken in the task world. All three of these may be working concurrently. When the checklist user performs a step,

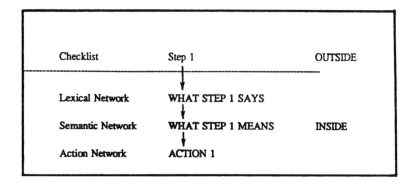

Figure 26.5. The networks activated in the performance of a step.

all three networks are activated. The shallow reading of the step itself produces a state in the lexical network. The working-out of the meaning of the step produces a state in the semantic network, and the performance of the actions that constitute the doing of the step produce states in the action network. The states in these networks are related to each other by the mediating structures (listed in Figures 26.1 through 26.4) that propagate states from one network to the next (see Figure 26.5). Let us now consider what might happen to this system with repeated performance of the task. As the user of the checklist reads each step in turn, the network that is dedicated to representing what the steps say is driven through a sequence of states that is repeated each time the checklist is followed. As a consequence, with repetition, the network learns the sequence of states produced by the shallow reading of the checklist, thereby internalizing the checklist. Here, by "internalizing the checklist" I mean specifically the development of a network which when placed in a state corresponding to the experience of "what step N says" will transition automatically to a state corresponding to the experience of "what step N+ 1 says."

Once such an internalized version of the checklist is developed, it may become the controlling structure for subsequent performances. This is shown in Figure 26.6. This amounts to the task performer having learned what the checklist says so that instead of reading the next step, he can "remember" what the next step says, use that to construct the meaning of the next step, and use that meaning to organize an action. A

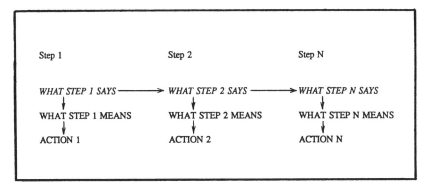

Figure 26.6. The lexical network has internalized the succession of states corresponding to the experience of reading the steps of the checklist. The horizontal arrows represent the learned state transitions in the lexical network. The vertical arrows represent the mediated propagation of state from the lexical to the semantic network via language skills, and from the semantic to the action network via planning and motor skills.

performance guided by the memory of the checklist is still a mediated task performance, but the mediating structure is now internal rather than external. The lexical network that encodes what the steps of the checklist say provides explicit representations of the steps of the procedure. It can move through a sequence of states, each of which corresponds to the experience of reading what a step on the checklist says. Moving from external to internal mediation also introduces new possibilities for the relations between the actor and the environment because the environment no longer need contain the mediating structure. The actor can deal with a wider range of environments. If the mediating structure was provided by the activities of another person, the actor who has internalized the structure can now act alone.[3]

Of course, at the same time that the neural network dedicated to the representation of what the steps say is being driven through a series of states, so is the neural network dedicated to representing the meanings of the steps. This is shown in Figure 26.7. Once this semantic network has been trained, the actor can remember the meanings of the steps, if necessary without reference to the memory of what the steps say. Because that other structure is around, however, and because people are

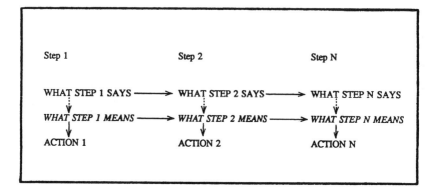

Figure 26.7. Automatization of the step meaning sequence by the semantic network. The semantic network has internalized the succession of states corresponding to the meanings of the steps of the checklist. The solid vertical arrows represent the mediated propagation of state from the semantic to action network. The dashed vertical arrows represent the available but not normally needed mediated propagation of state from the lexical network to the semantic network.

unrelentingly opportunistic, it is likely that both the memory of the meaning of the step, and the meaning derived from interpreting the memory of what the step says will be used in concert to determine the meaning of the step. Furthermore, a task performer may learn about the semantics of the domain and use that additional knowledge as yet another internal mediating structure in a sub-task of deriving constraints on the meaning of the next step to help in the reconstruction process that is remembering. This is an argument for the value of conceptual learning beyond rote learning.

But something else is happening too. In the use of both the external checklist and the internalized checklist, the neural apparatus involved in the performance of the task is driven through a sequence of states. Because of the nature of the structured interaction of the task performer with the environment, the sequence of states is repeated more or less consistently each time the checklist is followed. The network begins to encode the sequential relations among the successive states. Something of the organization of the $N+1$th state is in the potential of the network when the Nth state is present. Thus, the action network begins to inter-

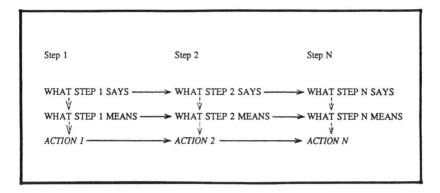

Figure 26.8. Automatization of the action sequence by the action network. The action network has internalized the succession of states corresponding to the actions taken in the task world. There is no longer a need for any mediation in the task performance. The entire structure is present, however, and could be invoked following any of the pathways present. The dashed vertical arrows represent not normally needed mediated propagation of state from the lexical network through the semantic network to the action network.

nalize the sequence of steps of the task in a different sense than the internalization of the words or meanings of the checklist itself. This latter internalization is implicit where the former two were explicit. With this encoding of the sequence represented implicitly in the connections of the action network, the network, once placed in state 1, can *do* the task automatically without reference to any explicit representation of the sequence. The mediated performances leading up to this state could be thought of as training trials for the network that produces the action. The system has now reached the condition described by Figure 26.8. In this condition, for a normal task performance, the action network no longer needs the organizing constraints of the mediating structure. Once placed in the initial state, the action network simply transitions through the states that constitute the doing of the task. This is the nature of automatized skill performances; automatized performances are performances that no longer utilize the organizing constraints of the mediating structure. Of course, if exceptional circumstances arise in the task world, the automatized performance may fail, requiring additional recourse to the mediating structure.

It is important to see that internalized memory of the checklist must become an automatized system before it can be used alone to control the states of the action network. Internalized mediation systems, while having explicit representational content in their states, rely for their controlling behavior on automatized implicit encodings of relations among their states. The issue of what is implicit and what is explicit depends upon the question being asked. The internalized memory for the checklist consists of states that represent explicit descriptions of the actions to be taken. But the sequential relations among those step descriptions are implicitly encoded in the pattern of connectivity of the lexical network much as the sequential relations among the step descriptions in the external checklist were implicitly encoded in their spatial relations on the checklist artifact itself. Consider briefly another common mediating structure, alphabetical order. It is used in many storage and retrieval schemes in our culture, so pains are taken to ensure that children learn it. In learning the alphabet song, the child is developing an explicit, internalized, automatized version of the alphabet structure. The content of the states, the words of the song, are explicit, but the sequential relations among them – which were provided by another mediating system, a teacher – are implicit. A child who knows the song can tell you what comes after "P" (perhaps after singing the first 17 letters) but that same child will have a difficult time saying why "Q" follows "P." There is simply no explicit representation of that in what the child knows.

The same thing would be true for the meanings of the steps were it not for the potential mediating role of conceptual knowledge in the task domain. If conceptual knowledge is tied to the meanings of the steps, some other network in the system may assume states that explicitly represent a reason why step $N+1$ follows step N. However, such a mediating structure need not be learned before the sequence of meanings of the steps is learned. Sometimes we discover *why* we do some task the way we do long after we have learned to do the task itself.

A common observation concerning automatized skill is that skilled performers may have difficulty saying how it is they do what they do. Two reasons for this fall out of this analysis. First, the automatized action network for the checklist is a way of producing in the relation of the person to the environment a sequence of actions that constitute the doing of the steps described by the checklist. Because it encodes a relationship between the person and the environment, the execution of the checklist by the automatized action network requires the cooperation of the environment in a way that remembering the checklist does not. For example, the attempt to do a step can be frustrated by the lack in the environment of something required by the step. Yet one may remember a description of a step even though the conditions required to carry it out are absent. In the example above, the actor may be forced by the lack of the required condition to do some other actions in preparation for the previously frustrated step. In giving an account of how to do a task, the task performer must assume a world, or perhaps more correctly, the report itself implies a world in which the described actions make sense. Except where the task in question occurs in a very stable set of environments, the assumed world is certain to differ from many of the actual worlds in which the task is attempted and the description will therefore fail in many of the worlds in which the task is performed. Second, the reports skilled performers can give are generally based on the mediating structures that were used to control their behavior while they were acquiring automatized skill. The accounts that are given, being descriptions of mediating structures, may be just what is needed to communicate the skill from one person to another because the only way to produce the automatized skill is to have the network learn it from experience and the only way for a novice to experience it is by use of mediating structure. However, if the memory for the mediating structure has atrophied as a result of long disuse during automatized performance, when we ask an expert how she does something, there may simply be no meaningful answer to be given. The automated system does what it has been trained to do, but it has no explicit representation of what it is doing. The *representation of* what it is doing exists only in the apparatus that provided the training, that is, the mediating structure which is now degraded.

Another situation that results in the expert task performer being unable to account for her own task performance arises when the mediating structure is present as constraints in the environment that shape the development of the action network directly, without the development of internalizations of explicit mediating representations. This seems to be the case for many motor skills. When asked to describe how the skill is performed, such an expert may describe events in which the skill was manifested. One view of such a response might be that the expert is being uncooperative, but when we understand that the mediating structure was in the environment of the skill acquisition, we see that describing events in which the skill was manifested is the best the expert can do to describe the mediating structure under which the skill developed.

With this example I have attempted to highlight the complexity and richness of interaction of mediation structures of different sorts in the performance of what seemed at the outset to be a relatively simple mediated task performance. I don't think this analysis should lead us to change our minds about the relative simplicity of using checklists. On the contrary, I hope it heightens our awareness of the diversity of kinds of mediating structures that come into play in everyday cognitive activities. In order to get useful mental work done, of course, the actor must be capable of bringing these structures into coordination with each other. As we saw with the coordination of the checklist with the task world, bringing mediating structures into coordination may require still more (meta-)mediating structures. The consequences of the lack of this ability are encoded in our folk wisdom about the differences between "book learning" and experience. One may have complete mastery over a major mediating structure for some task, but no development whatever of the meta-mediation required to put it to work in a real task environment.

In this view, what we learn and what we know, and what our culture knows for us in the form of the structure of artifacts and social organizations are these hunks of mediating structure. Thinking consists of bringing these structures into coordination with each other such that they can shape (and be shaped by) each other. The thinker in this world is a very special medium that can provide coordination among many structured media, some internal, some external, some embodied in artifacts, some in ideas, and some in social relationships.

Notes

1. Whether this internal representation is primarily auditory or visual or something else, I do not know. The important thing is that it be capable of permitting the actor to "remember" the lexical content of the step at a later time.
2. There is not sufficient space here to adequately explain how PDP systems actually work. In the following paragraphs, I outline some of their more interesting functional properties. I refer the interested reader to Rumelhart and McClelland, 1986.

3. This echoes Vygotsky's general genetic law of development with the two appearances of the mediating structure, one inter-psychological and the other intra-psychological.

References

Rumelhart, D. E., & McClelland, J. L. (1986). *Parallel distributed processing: Explorations in microstructure of cognition, Vol. 1, Foundations.* Cambridge, MA: Bradford Books.

Vygotsky, L. S. (1978). *Mind in Society.* In M. Cole, V. John-Steiner, S. Scribner, & E. Souberman (Eds.). Cambridge, MA: Harvard University Press.

27 Mind in action: A functional approach to thinking

Sylvia Scribner

I welcome this chance to talk to you. What I have decided to do is spend the time, not summing up past work, but introducing a new line of research that I undertook several years ago and that I think has important implications for adult learning and development.

I will introduce this research by asking you to imagine the following scene. My colleague and I are standing between stacks of milk cases in the refrigerated warehouse of a dairy. (My colleague's name, by the way, is Edward Fahrmeier and he is an important contributor to the research I will be telling you about.) Ed is armed with a sketch pad and pencil which he manipulates somewhat clumsily because he is wearing mittens. I am clutching a microphone and a tape recorder, having trouble holding on to them because I was not clever enough to *wear* mittens. We are watching a man called a preloader assemble just the right number of cartons of milk to fill a driver's order, and we are diagramming on paper and describing into the tape recorder exactly how he does this. Every now and then, when our hands and voices shake with cold, we run outside to sit on the factory steps. The 38 degree warehouse temperature collides with the 98 degree temperature of an August evening in Baltimore. Thawed, we return for more data collection.

In spite of the hazards of naturalistic observation portrayed in this episode, observation is an important component of the research project my title refers to – studying mind in action. What I am trying to do is analyze the characteristics of memory and thought, not as they appear in isolated mental tasks, but as they function in the larger, purposive life activities in which we engage. This approach contrasts with the dominant view in cognitive science today. The prevailing perspective views mind as a system of symbolic representations and operations that can be understood in and of itself, in isolation from other systems of activity. Accordingly, most researchers studying mental operations proceed by giving people isolated mental tasks to accomplish. If we study memory, we ask people to remember some information or event; if we study problem-solving, we ask people to talk aloud while solving problems. In these tasks, remembering and problem-solving are goals in themselves. When research is well developed, it is sometimes possible to specify the component operations in a task with sufficient precision to program them on a computer – a computer which sits in a room having no transactions with the external environment, a computer that is, so to speak, lost in thought.

This approach to cognition has many important achievements. Without minimizing them, it is fair to say that the metaphor "mind as computer" fails to capture significant aspects of human mental functioning. Memory and thinking in daily life are not separate from, but are part of, doing. We understand cognitive tasks, not merely as ends in themselves but as means for achieving larger objectives and goals; and we carry out these tasks in constant interaction with social and material resources and constraints. Unlike computers that *only* sit and think, people think while playing, working, creating art, and talking with one another. How does thought embedded in these ongoing activities compare with thought processes on isolated mental tasks? In recent years, as a result of the penetrating critiques of Cole, Bronfenbrenner, Neisser and others, we can no longer take for granted the optimistic assumption that laboratory-type tasks capture the critical characteristics of mental processes embedded in life activities. To discover the functional properties of thought in action requires that we take a look at the actual phenomena under natural conditions.

That is what my enterprise is about. I am attempting to place the study of naturally occurring activities at the center of cognitive inquiry. As my opening anecdote illustrates, I am grounding this enterprise in the study of activities which are of exceptional importance to youth and adults in our society – activities which we call work. In the workplace, tasks must be accomplished which require selection and retention of information, accumulation of knowledge, mastery of new symbol systems and on-line problem-solving – all in the service of getting other things done. How do adults cope with these demands? How, without formal instruction, do new workers acquire the intellectual skills these pursuits entail? And most importantly, how do cognitive skills in the workplace compare with those nurtured and demanded in academic settings? I went to the milk-processing plant in Baltimore to begin an exploration of these questions.

This is a preview of my research and my thesis. Before I take you back to the Dairy to tell you what we did and learned, I want to provide a brief account of how I came to this venture, the developmental questions it addresses, and the theoretical framework which guides it.

My interest in studying intellectual aspects of practical activities grows out of earlier attempts to understand the formative role of culture in cognitive development. In spite of the ambiguities that plague the field, cross-cultural research has revealed that the human intellect is not only universal in its *capacities* but diverse in its ways of *functioning*. After years of probing, psychologists and anthropologists have discerned some patterns in this diversity – patterns that reflect the impact of particular social institutions and practices. Most prominent in this line of work is the well-demonstrated association between Western-style schooling and features of performance on cognitive tasks.

While the interpretation of school-related cognitive skills is controversial, their very existence is a challenge to our theories. Even if we view such skills as specific rather than general in nature (and this view has been convincingly argued) we still confront a remarkable fact: an historically evolved and culturally rooted institution – school – fosters intellectual achievements that developmentalists, until recently, attributed solely to age.

Nor is school unique in its formative effects. New studies in Africa, the South Pacific, Pakistan have been documenting, sometimes with fine precision, the cognitive impact of other educative institutions – such as apprentice training and tutorial instruction in crafts and trades. This research has focused on the specialized knowledge and specific abilities that individuals acquire through participation in indigenous pursuits.

My own research among the Vai with Michale Cole has shown that literacy, too, has cognitive consequences of a specialized kind. The Vai people practice literacy in three scripts – two handed down without schooling and English acquired in government schools. We went to Vailand hoping to prove that literacy, with or without schooling, promoted higher mental abilities that humanists have long supposed it to do. Our expectations were dashed. Nonschooled literacies among the Vai were not like schooled literacy. We found no *general* effects of literacy as such and no higher skills common to all three literacies.

But we did find particular effects of particular literacies – memory skills associated with one, communication skills with another. In each case the specific skills linked to a given script closely paralleled the uses of that script in Vai society.

This outcome suggested to us the need to rethink the nature of literacy. Instead of conceiving of literacy as involvement with written language that is the same everywhere and involves some fixed inventory of capacities, we began to think of literacy as a term applying to a varied and open set of activities with written language. These activities might range from simple letter-writing to the composition of historical chronicles. In this view the cognitive skills that literacy fosters will also vary – with the kind of activities with writing that particular cultures develop and individuals within a culture are motivated to undertake.

At the conclusion of the Vai research, I put foward a conceptual framework to integrate these cross-cultural studies and guide future research on culture-based skill systems. I call this a practice framework of cognition. You may recognize it as bearing some resemblance to activity theory in Soviet psychology. My version is not a formal theory but a set of coherent constructs which may be helpful in re-thinking the relationship between mental skills and culturally organized activities.

Let me give you some unelaborated definitions and allow later descriptions to flesh out their meaning. By a practice, I refer to a socially constructed activity organized around some common objects. A practice involves bounded knowledge domains and determinate technologies, including symbol systems. A practice is comprised of recurrent and interrelated goal-directed actions. Participants in a practice master its knowledge and technology and acquire the mental and manual skills needed to apply them to the accomplishment of actions' goals. Navigation is a practice; so is letter-writing; and I will shortly point to others.

This practice framework implies a methodological principle. If skill systems are activity- or practice-dependent, one way to determine their characteristics and course of acquisition is to study them as they function in these practices. To put it somewhat differently, the practices themselves need to become the objects of study. Observational methods are necessary to determine what tasks are involved in certain practices and to describe their characteristics. Experimental methods are needed to refine these descriptions and analyze the component knowledge and cognitive skills involved in task accomplishment. In a rudimentary way, we attempted to carry out this progression from observation to experiment in the Vai research but were hampered by conditions of work in an unfamiliar culture. I came home, convinced I needed to be a native to undertake a research program that could test this methodology and elaborate the conceptual framework.

What practices should be selected for initial studies? I chose work for reasons of significance and strategy. Significance is apparent. Just as play represents the dominant activity of preschoolers, and school a dominant activity for children and youth, work is a principle activity for adults. Work occupies the bulk of our time. We tend to identify ourselves through our work: you are a psychologist, she is a surgeon. Work offers us many occasions for acquiring knowledge and developing expertise. While we are certainly not wholly defined through our participation in society's labor, it is unlikely we can fully understand the life cycle of development without examining what adults do when they work.

Considerations of research strategy pointed in the same direction and led me to concentrate my first effort in a single industrial plant. In developing methods for studying thought in activity, we benefit from an environment that imposes tight constraints on performance. A factory is such an environment. Its production system shapes occupational activities in both their social and technical aspects. Goals are predetermined and explicit. In choosing to study factory work we can bypass the need to proceed from fully explicit definitions of "practice" and "goal-directed actions." We can take advantage of natural categories available in the industrial environment, allowing *occupations* to represent *practices* and *work tasks* to represent *goal-directed* actions.

Finally, in many factory occupations, work is embedded in larger manual activities which have observable behavioral outcomes. Thought is related to action in ways that facilitate psychological reconstruction of the knowledge and operations brought to bear in accomplishment of a task. If we can achieve some rigorous analysis of tasks involving external operations, we might then go on to consider how such analyses might function as models for understanding cognitive tasks whose operations are primarily internal.

And so, through this detour, we arrive at the Dairy in Baltimore. We spent six months becoming acquainted with its operations, and, quite unfairly, you have to rely on a short segment of a videotape to give you a bit of background knowledge. I will be illustrating our research with a detailed case history of one job – and even a brief glimpse of what a milk-processing plant looks like will help you follow the description. The concrete details will tell you more about the intellectual intricacies of work tasks than sentences of glittering generalities.

(Tape)

Here is our research design in a nutshell. We selected three occupations and four work tasks for cognitive analysis. Two tasks involved physical objects – product assembly carried out by preloaders, and counting stock, an inventory job. Two tasks involved symbolic manipulations – pricing delivery tickets and forecasting the next day's orders, both the work of wholesale delivery drivers. In each instance, we began with observations of the job as it occurred under normal working conditions. We then constructed a model and simulated the task in experimental sessions. To explore the effects of job experience, we gave all job simulations to individuals from all occupations. Each occupation served as expert on its own task and novice on the others. We also included two distant novice groups – office workers in the Dairy and 9th grade students in a nearby junior high school.

I have selected product assembly for discussion. This job, considered one of the most unskilled in the Dairy, is carried out in the refrigerated warehouse which was the opening scene of my talk. Preloaders arrive at 6:00 p.m. to find awaiting them a sheaf of delivery orders called load-out order forms. Each form lists the products and their amounts that a wholesale driver has ordered for his next day's delivery. The preloader reads the form, locates the products and transports them to a common assembly area near a moving track which carries them past a checkpoint out to the loading platform. Speed counts – the preloader's shift lasts until all load-out order forms are processed and all trucks filled. Accuracy counts – the checker sends incorrect orders back to the preloader for reassembly.

An interesting feature of this job involves the symbol system used on the load-out order form to express quantities. Drivers place their orders for products in terms of the number of units needed – how many *half-pints* of chocolate milk they need or *quarts* of skim milk. Fluid products are not handled by unit within the plant, however, but by case. Since cases are standard size, the number of units they hold varies with the type of container – one case holds 4 gallons, 8 half-gallons, 16 quarts and so on.

When load-out order forms are produced, the computer cases out the drivers' orders by converting units into case equivalencies. If the required number of units does not amount to an even number of cases, the left-over amount is expressed in units. Rules of conversion result in some mixed orders being expressed as cases *plus* units, for example 1 + 6, and other orders as cases *minus* units, for example 2 − 7.

Thus preloaders confront mixed numbers on the load-out order form, numbers drawn from different base systems depending on the container size they qualify. How do they handle these? Do they always fill them as written – that is, do they always add units to an empty case when the order calls for a case plus units – as in 1 + 6 – or remove units from a full case when the order calls for that as in 1 − 6? Informal observations suggested that preloaders had worked out interpretative procedures for the number representations and often departed from literal instruction.

We planned a night of organized observation to obtain more systematic information, and two of us took up posts at a spot near milk products which had the greatest number of mixed case and unit orders. I have already described our procedures. Our diagrams and transcriptions permitted us to reconstruct for each order the exact array the preloader found on arrival, the moves he made, and the final state of the array. With these classes of evidence on hand, we analyzed the product assembly task as an example of problem-solving within the tradition of laboratory-based research.

The first thing we learned from our systematic observations is that the preloaders had a large repertoire of solution strategies for what looked like the "same problem." One order – 1 − 6 quarts – occurred six times while we were in the icebox. Remember there are 16 quarts in a case so that 10 were needed. On two occasions, this order received literal solutions: the preloader removed six quarts from a full case. But on four occasions, the order was rewritten behaviorally. All of these transformations took advantage of partially full cases to reduce the number of units that had to be moved to satisfy the order. In some instances the *take-away* (1 − 6) problem was changed to an *add-to* problem: 2 units were added to 8 in one instance and 4 units to 6 in another.

Nonliteral solutions such as these require that the assembler transform the original information into some representation that can be mapped onto quantitative properties of different arrays. We may infer that such solutions involve mental processing, or broadly speaking, mental work, over and beyond retention in short-term memory of the quantity given on the load-out order sheet (which literal solutions also require). When does a preloader elect to engage in such additional mental work? Are nonliteral solutions haphazard or rule-governed? We postulated a "law of mental effort": "In product assembly, mental work will be expended to save physical work." We tested this possibility against our observational records. These records provided us with a precise metric for scaling physical effort – the number of units an assembler moved in completing an order. By comparing various modes of solution in terms of the number of moves they required, we could determine which strategy represented a "least-physical-effort solution" under a given set of circumstances. We refer to these as optimal solutions.

Applying this definition to our observational records, we found that preloaders used literal strategies 30 times and 25 of these were least-physical-effort strategies. Nonliteral strategies were adopted 23 times; on every occasion such strategies represented a least-physical-effort solution. The evidence overwhelmingly favored the postulated relationships between mental and manual effort on this task.

At this point we moved to task simulation in our lab at the Dairy to further the analysis. We prepared facsimiles of load-out order sheets, restricting orders to quantities of less than a case. The informant, after reading the order, proceeded to an assembly area where we had set up an array consisting of a full case, an empty case and a partial case. The number of units in the partial case varied from trial to trial to fulfill parameters of the problem list.

Over two administrations and some 100 problems, preloaders distinguished themselves from all other groups. They selected optimal nonliteral strategies over 70% of the time – even under the artificial circumstances of our task. Rankings of other groups also highlight the role of experience. Inventory men and drivers who occasionally did product assembly were not far behind preloaders. Office workers with no experience in the task but familiarity with the Dairy used optimal, non-literal solutions in less than half the instances in which they were strategies of choice. As for students, complete novices, they were with few exceptions single algorithm problem-solvers. Instead of adapting solution strategies to the least-effort principle, they carried out literal instructions on almost all the problems.

Even when novices selected an optimal strategy,, they carried it out quite differently from preloaders. Audio and video records indicate they relied heavily on numerical solutions and counting operations, especially on early trials. Here is an example from an office worker's protocol. The order is 1 − 6 quarts (one case of 16 less six). She begins to fill the order and says:

> It was one case minus six, so there's two. four, six, eight, ten, sixteen (determines how many in a case; points finger as she counts). So there should be ten in here. Two, four, six, ten (counts units as she moves them from full to empty). One case minus six would be ten.

In contrast, preloaders often appeared to shortcut the arithmetic and work directly from the visual display. A preloader is discussing how he filled an order for 1 case − 8 quarts: (order of eight):

> I walked over and I visualized. I knew the case I was looking at had ten out of it, and I only wanted eight so I just added two to it . . . I don't never count when I'm making the order, I do it visual, a visual thing you know.

We have still additional evidence that different processes of comparison and solution characterize expert and novice assemblers. A particularly crucial phase of the assembly is the premovement period – the interval between a person's arrival at the array and execution of the first movement. All office workers on some occasion counted out loud during this phase; preloaders never did. We also measured the duration of the premovement period for all 90 problems which had optimal solutions. Decision time averaged 1.4 seconds per problem for preloaders, 3.2 seconds for office workers. This time differential supports the interpretation that preloaders were using perceptual information from the array to determine quantity while clerks used slower, enumerative techniques.

How does a product assembler become a skilled optimizer? No formal instruction is involved, although tips are undoubtedly passed on from old hands to newcomers. In studies now underway in our CUNY

Graduate School laboratories, we find that most high school students switch from literal to optimizing strategies on their own as they gain experience with the task; they learn through doing. These studies are also providing a nice confirmation of our hypothesis that optimizing in its initial stages involves expenditure of mental effort to save physical effort. We systematically varied the solution complexity of problems and found that those requiring fewer mental steps were among the first to be solved optimally. More intellectually demanding problems received literal solutions longer, and with some student apprentices, never became fully optimized.

I do not have time to describe problem-solving skills on all the other jobs we studied. But I will tell you a bit about our analysis of the delivery ticket pricing task to demonstrate that, in spite of marked surface differences across tasks, we are discovering some common, perhaps very general, characteristics of problem-solving on the job.

Pricing delivery tickets is all symbolic work. Wholesale drivers are responsible for determining the cost of their daily deliveries to customers. For this purpose, they use standard delivery tickets, preprinted with the customer's name and the products usually purchased. When a driver completes a delivery, he enters the amount of each product on the ticket, expressing this amount in units – 70 quarts of skim, 200 half-pints of chocolate. He then calculates the price for each line item and totals the dollar value of the entire delivery. Accuracy counts. Each driver is responsible for the exact value of products he takes out of the Dairy. Speed counts, too, for the driver's day begins at 3:00 a.m. and does not end until 1:00 or 2:00 in the afternoon. To help the driver price out, the company provides a mimeographed wholesale price list for all major products. All prices are expressed in units on this list because the price structure consists wholly of unit prices. Since the size of each product order is recorded on the delivery ticket in units, and prices are in units, the computation task seems straightforward: take the unit price from the price list or memory, multiply it by the number of units delivered, and enter the result in the appropriate column.

Informal observations revealed that drivers, no less than preloaders, frequently departed from this literal format. Mr. B., a driver I rode out with, provided one of the first instances of an alternate pricing strategy. He read the item "32 quarts lowfat" on his delivery ticket, found a price on a crib sheet in his pocket, doubled it and entered the answer. He had read "32 quarts" as "2 cases" and used a case price in his solution.

The milk case played an instrumental role in the product assembly task, both in its physical aspects as a container, and in its symbolic aspects – as a variable that could take certain number values. Pricing out is an activity occurring wholly in the symbolic mode. As a material object the case is without significance for this activity. Yet it appears here, too, as a variable in arithmetic operations. Unremarkable as this may first appear, one can think of the case price as a prototype of human sign-creating activities that play such an important role in theories of higher mental functions. An object which first possesses instrumental value in physical activity begins to serve a sign function and become incorporated in mental operations.

Through a series of simulations, proceeding in the manner described for product assembly, we learned that the use of case price techniques marked the performance of all experienced drivers. When unit quantities were evenly divisible into cases, they used case prices alone. On other occasions, they factored unit quantities into cases and units, and used both prices in various combinations. The versatility of some drivers was impressive. One man, about to retire after 37 years of service, was a mental math virtuoso: he used *25* different case and unit calculation strategies to solve pricing problems that had the identical units-times-unit-price format.

A problem by problem analysis of solution strategies showed that the case price technique functioned as an effort saver in a manner analogous to the nonliteral optimal solutions in the product assembly task – with an important difference. The effort saved here was *mental*, not physical. Use of case price either eliminated computation altogether or simplified it. This effort-saving interpretation is supported by our studies which mapped case price knowledge of individual drivers against their solution strategies. Drivers only used case prices when they knew them or had them readily available on personal crib sheets; no driver computed a case price on the way to a solution.

Our final observation is that drivers were not locked into a case price strategy any more than they were to a unit price strategy. In one experiment we prepared delivery tickets on which some problems could be simplified by use of *unit* prices – 101 quarts, for example, which can easily be solved as 100 plus one. Other problems lent themselves to *case* price solutions. Drivers were flexible problem-solvers, using the arithmetically simpler strategy in accordance with the problem's numerical properties. Students were inflexible problem-solvers. Most clung to a literal unit price strategy throughout. When some adopted a case price strategy, they used it for all problems, covering scratch sheets with long division to find a fraction of a case. White collar and warehouse workers fell between the two groups.

Some concluding remarks

Let me now try to establish ties with the broader questions that motivated these studies of practical thinking at work.

One motivation was a test of method. We wanted to determine if we could bring some rigor to the study of naturally occurring activities. Our entry into the real world was guided by a practice approach to cognition which helped us carve out units of behavior which we could subject to cognitive analysis. These units were work tasks within occupations. Using a research strategy that moved from observation to experiment, we succeeded in achieving a fine-grained specification of the knowledge and skill components of several tasks. My students and I – King Beach, Joy Stevens, and others – are now trying to extend the framework to new settings, different occupations and different kinds of cognitive skills, such as memory and spatial reasoning.

We cannot yet offer an assessment of how far we may travel with the approach we have taken but we have gained some confidence in the analyzability of intellectual components of work. As we proceed, certain old dichotomies that have impeded the adoption of an action-oriented approach to thought become increasingly irrelevant. Observation is not opposed to experiment, but may be the forerunner of it. Description is not opposed to explanation but may function as a first approximation to it.

A second purpose of this research was to examine the formative role of practical activities. We began with a theoretical orientation holding that cognitive skills take shape in the course of participation in socially organized practices. We elected to examine practices that involve neither esoteric bodies of knowledge nor high technologies. Yet the experience-based nature of skilled problem-solving was evident in all the tasks we analyzed. In every group comparison, the occupation with on-the-job experience provided the greatest number of experts. The job-related nature of cognitive skills was most readily discernible in contrasts between Dairy workers as a group and students as a group. The claim we make goes beyond the commonsense observation that "practice makes perfect." We have not been concerned, nor have we offered facts here, about *accuracy* or *speed* of performance. The changes we have documented are *qualitative*, not *quantitative*. Our analyses demonstrated that modes of solution change with experience. Practice makes for difference – the problem-solving process is restructured by the knowledge and strategy repertoire available to the expert in comparison to the novice. Other studies have shown such qualitative changes in pursuits such as physics and music. Our research suggests that a pattern of development from novice to expert performance may not be restricted to such demanding activities but may represent the course of adult skill acquisition in the mundane pursuits we commonly think of as "unskilled." The human implications of an approach to work which recognizes it as formative – as educative in the broadest sense of that term – are both exhilarating and sobering – exhilarating in terms of future possibilities and sobering in terms of many present-day realities.

A third purpose of this research was to increase our knowledge about the nature of this phenomenon that I call thinking-in-action, or practical thinking. Although we have examined only a half-dozen tasks, they share common features which offer interesting suggestions for a general theory of practical thinking at work.

One feature of skilled problem-solving is the dependency of problem-solving strategies on knowledge about the workplace. The industrial world as we found it was not only made up of things but of symbols that were in significant respects peculiar to that setting. Mastery of both knowledge and symbol systems was a precondition for skilled problem-solving. A preloader could only depart from a literal solution to an order when he understood the symbol "1 − 6" and knew its numeric value. A driver could only regroup 33 quarts into 32 and one for pricing purposes when he saw the cases in the numbers. Skill in the Dairy was not content-free.

Variability was an outstanding feature of skilled performance on all tasks. On first inspection, product assembly and pricing out appear as prototypical examples of repetitive industrial work. They both present the worker with recurring problems of the same kind, often of an identical kind. Yet workers brought a diversity of problem-solving operations to these same-problem formats. This problem-to-problem variability was not foreshadowed in laboratory research nor accounted for in formal models of problem-solving. Variability is often treated as a perturbation in an otherwise orderly system.

Bartlett's classic studies of thinking are an exception. He considered problem-solving to have the same characteristics of skilled performance in other modalities, and he held that a defining attribute of skill is variability. Moreover, skilled variability is rule-governed. He said:

> . . . all forms of skill expertly carried out possess an outstanding characteristic of rapid adaptation . . . so what is called the same operation is now done in one way and now in another, but each way is, as we say, "fitted to the occasion."

This is a fitting description of the kind of thinking we have seen in action at the Dairy and other work sites. Following Bartlett, we might consider these regularities as forms of adaption and put to future studies the following proposition: skilled practical thinking at work is goal-directed and varies adaptively with the changing properties of problems and changing conditions in the task environment.

Must we leave the concept of adaptive thinking on an analogical level? Our research raises a line of speculation that may be worth pursuing: practical thinking at work becomes adaptive when it serves the interests of economy of effort. Product assembly provided a vivid example of thinking saving manual effort; pricing out a parallel demonstration of thinking saving mental effort. Labor psychology laboratories in Paris and Dresden report that working people in those countries, too, evaluate their actions on the basis of an effectiveness criterion – a ratio of effort to result. This search for the economical, optimal solution appears to regulate many mental and manual activities in the workplace, spawning variation. Optimizing thinking stands in sharp contrast to the kind of thinking exemplified in the use of a single algorithm to solve all problems of a given type. Algorithms describe how *computers* solve problems. Variability and flexibility describe how *skilled* workers solve problems. Here we have a basic structural difference between formal, academic thinking and practical thinking at work.

These observations allow us to generate a speculative but intriguing model of the course of development of work-related skill systems. In contrast to the conventional psychological model of learning which assumes a progression from the particular and concrete to the general and abstract, skill acquisition at work seems to move in the direction of mastery of the concrete. The novice enters the workplace with a stock of knowledge, some school-based and some experience-based. Learning at work consists of adapting this prior knowledge to the accomplishment of the tasks at hand. Such adaptation proceeds by the assimilation of *specific* knowledge about the *objects* and *symbols* the setting affords, and the *actions* the work tasks require. Domain-specific knowledge reveals relationships that can be used to shortcut those stipulated in all-purpose algorithms. With domain-specific knowledge, expert workers have greater opportunity to free themselves from rules, and to invent flexible strategies. Skill in this model implies not only knowledge and know-how but creativity – an attribute of the work group as a social entity if not of each individual within it.

Work activities have certain peculiarities and cannot be considered representative of all practical thinking in action. Cognitive studies of work are only beginning; our models are tentative and our findings preliminary. But I hope that they suggest the theoretical and practical importance of studying the role of work in the developmental process. I hope, too, they convey a conception of mind which is not hostage to the traditional cleavage between the mind and the hand, the mental and the manual.

At the end of one interview, a seasoned delivery driver described to me the public's image of a milk man. He said, "Most people believe you only need a strong back to be a milk man. But, come to think of it, there is a lot of brain work involved." I think he is right.

Note

Invited Lecture, Biennial Meeting, Society for Research in Child Development, April 24, 1983.

28 Coordination, cooperation, and communication in the courts: Expansive transitions in legal work

Yrjö Engeström, Katherine Brown, L. Carol Christopher, and Judith Gregory

Introduction

Work in courts of law is among the most formal and rule-based processes in industrialized societies. However, the intricate division of labor in court organizations and the increasing complexity of the contents of cases give rise to various kinds of disturbances and unexpected contingencies in interactions inside and outside the courtroom.

In the United States as in many other countries, courts face rapidly growing caseloads without commensurate growth in the number of judges and other personnel. As Heydebrand and Seron (1990) show, the way to cope with this dilemma has been increasing rationalization. The means of rationalization include novel techniques of scheduling as well as increasing reliance on magistrates, probation officers, and law clerks instead of only judges. Most importantly, they include new mechanisms for resolving and settling cases before they enter the stage of a full-scale jury trial.

Rationalization is often regarded as synonymous either to bureaucratization in the Weberian sense or to assembly-line Fordism. On the basis of a careful historical and statistical analysis, Heydebrand and Seron demonstrate that rationalization in courts is a much more open-ended endeavor.

The growth and complexity of the organizational structure of courts is an undeniable development. But there are few signs that such growth is bureaucratic in the sense of Weber's model. Judicial case management has clearly played an important role in the rise of no-action and pretrial dispositions. Yet, the mandatory settlement conference or other

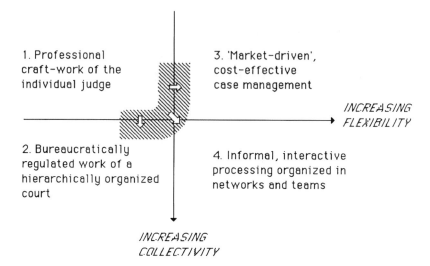

Figure 28.1. The hypothesized zone of proximal development for work in courts.

pretrial mechanisms of dispute resolution are not necessarily "bureaucratic" since they involve a host of informal procedures that deviate from the formal adversary-adjudicatory model alike. What is perhaps more crucial . . . is how these conferences are conducted, what mix of formal rational and informal-social elements they use, and what innovative alternatives they admit into their arsenal of conflict resolution techniques. (Heydebrand & Seron, 1990, p. 157)

Heydebrand and Seron (1990, pp. 156, 157) observe that the developments in court organizations particularly in metropolitan areas "point to the emergence of a highly elaborated network of organized activities" while many judges' orientations and policies may be changing "from that of formal adjudicators of cases to that of informal processors of disputes." In this light, we may hypothesize that the currently emerging zone of proximal development (Engeström, 1987) for work activity in American courts looks something like the gray field in Figure 28.1.

Figure 28.1 implies that the zone of proximal development is a terrain of constant ambivalence and struggle between at least three alternative directions (fields 2, 3, and 4). The struggle is manifested in ruptures, disturbances, and expansive innovations in the routine flow of work. We will look at one complex case of civil litigation that took place in the spring of 1991 in the superior court of a large city in southern California. The case involved a dispute over construction defects found in a 240-unit condominium complex. The homeowners association demanded approximately six million dollars from the developer for repair of the defects. After a year and a half of pretrial procedures and settlement attempts, the case went to a jury trial. The trial lasted two weeks, one week less than estimated by the judge and the attorneys. Forty-three witnesses testified and more than 200 exhibits were introduced (the two parties had originally prepared more than 700 exhibits).

This case exemplifies the increased complexity of many cases of civil litigation. It also represents a test case for the "independent calendar" and the "delay reduction program," a case management strategy for addressing the volume of litigation in which the judge handling this case is an active practitioner.

The county courts initiated the Delay Reduction Program, also referred to as the "fast track system," in the mid 1980s to improve the handling of the increasing number of time-consuming complex cases. The judge characterized the reform as a change from the traditional role of the court as a "passive receptacle" to the active management of a case assigned to an individual judge "for all purposes." Previously, the phases of a case – pretrial motions, settlement efforts, jury trial – were assigned to different specialized departments of the courts, each with a different presiding judge. The shift to the independent calendar means that, once a case has been declared complex, it is given to a superior court judge who will preside should the case go to trial. The judge acts as "master" of the case through all its phases.

Theorizing expansive transitions

In analyses of work, a crucial question is how to combine the subject–object and the subject–subject, or the instrumental and the communicative, aspects of the activity. Arne Raeithel (1983) and Bernd Fichtner (1984) suggest a three-level notion of the developmental forms of epistemological subject–object–subject relations. The three levels are called *coordination*, *cooperation*, and *communication*. We shall briefly sketch our interpretation of these levels and of the possible mechanisms of transition between them.

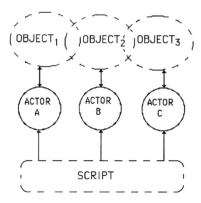

Figure 28.2. The general structure of coordination.

We call the normal scripted flow of interaction *coordination*. The various actors are following their scripted roles, each concentrating on the successful performance of the assigned actions, or on "the presentation of the self" (Goffman, 1959). The script is coded in written rules and places or tacitly assumed traditions. It coordinates the participants' actions as if from behind their backs, without being questioned or discussed (see Figure 28.2).

In a lawsuit, the script is largely coded in laws and statutes. It is also coded in the guidelines and instructions adopted locally by the particular court. Finally, there is an important component of unwritten tradition in the script. Obviously, the details of the script differ between different types of cases.

In Figures 28.2, 28.3, and 28.4, the unbroken boundaries indicate that the entities are in the focus of the subjects' critical attention. The broken boundaries indicate that the corresponding entities are not in the focus of critical attention for the subjects.

By *cooperation* we mean modes of interaction in which the actors, instead of each focusing on performing their assigned roles or presenting themselves, focus on a shared problem, trying to find mutually acceptable ways to conceptualize and solve it. The participants go beyond the confines of the given script, yet they do this without explicitly questioning or reconceptualizing the script. Transitions to cooperation may occur in interactions between various practitioners or between

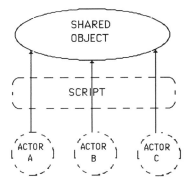

Figure 28.3. The general structure of cooperation.

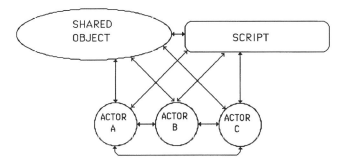

Figure 28.4. The general structure of communication.

professionals and lay clients. The general structure of cooperation is depicted in Figure 28.3.

By reflective *communication* we mean interactions in which the actors focus on reconceptualizing their own organization and interaction in relation to their shared objects. Both the object and the script are reconceptualized, as is the interaction between the participants. Transitions to communication are rare in the ongoing flow of daily work actions. The general structure of reflective communication is depicted in Figure 28.4.

The mechanisms of transition between the levels include disturbances, ruptures, and expansions (see Engeström, in press). Disturbances are unintentional deviations from the script. They cause discoordinations in interaction, which in turn may lead to (a) disintegration (e.g., confusion and withdrawal), (b) contraction (e.g., by authoritative silencing of some actors, or by softer evasion), or (c) expansion (i.e., collaborative reframing of the object by moving to cooperation or communication). Expansions may also occur without being triggered by specific disturbances.

While disturbances are deviations in the observable flow of interaction in the ongoing activity, ruptures are blocks, breaks, or gaps in the intersubjective understanding and flow of information between two or more participants of the activity. Ruptures don't ostensibly disturb the flow of the work process, although they may often lead to actual disturbances. Ruptures are thus found by interviewing and observing the participants outside or after the performance of work actions.

Disturbances, ruptures, and expansive transitions are crucially interesting as manifestations of the zone of proximal development of the activity system. We are especially interested in what facilitates expansive transitions, in particular, what kinds of linguistic and other tools are used and invented to initiate and complete them. We are also interested in how these might be institutionalized.

Disturbances and expansions in the court: The question of data

Since court proceedings are excessively scripted and well rehearsed, it is not easy to observe deviations from the normal in court. This is particularly true of trials where the parties are represented by skillful lawyers, much less so of cases where lay persons are directly involved (for examples of the latter, see Conley & O'Barr, 1990; Engeström, Brown, Engeström, Gregory, Haavisto, Pihlaja, Taylor & Wu, 1990; Merry, 1990). In the case analyzed here, the absence of visible deviations became a prominent problem. The litigating parties were very smooth, polite, and flexible in their interactions. Toward the end of the two-week trial, we were increasingly worried because so few instances of disturbances were evident from our videotapes and observation of the courtroom proceedings.

During the trial, procedural disagreements between the parties are commonly handled by what are called "sidebar" conferences or "sidebars." When one party objects to a move by the other party, one of the attorneys or the judge will usually call for a sidebar conference. These conferences are short breaks in the procedure where the judge hears the procedural arguments of both parties and makes his or her ruling accordingly. Sidebars often take place in the courtroom, in front of the bench but out of earshot of the jurors. In our case, they were held in the judge's chambers adjacent to the courtroom. An observer has no chance of hearing or recording the contents of the sidebars as they occur.

In our case, the judge habitually asked the official court reporter to attend and record the sidebars. This gave us the idea of analyzing the official sidebar transcripts as data on disturbances. Sidebars are indeed disturbances by definition. They interrupt the normal flow of interaction in the courtroom, and the judge is often quite conscious of the fact that they annoy the jurors, who cannot hear or understand what is going on in the sidebars. To our knowledge, sidebar transcripts have thus far not been systematically used as data in studies on court interaction.

During this trial, 19 sidebars were held in the presence of the official court reporter, lasting on average between two and four minutes. The transcripts of these sidebars are the data we analyzed for this paper. Courtroom transcripts prepared by ourselves from videotapes representing phases immediately before and after sidebars differed from the corresponding transcripts prepared by the court reporter only in very minor ways. This indicates a high verbatim accuracy on the part of the court reporter. In the excerpts presented below, we reproduce the official court reporter's transcripts, deleting only names and other identifiable terms and adding necessary contextual information in brackets [ ].

Returning to coordination by contraction

The most typical way of dealing with a sidebar is that of returning to business as usual by means of a quick unilateral decision by the judge. This is exemplified in excerpt #1.

Excerpt #1

[Direct examination of plaintiff's witness Mr. W by plaintiff's counsel Mr. G]

Mr. G: Mr. W, in – are you personally aware, given your special knowledge, skill and expertise, of how much it actually costs to move people from their homes and then to move them back into their homes?

Mr. W: I am aware of some of some of the costs, based on what we have done in the past.

Mr. G: All right. And based upon your special knowledge and expertise, what has it cost homeowners in the past in condominiums such as D [the name of the complex under litigation]?

Mr. V: [one of the two defense counsel]: Same objection, Your Honor.

Mr. G: It is facts.

Mr. V: The objection wasn't on foundation.

[The judge leads the parties into a sidebar. The following takes place in the judge's chambers without the presence of the jury.]

The judge: Maybe I am not tracking. Now, what is it that you say? There was actual discovery on this?

Mr. G: Oh, yes, Your Honor. It was in the deposition.

The judge: So, let's go back, then. What was the basis for the objection?

Mr. V: Beyond the scope of the expert designation in the case. There was a motion *in limine* granted to limit the experts to the scope of the expert witness declaration filed by counsel. Nowhere is Mr. W designated as an expert on moving costs. He is an expert on costs to repair. He is a general contractor. And this testimony goes beyond the scope of his designation, even if it was disclosed in deposition.

The judge: All right. It is overruled. I will consider the cost of repair. You can proceed.

[The parties return to the courtroom.]

The judge quickly eliminated this disturbance by means of one type of authoritative silencing. He heard the arguments of both parties, then decided in favor of the plaintiff without further discussion.

In spite of the rather straightforward nature of this interaction, certain hesitation and ambivalence may be observed. First the judge seems to regard the sidebar itself as unnecessary: "Maybe I am not tracking." He seems to be ready to make a unilateral decision right away: "So, let's go back, then." But he backs up and hears the defense argument. Only after that does he reconfirm his initial decision.

The pattern of contraction by authoritative silencing was followed in 12 of the 19 sidebars. In every single one of those there were interesting minor ambivalences, as if implying an emerging fundamental instability in this pattern.

Transitions to cooperation

There were six sidebars in which an expansive transition into cooperation took place (Figure 28.3). Instead of sticking to their respective assigned roles as adversaries and objective authority figure, the parties and the judge embarked upon joint construction of a novel problem and novel solution. The production of the new in these occasions resembles what Weick (1979) calls enactment and what Rittenberg (1985) characterizes as objectification of situated meaning. In excerpt #2, we give an example of such an expansive transition.

Excerpt #2

[Direct examination of plaintiff's witness Ms. P by the plaintiff's counsel Mr. G]

Mr. G: Other than the water stain beneath that window on the wall and the water stain in the living room ceiling, are there any other concerns or complaints about the condition of your condominium?

Ms. P: Yes, there are. I also have – Shall I go on?

Mr. G: Yes.

Ms. P: I didn't realize it was a problem, because the fire investigator –

Mr. V: Objection, Your Honor.

The judge: Sustained. What we are interested in are things that you know about rather than what somebody told you.

Ms. P: I know about it now, though, because –

The judge: I mean, that you observed, you know, your self, other than something that somebody said. Go ahead, Mr. G. You take over the questioning. (Laughter)

Mr. G: Thank you, Your Honor.

Ms. P: I don't understand. I am sorry.

Mr. G: What are you talking about? What condition have you seen that you are now concerned about?

Mr. V: Could I have a sidebar for a minute, please?

[The following held in chambers between the judge and counsel.]

Mr. G: I am doing the best I can.

Mr. V: I understand. I think the danger that we are running into now is the area where she is going to testify that a fire investigator – meaning Mr. H, in his volunteer fire department uniform – came into her house and took out her light fixture. That's the testimony that was the subject of a motion *in limine* –

The judge: All right.

Mr. V: – whether a fireman or a fire investigator determined that her light fixtures were a fire hazard. And that's the testimony that I wanted to avoid before we tried to unring the bell.

The judge: That makes sense. We've already talked about it. Can you – will she avoid that? Will you talk to her about that?

Mr. G: I will whisper in her ear and say, "Don't mention anything about what somebody else said, and don't mention what he was wearing."

Mr. V: If she is talking about Mr. W and the fire investigator in the chimney, I don't have a problem with that. But if we are talking about Mr. H in his fireman's uniform, that's where we have the problem.

The judge: Just spend a minute and lay out to her the fact that she should just avoid referencing Mr. H and what he was dressed in or what he represented himself to be. He already testified. The jury knows. And go from there.
Mr. V: I have no objection if Mr. G leads Ms. P through the testimony.
The judge: Okay. That's thoughtful. She is nervous, so that might help.

Here the counsel and the judge are facing an unexpected problem. Essentially, the witness does not understand a crucial part of the script, namely the "hearsay rule" which prohibits using what others have said as evidence rather than the witness's own direct knowledge and experience. The sidebar turns into shared problem solving. This is triggered by the initial disarming utterance of Mr. G: "I am doing the best I can." This unusually personal statement receives a sympathetic response from Mr. G's adversary, Mr. V: "I understand." Here the problem is redefined as no longer an issue of contest. It becomes an issue of finding a mutually acceptable way of coaching or guiding the witness.

The rather striking innovation produced in this episode is that the defense counsel actually suggests that it might be helpful if Mr. G "leads Ms. P through the testimony." In the script regulating court procedures, "leading the witness' is prohibited as strictly as using "hearsay." However, the boundary between leading the witness to a conclusion premeditated by the attorney and guiding or coaching the witness through the testimony is fuzzy and regularly contested. The traditional script expects that the parties watch that boundary restrictively and jealously. The use of the word "leads" by Mr. V – who generally adheres to the formal script quite consistently – may not be accidental. It delivers a signal constructing and confirming the mutual understanding that here we shall bend the rule and collaborate above and beyond the jealous watchdog mentality implied in the adversarial courtroom script. In other words, to avoid breaking the hearsay rule, another rule must be bent and a different mentality – or a different notion of the object – must be achieved by joint decision.

A range of formal and informal linguistic devices are employed creatively by the attorneys and the judge. These are important to the problem solving processes which take place. They both signal and facilitate the collaboration between the attorneys and the judge. Mr. G and the judge use the linguistic tools of personalization and familiarization – recourse to everyday language – to achieve this expansive transition. The judge concludes the sidebar using the nonlegalistic words "thought-

ful," "nervous," and "help." On the other hand, Mr. V uses the meta-
linguistic tool of reflecting on the preceding discourse: "And that's the
testimony that I wanted to avoid before we tried to unring the bell." The
judge joins in, reflecting on a longer history of previous discussions:
"That makes sense. We've already talked about it." Perhaps the most
sophisticated tool is used by Mr. G when he employs reported speech
(Volosinov, 1971; Goffman, 1974; Goodwin, 1990) in a proactive, antic-
ipatory fashion: "I will whisper in her ear and say, 'Don't mention anything about what somebody else said, and don't mention what he was
wearing.'"

In the other five sidebars displaying a transition to cooperation,
similar tools were used. Excerpt #3 provides another example of the
effective use of personalization.

Excerpt #3

Mr. S: ... I could be wrong, Bob [addressing Mr. G], and if you have something.
The judge: All right. I am going to allow you to cross on this and if you are correct
you'll look fine. If you are not correct ...
Mr. S: I'll look silly.
The judge: Then you wouldn't look fine.

In a similar vein, excerpt #4 demonstrates the use of familiarization.

Excerpt #4

Mr. G: My thinking is that, in the first 5, 10, 15 minutes that they [the jury] are in
there, we can quickly consider those items and get them into them –
The judge: Sure.
Mr. G: – while they are still talking about the C's [name of the local baseball team].

Attempts at reflective communication

In one of the sidebars, there is a piece of discourse that seems
to differ qualitatively from both authoritative silencing and cooperation.

Excerpt #5

[Held in the judge's chambers without the presence of the jury]

The judge: All right. I am going to allow him. But this is the other side of a problem
that Mr. S experienced. And you can now – both of you can – so that – the
problems it causes, when new figures come in, and by making somebody available the night before at 5:15 p.m. really doesn't comply with what I have in
mind in terms of the "spirit of cooperation." It might have been the only time
that he was available or the time that you were available, but, really, when I –

if I make this kind of ruling in the future – what I mean by that, to both counsel, is that you set up a time that's convenient for the other person and really break your backs to get that information.

In this excerpt, the judge is teaching or reminding the attorneys to follow the rules of cooperation. In that sense, both the script itself and the interaction of the participants become the foci of attention. These are hallmarks of reflective communication (recall Figure 28.4). Yet there is something peculiarly non-communicative in the discourse. The judge is in effect presenting a monologue to which the attorneys do not respond in any noticeable way. The content is reflective communication; the form is non-communication.

When the judge refers to the "spirit of cooperation," he is not just talking about a general principle. He is referring to the contents of an issues conference, a special meeting he had with the attorneys immediately before the trial. This meeting is actually a tool with which this judge attempts to achieve reflective communication between himself and the parties of the trial.

The delay reduction program officially adopted by the court requires that a mandatory *disposition conference* be held in good time before the trial. The *issues conference*, however, is the judge's own invention. In his interview, he characterized the two types of pre-trial conferences as follows.

The judge: The delay reduction program really is generated by the control of the case from the very first time that it's filed and answered, with mandatory deadlines for certain things to happen. And about two months before trial, the final thing before trial is the disposition conference. And they have to prepare a joint document, both sides or all sides, listing all their witnesses, all the issues they say are still unresolved, instructions, things that were unheard of to do ahead of time. Back when I still was practicing, you never knew who the other side's witnesses even were, and now you know two months ahead of time.

Interviewer: Did you have a disposition conference in this case?

The judge: No, because I had the case managed so that I told them to file their witness list and things, they did it on an informal basis.

Interviewer: So you didn't have to have it all at once in writing?

The judge: Exactly. And they were working well enough together so I didn't require them to file this formal disposition conference document that requires both their signatures. But that funnel-shaped item is a reduction with dates and fines, money fines, sanctions, if you don't live up to them. Very negative.

Interviewer: Now the issues conference, that is really your own tool. How is that related to the disposition conference?

The judge: That disposition conference, that's a formal document. And I take the disposition conference report, and I say, okay, this is what you've said, but now we're right down to trial, and what is the reality of this?

Interviewer: So the issues conference is really about the trial in actual practice?

The judge: Right, exactly. And we are going to trial on this. They've been sent out – Every case, two months ahead of time, files a disposition report, conference report. But not every case goes down to trial. And these people actually are, they show up at my door step, supposedly ready for trial. Now, because I'm usually in trial, I'm not ready for 'em that day. So I'll have an issues conference for them, which says, now you've said you're ready for trial, but let's make sure we are.

The judge: I mean, we talked over some potential things. It gets timelines set up and gets when people expect things to happen, and gets 'em in the frame of mind that I want them in when they try a case here.

Interviewer: Did you invent that or did you learn it from somebody else?

The judge: No, I invented it because I found that I was talking about the same things with these people in front of me, the same time, so I just started keeping a list and then I'd add something. Then I made the list, then I typed it out. Then I put, y'know, it just grew, just one of those things that grew. But it's helpful.

The list to which the judge is referring is an artifact he created to sustain and consolidate the innovation. It is his standard agenda for an issues conference. It contains 17 items. The last item on it is simply "Work together." According to the judge, one of the aims of the issues conference is to make sure the parties will focus on the essential questions in the case, not confusing the jury by diverting attention to insignificant details. Another aim is to reduce the anxiety of the parties, to get them to collaborate and interact self-consciously. These aims speak of the judge's intention to reach reflective communication in the process of complex litigation.

We tape recorded the two-hour issues conference preceding the case. The contents of the conference corresponded to the agenda.

On the quality of interaction:

The judge: Ah, so, I just want you to understand that I don't, I don't want me, er, to sound like I'm lecturing you but that is a real important thing, as I sit here, that I wasn't as sensitive to, ah, when I was sitting where you are. So I am now, and that will be a lot of my, my feeling as to keep the jury, ah, respectful of the process. It's real important. Now, with that in mind, it's the philosophy I want between you two, and I say two because of the size, I don't know who will be trying the case, is that I want you to assist each other in putting your cases on. The time for gamesmanship, or trial by ambush or, ah, tactics that make the other attorney look bad, ah, are over, as far as I'm concerned. So, when – when Mr. G, when your witnesses are going on, on Monday afternoon, or Tuesday, ah, I want you to tell Mr. S who they are going to be, and about how long they'll take. I'll direct, Mr. S, I want you to do exactly the same thing. Everything in this courtroom applies both ways, so, eh, when your case is on, I want you to cooperate with each other.

On the mutual definition of the object:

The judge: . . . Ah, take a look at his verdict form. The only reason that I want, and I want you, if there's something dreadfully wrong with it or if it doesn't, or if it isn't this case that we're trying, then I want you to prepare a verdict form that you think reflects the case. The reason is simple. PM [name of another judge] was talking about this early, about a year and a half ago when I first started. And I thought it was ludicrous until I had about 20 trials where at the last day of trial nobody could agree on the verdict form because they had been trying, essentially, a different case. They said, "Well, gee, we, we didn't present any evidence on these elements here, you know, because we thought we were trying this case over here." And this is the last day of trial. Then what will I do? Well I've learned if, if you at least show each other the verdict form early in the case, ah, if there's a great deal of difference then, ah, let me know. I mean, I'll look at them both and it will give me an idea anyway. At least I know that you agree on what elements of each, ah, cause of action. . . . Ah, I don't care if you agree at this point. I just want you to have exchanged one. Or if you're satisfied with the one that's produced, fine. We're trying the same lawsuit. You don't have to agree to individual language. But you know what I'm talking about.

Mr. G: Yes, sir.

The judge effectively uses reported speech, among other means, as a tool to convince the attorneys. Yet there is no interaction except the mandatory "yes, sir" from one of the attorneys. In the issues conference, the attorneys took initiative and talked actively only in matters requiring technical coordination for the trial. In other words, the communicative contents were all but nullified by the non-communicative form of the discussion.

What could be the reason for this? Obviously it may the judge's habitual dominating or lecturing style that precludes interaction. But the attorneys were experienced and not at all timid. They could have responded more actively if they had wanted to.

A more plausible explanation is found in the post-trial interviews of the attorneys. First the plaintiff's side.

Interviewer: He [the judge] also uses what he calls the issues conference just before the trial. We were actually present when that took place on Friday just before the trial. And, I was wondering, did you find it useful? First of all, is it common procedure?

Mr. G: Oh, it's usually that it's a month before the trial. And it is important to do that three weeks to a month, from both parties' point of view. And I was critical of the judge for having and holding that issues conference so soon before trial. Things occurred in trial. Now, it was a very efficiently run trial and it went fast. But there were several sidebars there that occurred that wouldn't have occurred had they been talked about in the issues conference. We also call it a disposition conference, the terms are used interchangeably. And, you talk about the law. Like, what's the law here? [laughs] What are you going to tell the jury the law is? And, let's rule on the admissibility of some of these exhibits before we go and prepare them or blow them up.

Then the defense side.

Interviewer: There is a particular situation where we were actually present. And that was what he [the judge] calls the issues conference, which was just the last Friday before the actual trial. And it seemed to be somewhat of an invention of the judge. He has this list of things that he went through. What did you think about it, was that useful or sensible?

Mr. S: Actually it's very useful and that's one of the new things that our court system has, it's called "the fast track." And this is part of the fast track procedures. The idea is that we're gonna have this issues conference, usually that occurs about a month before trial, to sit down and make the attorneys have this case ready for trial a month beforehand. So that when the trial comes, we can get it done a lot more quickly and efficiently. They tell you, you determine what evidence is gonna come in, what witnesses are gonna be there, work out all your problems, come with a list of what the exhibits are, and basically you're ready to go with trial and it's gonna go smoothly on this game plan.

Interviewer: This time you had it just before the trial.

Mr. V: Because the subs [the subcontractors] were still in.

Mr. S: It was all because the subs were still in and he didn't want to have it until he made a decision as to whether or not the subs were gonna get out. Because if the subs were involved, it would have been much more complicated.

Interviewer: Did you feel it was problematic so close to the actual trial date?

Mr. S: We didn't. The plaintiff did.

So both attorneys confuse the issues conference with the disposition conference. This is something the judge explicitly rejected in his interview cited above, emphatically pointing out the crucial difference between the two conferences. Somehow the judge's entire innovation has been misunderstood by the litigating attorneys. This is a prime example of a rupture that effectively prevents an expansive transition from being realized. One wonders what would have happened had the judge prepared the attorneys by simply telling them the same things about the issues conference he told us.

The invisible battleground

The data presented above tell about the zone of proximal development in an invisible battleground. Even though the reforms officially introduced in the court are driven by market forces, costs, and the volume of cases, they open up room for inventiveness by the judge and others, providing space for rethinking and re-creating aspects of the activity system. In the ongoing work activity, disturbances occur continuously. Disturbances are dealt with both regressively and expansively. Innovative solutions appear. But innovations may be blocked by ruptures in the intersubjective understanding between the participants of the activity system.

In Figure 28.1, we presented a tentative picture of the zone of proximal development in the work activity of courts. The judge in the present case was an active proponent of the delay reduction program and the so called "independent calendar" adopted by the court. Both are reforms that might be placed in the individually mastered cost-effective case management represented by field 3 of Figure 28.1. However, the judge's attempt to reach reflective communication by means of the issues conference is more characteristic of the informal and interactive teamwork represented by field 4 in Figure 28.1. Perhaps the persistent lecturing style in his approach to the attorneys represents the heavy tradition of field 1.

The expansive transitions found in the sidebars could not have been achieved by the judge alone. To the contrary, excerpt #2 is a good example of a transition in which the innovation emerges through an effort fairly equally distributed between the two attorneys and the judge. What is missing is conscious input from the lay witness, or lay clients more generally. Perhaps this would be going to the far end of the current zone of proximal development in complex litigation work.

References

Conley, J. M., & O'Barr, W. M. (1990). *Rules versus relationships: The ethnography of legal discourse.* Chicago: The University of Chicago Press.

Engeström, Y. (1987). *Learning by expanding: An activity-theoretical approach to developmental research.* Helsinki: Orienta-Konsultit.

Engeström, Y. (in press). Developmental work research: Reconstructing expertise through expansive learning. In M. I. Nurminen, P. Järvinen, & G. Weir (Eds.), *Human jobs and computer interfaces.* Amsterdam: North-Holland.

Engeström, Y., Brown, K., Engeström, R., Gregory, J., Haavisto, V., Pihlaja, J., Taylor, R., & Wu, C. C. (1990, November). *The tensions of judging: Handling cases of driving under the influence of alcohol in Finland and California.* Paper presented at the 89th Annual Meeting of the American Anthropological Association, New Orleans, LA.

Fichtner, B. (1984). Co-ordination, co-operation and communication in the formation of theoretical concepts in instruction. In M. Hedegaard, P. Hakkarainen, & Y. Engeström (Eds.), *Learning and teaching on a scientific basis: Methodological and epistemological aspects of the activity theory of learning and teaching* (pp. 207–227). Aarhus: Aarhus Universitet, Psykologisk Institut.

Goffman, E. (1959). *The presentation of self in everyday life.* New York: Doubleday.

Goffman, E. (1974). *Frame analysis: An essay on the organization of experience.* Boston: Northeastern University Press.

Goodwin, M. H. (1990). *He-said-she-said: Talk as social organization among Black children.* Bloomington: Indiana University Press.

Heydebrand, W., & Seron, C. (1990). *Rationalizing justice: The political economy of federal district courts.* Albany: State University of New York Press.

Merry, S. E. (1990). *Getting justice and getting even: Legal consciousness among working-class Americans.* Chicago: The University of Chicago Press.

Raeithel, A. (1983). *Tätigkeit, Arbeit und Praxis: Grundbegriffe für eine praktische Psychologie.* Frankfurt am Main: Campus.

Rittenberg, W. (1985). Mary; A patient as emergent symbol on a pediatrics ward: The objectification of meaning in social process. In R. A. Hahn & A. D. Gaines (Eds.), *Physicians of Western medicine* (pp. 141–153). Dordrecht: Reidel.

Volosinov, V. N. (1971). Reported speech. In L. Matejka & K. Pomorska (Eds.), *Readings in Russian poetics: Formalist and structuralist views.* Cambridge: The M.I.T. Press.

Weick, K. E. (1979). *The social psychology of organizing.* New York: Random House.

Power and discourse

29 The politics of representation

Michael Holquist

> But the social order is a sacred right which serves as a foundation for all others. This right, however, does not come from nature. It is therefore based on convention – The question is to know what these conventions are . . .
>
> Rousseau, *The Social Contract*

We meet under the aegis of the English Institute. As an outsider, I am aware that departments of English have recently demonstrated a quite remarkable openness to non-Anglo-Saxon ideas about the nature of literary study. However, this new cosmopolitanism has not been all-inclusive; it has stretched to Paris, but such places as Prague and Tartu still seen a bit exotic. As someone, then, who comes out of neither an English nor a French background – and who is yet anxious not to be perceived as coming out of left field – I would like to make a few preliminary observations about the assumptive world from which I have come here as a visitor.

The one thing we would now all appear to have in common is an overriding interest in the nature of language. But each different national tradition seems to have a different idea as to what that nature might be: the word *language* is in danger of losing its status as a noun as it shades more and more into the category of what Jakobson calls shifters, a word such as a pronoun, that indicates nothing more than position in discourse. From the no doubt slightly skewed perspective of an American Slavist, there would seem to be at least three such positions, three different conceptions of language abroad in the academy today (I begin by excluding a fourth conception – the one reigning in departments of linguistics – which is arguably the most outlandish of all).

389

In departments of literature, the three dominant ways language has come to be understood may most economically (if not responsibly) be characterized according to how each conceives the ownership of meaning. A first conception, which I shall call *Personalist*, has been associated on the continent with names like Wilhelm Wundt, Karl Vossler, Benedetto Croce, and Edmund Husserl. But, in less evident forms, it has long been regnant in English studies as a more or less unspoken first principle. This view holds that "*I* own meaning." A close bond is felt between the sense I have of myself as a unique being and the being of my language.

Such a view, with its heavy investment in the personhood of individuals, is deeply implicated in the Western Humanist tradition. As such, it is at the opposite pole from another view of language which has recently come to dominate departments of French and comparative literature, as well as many English departments. This second, or *Deconstructionist* view, holds that "*No one* owns meaning": the very conception of meaning, to say nothing of persons, invoked in most traditional epistemologies, begins by illicitly assuming a presence whose end Nietzsche really was announcing when he let it be known that God had died in history.

A third conception of language, which I shall call D*ialogism*, is one found increasingly in Slavic departments. Like the second, it has roots in Geneva. By analogy with leftist and rightist Hegelianism, we might say that it is a right-wing Saussurianism, as opposed to Deconstructionist leftism. If the Left has evolved ever increasingly radical implications of *Langue* and text, the Right has continued to mediate the complexities of *Parole* and context. The Slavic view holds that "*We* own meaning." Or – as I am reaching more familiar ground, I feel the need to be more precise – "If we do not own it, we may at least *rent* meaning." If Personalists maintain that the ground of meaning is in the unique individual, and Deconstructivists locate it in the structure of difference itself, this third view holds that meaning is rooted in the social, but the social conceived in a particular way.

The contention here is that meaning comes about *not* as the lonely product of an intention willed by a sovereign or transcendent ego. Nor is meaning ultimately *impossible* to achieve because of the arbitrary play of differences between signs. In the first instance, meaning would give itself as an immediate presence; as such, it would be subject to all the powerful criticisms Deconstructivists have mounted since at least Derrida's 1967 attack on Husserl.[1] In the second instance, such criticisms may (partially) be avoided, or at least robbed of their worst sting, through the deference one pays them in ordering his own discourse. But the price of such tact – which can be very impressive in its stoic way – is the perpetual elusiveness of meaning as it fades away in the phantom relay of the signifying chain.

The Personalist view is simultaneously logo- and phono-centric: the assumption is that I can by *speaking* appropriate to my own use the impersonal structure of signs, which is always already there. The breath of my life is the material of words; my voice welds me to language. The second view goes to the opposite extreme: in it, the human voice is conceived merely as another means for registering differences – one, moreover, not necessarily privileged: it is far less powerful than writing.

Russians, Poles, and Czechs such as Baudouin de Courtenay, Nikolai Kruszevski, Mikhail Bakhtin, Lev Vygotsky, Sergej Karcevskij, Jan Mukařovský, and of course, Roman Jakobson himself have sought since at least the early 1920s to avoid both these extremes. They would argue that the apparently mutual contradiction between phonocentrism on the one hand, and grammatology on the other – the *tertium non datur* of an overconfident monolog, or an excessively ascetic silence – obscures a third possibility for conceiving language. It is the one that maintains: I can mean what I say, but only *indirectly*, as a second remove, in words I take and give back to the community according to the protocols it establishes. My voice can mean, but only with others: at times in chorus, but at the best of times in a dialogue.

Meaning in this view is made as a product, much as a work of folklore is "made" in societies that strictly hold to their traditions: "A work of folklore comes into existence only at the moment it is accepted by a particular community."[2] There may be many versions put forth, but only one will be capable of resisting the structural amnesia of the group. Its acceptance by the community is the actual – if chronologically secondary – birth of the text. As metaphor for an account of meaning, this process is, of course, extremely crude; but it has at least the virtue of highlighting what is of central importance in East European philosophy of language from Kruszevski up to, and including, the work of such people as Jury Lotman: that my words will always come already wrapped in contextual layers sedimented by the many intralanguages, various social patois, the sum of which will constitute "the" language of my culture system.

If we were to compare current ideas about language in terms of the semantic space characteristic of each, it might be said that for Personalists it is inner; for Deconstructivists elsewhere; and for East Europeans somewhere in-between: I emphasize "in-between" here not only to suggest meaning's need always to be shared, but to underline as well the degree to which multiplicity and struggle characterize this heteroglot view of language. At the highest level of abstraction, the contest may be conceived as Manichean struggle. On the one side are ranged those forces that serve to unify and centralize meaning, that conduce to a structuredness that is indispensible if a text is to manifest system. On the opposing side stand tendencies fostering the diversity and randomness needed to keep open paths to the constantly fluctuating contextual world surrounding any utterance. The normative, systemic aspects of language have attracted the attention of most linguists, whether New Grammarians or Structuralists, and until quite recently the same could be said of most students of literature as well. It is this imbalance that the Russians seek to redress by devoting the majority of their considerable energies to studying the centrifugal forces in language, particularly as they are made specific in the various professional, class, generational, period, and other patois that the academic fiction (a necessary fiction) of a unitary national language seeks to contain. "This stratification, diversity and randomness [which Russians call *raznorečie*, or heteroglossia] is not only a static invariant in the life of language, but also what insures its dynamics. . . . Alongside centripetal forces, the centrifugal impulses of language carry on their ceaseless work. Alongside . . . centralization and unification the uninterrupted processes of decentralization and disunification go forward."[3]

Stated in such general terms, the struggle must appear a bloodless clash of abstractions; however, this is far from being the case. This conflict animates every concrete utterance made by any speaking subject: "The utterance not only answers the requirements of its own language, as an individualized embodiment of a speech act, but it answers the requirements of heteroglossia as well – indeed, any particular utterance is an active participant in such speech diversity – a fact that determines the linguistic profile and style of the utterance to no less a degree than its inclusion in any normative centralizing system of a unitary language."[4]

The most comprehensive statement of the dialogic exchange between static signs and a constantly fluctuating reality was made in 1929 by Saussure's Russian student (and respectful opponent) Sergej Karcevskij (1888–1955): "the signifier (sound) and the signified (meaning) slide continually on the 'slope of reality.' Each one 'overflows' the member assigned to it by its partner: the signifier seeks to express itself by means other than by its sign . . . it is thanks to the asymmetric dualism of the structure of its signs that a linguistic system can evolve: the 'adequate' position of the sign is continuously displaced through its adaptation to the exigencies of the concrete situation."[5] Or, as Edward Sapir never tired of repeating, "All systems leak."

Instead of a neo-Platonic gap between *langue*'s dream of order and *parole*'s necessary deviance, Dialogists propose a continuum between system and performance, the complimentarity of both. The common element connecting both levels is the never-ending contest between canonization and heteroglossia, which is fought out at each level. The process is fairly obvious at the highest levels of generalization, if only because there the struggle has served as traditional subject for philology, which has always studied the victory of one language over another, the supplanting of one normative dialect by another – indeed, the life and death of whole languages. Philology, of course, has emphasized the role of the great centralizing forces as it pursued its utopian quest for a single *Ursprache*, a tendency that finds its comic extreme in August Schlelcher's short story *avis akvãsas ka*, "The Sheep and the Horses" (1868), a work written in a totally concocted proto-Indo-European.

It bears repeating that the contest is present as well in individual utterances. It is more difficult to perceive at the most immediate levels because neither traditional linguistics nor stylistics, as it is usually practiced, has provided units of study adequate to the struggle's complexities. The concentration of linguists on such invariant features as grammatical or phonemic markers misses the point because so much of the battle is prosecuted through the interplay of codes, each of which may be socially distinct, but all of which employ the same grammatical and sound system (a point used by Stalin in his 1950 *Pravda* attack on the hapless Nikolai Marr, a linguist who argued language was a phenomenon of ideological superstructure rather than economic base). The attention stylistics has devoted to units such as whole sentences and paragraphs fails to take into account that the contest may be fought out as a duel of two social codes within a single sentence – indeed, within a single word.

For this reason, Bakhtin has proposed as a more sensitive stylistic unit of study what he calls hybrid constructions, that is, "an utterance which belongs, by virtue of its grammatical (syntactic) and compositional markers to a single speaker, but which actually contains mixed within it *two* 'languages,' two semantic and axiological belief systems." As an example, he cites a passage from Dickens's *Little Dorrit*: "That illustrious man and great national ornament, Mr. Merdle, continued his shining course. It began to be widely understood that one who had done society the admirable service of *making so much money out of it*, could not be suffered to remain a commoner. A baronetcy was spoken of with confidence; a peerage was frequently mentioned."[6]

In this passage there is first of all the author's fictive solidarity with

The hypocritically ceremonial general opinion [held by most people] of Merdle. All epithets referring to Merdle in the first sentences derive from [such a] general opinion, that is, they are the concealed speech of another. The second sentence – "it began to be widely understood" etc. – is kept within the bounds of an emphatically objective style, representing not subjective opinion, but the admission of a . . . completely indisputable fact. [However,] the phrase "who had done society the admirable service" is completely at the level [once again] of common opinion, repeating its official glorification; but the subordinate clause attached to that glorification ("of making so much money out of it") is made up of the author's words (as *if* put into parenthesis) [but actually without any distinguishing punctuation at all]. The last sentence then picks up again at the level of common opinion. [This is] a typical hybrid construction, where the subordinate clause is in an authorial speech that is relatively *direct* [by contrast with] the main clause [which is] in someone else's speech. The main and subordinate clauses are constructed in different semantic and axiological conceptual systems.[7]

Dialogism argues that what in the English comic novel is often written off as mere irony, actually constitutes a paradigm for all utterance: I can appropriate meaning to my purposes only by ventriloquating others.

A first implication of this principle is that as speakers we all participate in the rigors of authorship: we bend language to represent by representing languages. As an illustration of this process, I would like once again to use Bakhtin as an example; this time, the example provided by the relation he himself bears to certain texts he authored. In order to proceed in this way, some historical context will be necessary. In the year 1929, three important events occurred in Bakhtin's life. The first was publication of his book *Marxism and the Philosophy of Language*; the second was his arrest and subsequent exile to Kazakhstan; the third was publication of another of his books, *Problems of Dostoevsky's Poetics*. Each of these events had its curious twist. The arrest and exile were never officialized: there were never any formal charges brought and no trial. The only procedures involved were lengthy interrogation (which Bakhtin found quite interesting) and a certain amount of uniquely Soviet plea bargaining; that is, should he be sent to certain death in the forced labor camps of the Solovki islands, or merely exiled to a remote area for a fixed period? In the end he got off with six years exile, but because the whole thing was officially a nonevent, Bakhtin could never officially be rehabilitated. The Dostoevsky book appeared while Bakhtin was already in jail undergoing questioning. It was highly praised when it came out, by, among others, a leading member of the government, Anatoly Lunacharsky, who made strong claims for the work in a long review article. Thus you have a book written by a man who at that very moment was being held in the Lyubyanka prison being advanced as a model by the Soviet minister for education.

Strangest of all, however, are the facts surrounding the other book Bakhtin published that year, *Marxism and the Philosophy of Language*. I wish to dwell on the eccentric textology of this book, but let me first quickly recapitulate its main thesis. My reason for doing so is that I hope to apply some of its own dicta about the nature of representation in general to the specific act of representation constituted by the text itself.

Anticipating George Herbert Mead's and C. Wright Mill's concept of the "generalized other," Bakhtin points out that

the word is always oriented toward an addressee, toward who that addressee might be . . . each person's inner world and thought has its stabilized *social audience* that comprises the environments in which reasons, motives, values and so on are fashioned . . . the word is a two-sided act. It is determined equally by whose word it is and for whom it is meant. As word it is precisely the product of the reciprocal relationship between speaker and listener, addresser and addressee. Each and every word expresses the one relation to the other. I give myself verbal shape from another's point of view, ultimately from the point of view of the community to which I belong. A word is territory *shared* by both addresser and addressee, by the speaker and his interlocutor.[8]

It is this territorial concept of the word which necessitates a politics of representation: How is the territory governed? What legislates the way meaning is parcelled out in any given utterance?

In order to take up these questions, let me return to the peculiarities surrounding the appearance of *Marxism and the Philosophy of Language* in 1929. A first irregularity concerns the fact that the book, although written by Bakhtin, was actually published under the name of his friend Valentin Nikolaevič Vološinov. This is not the only case of plagiarism in reverse to be laid at Bakhtin's door during the 1920s. He published another book (*Freudianism: A Critical Sketch*, 1927) and an article ("Discourse in Life and Discourse in Art," *Zvezda*, no. 6 (1926), pp. 244–67) under Vološinov's name; a book attacking the Formalists under the name of his friend P. N. Medvedev (*The Formal Method in Literature Study*) in 1928, plus an article on Vitalism in a science journal in 1926 under the name of another friend, the eminent biologist I. I. Kanaev.

This is not the place to rehearse the long and complex proofs of Bakhtin's authorship of these books and articles. Suffice it to say that there is no doubt that he is their actual begetter (I do not say "onlie," because in Bakhtin's theory there are no "onlie" begetters). It is germane to our argument, however, to pause for a moment on his reasons for entering into what might be called, in his own terminology, such a *polyphonic* arrangement with his friends. These reasons are complex, and different in the case of each book or article involved, but essentially they all boil down to expedience: Bakhtin was notorious in Leningrad intellectual circles as a *cerkovnik*, a devout Orthodox Christian (of the unorthodox sort Russian intellectuals become when they give themselves to the Russian Orthodox Church). He was associated with the *Vosskresenie* group, which gathered weekly for prayer and discussion. From early on (1918–24) in his career, while still living in Byelorussia, in retreat from the capital, Bakhtin had been working on a magnum opus that he hoped would succeed in doing for the Russian religious tradition what Hermann Cohen had failed to do in his last book, *Religion der Vernunft* (1918), for Judaism: that is, to completely rethink West European metaphysics in the light of religious thought; to show, as it were, that philosophy had in a sense always been anticipated by religion. The problems metaphysics had not solved within *its* categories could be shown to avail themselves to theology. This intention took the shape of an enormous book Bakhtin wrote during the early 1920s in the area of moral philosophy.

Only portions of the manuscript have survived, written out in pencil on crumbling student note pads. It bears no title, but internal evidence suggests it might be called *The Architectonics of Responsibility*.[9] It is a full-blown axiological theory having clear ties with both Neo-Kantianism and Husserlian phenomenology. The theory is couched in its own highly idiosyncratic language, which exploits Russian for its unique coining capacities – much as Heidegger plays with German and Greek.

We shall not have time to dwell on this work, but in order to proceed it must be kept in mind that *it contains, in embryonic form, every major idea Bakhtin was to have for the rest of his long life*. The whole conception of the work (a kind of phenomenological meditation on Christ's injunction to treat others as you would yourself be treated), to say nothing of its lyrico-metaphysical style, was wildly at odds with the time and place in which Bakhtin lived. He attempted to publish a watered-down version of one section in 1924, but the journal that had been fool-hardy enough to accept it was closed down before the fragment could be published. Bakhtin's problem, then, was to find ways he could translate his idiosyncratic religious ideas into a language and a genre that would be publicly acceptable in the Soviet Union at a time when that country had already begun its march into the dark night of the 1930s.

The problem became even more urgent in the latter half of the 1920s, since Bakhtin could find no work. He and his wife lived the most ascetic of lives, existing for long periods on little more than strong tea, and smoking endless, even stronger cigarettes in an effort to keep warm. At this point, the theoretical epicenter of his work – how to reconcile modern linguistics with the biblical assurance that the Word became flesh – overlapped with his own most pressing practical needs: How was he to find an appropriate ideological flesh for the spirit of his own words so that he could sell his work before wasting completely away?

His answer was to conceive a number of books, each of which would convey one or another aspect of the general theory of his *Architectonics*, but all of which could be presented in the Marxist idiom of the day. Thus a major thesis of his axiology had been that human existence is the interaction between a given world that is always already there (*uže stavšee bytie*) and a mind that is conjoined (*priobščen*) to this world through the deed (*postupok*) of enacting values. What Bakhtin does in *Marxism and the Philosophy of Language*, for instance, is to define the always-already-there aspect of the world as the "socioeconomic base." A central obsession in the axiology had been the relation between the "I" and "the other," an irreducible duality conceived in terms of the need to *share* being. Bakhtin's term for the distinctiveness of human existence is *sobytje bytija*, a pun implying that such existence is both a coexisting (*sobytie*) and an event (*sobytie*). In the Vološinov books, Bakhtin continues to foreground the primacy of shared being, but this time in terms of social existence. In his book on Freud, Bakhtin says "*dialectical materialism* demands that . . . human psychology be socialized."[10] We might add this is not only the demand of "dialectical materialism," but of Bakhtin's own system of ethics as well, in which there is no "I" without "the other."

Marx is sometimes present in the works published in the late twenties as an honored philosopher who very early saw the systematic implications of man's social being. Thus his *Sixth Thesis of Fenerbach* can be quoted with approval: "The essence of man is not an abstraction inherent in each separate individual. In its reality it is the aggregate of social relationship."[11] This emphasis on the collective and social dimension in human beings is not, of course, an exclusively Marxist attitude (another area where such a position is an enabling a priori is, obviously, the study of language: Zellig Harris relates that after Leonard Bloomfield read *Capital* in the thirties he "was impressed above all with the similarity between Marx's statement of social behavior and that of linguistics").

Marxist terms are, however, most often present in Bakhtin's books from this period as a kind of *convenient*, in the abstract, not necessarily *inimical* – but above all, *necessary* – flag under which to advance his own views: If the Christian word were to take on Soviet flesh it had to clothe itself in ideological disguise.

It would have been impossible, of course, for Bakhtin himself, in the tight circle of the Leningrad intelligentsia, to publish self-dramatizingly Marxist works, even had he wished to; everyone knew of his religious beliefs. Two of his *friends*, however, could publish such works without straining credulity: Vološinov because of his relative obscurity – he was a minor poet, amateur musicologist, and student of linguists, about whose personal convictions very little was generally known;[12] and Medvedev, because he was not only a Marxist, but a well-known and energetic member of the party, former chairman of the Central

Committee in Vitebsk province, and, in Leningrad, a frequent go-between in the party's dealings with people in the theater and other intellectuals. Each of these men had his own reasons for entering the deception: Vološinov, because he wanted to help his beloved friend and mentor; Medvedev, because he felt such a book might raise his stock both in the party and among the ranks of the intelligentsia. So it was that the three books were published as if they were contributions to Marxist theory put forward by committed Soviet Marxists. The parts Vološinov and Medvedev were assigned required both actors to have well-established *emplois*.

Did Bakhtin – as did do many others – have to completely *misrepresent* his personally held beliefs in order to publish in the unusual conditions obtaining in the Soviet Union? The answer, while it must, of course, be highly qualified, is that he did *not*. The Vološinov and Medvedev books are, among other things, investigations into the mystery of the voice. They probe the surprising complexities that lie hidden in the apparently elementary question, *"Who* is talking?" When discussing the phenomenon of "reported or indirect speech" (*čužaja reč*; literally the "speech of another"), there is a point in each of the books where Bakhtin leaves an opening in the manifest rhetoric he has woven around his argument. He creates a kind of authorial loophole (*lazejka*), in which he describes exactly what he is doing.

In *Marxism and the Philosophy of Language*, one such loophole is constituted by his discussion of the situation that occurs in fiction when the character and author speak with a *single* voice:

The absolute of acting out we understand to be not only a change of expressive intonation – a change logically possible within the confines of a single voice, a single consciousness – but also a change in voice in terms of the whole set of features individualizing that voice, a change of persona ("mask") in terms of a whole set of individualizing traits of facial expression and gesticulation, and finally, the complete self-consistency of this voice and persona throughout the entire acting out of the role.[13]

In other words, the text of *Marxism and the Philosophy of Language* itself constitutes the kind of dialogic space Bakhtin is talking about within it. Bakhtin, as author, manipulates the *persona* of Vološinov, using his Marxist voice to ventriloquate a meaning not specific to Marxism, even when conceived as only a discourse.

The recurring motifs of *Marxism and the Philosophy of Language* – "the concrete utterance," "the living word," and "the word in the word"

– bespeak in their Marxist context an emphasis on the here and now, on the intensely immediate exchange between living people in actual historical and social encounters. Does not this emphasis on the material world of the present preclude any religious interpretation? Some background is necessary here. Such motifs are present in the Russian religious tradition as well, even the insistence on materialism (Nicolas Zernov has recently pointed out that "the fundamental conviction of the Russian religious mind is the potential holiness of matter").[14]

This concern for the materiality of things is nowhere more insistently present in Orthodoxy than in its ancient obsession with the corporeality of Christ, the emptying out of spirit, *kenosis*, when the Word took on flesh during the life of Jesus. From the time of their conversion as a nation, the Russians have venerated Christ not as the Byzantine Pantocrater, but as a humble man, a tradition that continued to live in the twentieth century in the fascination exercised by "God-Manhood," not only on such would-be mystics as Merezkovsky, but even on political radicals such as Gorky, who preached God-building (*bogostroitel'stvo*) from the rostrum of the Writers' Union Congresses as late as the thirties.

There is no time to trace this "kenotic" tradition in any detail, but we should keep in mind that the first Russian saints, Boris and Gleb, were canonized not because they were martyrs for the faith. Their deaths were cold-bloodedly political; they were assassinated by their brother Sviatopolk and his followers to insure Sviatopolk's inheritance of his father's throne. They submitted humbly and meekly to the knives of their attackers, and it was this humility, this following of Christ's example (Russians shy away from the idea of "imitatio") that served as grounds for their being made saints. G. P. Fedotov, a member of the *Vosskresenie* group that Bakhtin frequented, in his history of the Russian religious mind (written after Fedotov's emigration) points out that St. Theodosius, founder of the greatest of the old Russian monasteries, was opposed to any mysticism. In this, he "is the spokesman of ancient Russia. . . . The terms in which he speaks of his love for Christ are quite remarkable: the Eucharistic bread speaks to him not only of Christ, but especially of Christ's flesh."[15]

This tradition was kept alive in Russian religious experience throughout the centuries: at times the obsession with Christ's corporeality took extreme forms, such as the sect of the *Khlysty*, an Orthodox version of

Tantrism, in which sexual orgies were an inveterate feature (and whose importance in the twentieth century was highlighted in the central role played by Rasputin at the court of the last Romanov czar).

Bakhtin's work in axiology was a philosophical contribution to this tradition. Its basic thesis was that men define their unique place in existence through the responsibility they enact, the care they exhibit in their deeds for others and the world. Deed is understood as meaning *word* as well as physical act: the deed is how meaning comes into the world, how brute facticity is given significance and form, how the Word becomes flesh.

Marxism and the Philosophy of Language, if treated as an utterance – that is, a statement whose meaning depends on the unrepeatable historical and social context in which it was pronounced, as well as on the repeatable words of the text – is, then, a very complex example of the transcoding possibilities in indirect speech, *čužaja reč'*, the speech of the others. Bakhtin has appropriated the code of one ideology to made public the message of quite another.

One of the more popular accounts of representation imported recently from France has been Pierre Macherey's application of Louis Althusser.[16] It is a highly sophisticated model for mapping the relationship between an individual consciousness and the expressive means a society makes available to such a consciousness. As such, I would like (in passing) to point out why it cannot account for Bakhtin's ideological transcoding. Pierre Macherey still assumes the necessity of bad faith, the inescapability of false consciousness. In this view, authors can never express the actual place they occupy among the reigning myths of their own time and place. It is a Marxist version of "blindness and insight," in which a text is always incomplete insofar as it will always leave out its author's complicity in the web of his own – unavoidable – misrecognitions. Thus, Jules Verne might "figure" the ideology of the Third Republic's colonializing bourgeoisie, but a discerning (subsequent) critic will be able to perceive a gap in his texts where, all unknown to the historical subject Jules Verne, he is actually "representing" a powerful critique of that ideology. There are, as it were, two voices, two ideologies to be found in a single text, but only as it is constituted by the astute reader who can overcome its delusion, the delusion of its author, that it (he) is monologic. Clearly such a theory cannot account for Bakhtin's very consciously wrought creolization of different ideologies in the texts he published as Vološinov. In his case, we get the very opposite of what Macherey proposes: it is precisely the *author* who knew more about the ideologies concealed in the gaps of his text than his "discerning readers" in the office of the Soviet censor.

The theory of representation most capable of accounting for Bakhtin's dialogic practice is, not surprisingly, his own.

In his book on Freud, Bakhtin redefines the distinction between the conscious and the unconscious. This part of the argument is initiated by a bold act of substitution. Bakhtin reformulates the distinction between conscious and unconscious as a difference not between two different kinds of reality, for they are both variants of the same phenomenon: *both* are aspects of consciousness. Instead of positing an ontological difference between the two, Bakhtin perceives the distinction as differing degrees of ideological *sharing*. The unconscious is a suppressed, relatively idiosyncratic ideological realm (insofar as ideology can *ever* be idiosyncratic), whereas the conscious is a public world whose ideologies may be shared openly with others. He calls Freud's *un*conscious the "unofficial conscious," as opposed to the ordinary "official conscious."

The language of unofficial conscious is inner speech, the language of official conscious outward speech, but they both operate according to the general rules of all human verbal behavior. *"The verbal component of behavior is determined in all fundamentals and essentials of its content by objective-social factors. . . .* Therefore nothing verbal in human behavior (inner and outward speech equally) can under any circumstances be reckoned to the account of the individual subject in isolation; the verbal is not his property but the property of his *social group* (his social milieu)."[17]

There is, of course, a *hierarchy* of causes and effects which stretches from the content of the individual psyche (understood as *individual*, but never isolated) to the content of a large-scale system of culture. The route between the two extremes is, however, a highway governed by the same rules of the road: "At all stages of this route human consciousness operates through *words*."[18] It follows that:

Any human verbal utterance is an ideological construct in the small. The motivation of one's behaviour is *juridical* and *moral* behaviour on a small scale; an exclamation of joy or grief is a primitive lyric composition; pragmatic considerations of the causes and consequences of happenings are germinal forms of *scientific* and *philosophical* cognition. . . . The stable, formulated ideological systems of the sciences, the arts, jurisprudence and the like, have sprung and crystallized from that seething ideological element where broad waves of inner and outward speech engulf our every act and our very perception.[19]

But if there are important similarities between the *modus operandi* of individual psyches and whole culture systems, there are also significant differences. In outlining these, we first become aware of the reasons for Bakhtin's substituting unofficialism for Freud's unconscious/conscious distinction.

Although the systems of individual psyche and whole societies are both ideological through and through, ideology has a different status in each. The primary difference consists in the achieved, stable quality of official ideologies that are shared by the group as a whole. They are, in Bakhtin's own terminology, "finished off" (*zaveršen*), the source of what he will call, in the thirties' version of the same distinction, the discourse of authority (*'avtoritetnoe slovo*). Because of its rigidity, it is always-always-there, it is "pre-located discourse" (*prednaxodinoe slovo*), the language, then of the fathers, a past that is still very present.

Against this fixed system of values, Bakhtin poses another system, which he calls behavioral ideology, "that inner and outward speech that permeates our individual, 'personal' behaviour in all its aspects."[20] As opposed to broad-based social values, behavioral ideology is "more sensitive, more responsive, more excitable and livelier" than an ideology that has undergone formulation and become 'official.'" It is not finished off, and corresponds to what Bakhtin will call innerly persuasive discourse (*vnutrenno-ubeditel'noe slove*) in the thirties. It is unfinished, not completely formulated, because it is the world ideologized from the point of view of an individual consciousness who lives in "the absolute future" of still unrealized possibilities.

The opposition Bakhtin sets up here, although carefully camouflaged in Marxist terminology and neutral adjectives (i.e., "social," "behavioral"), is still the master opposition at the heart of his *Architectonics*: the conflict between a set of values grounded in the self, and a set of values grounded in the other. What Bakhtin is saying in his distinction between behavioral ideology and social ideology is that there is a *gap* between the two. Individual consciousness never – even among the most wholly committed ideologues – fully replicates the structure of the society's public values. To assume that it *can* is the great mistake of "vulgar Marxists" who seek a one-to-one correspondence between individuals and their social origin, who seek to close the space between individual consciousness and class consciousness.

In his *Architectonics*, Bakhtin had explained the gap in ontological terms; the self and the other were seen to constitute two different realities, which could never fuse on a single plane. In the book on Freud, the explanation for the gap is developmental, that is, behavioral ideology is conceived as still inchoate, a primitive form of more public ideologies: when behavioral thought finds its highest expression, it will be fixed in the *shared* values of an official ideology. The switch to such developmental categories was a perhaps necessary dissembling if so radical a distinction was to be maintained at all. But, even so, the clear implication is that the traffic between the social and the individual is not *all one way*. An ideology, once formulated, has enormous impact on individuals comprising the society whose values it defines. The *opposite* is also the case, however, for "in the depths of behavioral ideology accumulate those contradictions which once having reached a certain threshold, ultimately burst asunder the system of the official ideology."[21] (This surely is what Erik Erikson has in mind as well when he characterizes the collision between the individual histories of Luther and Gandhi and the collective histories of their societies as the willingness of such men "to do the dirty work of their ages.")

What Bakhtin has done is to realize, in a recognizably Russian scenario, Freud's metaphor of censorship: the *un*conscious, as unofficial *conscious*, operates like a minority political party opposed to certain aspects of the politics reigning in the surrounding culture. The more of these aspects it opposes, the more "censored" it is, because the difference between its values and those of the majority will be expressed as a difference in the intelligibility of languages; the less the unofficial party has in common with official ideology, the more restricted will be its expressive means. Insofar as the minority cannot *share* its values, it is condemned to a relative silence. It is as if an Eskimo revolutionary group, seeking independence from the United States, were to flood New York City with manifestoes written in Athabaskan – even though *willing* a conflict with the majority culture, the group is condemned to inaction by the structure of communication, the architectonics of value. In a very real sense, what Bakhtin is doing may be likened to the efforts of early Christians to spread their message by parable and allegory. The clandestine church in Leningrad during these years was called "the catacomb church" because its members felt they lived in times very similar to those first-century sectarians who met by night in cellars below the imperial marble of a hostile Rome.

It is here we should seek the reasons Bakhtin feels compelled to revise Freud's scenario of conflict between the official and unofficial conscious. When he writes that "the wider and deeper the breach between the official and unofficial conscious, the more difficult it becomes for motives of inner speech to turn into outward speech . . . wherein they might acquire formulation, clarity and vigor,"[22] he is describing his own dilemma, the increasing gap between his own religious and metaphysical ideas and the Soviet government's ever more militant insistence on adherence to Russian Communism. Bakhtin says that "motives under these conditions begin to . . . lose their verbal countenance, and little by little really do turn into a 'foreign body' in psyche," but it is clear he also means that they become foreign bodies in the state as well.

His daring insistence on the uniplanar coexistence of rules of governance in the *psyche* with rules for governance in the *state* is not merely one more way to conceive Freudian theory. It also explains Bakhtin's practice of sending out transcoded messages from the catacombs. He has just said that the gap between official and unofficial conscious can become so great that finally the content of the unofficial conscious is snuffed out. But if we remember that the traffic between the terminus of an individual psyche and that of a whole culture moves in *both* directions, a more optimistic scenario may be conceived for unofficial forces: it is not true

that *every* motive in contradiction with the official ideology must degenerate into indistinct inner speech and then die out – [one of them] might well engage in a struggle with that official ideology [and] . . . if it is not merely the motive of a declassé loner, then it has a chance for a future and perhaps even a *victorious future* . . . at first a motive of this sort will develop within a small social milieu and will depart into the underground – not the psychological underground, but the salutary political underground.[23]

For Russians, utterance has ever been a contest, a struggle. The need to speak indirectly has resulted in a Russian discourse that is always fabular precisely when it is fueled by the most intense desire to mean. Such indirection has resulted in an allegorical mode known as "Aesopic language." Bakhtin's achievement is to refine, out of the particular features that have created such a situation, a synthetic philosophy of language.

If he is correct, utterance cannot avoid contest and struggle. The dictum that "War is the prosecution of diplomacy by other means" may in Bakhtin's case be paraphrased as "Allegory is the prosecution of semantic intention by other means." As such, Bakhtin's example provides at least the beginning of an answer to some troubling questions raised recently by Paul de Man in his reading of Pascal: "From a theoretical point of view," de Man writes, "there ought to be no difficulty in moving from epistemology to persuasion. The very occurrence of allegory, however, indicates a possible complication. Why is it that the furthest reaching truths about ourselves and the world have to be stated in such a lopsided, referentially indirect mode?"

The answer provided by Bakhtin in both his theory and his practice, although not adequate to all the implications of de Man's question, suffices at least to point us in a further direction. If we begin by assuming that *all* representation must be indirect, that *all* utterance is ventriloquism, then it will be clear – even, or especially, from a theoretical point of view – that difficulties *do* exist in moving from epistemology to persuasion. This is because difficulties exist in the very politics of any utterance, difficulties that at their most powerful exist in the politics of culture systems.

If the actual source of prohibition is recognized, however, the possibility of deceiving the censor becomes an option. I would like now, very briefly, to return to the three views of language with which I began. Such a tripartite division is, of course, already overschematized. I hope, however, such categorization will take any further strain put upon it by suggesting that each view of language results in its own characteristic genre. Personalism has a natural affinity with the *Bildungsroman*; it is full of "Great Expectations." Deconstructivism has an affinity with lyric and fragment; it concerns itself with traces such as the message that never gets delivered in Kafka's fragment, "The News of the Building of the Wall."

Dialogism has a taste for carnival and comedy, an affinity perhaps best caught in Bakhtin's lifelong affection for the first story of the *Decameron*, "How Ser Ciapelletto Became Saint Ciapelletto." You will remember it is a funny – but somewhat eerie – tale about an evil merchant who has lied, cheated, and indiscriminately fornicated all his life. He falls ill and recognizes that he is about to die while visiting a strange town where no one knows him. He calls for a priest in order to make his final confession and, by a series of subtle indirections convinces the priest he has led a life of the most unexampled virtue. After the evil merchant's death, the priest to whom he confessed tells everyone about his discovery of a secret saint. Soon pilgrimages are made to the merchant's tomb, and, before very long, miracles begin to occur on the site.

In conclusion, I would like to suggest that this tale of how subversive intentions get canonized is not only a parabolic expression of Bakhtin's biographical project. It serves as well to remind us that although the politics of representation are vexed, it is still a politics insofar as it is an art of the possible. Paraphrasing Stephen Daedelus, we may say that silence is not mandatory, exile may be overcome, as long as cunning reigns.

Notes

This article is reprinted from *Allegory and Representation*, Stephen J. Greenblatt (Ed.), with the kind permission of The Johns Hopkins University Press.

1. Jacques Derrida, *La Voix et le phénomène* (Paris: Presses universitaires de France), 1967. Translated by David Allison, as *Speech and Phenomena* (Evanston, Ill.: Northwestern University Press, 1973).
2. Roman Jakobson (with P. Bogatyrev), "Die Folklore als eine besondere Form des Schaffens," Selected *Writings* (The Hague: Mouton, 1966), 4:13
3. M. M. Bakhtin, "Slovo v romane," *Voprosy literatury i estetiki* (Moscow: Xudožeztvennaja literatura, 1975), p. 85. The essay here quoted, "Discourse in the Novel," together with three other pieces on theory of the novel and philosophy of language, will be published in English translation in 1981.
4. Ibid.
5. Sergej Karcevskij, "Du dualisme asymétrique de signe linguistique," *Travaux du Cercle linguistique de Prague* (Prague, 1929), 1:88. See also Wendy Steiner's fine piece comparing Saussure and Karcevskij "Language as Process: Sergej Karcevskij's Semiotics of Language," *Sound, Sign and Meaning: Quinquagenary of the Prague Linguistic Circle*, ed. L. Matejka (Ann Arbor: University of Michigan Press, 1978).
6. Bakhtin, "Slovo v romane," p. 119.
7. Ibid., p. 120.
8. M. M. Bakhtin, *Marxism and the Philosophy of Language*, trans. Ladislav Matejka and I. R. Titunik (New York: Seminar Press, 1973), pp. 85–86.
9. A longish portion of this work (one of five sections) was published under the calculatedly neutral title of "Author and Hero," in the latest collection of Bakhtin's writings to be published in the Soviet Union. See "Avtor i geroj," *Estetika slovesnogo tvorčestva*, ed. S. Bočarov (Moscow: Isskustvo, 1979), pp. 7–180.
10. M. M. Bakhtin, *Freudianism, a Marxist Critique* (the translator has changed the original title which was *Marxism: A Critical Sketch*), trans I. R. Titunik (New York: Academic Press, 1976), p. 22.

408   *Michael Holquist*

11. Ibid., p. 5.
12. There has been a good deal of confusion surrounding Vološinov, due to a rumor that has several times found its way into print in the West. The assumption that Vološinov was arrested in the purges of the 1930s is, however, utterly unfounded. Unlike Bakhtin or Medvedev, Vološinov was never even arrested. He died of tuberculosis in 1936.
13. Bakhtin, *Marxism and the Philosophy of Language*, pp. 156–57.
14. Nicholas Zernov, *The Russian Religious Renaissance of the Twentieth Century* (London: Duckworth, 1963), p. 285.
15. G. P. Fedotov, *The Russian Religious Mind* (Cambridge: Harvard University Press, 1966), 2:317.
16. Pierre Macherey, *A Theory of Literary Production*, trans. Geoffrey Wall (London: Routledge & Kegan Paul, 1978).
17. Bakhtin, *Freudianism*, p. 86.
18. Ibid., p. 87.
19. Ibid., p. 88.
20. Ibid.
21. Ibid.
22. Bakhtin, *Freudianism*, p. 89.
23. Ibid., p. 90.

30   Wisdom from the periphery: Talk, thought, and politics in the ethnographic theater of John Millington Synge

R. P. McDermott

> In Ireland, for a few years more, we have a popular imagination that is fiery and magnificent, and tender; so that those of us who wish to write start with a chance that is not given to writers in places where the springtime of the local life has been forgotten, and the harvest is a memory only, and the straw has been turned into bricks.
>
> John Millington Synge, 1907, *Preface to*
> *The Playboy of the Western World*

It is the legacy of Mikail Bakhtin (1934–35, 1940) to have shown us that systems of articulation and thought are always on their way somewhere. They are irremediably in progress by virtue of how they are constructed and maintained by people working, variously and inventively, with the constraints that organize their lives together. Communities are made of voices and voices of words, and every word helps to structure a recognizable community to the extent that it can be wrestled to a common ground, to an ideological core, where the word can be said to have specific and even uniform meanings and consequences. These are rough waters on which to build a coherent system of thought; it is not that people do not manage coherence, rather that they do so only with violence to all the other things that might have been said by their every word.

A primary social tension exists between periphery and core uses of our conversations with each other; all words are pulled by speakers, listeners, and the powers that be to an institutionally enhancing use, while at the same time each word represents a scream for alternative formulations of the world.[1] It is this tension that guided Bakhtin's interest

409

in the multiple languages at the periphery of society, in the languages of the folk poets, clowns and carnival masters. People who live on the periphery run the greatest risk of having their words taken from them. They are institutionally coherent to the extent that their words are appropriated to the ideological core, and they are similarly unintelligible, and deemed unintelligent, to the extent that their words resist a further contribution to core values.

This brief report examines the play of a core–periphery tension in the search for an adequate language of expression in early twentieth century Ireland, particularly in the six ethnographic dramas of J. M. Synge. In the course of articulating and negotiating the core–periphery tensions of his time, Synge confronted first hand the most basic problems facing a comparative study of human cognition. Over the decade that Synge "collaborated" with the people of Ireland in the development of his plays, his mastery of their talk, his sense of their contexts, and his appreciation of their intelligence was greatly enhanced. This experience should be familiar to readers of this journal, who stand for the possibility that if people on any periphery[2] do not make sense, it is likely they are being judged by mainstream yardsticks; with a little more time in their world and better eliciting tools, their peripheral wisdom can be understood and displayed in core terms (Hanunoo love poets, Pulawat navigators and Harlem street gang adolescents, for example, can be shown to be smart).

But Synge's story has a deeper moral. The separation between core and periphery is marked by more than neutral linguistic or cultural differences. Core and periphery are separated by a systematic differentiation of persons and activities along a continuum of access to resources and power. Synge did more than learn to describe and explain the different kinds of people on the periphery. Rather he learned to contextualize their wisdom well enough to reproduce it on stage. He did not speak for the people as much as he allowed them to speak through him, and then simply for his pleasure. And speak they did, and far louder than he ever anticipated. His plays were met with outrage from official Irish consciousness. All kinds of Dubliners, with the most nationalist leading the pack, literally rioted for a week in response to his carnivalization of core values in peasant garb. In the long run, his characters carried their own voices, and Synge's dialect theater became, in Yeats's words (1935), part of "the stir of thought which prepared for the Anglo-Irish war." Within a decade of Synge's death (in 1909, at age 38), their voices had moved for the moment from the periphery to the core. The work Synge had done to contextualize their words helped to give them a new forum for the verbal revolutions they had been attempting for decades before.

The status of the Irish peasantry as peripheral is uncontested. Long an outpost for European civilization and a refuge region for European markets, the Irish of the turn of the century were living in the face of a massive depopulation by starvation and migration, 300 unpleasant years of British rule, the imminent extinction of their Gaelic language and fading access to the educational treasures of their own culture. A first level of tension exists between the emerging Irish state (periphery) and the British empire (core), and a second level between the Catholic peasants of Ireland (periphery) and the Anglo-Irish, Protestant population that controlled both cultural and economic reproduction within Ireland (core). Both tensions are played out in the languages available for the different communities within Ireland to express themselves, namely, the fast disappearing Gaelic of the peasants, an Hiberno English dialect used by the bulk of the people at the very least in the local marketplace, and a proper British English useful for official and educational conversations and participation in the international marketplace.[3]

Within this configuration, Synge was something of an urban gentry, but nonetheless Irish and nonetheless in search of a language and intellectual tradition. He went to the peasants for their wisdom, to the blind beggars of the countryside, the fishing folk of the islands, and the tinkers of the roads and ditches, "where the imagination of the people, and the language they use, is rich and living." It was among them that he found his own tongue. Lady Gregory and William Butler Yeats joined the search for Celtic riches. Other luminaries of the literary renaissance took different directions: George Russel (AE) and (again) Yeats sought another kind of wisdom in spiritualist traditions; Sean O'Casey mined world politics for the stuff of his Irish based writings; and James Joyce went still another way, pushing language in the direction of music. What made all these voices the same was the search for a way to talk through the tensions between speaking as the world could hear, that is to say, in the British English language of the cultural and economic marketplace, and speaking in a language fitted to the experience of the people, in the language of resentment that comes from poverty, oppression and degradation.[4]

Synge lived these tensions to their fullest. A member of the Protestant ascendancy, he was educated in the finest English traditions available in late nineteenth century Dublin. At the same time, his Gaelic was excellent, and he walked the roads with the most peripheral Gaels ever to be locked out of European civilization. Always in the middle, he rested with neither extreme and gave the bulk of his creative efforts to fashioning an Hiberno English into an artistic medium. He was proud to note that in his plays he "used one or two words only that I have not heard among the country people of Ireland, or spoken in my own nursery before I could read the newspapers."

Peripheral to British powers, but core to the even more peripheral peasantry, Synge was in the position of many ethnographers. From his travels in the tradition bound Aran Islands from 1898 to 1902, he confronts the so-called problem of primitive mentality:[5]

In some ways these men and women seem strangely far away from me. They have the same emotions that I have, and the animals have, yet I cannot talk to them when there is much to say, more then to the dog that whines beside me in a mountain fog.

There is hardly an hour I am with them that I do not feel the shock of some inconceivable idea, and then again the shock of some vague emotion that is familiar to them and to me. On some days I feel this island as a perfect home and resting place; on other days I feel that I am a waif among the people. I can feel more with them than they can feel with me, and while I wander among them, they like me sometimes, and laugh at me sometimes, yet never know what I am doing. (1907, p. 83)

The natives seem to think just the way we do, but they do not seem to know very much. They do not seem to have inquiring minds. Synge can know their world, but they have no frame of reference for understanding his world.

If the heads of the Aran Islanders appear to be half-empty, the anthropological instinct is to locate the wisdom that fills up the other half of their glass of intelligence. Even if the natives do not make sense in core terms, their wisdom might be found in their understanding of local fishing or farming, or in the complexities of their kin reckoning. Synge worked on the possibility that the traditional people had access to a sensibility of another kind, that what they lacked in a wide range of knowledge was made up for in a depth of vision into their own "race worn with sorrow." In a paragraph following the ones cited above, Synge reformulated his question about their mental life into an appreciation:

In the evenings I sometimes meet with a girl who is not half way through her teens . . . As we sit on stools on either side of the fire I hear her voice going backwards and forwards in the same sentence from the gaiety of a child to the plaintive intonation of an old race that is worn with sorrow. At one moment she is a simple peasant, at another she seems to be looking out at the world with a sense of prehistoric disillusion and to sum up in the expression of her grey-blue eyes the whole external despondency of the clouds and sea. (p. 83)

Synge shared the ethnographer's sense of the people of Aran as half full rather than half empty.

Beyond anthropology, there is Bakhtin's instinct. People locked away from core culture may have something quite powerful to say about that very core, even if their critique is not easily intelligible in core terms. After Synge's magnificent *Playboy of the Western World* caused an uproar in Dublin, Bakhtin's point seems well secured. Synge was ready for the peasants to be smart, but he had no idea that his reconstruction of their wisdom would speak so loudly and so systematically to the core.

It was in the Aran Islands that Synge first heard the story that grew into his *Playboy*, the story of young Christy Mahon, who thinking he had killed his own, and most oppressive father, escapes to a distant village where they treat him as a hero, at least until his not so mortally wounded father shows up looking for him, and he is then degraded by all. In the rise and fall of such a playboy, one who would even murder his own Da, Synge found a vehicle for articulating the main constraints of the lives of the country people: poverty, paternal oppression, women in need of a road out, they all take a turn announcing their sway. Fifty years of ethnography, from Arensberg (1937) to Wilson (1984), is still filling in a structural description of the constraints Synge identified. Synge had Christy Mahon speak in an Hiberno English, and he used it to say all that any man in his situation could ever say, and he said it so well. By Synge's hand, Christy Mahon became one of the great orators of our time, and Hiberno English became an artistic medium that spoke directly to the political tensions between Irish and English people and their respective languages. In making the transition from ethnographer to playwright, in retelling their stories in ways consonant with what they understood in their telling them, Synge opened the stage for the voices of the people to emerge in new clothing.

For the century before the opening of the Abbey Theater in Dublin, the Irishman complete with his Hiberno English played the fool, the ruffian, and the drunk on the British stage (Waters, 1984). The Abbey, headed by Yeats and Lady Gregory, was charged with building a national theater that could go beyond the stereotypes. The Irish were to be presented on the Abbey stage as respectable members of the core culture, no longer to be laughed at, but appreciated in core terms. Synge's *Playboy* challenged this mission. Christy Mahon was no fool, and his Hiberno English was as good a vehicle for cleverness as had ever been heard. But he was no respectable member of core culture either.[6] Not only had he killed his father, good fodder for the farce Synge was trying to put on, he also brought with him the reality of the countryside and its honesty vis-à-vis the efforts of the Dublin aristocracy to claim freedom for the Irish in the name of their respectability, rather than in the name of the suffering peasants. While Dublin rioted in response to the continued presentation of the *Playboy* at the Abbey, the newspapers were filled with scathing reviews and occasional defenders of Synge's efforts. One review had it that:

> ... the Stage Irishman is a gentleman in comparison with the vile wretch whom Mr. Synge presented to an astonished Irish audience as the most popular type of Western peasant. The chief faults of the stage Irishman are excessive flamboyance and curious eccentricities of costume and brogue. But the Abbey street stage Irishman ... is a foul-mouthed scoundrel and parracide. (Kilroy, 1971, p. 19)

The voices of the periphery were not welcome among nationalists who lived, however unconsciously, under the sway of British views of the world. If the question was "Who can speak for Ireland?" a more important question was, "To whom?" (Kiberd, 1984). To the aristocracy that rioted at Synge's *Playboy*, all speaking had to be addressed to, and understood in terms of, the British core. For Synge's peasants, the voices necessary for speaking to either the British or the cultured elite of Dublin were systematically unavailable. Synge made those voices available and only a few Dubliners were able to hear; others could only respond to the tensions in the system articulated by the pains and sorrows of life in the countryside, and they screamed back.

Yeats made the claim that Synge was in the long run hailed as a great spokesman for the Irish periphery precisely because he was "the only man I have ever known incapable of a political thought or of a humanitarian purpose. He could walk the roadside all day with some poor man without any desire to do him good or for any reason except that he liked them" (1935). Bakhtin's point, of course, is that exchanging voices with people is an intensely political act. When Synge went for the voices of the people and tried to recapture, in a way larger than life, as any stage requires, the contexts that organized those voices and how they were to be appropriated by the core or banished to the periphery, he came up with revolutionary materials. The periphery can speak that clearly and that forcefully to the core if the proper forum and medium are made available. For the peasants on the Irish periphery at the turn of this century, John Synge and the Abbey Theater group were the medium and the forum.

The revolutionary impact of Synge's theater should leave us with both a celebration and an uneasiness. The celebration is for all those left inarticulate by their place within the system. Any non-appreciation of the wisdom of people on the periphery is rarely an accident; they are speaking and thinking often in antithesis to what we might expect, in antithesis to what we might insist on by the canons of good, common sense, but they can make sense. The uneasiness is for those of us who think of ourselves as listeners. If listened to carefully enough, the babble from the periphery may tower over our more ordinary lives with a devastating critique of its constraints and contradictions. As students of comparative human cognition, we are now prepared to find the disenfranchised being smart in ways that are difficult for us to recognize. If Bakhtin is right, we should be prepared to find them smart in ways we cannot handle. In articulating the roads not available in their lives, people from the periphery might identify roads we might be afraid to walk. Any ethnography of people cut from the mainstream that does not terrify or infuriate its readers is likely not to have pushed far enough.

Notes

1. Bakhtin's radically dialectical theory of word meanings should not be confused with the naive stand that any word can mean anything (as can be had, for example, from an unsympathetic reading of Malinowski). Bakhtin was fully aware that words came prepackaged, that a rose is a rose; he was also aware that the packaging was arbitrary except within a system of values enforced by a community of voices. It is precisely because a word's meaning is maintained on the strength of a collusion on the parts of many speakers that every utterance suggests its opposite, and screams for lighter alternatives (McDermott and Tylbor, 1983). Early in life, Synge held the naive stand and made up his own words for many objects in the world. His mother convinced

him it was a sin, and he had to give it up (Kiberd, 1979). Later in life, as we shall see, he was closer to Bakhtin's position, choosing his words carefully to fit the communal contexts in which he heard them, and moving them to new contexts in which they exploded. He had committed another sin, this one leaving much of literate Dublin screaming at each other.

2. By periphery I mean particularly people disenfranchised by geographic or economic isolation. Bakhtin's account cuts deeper and identifies some of us core culture persons as fairly permanently peripheral (Bateson's schizophrenics) and all of us constantly, on an every other moment basis, peripheral to the very worlds we are helping recreate. For an important account of kinds of peripheries and social economies available in western Ireland over the last century, see the work of Taylor (1980).

3. There is an abundance of intelligent accounts of the literature and politics of the times. See, for example, Brown (1972), Kenner (1984) and Lyons (1979).

4. In 1928, James Joyce asked H. G. Wells to support his efforts to produce a new kind of novel (*Finnegans Wake*). Wells turned him down and his answer sums up with shocking clarity some of the tensions between British and Irish versions of both language and situated conversations:

> Your training has been Catholic, Irish and insurrectionary; mine, such as it was, was scientific, constructive and, I suppose, English. The frame of my mind is a world wherein a big unifying and concentrating process is possible (increase of power and range by economy and concentration of effort), a progress not inevitable but interesting and possible. That game attracted and holds me. For it, I want a language and statement as simple and clear as possible. You begin Catholic , that is to say, you began with a system of values in stark opposition to reality. Your mental existence is obsessed by a monstrous system of contradictions. You really believe in chastity, purity and the personal God and that is why you are always breaking out into cries of cunt, shit, and hell . . . And while you were brought up under the delusion of political suppression I was brought up under the delusion of political responsibility. It seems a fine thing for you to defy and break up. To me, not in the least.

Almost to the year, Bakhtin was stating, under another person's name, a more formal version of such tensions between the many voices that make up a community (Volosinov, 1929). A supporting voice of my own, one belonging to William Peter Murphy, was good enough to send the Wells letter to me.

5. Compare the notes of another nascent anthropologist only 20 years before. Franz Boas wrote of the Eskimo: "I had seen that they enjoyed life, and hard life, as we do: that nature is beautiful to them; that feelings of friendship also root in the Eskimo heart; that, although the character of their life is rude as compared to civilized life, the Eskimo is a man as we are; that his feelings, his virtues and his shortcomings are based on human nature, like ours" (cited in Kardiner and Preble, 1961, p. 119). Diamond (1974) has been good enough to show that the problem of primitive mentality is less something to be discovered in the world and more a statement of our relations to various kinds of disenfranchised people.

6. Bakhtin's account of the peasants in Rabelais shared many of the traits of Synge's new heroes. Holquist (1984, p. xix) has noted that Bakhtin "employs his most glowing colors to highlight attributes of the folk precisely and diametrically opposed to those celebrated in Soviet *folklorico*. His folk are blasphemous rather than adoring, cunning

rather than intelligent; they are coarse, dirty and rampantly physical, reveling in oceans of strong drink, poods of sausage, and endless coupling of bodies . . . Bakhtin's claim that the folk not only picked their noses and farted, but enjoyed doing so, seemed particularly unregenerate. The opposition is not merely between two different concepts of common man, but between two fundamentally opposed world views with nothing in common except that each finds its most comprehensive metaphor in 'the folk.'"

References

Arensberg, C. A. (1937). *The Irish countryman*. New York: Anchor.
Bakhtin, M. M. (1934–35). Discourse in the novel. In M. Holquist (Ed.), *The dialogic imagination* (2nd ed., 1971). Austin: University of Texas Press.
Bakhtin, M. M. (1940). *Rabelais and his world* (2nd ed., 1984). Bloomington: Indiana University Press.
Brown, M. (1972). *The politics of Irish literature*. Seattle: University of Washington Press.
Diamond, S. (1974). *In search of the primitive*. New Brunswick: Transaction Books.
Holquist, M. (1984). Prologue to M. Bakhtin's, *Rabelais and his world*. Bloomington: Indiana University Press.
Kardiner, A., & Preble, E. (1961). *They studied man*. New York: Mentor.
Kenner, H. (1984). *A colder eye*. Baltimore: Penguin.
Kiberd, D. (1979). *Synge and the Irish language*. Totowa: Rowman & Littlefield.
Kiberd, D. (1984). *Anglo-Irish attitudes*. Derry: Field Day.
Kilroy, J. (1971). *The "Playboy" riots*. Dublin: Dolmen Press.
Lyons, F. S. L. (1979). *Culture and anarchy in Ireland 1890–1939*. Oxford: Clarendon Press.
McDermott, R., & Tylbor, H. (1983). On the necessity of collusion in conversation. *TEXT, 3*, 277–297.
Synge, J. M. (1907). *The Aran Islands*. Oxford: Oxford University Press.
Synge, J. M. (1935). *The complete plays*. New York: Vintage.
Taylor, L. (1980). The merchant in peripheral Ireland. *Anthropology, 4*, 63–76.
Volosinov, N. (1929). *Marxism and the philosophy of language*. New York: Academic Press.
Waters, M. (1984). *The comic Irishman*. Albany: State University of New York Press.
Wells, H. G. (1928). Letter to James Joyce. In R. Ellmann (Ed.), *James Joyce* (2nd ed., 1982). Oxford: Oxford University Press.
Wilson, T. (1984). From Clare to the Common Market. *Anthropological Quarterly, 57*, 1–15.
Yeats, W. B. (1935). *The autobiography of William Butler Yeats*. New York: Collier Books.

31 Learning to be deaf: Conflicts between Hearing and Deaf cultures

Carol Padden and Harry Markowicz

Introduction

In most social groups, membership is a result of being born into a particular family. The deaf community represents a unique situation in that, at most, ten per cent of all deaf children have parents who are themselves deaf (Mindel & Vernon, 1971). Other deaf children are socialized into the deaf community outside of the home and at different periods in their lives when they enter schools and meet other deaf people (Meadow, 1972). The experimental group under investigation here consists of 21 young deaf adults who entered Gallaudet College, a college for deaf students, as first-year students. Although 15 of our subjects had hearing impairments either at birth or before the age of two, at the time of their enrollment at Gallaudet, most had never met or socialized with other deaf people. Additionally, the primary means of communication among deaf people on campus – sign language – was a foreign language for our subjects. The subjects' arrival on the Gallaudet campus represented a sudden transposition to an alien culture of whose existence they had been mostly unaware until that time. At the time of this report, all subjects had had at least six months of contact with other deaf students at Gallaudet College. Predictably, this complete immersion had effected a change in their self-perception and how they view their social identity. Realizing that these adjustments and changes are likely to continue over a period of several years, we report here on the more immediate consequences of these changes as experienced by our subjects.

418

The experimental group

Our observations of cultural conflicts are based on a group of hearing-impaired Gallaudet College students who were socialized in the hearing society. The experimental group was selected on the basis of their unfamiliarity with deaf culture. Included in the study were students who met these criteria and who enrolled at Gallaudet for the first time during either the summer or the fall. We eliminated from the experimental group foreign students who would introduce other conflicting cultural patterns.

This selection yielded 21 subjects, 14 females and 7 males.

1. Fifteen of the subjects suffered hearing losses either at birth or at/before age of two (10 females, 5 males).
2. Eight of these subjects had been enrolled in a postsecondary program prior to their entrance at Gallaudet. Length of enrollment ranged from one semester to two years. None of these postsecondary institutions had special programs for the hearing-impaired. All 8 subjects reported severe difficulties in the college classroom which had influenced their decisions to seek out other educational opportunities.
3. Eight subjects were 20 years old or older and encountered some initial problems in forming peer relations with their preparatory and freshman classmates.

Interviews and observations

The methodology of investigation consisted largely of individual interviews, usually of one hour duration or longer. The interviews were conducted in spoken English, a mode of communication in which our subjects do not have great difficulty in a face-to-face situation.

Interviews usually started with general questions about the subject's age, where he/she lived, type of school attended, and how the subject judged the extent of the hearing loss.

The informal interview was then steered toward a more in-depth discussion of the subject's parental and educational background, how he/she was introduced to Gallaudet, reactions from family and friends to the decision to attend Gallaudet, and eventually, reflections on how his or her present Gallaudet life-style differed from his/her life-style elsewhere.

Our subjects report that deaf individuals use certain facial expressions they have never seen used among the American hearing public. Some subjects say that facial expressions of Deaf students are "exaggerated" or "attention-drawing." Not only do subjects recognize that some facial expressions used by Deaf students are different, but the subjects have reported that they could not always understand the meaning of these facial expressions. At the same time, other subjects say that, when in a conversation with Deaf students, the facial expressions which they use at home may either be misinterpreted or not understood by Deaf students.

At this point, we would speculate that some of the confusion and misinterpretation on the part of the subjects and the Deaf students result from cross-linguistic and cross-cultural conflicts since members of the two opposing cultures do not share the same language and appear not to share the same nonverbal codes as well.

Summary

Excluding potential intruders is a mechanism by which an ethnic group seeks to protect its group identity. Deaf people, being surrounded by a larger and dominant Hearing community, allow intimate interaction with their members only if the individual exhibits appropriate behavior and language skills.

This experimental group of students experienced exclusion at the time of their arrival at Gallaudet. If the subjects, in order to gain acceptance, must abandon behavior they previously considered crucial to survival we can describe that behavior as incompatible with distinctions among subgroups' use of a particular identifying variety of ASL. Finding an interacting role in the Deaf community necessarily requires the ability to recognize sociolinguistic patterns of subgroups and the means by which a member can identify the social status of an individual from his use of a particular language variety.

Another intriguing problem faced by our subjects is that of conflicts arising from a specific kind of misinterpretation attributed to facial expressions and other body movements. From our subjects' descriptions, these misinterpretations did not seem to be related to a verbal exchange, but rather to nonverbal behavior.

Nonverbal behavior is distinguished from verbal communication in that nonverbal communication employs the use of signals not directly involved with the language code itself. Thus, one can verbalize, "Why did you do that?" and convey nonverbally, fear, anger, distrust, sympathy by use of posture, face, eyes, body, hands, and other parts of the body.

Literature on nonverbal communication in spoken languages describes how the use of the eyes alone can communicate nonverbal signals (Birdwhistell, 1967). In American Sign Language, however, the eyes are used not only nonverbally, but verbally as well. Eyes have been shown to identify clause boundaries (Stokoe, 1972), as in marking the boundary between subordinate and main clauses and also in determining pronouns (Lacy, 1974). Eye-to-eye contact between native ASL signers is essential in its function both as grammatical determinants and in conveying nonverbal information in a fashion distinct from that of English (Battison, personal communication). Native signers have on occasion complained that nonnative signers move the eyes away from the other signer's face at "the wrong time."

Seven subjects proved to be particularly informative about their experiences and were asked to return for further interviews.

For all of our subjects, we have compiled case histories detailing their family and educational backgrounds as well as their own reflections on the progress of their socialization into the deaf culture through their association with the deaf community at Gallaudet.

Additionally, upon the students' arrival at Gallaudet, they were placed in sign language classes and for the first time, encountered a deaf person as their teacher. From our observations of subjects in their sign language classes, we were able to obtain information on how the subjects interacted with each other and with the teacher.

Deaf culture

At this point, a question may be raised: How does one determine that a deaf culture exists, separate from the culture of the hearing people around them? There have been numerous studies of the deaf person as individual, but with the introduction of work by Boese (1964), Vernon and Makowsky (1969), Reich and Reich (1974), and Schein

(1968), it was noted that deaf individuals form cohesive groups in which they carry out social obligations to each other. In a first definition, Schein (1968) labels this group of deaf individuals as a *deaf community* and defines certain criteria for inclusion in the community, one of which is an audiological impairment. In addition to those members who have severely limited audiological capabilities, a smaller number of individuals whose hearing loss is "sufficient to interfere with, but not necessarily to preclude, the normal reception of speech" are also considered to be members of the deaf community. This subgroup is referred to as *socially deaf* persons. However, a strictly audiological definition of the deaf cultural group cannot be applied, since the group of students we are investigating meet the audiological criteria for membership without, however, being accepted as members by other deaf people.

Schlesinger and Meadow (1972) note other criteria that determine group membership. Their criteria for social group identification specify that the deaf community is essentially one defined by the language it uses. In reference to other social groups, it has been observed that "language has unifying effects upon a community. A common language, especially a language of a minority group, may foster a sense of togetherness and corporate identity" (Aceves, 1974). Although we agree that language acts as a powerful cohesive force, we suggest that language is only part of the cultural characteristics shared by its members. The conflicts our subjects experienced involved differences in not only language but behavior and manner associated with being a member of the deaf ethnic group. Their experiences corroborate recent anthropological studies in which an independent value system and set of behaviors associated with the Deaf[1] cultural group have been identified (Padden, 1980; Baker & Cokely, 1980; Erting, 1977).

The approach taken in this article follows that of Barth in which we define ethnic membership as a result of ascription – or if one identifies with an ethnic group and is identified by others as a member of that group, then he is a member of the said group. Membership is determined by those particular physical and cultural characteristics considered to be significant by members and outsiders, ". . . often such features as language. . . . general style of life, and basic value orientations. . . ." (Barth, 1969). Consequently, membership in the ethnic group is not solely conditioned by the degree of hearing loss, whereas the use of American Sign Language and display of appropriate social behavior are necessary social requirements, thus indicating cultural characteristics shared by the members.

The traits which mark membership in a social group are specified by a basic identity shared by the members. Implied in this basic identity is a commonality of experiences and values which can be expressed in a mutually understandable language. Two individuals who recognize each other as members of the same group know that they are likely to share similar criteria for judgments of values and evaluation of performance. On the other hand, members of different groups know that such a shared understanding of values and performance cannot be assumed and that interaction may be limited to areas of mutual interest (Barth, 1969). Thus, interaction within a group is generally easier and more extensive than with outsiders. This differentiation between members and non-members determines a boundary which serves to maintain the group's self-identity.

Interviews with our subjects illustrate this definition of membership and exclusion with repeated references to "the Deaf people, the ones who attended schools for the deaf all their lives." Residential schools for deaf students serve as a powerful socializing force since they group together deaf students on a regular basis and expose them to contact with other deaf adults.

For most subjects, the reality of their deafness was accepted by themselves before arriving at Gallaudet. When asked whether they differ from the other students at Gallaudet, they answered that there is no difference. "We all have hearing losses." However, during the same interview they stated that other Deaf students behave differently, that they are "immature" or they "lack manners." The kinds of acceptable social behaviors they observed in other Deaf people struck them as very different from those of hearing people. Their value judgments in this respect are similar to those of early missionaries who reported South Pacific islander behavior as "childlike" or "irrational."

An almost universal reaction from our subjects upon their arrival at Gallaudet was one of surprise. For them, deafness was conceived solely as a hearing loss, a physical handicap with social consequences which affect relations with hearing people. None of the subjects were prepared to find a minority with its own culture and its own language. They expected to be among others like themselves. Instead they found that they could not interact easily with other students. The first barrier they encountered, of course, was that of language, but behavioral differences struck them immediately as well. For example, within less than forty-eight hours of his arrival on campus, one subject was tapped on the shoulder by another student, a perfect stranger, who ordered him to stop using his voice. As he was to learn quickly, the valued mode of communication among Deaf people is not speech, but use of the visual-manual mode of sign language.

These feelings of being outsiders experienced by our experimental group often resulted from their contacts with the Deaf fellow students. One subject was baffled by an incident involving a Deaf student she had never seen before. He approached her and informed her that she did not belong at Gallaudet, that she should attend a hearing college. Our subjects realized quickly that a boundary exists between themselves and Deaf students at Gallaudet. This distinction of member and non-member is well exemplified by the number of pejorative vocabulary reserved specifically for reference to those deaf students outside the group. For example, the sign ORAL is a play on a sign meaning exaggerated mouth movements.

Acceptance, as one subject explained, involves:

Subject: 1) Communication easier.
            2) Start thinking in the same way as a Deaf person: vocabulary, ideas, how
                you act, everything.
Interviewer: How do you "act" like a Deaf person?
Subject: I don't know. . . . not like you're above the people here – equal. Don't walk
            around, you know, like stuck-up to other people. Act the same. Think of other
            people as equal – the same.[2]

In a minority culture where its language and values are disparaged in favor of those of the majority group, there is fierce protection of group identity and behavior within the boundaries of the minority group. By persisting in use of hearing group behaviors around other Deaf students, our subjects found themselves judged severely for their behavior.

We must stress again that the degree of hearing loss is not a consideration since the range of hearing impairment of the subjects is similar to that of other Gallaudet students.

Speaking is one of the first noticeable characteristics by which a Deaf student identifies outsiders. Our subjects found talking and accompanying behavior crucial in surviving as members of their hearing communities. In the process of their socialization in the hearing community, they were encouraged to function as hearing members, which also meant displaying normal speaking behavior when possible. As we observed in their first few sign language classes, some subjects risked miscommunication by exhibiting conversing behavior they associated with that of a normal hearing person. They engaged in rapid talking, little eye-to-eye contact, and limited the use of their hands. Their concern that they appear as "hearing" as possible dominated their need for effective communication.

However, when in the presence of other Deaf individuals, the subjects' talking behavior did not allow them to be accepted into activities among Deaf people. For many Deaf students, speaking has negative connotations: it represents attempts by the majority culture to replace sign language with speech, and to deny the value of sign language as a preferred means of communication.

Some subjects have quickly assessed the effects of this behavior and have confined their talking to certain individuals at certain times. Others, from long-time associations with their more familiar culture, find it difficult to make drastic changes in their behavior, including the manner in which they converse with others.

In contrast to their difficult position as outsiders when they arrive on campus, a number of our subjects found themselves cast in a respected status position as cultural brokers. Since they are seen by other Deaf students as members of the dominant hearing community, they are often asked to provide information about its culture to their fellow Deaf students. Some alumni of residential schools for deaf students view our subjects as wise in the ways of the world, and consequently, several have become counselors for their dormitory mates. One of these subjects remarked that the same girls who seek her advice ignore her when they see her outside of her dormitory room. This apparent contradiction can be understood when viewed in terms of interactions across ethnic boundaries, as suggested earlier (Barth, 1969). The cross-cultural interactions made possible by the roles of counselor and cultural broker are structured in that these roles are limited as to where interactions can take place and to certain areas of common interest.

Socialization in a second culture

Research in second language learning shows that success in learning a new language correlates inversely with the strength of the learner's ethnocentric views or his negative attitude toward the new group (Lambert, 1967).

Ethnocentrism alone, however, does not account for one's resistance to a new culture. In a situation where the learner feels insecure about his performance, he may revert to accustomed behavior when interacting with members of the unfamiliar culture. Occasionally, on the basis of an initial encounter an individual may pass for a member of a group, only to be exposed later by further interaction (Goffman, 1963). Fear of public embarrassment ensuing from incorrect performance or inappropriate behavior may cause an individual to adhere purposely to older behavior, thus marking his status as an outsider.

We have on record a subject's detailed description of her first excursion into behaving like a Deaf person. During a three-day vacation to New York City with some Deaf friends, she modified her usual behavior to indicate clearly her deafness to others around her. The change in her behavior received immediate notice and surprise from her Deaf friends. However, their support for her new behavior could not persuade her to continue upon her return to Gallaudet. Her reluctance to use new learned behavior stems from her fear of being held up to ridicule and embarrassment by other Deaf students should she accidently display inappropriate behavior.

. . . if I do something wrong, I would feel more embarrassed than not doing anything. . . . I'm not one who likes to change a lot quickly. You know – if they knew me before, and saw me before – and then change, you know – think, "What's wrong?" "What happened?"

The transition from one social group to another can be characterized as a gradual process during which new ways of behaving, both social and linguistic, are learned and tested. Old behavioral patterns cannot be abandoned entirely until the individual has adequately mastered the new patterns in order to function as a member of the new group.

Language variation and community structure

Sociolinguists have presented the theory of language variation as an attempt to describe actual language usage within a community. Linguists have recognized that for spoken languages, "there are no single-style speakers" (Labov, 1970), since different social situations and topics of conversations require different styles of language (Gumperz, 1972).

Research studies since 1960 have recognized American Sign Language (ASL) as a language distinct from English, with its own vocabulary and grammar and with a set of complex rules for their appropriate use in the Deaf community (Stokoe, 1970).

ASL is not an exception to the phenomenon of language variation. All signers, either native or fluent, vary the formation, vocabulary, and grammatical rules of their signing depending on the participants in the conversation, the subject being discussed, the formality or informality of the setting, and many other social variables (Stokoe, 1970). Language variation in ASL, as in any other language, is rule-governed, that is, social conditions determine what variety is acceptable to use in a partic-ular context.

A frequent example of variation in ASL occurs with younger Deaf signers' use of a more formal variety when conversing with older members of the community. Such dialect switches anticipate that the older Deaf persons may not recognize certain signs used by younger members of the community. This situation is the equivalent of that found in any hearing society, where it can be easily observed that children do not talk in the same way to their parents as they do to their peers.

Not unlike the languages of other minority groups in North America, ASL is greatly influenced by the dominant American English speaking society. One particular type of variation occurring in the Deaf commu-nity has been described (Vernon & Makowsky, 1969) as a continuum of varieties extending from *competence in ASL to competence in English*,[3] idealized in the following graphic representation:

Continuum:
ASL ◄—————► English

A language variety may vary from the extreme left, where it is most like ASL and least like English, to the middle, which consists of char-acteristics of both languages, and to the extreme right where the variety shows marked separation from ASL. Thus, in the middle of the con-tinuum, one cannot easily determine what is American Sign Language and what is English. Individuals differ in the range of the continuum they control.

Native signers of ASL who are also fluent in English often incorporate more English elements in their signing, replacing certain elements of ASL vocabulary and grammar. We are also familiar with hearing individuals who, with no competence in ASL, will use a language variety close to English. Often, when a hearing person joins a conversation already in progress among Deaf individuals, the Deaf signers, in order to accommodate a person not fluent in ASL, will switch to a variety closer to English and may begin to use speech as well. The switching to a more appropriate language variety allows the hearing person to interact more comfortably with the Deaf signers. This switching is triggered by a social constraint which requires the use of English with outsiders (Stokoe, 1970).

Hearing people are not given the opportunity to interact in ASL; for the most part, this accounts for the fact that they rarely learn that language. In this respect, our subjects are treated like hearing people by their fellow Deaf students, as the following quotation from an interview illustrates. The subject is referring to her Deaf roommate who is engaged in a conversation with a Deaf girlfriend:

She was talking to her without voice, you know, using sign language. And when she turned around to talk to me, she used her voice and sign language. I asked her "Why?" She can't help it, it depends on who she's talking to . . . you know?

As discussed earlier, the presence of language varieties in ASL necessarily corresponds to appropriate rules for the usage of these varieties. A member of the Deaf community is usually capable of switching varieties to accommodate a particular social situation.

Thus, it can be seen that socialization in a second social group involves more than learning the vocabulary and the grammar of its language. An essential condition is the acquisition of the varieties of that language and the rules for their appropriate use.

Although our subjects have been formally taught sign language, their competence in ASL and their understanding of the social situations that determine variation within ASL is minimal. They repeatedly state that their language is not the same as other Deaf students – describing the latter's signing by comparing it to English. Many interpret these language differences with value judgments. We commonly hear complaints from our subjects that Deaf students at Gallaudet persist in using incomplete English or that they talk only in ideas and concepts, a common misunderstanding about ASL.

The sign language variety a member of the Deaf community uses most often corresponds to his social status in the community. Different varieties of sign language have been described (Stokoe, 1970; Woodward, 1973) and usage has been correlated with variables such as $+/-$ deaf parents,[4] $+/-$ learned ASL after age of six, $+/-$ attended residential school, and $+/-$ attended college (Woodward, 1973).

Limited experience with sign language allows our subjects to make gross decisions about how their use of signs differs from the ASL of Deaf students at Gallaudet. However, most of them cannot yet perceive finer values shared by Deaf people.

Ethnocentric attitudes and behavior often present serious conflicts when an unaware individual seeks to interact with Deaf people, as evidenced by the conflicts our subjects are experiencing. The process of making adjustments to these conflicts is a long and difficult one. The subjects' anxieties about changing their familiar behavior to accommodate newer, more acceptable behavior must be understood as a reaction toward conflicts arising from two cultures in contact.

This study points to the need to recognize Deaf people as comprising a separate cultural entity, particularly for those who wish to join it as new members, but also for outsiders who deal with Deaf individuals in a professional capacity. By helping outsiders learn more about conflicting values, we can encourage respect and meaningful interaction between Deaf and Hearing people.

Notes

The study reported here was supported in part by NIH grant #NS-10302 and NSF grant #SOC 74147224. We gratefully acknowledge the assistance and support of Dr. W. C. Stokoe, Director of the Linguistics Research Laboratory at Gallaudet College.

We would like to thank Robbin Battison, Dr. Veda Charrow, Dr. Carl Jensema, and Dr. James Woodward for their helpful comments. Although we have tried to incorporate as much of their insightful suggestions as we could, the final paper remains our own responsibility. The assistance of other professional members of the Deaf community, Dr. I. King Jordan, and Dr. Allen Sussman was invaluable in the development of this research investigation.

1. Throughout the remainder of this article, we shall use the convention of capitalizing the first letter of the word "Deaf" when we are referring to the ethnic group, its culture, or its membership. We shall continue to write "deaf" without capitalization to indicate an audiological condition of deafness.
2. Quotations used in this article are taken from transcripts of videotapes made during the interviewing sessions. The subjects' competence in English is not truly reflected

in the quotations because they were generally speaking and signing simultaneously, requiring them to make adaptations in their speech.
3. Competence is the knowledge of the abstract rules of a language that allows one to produce and comprehend sentences appropriate to that language.
4. Presence of the variable is indicated by the symbol +; its absence is shown by the symbol −.

References

Aceves, J. B. *Identity, survival, and change: Exploring social/cultural anthropology.* Morristown: General Learning Press, 1974.
Baker, C., & Cokely, D. *American Sign Language: A teacher's resource manual on grammar and culture.* Silver Spring, MD: TJ Publishers Inc., 1980.
Barth, F. (Ed.). *Ethnic groups and boundaries: The social organization of culture difference* (Introduction). Boston: Little Brown & Co., 1969.
Birdwhistell, R. L. Some body motion elements accompanying spoken American English. In L. Thayer (Ed.), *Communication: Concepts and perspectives.* Washington, DC: Spartan Books, 1967.
Boese, R. J. Differentiations in the deaf community. Unpublished study submitted to the Department of Sociology, University of British Columbia, 1964.
Erting, C. Deafness as ethnicity: Implications for language policy. Manuscript, Research Department, Kendall Demonstration Elementary School, Washington, DC, 1977.
Goffman, E. *Stigma: Notes on the management of spoiled identity.* Englewood Cliffs: Prentice-Hall, 1963.
Gumperz, J. J., & Hymes, D. (Eds.). *Directions in sociolinguistics: The ethnography of communication.* New York: Holt, Rinehart and Winston, 1972.
Labov, W. *The study of nonstandard English.* Champaign, IL: National Council of Teachers of English, 1970.
Lacy, R. Putting some of the syntax back into semantics, manually. Paper presented at the 49th Annual Meeting of the Linguistic Society of America, New York, December, 1974.
Lambert, E. A. A social psychology of bilingualism. *Journal of Social Issues,* 1967, *23* (2), 91–109.
Meadow, K. P. Sociolinguistics, sign language, and the deaf subculture. In T. J. O'Rourke (Ed.), *Psycholinguistics and total communication: The state of the art.* Washington, DC: American Annals of the Deaf, 1972.
Mindel, E. D., & Vernon, M. *They grow in silence: The deaf child and his family.* Silver Spring, MD: National Association of the Deaf, 1971.
Padden, C. The deaf community and the culture of Deaf people. In C. Baker & R. Battison (Eds.), *Sign Language and the deaf community.* Silver Spring, MD: National Association of the Deaf, 1980.
Reich, P. A., & Reich, C. M. A follow-up study of the deaf. Toronto: Research Service, Board of Education, 1974, No. 120.

Schein, J. D. *The Deaf community: Studies in the social psychology of deafness.* Washington, DC: Gallaudet College Press, 1968.

Schlesinger, H. S., & Meadow, K. P. *Sound and sign: Childhood deafness and mental health.* Berkeley: University of California Press, 1972.

Stokoe, W. C. Jr. Sign language diglossia. *Studies in Linguistics,* 1970, *21,* 27–41.

Stokoe, W. C. Jr. A classroom experiment in two languages. In T. J. O'Rourke (Ed.), *Psycholinguistics and total communication: The state of the art.* Washington, DC: American Annals of the Deaf, 1972.

Vernon, M., & Makowsky, B. Deafness and minority group dynamics. *The Deaf American,* 1969, *21,* 3–6.

Woodward, J. C. Jr. Some observations on sociolinguistic variation and American sign language. *Kansas Journal of Sociology,* 1973, *9* (2), 191–200.

32 Why must might be right? Observations on sexual herrschaft

Esther Goody

The politics of sexual herrschaft is about control. This is very complicated politics because it emerges from the interaction of the consequences of biological differences between males and females, the conceptualization of these differences including the myths and ideologies formed around the concepts, and from the constraints of social institutions, particularly those linked to domestic and political roles. Each of these frames affects the others, and it is within this multidimensional field that individual men and women live and contend for control. No one frame can "explain" the patterns of control which emerge, since these are a product of their interaction. This circumstance also makes analysis difficult; the selection of one element to discuss implies its greater importance when this is not intended. To comment on these issues is also difficult because of the large amount of unusually high quality work already published. It is neither possible to do justice to these studies in the space available, nor valid to ignore them. Of necessity major contributions and unresolved debates, proper subjects of essays in themselves, are here relegated to footnotes.

A basic learning mechanism for higher animals, including humans, is the reward/punishment complex studied by behavioural psychology.[1] Our behaviour is constantly shaped by this learning organized around seeking gratification and avoiding pain. While this has obvious implications for childrearing and education generally, it is in fact also fundamental to social institutions. It is through rewarding conformity and the threat of negative sanctions that norms are established and maintained. Such sanctions need not be formal such as those embodied in courts and police. Evans-Pritchard wrote of Nuer social order being maintained by the threat of the feud (Evans-Pritchard, 1940). Yanomamo villages retain their autonomy by being feared as fierce and ready to attack others (Chagnon, 1968). Relations between street gangs in modern cities follow much the same lines (Keiser, 1969). There is thus at a basic level an association between force and the normative order. The polemics of modern governments seeking to justify massive overkill capacity are always framed in terms of defending the good (democracy/socialism) against the evil (capitalist/socialist) dictatorship. But of course this very relativity of who and what is right throws into high relief the danger of accepting the simple equation Might = Right. In simple societies there is generally a straightforward pattern: My people/descent group/village are right and we will fight to defend ourselves against your people/descent group/village who are our enemies because you are fighting us. Because you are our enemies you are wrong (and we are right).

Individuals with ties to two hostile groups often act as go-betweens and mediators; or they may be caught between the two and seen as potential enemies by both. The moral element in such conflicts is sometimes expressed in the idea of a duel, tournament or battle as an ordeal, with the victory going to those who have the Lord (i.e., morality) on their side. State systems have evolved a wide variety of institutions for constraining open contests of strength within their boundaries, and for separating right (law) from whether one individual or his group is stronger than another. Significantly, at the level of relations between states (or in a civil war, between the opposing sides) Might is still used as a measure of who is Right. A successful coup or revolution is followed, eventually if not immediately, by the recognition by other nations of the new government. Winning a war results in the redrawing of boundaries, and the re-design of constitutions. The side which wins gets to make the new rules.

However, this paper is not about legal systems or national polities, but about the interaction between power and morality in relations between men and women. That these are not totally separate problems can be seen in the way in which many simple societies describe their origins in terms of the overthrow of the rule of women (see below).

Paradoxes of herrschaft at the level of social structure

Women, Levi-Strauss has shown, are objects of transactions by men (Levi-Strauss, 1969). In small traditional systems marriages were often based on the exchange of sisters between men, since because of incest conventions, men cannot marry their own sisters. In other societies, such exchanges were transformed to bridewealth transactions, in which a conventionally determined valuable was exchanged for rights to marry a kinswoman; the kinsman who received bridewealth could then exchange it with another family for a bride for himself or his son. In more complex societies fathers sought prestigious suitors for their daughters with valuable dowries (Goody & Tambiah, 1973). In many places it was accepted that men could seize wives in raids, or as the prizes of war, or as the prerequisites of slave ownership. But always it was men who transacted the rights to marry women and not the women themselves (although they might have some influence behind the scenes). The obvious question would seem to be, why in these many, many independent systems didn't women use the fact that their sexual and reproductive capacities were a valued resource, to take control over their own bodies and transact on their own account? For according to exchange theory, the party to a transaction who holds the greater resources, commands the greater power (Blau, 1968; Homans, 1958). Yet women yield this resource to men, who use it to gain wives, establish alliances between kin groups – and determine the domestic destiny of the women themselves. Societies vary in the extent to which marriages are arranged by one or another of these institutions, but in no society do women transact in the marriages of men.

The Marxist premise is that control over the means of production leads to economic power which is the ultimate basis for political power. Yet this equation does not seem to operate in the relationship between the sexual division of labour and economic and political power for women. In simple technology societies women tend to contribute heavily to subsistence: In most types of hunting and gathering systems it has been estimated that they provide well over 50% of subsistence consumption (Lee, 1968), while in the rudimentary agriculture of New Guinea, Amazonia, aboriginal North America, and much of Africa, women were cultivators, and often produced most or all of the staple food (Friedl, 1975). Yet it is rare for women to hold positions of either economic or political authority in these societies. In foraging systems it is men who are hunters, although the supply of meat they provide is irregular and often small. However, meat, unlike gathered foods, serves as the basis for gifts and exchange outside of the domestic group and may be built into claims for wives as among the Tiwi of Australia (Hart & Pilling, 1960), or into systems of prestige and even office (as in the potlatch system of the Indians of the northwest coast of North America). Even in those simple agricultural systems in which women do all the cultivating of staple foods (frequent in New Guinea, and in many societies in Africa and Amazonia) this gives them no claims on external economic roles or political office. It is always men who initially clear the land, and who construct and hold social ownership of land which gives them claims on the crops it bears (Friedl, 1975). It thus cannot be argued that women hold less power and prestige *because* their absorption in bearing and rearing children has prevented them from contributing to subsistence production. On the contrary, they seem to be subordinate in many societies *in spite of* being the major subsistence producers (Kaberry, 1952). What seems to happen in these societies is that men's contribution to the division of labour is based on superior strength, and possibly on the greater risk of injury or death. Both hunting and clearing of land are the basis of political and economic transactions between men in which women do not participate. These transactions create a superstructure of power and authority roles that feeds back into the definition of male and female domestic roles, and the overall pattern of male dominance. As Rosaldo argued in her seminal paper (1974), the pre-occupation of women with childrearing and the domestic domain produces societal systems in which men hold legitimate authority and manage relations *between* domestic groups.

But the final paradox is that men, holding the dominant roles in the public sphere in virtually every society[2], should find it necessary to label women's power, when it does emerge, as illegitimate and wrong. For in cosmologies, myths of origin, and beliefs about causes of misfortune, one repeatedly finds that the subordination of women is their own fault; either women committed some original sin which doomed them to eternal inferiority, or it is in their nature as women to be in some way to blame, to be guilty, or evil, or simply stupid. This being so, men are "naturally" and "inevitably" dominant. Such a coincidence between *de facto* distribution of power and beliefs about the nature of the world both serves to reinforce the position of the dominant and argues to the sub-ordinated that they cannot change their situation. But of course it is not a coincidence. Why does Might claim to be Right? And why is this claim accepted by those whom it blames for their own subordination?

In discussing the nature of social stratification, Beteille has argued (1983) that complex societies in which there is an ethic of equality are in fact faced with the reality of marked inequalities. They tend to respond by producing various rationalizations as to why some are better off and others disadvantaged, and these rationalizations tend to be based on some sort of supposed "natural order."[3] This displaces the responsi-bility for the reality of inequality from human beings to nature, which, since there is a very strong commitment to the ideal of equality, is more comfortable than having to accept that the contradiction has a human social basis. Beteille is concerned with social divisions, class and caste. But there are striking parallels in the ideological rationalizations of very diverse societies for the domination of men over women. The parallel occurs at two levels: First, in the elaborate ideologies which explain the origin and necessity for this dominance; and second, in the tracing of the cause to the "natural" attributes of women. There is also a third element which I suspect may appear in ideologies justifying socio-economic stratification. This is based on morality. Women are inferior because they have sinned, or are in essence sinful. This twist to the argu-ment allows men to feel not only superior, but righteous. The women brought it on themselves, and deserve to be punished. So one is forced to ask why should these ideologies legitimating dominance make the weaker also be guilty of some form of immorality? Why must Might also be Right?

One could draw illustrative material for this pattern of the social con-struction of reality from a very wide range of historical and ethnographic examples. I shall consider just a few cases in sufficient detail to make clear the culturally specific patterns and then return to the question of the underlying dynamic.

South American Indians: Origin myths and control of women

There are two strikingly similar complexes of South American Indian origin myths, both linked to male adolescent initiation, one from the extreme southeast of the continent, and the other from the tropical forest area of the northwest Amazon and central Brazil. Bamberger has described these as "myths of matriarchy" and "myths about the Rule of Women" for they focus on an account of how women in the beginning controlled sacred knowledge, and made men raise manioc, do the domestic work and take their orders (Bamberger, 1974). In other versions men originally were dominant, but women seized the sacred objects and took control. In both variants, the men attacked the women and gained (regained) control of the sacred objects, thus ensuring their control over women's labour and their subservience and establishing the natural order of dominance which continues today. The Ona myth (Tierra del Fuego) described by Bridges on the basis of his own initiation (early 20th century) contains the main features of the set:

In the days when all the forest was evergreen, . . . in the days when the Sun and Moon walked the earth as man and wife . . . in those far off days witchcraft was known only by the women of Ona-land. They kept their own particular lodge, which no man dared approach. The girls, as they neared womanhood, were instructed in the magic arts, learning how to bring sickness and even death to all those who displeased them.

The men lived in abject fear and subjection. Certainly they had bows and arrows with which to supply the camp with meat, yet, they asked, what use were such weapons against witchcraft and sickness? As this tyranny of the women became worse, the men decided to kill off all the women; "and there ensued a great massacre, from which not one woman escaped in human form." After this debacle the men were forced to wait to replace their wives until young girl children matured. Meanwhile the question arose: how could men keep the upper hand now they had got it? One day, when these girl children reached maturity, they might band together and regain their old ascendancy. To forestall this, the men inaugurated a secret society of their own and banished forever the women's Lodge in which so many wicked plots had been hatched against them. No woman was allowed to come near the Hain (men's Lodge) on penalty of death . . . (Quoted from Bridges, 1948, pp. 412–413 in Bamberger, 1974, p. 270)

From the Amazon Barasana Indians of a quite distinct culture area, Stephen Hugh-Jones recorded the following myth:

1. Romi Kumu's father, Poison Anaconda, told his sons to get up early and go down to the river to bathe, vomit water and play the *He* (sacred flutes).
2. In the morning the sons stayed in bed but Romi Kumu got up early and went down to the river where she found the *He*.
3. (Variant: the women/woman did not know what to do with the Yurupary (flutes). They put them over all the orifices of their bodies but not in their mouths. Finally a fish, jacunda (*Crenicichla sp.*) showed them what to do by signalling with its big mouth.)
4. The father was at first pleased when he heard the noise of *He* but when he saw his sons still asleep he realized what had happened and was very angry.

5. The men ran down to the port but Romi Kumu had already gone, taking the *He* and all other sacred equipment of the men with her.
6. They chased after her, following the sound of the *He*, but each time they got near she ran off again. She walked along the rivers and one can still see her footprints (carved) on the rocks in the Pira-Pirana area. There the men caught up with her and took back the *He* and ritual equipment.
7. The men punished Romi Kumu and the other women by making them menstruate. (Variant: When the women stole the Yurupary they talked a lot and were drunk. The men attacked the women and rammed the instruments up their vaginas.)
8. When the women stole the *He* from the men, the men became like women: they worked in the manioc gardens producing manioc, they had a bend in their forearms like women, and they menstruated. (S. Hugh-Jones, 1979, pp. 265–266.)

Hugh-Jones comments that the version he has given here is:

> in some respects a "weak" version: in most of the versions told to me it was stated that when the women were in possession of the *He*, the men did not merely cultivate manioc but were also subject to the political dominance of women. This theme of social revolution in which women overthrow the power of men is common to all the versions of the Yurupary myth from the Vaupes-Incana region and is also widespread amongst the Indian groups of lowland South America. (S. Hugh-Jones, 1979, p. 127)

Throughout the areas where these myths are the basis of the cosmology, explaining the power of the sacred flutes and providing the basis for male initiation, it is forbidden for women even to see the flutes, and transgression was punished by death. Whether this is accounted for by the women's original crimes (witchcraft, bringing disorder) or by the crime of usurping male power by stealing the ritual instruments and "contaminating their sacredness by viewing or touching them" (Bamberger, 1974, p. 274), women are shown to be dangerous and bad. Women are described as lazy, insatiably curious, greedy, promiscuous, and unable to keep secrets. They are "naturally" this way, and thus incapable of holding power effectively. Hugh-Jones says that the Barasana believe that if women did see the sacred flutes they would come to have the same ritual knowledge and power as men, and there would be a period of chaos when people fought each other. It is to avoid this that women are kept away. In both the Amazonian and the Fuegian myths the theme of punishing the women is very clear. In the Ona myth all adult women are killed; in the Barasana myth they are subjected to gang rape and have the flutes rammed up their vaginas. And of course today punishment awaits any woman (or girl) who looks at the sacred flutes, or intrudes in the men's initiation rituals. The anchorage of this moral weakness in the natural order is also clear. The fact that women menstruate and that they are totally excluded from ritual knowledge "proves" that the myth is about the true relation between men and women. It is wrong for women to have either secular or ritual power; they were punished for taking it once and will be punished again should they attempt to assert equality with men. This much is clear from the texts, and from the threats ensuring the continued exclusion of women from the rituals that accompany recitation of the myths. However, Hugh-Jones does not consider that the Barasana see these as myths and rituals about morality:

> Sin, to me, smacks of a universal morality which seems to be lacking in Amazonia. Morality is always contextually defined. I can think of no context in which women as a class are deemed sinful or immoral. . . . I don't really think that women's subordination is their own *fault* (except in the marginal sense of them failing to win a battle for supernatural power). (S. Hugh-Jones, 1985)

This highlights the need to distinguish between the actors' view (which Hugh-Jones expresses), and an analytical interpretation (on which he and I differ). For I would contend that at an analytical level the Barasana myth does describe punishment in the sense of "To afflict with pain, loss or suffering for a crime or fault" (*Webster's Collegiate Dictionary*) when it describes "failing to win a battle . . ." as followed by "The men attacked the women and rammed the instruments (the sacred flutes) up their vaginas" (S. Hugh-Jones, 1979, p. 266). In the other version Hugh-Jones gives, his translation of the myth reads: "(7) The men punished Romi Kumu and the other women by making them menstruate" (p. 266). In the myth, then, the women's action in seizing the sacred flutes is explicitly judged as wrong in that the men are described as "punishing" the women by making them menstruate. This is a judgement on all women, as a class, since it is all women who must, forever afterwards, menstruate, and not just the few who seized the sacred flutes. Hugh-Jones' comment raises sharply the question of whether it is appropriate to speak of morality outside of the framework of a universalistic ethic. His translation of the Barasana myth suggests that here, at least, it is necessary to find some way of expressing the idea of transgression and punishment. But this also raises another question: What defined the action of the women as meriting punishment? His comment suggests that if the women had won the battle for supernatural power instead of losing it, they would have not been in the wrong. At least they would not have been punished! It was winning, "Might" that defined who was "Right." Now an interesting common feature of both the Amazonian myths and the Ona myth is that when men decided to take the super-natural power away from women they were able to do so because they were stronger. This equation of dominant physical force and legitimacy is quite explicit, and it is further reinforced by the sanctions which main-tain the now legitimate male dominance: If, today, women attempt to regain control over the supernatural sources of power, they will be raped or killed because the men are stronger and can do so. Significantly, here male force is linked to the normative social order. Men act together in defense of what (as the myths have demonstrated) is the correct distribution of power and authority.

The Amazonian myths are, however, too rich to be reduced to a two-dimensional silhouette of force and morality. Accounts of Barasana myths (S. Hugh-Jones, 1979, 1985) and Mundurucu myths (R. Murphy, 1958; Murphy & Murphy, 1974; Nadelson, 1981) emphasize that only women have the sacred power to reproduce humans. They are seen by men as full of uncontrolled power – to menstruate and to make babies – both of which are not open to human control. Men fear this mystical power of women, which is seen as linked to their power to grow veg-etable food, and feel that it threatens their secular control over politics, community relations and the women themselves. "Men have a neurosis about the insecurity of their control and dominance over women" (Hugh-Jones, 1985). Sanday's probing study makes the same link between the reproductive powers of women, their critical influence over the growth of crops, and the fear and respect in which they are held by men (1981). And indeed, these myths are about this very fear: that women will cease to accept male domination and use their own kind of power to seize formal authority from men. In this connection Hugh-Jones writes: "I would read the myths as saying that it is only through their aggressive exertions that men came to have power" and of the Ona myth, "What the women did was to practice witchcraft (which men do today). What was amoral was that *women* [my ital.] used such power, not the power itself" (Hugh-Jones, 1985). Men's fear of women's non-formal power seems to be a key theme in the wider problem of relations between force, legitimacy and the denigration of women.

Australian Aborigines: Origin myths and male initiation rites

Extended male initiation at puberty is even more central to Aboriginal society than for the South American Indian peoples. It typically involves a period of several weeks or even longer during which youths are taken by the men apart from the women, their mothers, and ritually "killed," taught sacred lore, and finally "reborn" as men. The rituals are performed to a mythical score which gives symbolic, and sometimes explicit meaning to what is taking place. There seem to be two basic variants of these myths, both of which provide a model for the killing and rebirth of the youths. In the first, for which Warner's account of the Murngin myth serves as a paradigmatic example (Warner, 1937, pp. 250–259),[4] two women, one pregnant, the other with a child, both by incestuous unions, wander over the earth giving names to plants, animals and natural features. The women pollute a sacred water hole with the blood of childbirth and menstruation, which insults the great Yurlunggur serpent who emerges to swallow the women and their sons. Later the serpent regurgitates them into an ants' nest where the stings revive them. In the second variant a woman (two) is entrusted with the care of (her/others') children but eats them. When the men discover what has happened they kill the women and find ritual means to revive their sons. The following Murinbata myth associated with the Punji rite (recorded by Stanner) provides an example:

The people said to Mutingga, the Old Woman: "We shall leave the children with you while we find honey; you look after them." She agreed, and the people went off to hunt. After the children had bathed, they settled down to sleep near her. Bringing one close on the pretext of looking for lice, she swallowed it. Then she swallowed the others, ten altogether, and left.

A man and his wife returned to the camp for water and realized what must have happened. They gave the alarm, and the others came back. Ten men set off in pursuit and eventually overtook Mutingga crawling along a river bed. A left-handed man speared her through the legs and a right-handed man broke her neck with a club. Then they cut her belly open and found the children still alive in her womb. They had not gone where the excrement is. The men cleaned and adorned the children and took them back to the camp. Their mothers cried with joy on seeing them and hit themselves until the blood flowed. (Stanner, 1959–63, pp. 40–42, quoted in Hiatt, 1975, p. 151).

There are many themes in these myths and the associated initiation rituals.[5] However, the one I wish to stress here is that in both forms of myth which provide charters for the adolescent initiation ceremonies, women are punished for abominable behaviour – pollution of sacred sites, incest, cannibalism – and in addition to the actual culprits being killed, all women are subsequently and forever deprived of control of their adult sons. That is (1) women are punished because they are/were evil; and (2) the initiation of their sons by men and the complete exclusion of women from this ritual which forms the basis of sacred knowledge serves to deprive women of the possibility of aligning their sons with them against their fathers. There is here a double sense in which women cause trouble, first by failing to respect the rules of decent society (against pollution, incest, cannibalism), and second by trying to seize power through their sons. Obviously, women can't be trusted (Hiatt, 1975, p. 156).

As further versions are recorded and analyzed the Wawilak myth emerges as even more rich and complex. Knight has recently argued that there are two different "messages" in this myth: In one the serpent represents the force of male dominance which controls women, and represents a phallus, male rule and possible rape. The two sisters pollute a male sacred site and are sexually punished as a result. "This is certainly the story which the women are supposed to swallow and it is also the message which most social anthropologists appear to have accepted more or less at face value" (1983, p. 25). However, there is another "inner" message according to Knight's analysis, for he contends that the myth conveys different messages to the uninitiated – women and children – and to the initiated – men. The message for the initiated men is that the women have tremendous power, through menstruation and the ability to bear children, and that they must be kept in ignorance of this power, and under control by men. Women are doubly dangerous, because of the potency of their blood and reproductive activity as individual women, and because if they realized their power they might act together, as men do, seize men's ritual and secular power, and reverse the entire natural order of male dominance.

To return to herrschaft and the problem of evil, perhaps it is precisely because men fear this reproductive potency women have as a source of power greater than their own that myths portray women as unfit to hold socially significant power. This has been persuasively argued at the level of individual psychodynamics by B. and J. W. M. Whiting (1965, 1975) and Y. and R. F. Murphy (1974): Each male needs to deny his childhood dependence on an identification with his mother, i.e., her overwhelming power; myth and ritual support this denial and establish adult male identity on the basis of "natural" and supernatural dominance of men over women.

This combination of myths about the overthrow of women's power in which women are punished for wrong or dangerous behaviour, and where there is also evidence that men greatly fear and respect women's reproductive power, occurs widely in aboriginal South America and Australia, and both Hugh-Jones and Hiatt comment on the strong parallels with New Guinea material.[6] Why should men in these societies particularly need to buttress their male identity and authority with myth and initiation ritual and the moral discrediting of women? La Fontaine suggests that these are societies in which there is very little institutionalized male hierarchy, but constant competition among men for preeminence (1985). In other words, control over women's power becomes the focus of fear, myth and ritual when dominance between men is unstructured, and therefore contested. This view parallels closely the picture which emerges from a consideration of witchcraft in Africa.

African witchcraft

There are two main models for African witchcraft patterns. One is the evil witch who kills and injures relatives, including her own children, from malice, jealousy and greed, or because of blood debts to the coven. The second is the socially responsible witch who uses mystical powers in defense of the group, often to repel attacks by evil witches. Tiv elders, Azande princes and Gonja chiefs are all "known" to be "good" witches in this sense. Now clearly it is not possible to use (mystical) power on behalf of the community unless one is recognized as acting on behalf of the community. Thus Azande commoners were accused of witchcraft and required to renounce the attack on a particular victim, but princes were not accused in this way.[7]

In West African traditional societies, when serious illness, misfortune or death occurs, a diviner is consulted to discover the cause and what may be done. If the verdict was that an evil witch was responsible there were in pre-Colonial times several forms of counteraction possible. One was an ordeal which killed the guilty and exonerated the innocent. Another (still common) was to place the person under the control of a shrine believed to be mystically powerful enough to turn the attacks against the witch herself. Sometimes there was a form of judicial process followed by driving the witch out of the community, or by execution.[8] Significantly, the forms of ordeal (throwing a bound witch into the river; reaching into boiling oil) and forms of execution (burning alive) resemble strongly medieval European practices. Few can have survived the ordeals and the manner of the witches' deaths clearly represents exaction of vengeance against a feared and hated enemy.

When I began fieldwork in Gonja (northern Ghana) I had no intention of studying witchcraft, but was forced to respond to the deep concern of the people themselves to what was for them a constant threat. The picture which emerged was of men who boasted of being witches – and were therefore powerful and to be feared and given way to; and of women who were terrified of being accused of witchcraft, since it meant at best ostracism or flight from their home village, and possible death. These were not imaginary fears. I was involved, as bystander, witness, and in one case unwitting cause of a jealous attack, in many witchcraft incidents. All of those defined as evil (*libi*), in that they led to direct accusations and to counteraction, concerned women witches. I began to ask the women: "Why is it women who are bad witches?" (For women accuse each other, along with the men; bad witches are seen as a threat to all.) "Because," they said, "we are evil." And they went on to recount the various antisocial feelings which they knew themselves to have: jealousy of co-wives, and co-wives' children, resentment of neglectful husbands, anger against kin for favouring others or for not supporting them. The inevitable strains of social interdependency are here attributed to women, as part of their "nature"; women are likely to have evil feelings and motives, they are bad witches because of their feelings and motives, and the fact that they are identified in divination as responsible for illness and death "proves" them as evil. (See E. N. Goody, 1970.)[9]

On the other hand, men in positions of political and often ritual power are "known" to be witches. They may boast of these powers in claiming rights to office, and competition for office may be carried out partly on the level of (assertions of) mystical attack and counterattack. Thus the Gonja say that no man can succeed in becoming chief unless he is a strong witch, and when a chief dies it is assumed that a rival's witchcraft overcame his own. My records of witchcraft episodes linked to men include attribution in gossip of specific deaths within the community to chiefs and to Muslim scholars. But no direct accusations were made, and no counteraction taken against them. These chiefly witches are not "evil." They are believed to need strong mystical powers to defend their people against the attacks of evil witches, both outside and within the community. Similarly, in Tiv society, which has no formal political offices, the elders are believed to meet at night as witches and may even sometimes kill and eat a member of their own lineage in order to maintain their powers of defense against outside attack (Bohannan & Bohannan, 1953). The striking thing about male witches in these societies is that there is no attempt to say that they do not use the same forms of mystical aggression (mystical poison, invisible arrows that travel many miles to seek their target,[10] the power to change shape, etc.) as those for which evil witches are blamed and killed. But when these forms of mystical aggression are used, they are seen as attributes of office, or the struggle for office, and become a source of reputation and legitimate political power.

In these societies mystical aggressive powers used by men are proof of political authority; used by women they are frightening, dangerous, and so evil that they lead to the execution of the female witch by methods that are in many cases extremely sadistic.[11] There are also African societies in which male witches are feared and become the object of counteraction. In Azande, male commoners, i.e., those who do not hold legitimating positions in the political system, are required to blow on a chicken wing as proof that they will cease their attacks. However, it is striking that Azande male witches were not, apparently, exiled or executed, even when they were thought responsible for a death. Rather, counter witchcraft was used against them – the battle played out on the mystical plane.

There is another very interesting set of societies in which mystical powers are sometimes legitimate and sometimes not. These tend to be systems in which lineage office exists, but is weakly developed; lineage heads are recognized, and they have quite specific powers over junior lineage members, including control over critical economic resources. However, the process of succession to these lineage offices is linked to lineage fission, and thus gives rise to regular succession crises (Cewa, Lugbara). Accusations of witchcraft tend to focus on competitors for lineage authority. Here, to accuse a man of witchcraft is to accuse him of illegitimate mystical attack, and thus to dispute his *right* to the contested office, and indeed, his right to split the lineage. Where mystical powers are considered legitimate, as in the invocation by the head of the Lugbara family cluster of the ghosts of his patrilineal ancestors, it is not categorized as witchcraft – although Lugbara use the same word (*ole*) for both ghost invocation and witchcraft.[12] Significantly, the close followers of a man accused of witchcraft may not define his actions as witchcraft at all, and thus can continue to support their candidate (Lugbara). In these societies witchcraft itself is evil, and what is at issue is whether a given act is an expression of witchcraft powers (evil) or of legitimate authority (strong/good).

If we map the male/female dichotomy onto the distinction between evil and good mystical powers, and see these in relation to the holding of office, the model is roughly:

Women No offices;
 evil witchcraft;
 severe punishment.

Men (i) Succession to office weakly defined, linked to lineage fission. Mystical aggression used in competition for power is situationally defined; "witchraft" is evil.

Men (ii) Clearly defined offices; political system not based on lineages. Male officials expect to use mystical power. Witchcraft in competition for office = fair fighting.

The underlying pattern here seems to be that holders of clearly legitimate authority can use dangerous powers safely because there is a structural assumption (the legitimacy of office) that they are acting in the public good. If those who are competing for power in a fluid system use dangerous (mystical) weapons, their allies will consider this evidence of strength, and fair, but their enemies will consider it wicked and antisocial. The position of women is particularly interesting here, because there are very few situations in which anyone considers their use of dangerous (mystical) power as evidence of legitimate strength used for the social good. On the contrary, they risk being branded as evil witches, exile or execution.

Although Gonja obviously represents only one kind of African system, it is a particularly interesting case for the present problem because there are a few political and ritual offices for women. The model for the legitimacy of male mystical power suggests that women holding office should be either free to use mystical power legitimately or perhaps expected not to need it. However, case material shows clearly that office-holding women are sometimes thought to have killed with witchcraft. When this happened they were ostracized and terrified, but were not killed (though this was in the 1960s when executions for witchcraft had been prevented for 50 years). While their offices may have cushioned them from the full force of counteraction against evil witches, they clearly did not gain strength and political legitimacy from being recognized as witches, as male officials still do today.[13] For women, then, the structural assumption of legitimacy provided by office does not work. In Gonja, women who use mystical power are evil, whatever their position in the politico-jural structure. It is as though men may use mystical power safely if they have the right position in a political structure that defines authority roles and succession to these clearly. It is dangerous for men to use mystical power (which is of course difficult to observe and control) where the political system itself is loosely structured and competition between men for power threatens the stability of constituent elements of the system. This leads to situational legitimacy: "The ancestors are acting for us: You are using witchcraft." But there are virtually *no* conditions of structural legitimacy that permit women to use mystical power. The same logic would argue that in some way for women to be allowed mystical power *always* is experienced as threatening to the stability of the society.

Most African societies seem not to have myths of origin which justify the subordination of women as do those of South America and the Australian aboriginals. However, the reservation of the legitimate use of mystical power for men, and the hysteria surrounding the evil witchcraft of women, carries much the same underlying message. Women cannot hold legitimate power; women who try to exercise power are evil.[14]

The Judeo-Christian tradition

From the examples considered so far – South American Indians, Australian aborigines, African tribes – it might seem that it is only preliterate small-scale societies in which the ideology of legitimate power was based on the premise that women are originally or fundamentally anti-social or evil, and therefore, necessarily excluded from authority outside of the domestic domain. Surely the most widely disseminated myth of this sort is that of the Judeo–Christian tradition. As it is set out in the Book of Genesis, on the sixth day of creation God made man in his own image, and put him in the garden of Eden to care for it, admonishing him not to eat of the tree of knowledge of good and evil. Then seeing that the man was alone, he took one of his ribs and made a woman as "a helpmate for him." Man, who had named all the creatures God had created, then named his helpmate, "woman" because she was taken out of "man" (Heb. *ishshah*, from Heb. *ish*). But the serpent, who was more subtle than any other of the wild creatures God had made, told Eve that nothing bad would happen to her if she ate the forbidden fruit, but that if she ate she would become like God, knowing good and evil. So Eve was tempted, and she took the fruit and ate; and she also gave some to her husband and he ate. "Then the eyes of both were opened, and they knew they were naked; and they sewed fig leaves together and made themselves aprons" (thus the beginning of culture). And God punished the serpent, and Eve and Adam.

Eve's punishment was that although she will bear children in suffering, yet "her desire shall be for her husband and he shall rule over her." Adam's punishment was perpetual toil to wrest daily food from the harsh soil, for God drove him from the garden of Eden "lest he put forth his hand and take also of the tree of life, and eat and live forever." (Genesis 2: 3).

If this account is taken literally, Eve was the cause of all the later sufferings of men and women, because she listened to the subtle serpent, and then led her husband astray. Man explains his disobedience to God by saying, "The woman whom thou gavest to be with me, she gave me of the tree, and I did eat." The issue between God and his creatures is control. Man is punished for disobedience by toil and expulsion from Eden. Eve is punished for being foolish *and* disobedient, and placed under the control of man. She was the cause of the original sin because she acted independently, under the control of neither man nor God. God's reason for driving them from Eden is the fear that they may, having knowledge, also eat of the tree of life, thus gaining immortality as well. Since man was made in the image of God initially, with knowledge and immortality also there would be no difference between man and God, and no possibility for God to control man (or man/woman?).

But notice that in the text that has come down to us in the Bible, while God responds to this disobedience by driving man out of the garden of

Eden ("God sent him forth from the garden of Eden, . . . he drove out the man" . . .) he places man firmly in control of women. As Sanday notes in her stimulating essay on the formation of the Christian tradition (1981, Epilogue) later Christian writers took up this theme and were more explicit. In a letter to Timothy, Paul admonishes:

> Let a woman learn in silence with full submissiveness. I do not allow any woman to teach or to exercise authority over a man; she is to remain silent, for Adam was formed first, and then Eve and furthermore, Adam was not deceived, but the woman was utterly seduced into sin . . . (2 Timothy 2: 11–14).

And Paul wrote to the Corinthians: "But I want you to understand that in the head of every man is Christ, the head of woman is her husband and the head of Christ is God" (1 Corinthians 11: 3), while elsewhere in the New Testament it is simply written, "Let the wife see that she fear her husband."

Research on recently discovered Gnostic texts suggests that this strong masculine dominance of the established New Testament was only achieved by suppressing other texts, and indeed demoting Mary Magdalene from the status of disciple to passive follower (the Gospel of Philip, the gospel of Mary, in Pagels, 1979). The relative egalitarianism of the Gnostics, who allowed women to read the scriptures and preach in religious services and to conduct rituals, was fiercely contested by the orthodox Christians. The North African theologian Tertullian (c. 190 A.D.) considered the religious activities of women among the Gnostics as actions of heretics. By the late second century, "Orthodox Christians came to accept the domination of men over women as the proper, God-given order – not only for the human race, but also for the (internal hierarchy) of the Christian churches." (Pagels, quoted in Sanday, 1981, p. 229).

Christianity, then, has taken the Genesis myth of Eve's foolishness, guile and original sin (she ate the apple first), as a charter for firmly legitimating the control of a wife by her husband, and of women by men (as in the organization of the churches). For a brief moment Eve had knowledge and power equal to God's but her possession of them was the supreme sin, and the cause of all subsequent human suffering. This absolves both man ("The woman whom thou gavest to me, she gave me of the tree and I did eat") and God ("Because you have listened to the voice of your wife . . ."). But the early Christians seem to have reenacted the scenario, as the emerging orthodoxy and hierarchy of church authority excluded women from any role in the conduct of religious observances, and relegated them again to the authority of their husbands. From sharing in the conduct of the new religion, women became only objects of control, by conscience, by priests, and of course, by their husbands who conducted the family services (e.g., Morgan, 1944). It has been persuasively argued that the linking in Christian teachings through the centuries of legitimate authority of husband over wife to Eve's betrayal has formed the implicit basis for our attitudes today (Dobash & Dobash, 1979).

Interpreting the "messages" of ideology

There is a striking parallel in the nature of Eve's sin – which gave humans knowledge that ought to have been reserved for God – with the South American myths which tell of the time when women controlled ritual knowledge (which had to be rescued from them), and in a somewhat different way with the African premise that women who have mystical knowledge of witchcraft must be using it for evil. What is portrayed as dangerous is the possession of knowledge by those who ought to be subordinate. Clearly knowledge is power. And significantly, it is power which does not depend on physical strength, so that if women control knowledge this would challenge the physical advantage men hold.

In looking at the relationship between domination and ideology it is useful to distinguish between:

- the current function of ideology in relation to existing patterns of domination.
- how an ideology comes to be formulated. (Preliterate cases must be treated separately from those in literate societies.)
- how an ideology comes to be institutionalized – made "official" (i.e., encapsulated in myth, or made the basis for public justification of action).

Each of these is a separate, and major, problem. They are set out here, not because it is presumed to resolve them, but to avoid confusing the comments relevant to different ones.

The contemporary functions of this sort of ideology, once it is established, are clear. It serves to justify and to reinforce the domination of men in several ways: (1) It means that in a given relationship domination is not an individual, arbitrary control, nor, often, is it seen as the way of a particular community or society. It is pre-ordained, "natural," "the will of God" (Ortner, 1974; Ortner & Whitehead, 1981; Beteille, 1983). (2) It is thus impossible to conceive of altering the balance of power. This is so in a very literal sense – it is impossible to *think* otherwise. The conceptual tools and premises preempt alternative formulations. (3) For those who are dominated it leads to acquiescence, to the acceptance of the inevitable, and quite possibly to less resentment and pain than if *de facto* domination were combined with an ideology of equality. This would be a clear example of what Beteille has called a disharmonic system (1983). (4) Very probably less actual power differential is necessary to maintain dominance where it is reinforced in this way by an ideology (harmonic system) than when it is not (disharmonic system). (5) Other, more specific functions can be worked out for particular cases. Bamburger's paper on South American Indian "myths of matriarchy" sets out several (Bamburger, 1974).

However, the very interesting questions of how such belief systems come into being, and how they come to be institutionalized as the "official view" of things are much more difficult. One problem is that it is impossible to watch the emergence and institutionalization of beliefs in any particular simple society. At a given time certain beliefs are already "official" and we don't really know how to identify emergent ones. Nor, if we look at contemporary societies and reason backwards as to how it might have been, can we do more than speculate? It is probably not fruitful to look for general answers. But in particular cases there may be hints from observing contemporary, but parallel, situations, particularly if this observation is combined with comparative analysis of the same phenomenon in many different societies. What general patterns have appeared in the cases so far considered?

- In these several sets of societies men are in fact dominant over women in the sense of managing political, religious and economic affairs outside the household, and in the sense of being "head of the household" – the one who gives orders and is deferred to. In most (all?) of these societies men "chastise" their women physically when they deem it necessary.

- There is a belief system, cosmology, or set of ideas about causes of misfortune which defines women as at best weak and foolish, and in some cases as basically, naturally, sinful or evil.
- Men have legitimate authority roles, and women's power, where it is acknowledged, is frightening (Amazonia, Australia) or evil (African witchcraft). *De facto* male domination over women in these systems is thus justified morally.

The fact that this association of legitimate male power and the non-legitimacy, or even wickedness, of female power recurs so frequently suggests that it is generated by the interaction between men and women in widely different societies, independently of different cultural frames. Or rather, that the cultural frames emerge to give form to this aspect of the interaction. What are the dynamics here? Fortunately this is an instance in which detailed studies of a relevant contemporary phenomenon are available.

Power and legitimacy in conjugal relations in contemporary Western society

Since the 1970s, both in England and in the United States, there has been a growing concern about cases of violence against women by the men they live with. In England this led to a Parliamentary Select Committee on Violence in Marriage whose report in 1975 laid the basis for national legislation specifically designed to provide legal protection for women who were victims of domestic violence. There has since then been considerable research on this problem in these countries, but the authors of a recent international study of family violence could find little data elsewhere except in Canada (Gelles & Cornell, 1983). There is anecdotal evidence that violence against wives has been an obvious occurrence since the early middle ages in Europe (Dobash & Dobash, 1979) and since the 18th century in the United States (Dobash & Dobash, 1979; Moore, 1979). It is impossible to know whether the recent upsurge of interest is due to generally greater awareness of women's issues, or whether there has been an increase in domestic violence. It seems very probable that growing emphasis on sexual equality makes conjugal violence more frequent (because of conflicting expectations of the two spouses) and less tolerable to the victim.

The question of the incidence of physical violence in current marriages is no less difficult. Research-based projections vary from 50–60% of all couples in the U.S. (Straus, Gelles, & Steinmetz, 1980) to 21% of ever-married women based on a large California sample (Russell, 1982). Much of the difference between those two figures can be attributed to differences in definitions used; however, both were based on random samples of the general population.[15] These are figures for women beaten at least once by a husband or co-habitee. There is reason to believe that a single beating can permanently structure the nature of a conjugal relationship by establishing the husband's physical dominance, and thus the inevitable outcome of any future confrontation (Gelles, 1972). Within this context it is necessary to distinguish between couples who have experienced one or two episodes of violence and those in which violence has become an established pattern. In a few marriages the wife is subjected to frequent, or even daily, beatings – which may escalate in severity (Dobash & Dobash, 1979); it is women subjected to repeated injury and who remain in this violent situation who are referred to in the literature, and by the media, as "battered wives." It is quite impossible to calculate the incidence of regularly violent marriages. The usual source of information is case material from victims which cannot be related to the wider population. Police reports can provide incidence of violence in relation to a given population, but the level of unreported cases is so high (the Dobash study estimated 2 out of 98 were reported to police) that they cannot be used reliably. There are clues: repeated physical violence is cited between 17% and 57% in various studies of women seeking divorce (Moore, 1979; Levinger, 1966). And both in Britain and the United States, refuges for battered wives seeking to leave the marriage are extremely overcrowded; newly opened refuges fill up immediately and often have waiting lists before they open their doors (Moore, 1979).

The definitions used in collecting and analysing data in one national American study suggested that wives also used violence against husbands frequently, leading to discussion of a "battered husband syndrome" (Straus, et al., 1980; Steinmetz, 1977, 1978). This has not proved a robust finding; the type of violence used by wives is significantly less severe; husbands do not take wifely violence seriously much of the time

(Adler, 1981), serious attacks by women are almost always in self-defense, and it is women, not men who are seriously injured or killed in domestic disputes. For instance in a study of police cases of family violence in one year in Scotland, the Dobashes found males to be the aggressors and females the victims in 94% of the cases (Dobash & Dobash, 1978).

In violence between spouses . . . usually the male is the stronger and is only the victim when this physical advantage is negated by use of weapons, or more frequently, he refrains from using his full strength . . . it is rare for the male to be the victim and once he releases his full physical force inhibition and even resorts to weapons, few women stand a chance. (Gayford, 1983, p. 124).

Some researchers argue that verbal aggression is as damaging to wives as overt physical violence. In terms of the importance for women of a sense of competence in domestic/conjugal roles, this could be so, since a sense of competence can be verbally destroyed. However, the consequences of being physically beaten up by a person with whom she is in direct daily interaction must be separately assessed. Gelles quotes from a long interview with an American couple who asserted proudly that they never fought, but where an allusion is made to a single occasion at the beginning of the marriage when the husband became so angry that he "had to do something" and did beat his wife. Since then, he said, she had never challenged him, and they had lived on excellent terms. One confrontation established the physical dominance of the husband, and thereafter conflict was avoided by the wife's submission (Gelles, 1972). This corresponds with ethological descriptions of the establishment of dominance hierarchies among many species, from chickens to chimpanzees. Among humans it is probable that play during adolescence teaches girls that males are stronger, and that therefore many conjugal relationships never include a direct challenge or physical confrontation at all.

It is clearly important to distinguish between the implicit premise of male physical dominance, which may operate in many non-violent marriages or those in which violence is occasional, and the routinized violence of wife battering in which this dominance is acted out. In a sense the myths and theologies legitimating male power over women may act to make this premise explicit *and link it to the legitimate moral order.* That it is not fully legitimate in our society is indicated by the titles of recent books on violence against wives: *Scream Quietly or the Neighbors will Hear You* (Pizzey, 1974) and *Behind Closed Doors* (Straus et al., 1980). The feminist movement generally sees conjugal violence as arising from what they term our patriarchal society. In other words, it is because men are dominant in the social institutions that they consider it legitimate to use physical violence against their wives if they want to. The failure of the (male dominated) society to prevent them itself acts to reinforce their view that this is right. At this level we are in the same situation as when seeking to understand societies in which origin myths and witchcraft beliefs already "in place" reinforce the system of male dominance.

In fact, one must agree with this analysis as far as it goes. It is clear from studies of police response, and from court records showing how few are the cases of wife assault brought to court, and of these, how few result in conviction of the husband, that it is extremely rare for "society" to act against a violent husband, even when serious injury has been done (Farragher, 1985; Freeman, 1979, 1985; Johnson, 1985; Paterson, 1979). And there is plenty of confirmation in interview material that some violent men really do consider that "My home is my castle and in it I can do as I please" (Frankenberg, 1977; see also Dobash & Dobash, 1979).[16]

The dynamics of extreme domestic violence

However, my puzzlement about the link between morality and force began with the women of Gonja who themselves said, "We are evil." The interest of recent research on domestic violence lies in a striking parallel. For one of the themes to appear constantly is that after an initial period of disbelief, and of hoping that the husband's violence is a temporary aberration, the woman comes to expect and accept it (in the sense that she realizes that it is a permanent part of the conjugal relationship) and frequently she concludes she must be in some way to blame. Of course part of the reason for accepting blame is that the husband tends to link his violence with accusations and complaints. These focus repeatedly on two things: sexual infidelity and domestic failure. Sexual jealousy is likely to precipitate a beating when the wife is not allowed to leave the house even to visit her mother, as well as when she moves freely outside the home. And domestic crimes include failing to keep dinner hot until midnight, or allowing the baby to cry. Very often in the interview material the wife will insist that she has not been unfaithful, and that whatever she does, the husband complains about her cooking or the care of the children. I am not here concerned with whether these allegations are in fact true; the significant thing is that they are so frequently part of the pattern of conjugal violence. Perhaps even more significant, those very women who say that they have not done the things their husbands accuse them of still feel that the *situation* is in some way their fault; that it is somehow up to them to "make the marriage work" and that in marrying they have "made their bed and must lie in it" (folk phrase quoted in interviews both from the United States and the United Kingdom).[17] For many of these women this sense of guilt lies behind their failure to leave a domestic situation in which they are regularly injured by the husband. It also makes it impossible for some to seek help from kin or to take the children back to their natal family. Indeed, it is this sense of desperation, and of having nowhere to turn among family and friends, that accounts in part for the flooding of women into refuges. Despite the discomfort of overcrowded conditions, women say of living in the refuge that it was a tremendous relief because there they found others who had similar experiences, and at least they realized that they were not in the wrong. Those who run the refuges say that one of the main problems for these victims of extreme domestic violence is their terrible lack of self-confidence. It is difficult for them to do anything constructive when they first arrive. They cannot deal effectively with officials – from the social services, housing department, school – and they do not have the confidence to find work.[18] Several recent studies of domestic violence discuss this crippling sense of guilt (Pagelow, 1984; Morgan, 1982).

This sense of guilt and lack of confidence probably has at least three sources, all relevant for a model of domination. First, there is the element of cultural norms and family norms. Our society does expect women to put up with difficulties to make a marriage work (see above). In fact failure may well cause a deeper sense of personal inadequacy in a society with a strong norm of egalitarian and companionate marriage than where women expect husbands to be physically dominant and this matches reality. For at least a few, their own parents' marriage provided a model of marital violence, so they may see it as "normal."[19] But even these women feel they are supposed to be able to "make it work," and as they cannot cope, they have obviously failed. If husbands are "naturally" violent, they should be able to handle this without going to pieces. Either way it is their fault. This of course takes us back to the same position we were in with the preliterate cases. How does a society come to generate such norms?

This aspect is linked to a second, which is the nature of the roles which women define as goals. During the first half of this century, girls were raised to expect to marry and have a family. They wanted to do this, and most of them did so. "Wife" and "mother" were core roles. While those less well-off may have had to work, very few had careers. I would suggest that it is axiomatic that a person's sense of competence is closely linked to his/her ability to perform to their own and others' satisfaction in core roles. Thus, when a woman feels she has failed to make a go of her marriage, it isn't only a matter of the particular interpersonal relations involved. It is her social identity which has been destroyed. It might be argued that a man must also realize his marriage has been unsuccessful if he constantly "has to" beat his wife. But of course he may see this as the proper expression of *his* role as a dominant male, and in some societies this is so, e.g., in the Mediterranean (Loizos, 1978). Even assuming that the husband does feel his marriage is a failure, the conjugal role is far less central for men than it is for women. I am not suggesting that it is unimportant, only that in terms of social roles comprising the social persona, it is less central. There is, in our society, a real sense in which for a man it is a personal failure, but not a social failure.[20] Thus in society's terms a woman has indeed "failed" in not finding herself an effective conjugal/maternal/domestic role, where a man has not defaulted on his main core roles in the same way. The question begged by this formulation is whether domestic roles are central for women in all societies, and whether if they are universally so, this centrality is best viewed as a social or a biological phenomenon? These questions have been the subject of much recent scholarship and to discuss them adequately is not possible in the space available (see Brown, 1970; Divale & Harris, 1976; La Fontaine, 1981; Maccoby, 1966; Ortner, 1974; Ortner & Whitehead, 1981; Parker & Parker, 1979; Reiter, 1975; Rosaldo & Lamphere, 1974; Sanday, 1973, 1981; van den Berge & Barash, 1977, etc.). My own view is that biology sets constraints that, like the grit in an oyster, produce complex and amazing responses which, as ideologies and institutions in turn shape social roles, including the division of labour. The optimal female reproductive strategy of maintaining claims on a man for support and protection in order to maximize successful investment in her few children (Hinde, 1984), would certainly make both wife and mother roles central on a species-wide basis. But even on the most immediate level, one would have to argue that where women's core social role *is* the conjugal domestic role, then women are highly vulnerable in situations where they cannot fill this role effectively. Thus when a husband complains, the wife is more threatened in terms of social competence than if a wife complains about the role performance of her husband. Incidentally, the non-legitimacy of women's complaints is nicely caught by the stereotype of the "nagging" wife, i.e., the irritating repetition of the same comment or request (presumably because the husband has not responded).

The very widespread acceptance that women have a duty to succeed in the conjugal role is reflected in the view not infrequently expressed by social workers, as well as by police, that women who are the victims of conjugal violence "bring it on themselves." This refers particularly to "provocative" behavior – taunting or indirect aggression, including verbal aggression – which so annoys the spouse that he loses his temper and hits his wife. They say that such women enjoy the excitement of a fight, and even perhaps in a masochistic way, enjoy being injured. A surprising recent advocate of this position is Erin Pizzey, a pioneer in England of women's refuges (Pizzey & Shapiro, 1982). All these people, social workers, police, and certainly someone as intimately involved with victims of violent husbands as Pizzey, are speaking from close and extended familiarity with conjugal violence. Yet this argument has a strong similarity to the beliefs in simple societies that "women are naturally weak and unable to keep secrets, quarrelsome." What is the reality to which this modern version of "women are evil" corresponds?

It is useful here to distinguish between two (admittedly related) problems: (1) Why are men more violent towards their spouses than their wives are towards them? (2) How do women living with violent men manage this violence? One view (Pizzey, etc.) is that a man would not hit a wife unless provoked, which implies that women initiate the fights in which they are battered. However, given male aggressiveness in warfare, hunting, street gangs, not to mention rape, this seems unlikely as an explanation for more than a small proportion of domestic violence. If we can for the moment accept the view which is increasingly well documented, that men are more prone to aggressive response than women

(Konner, 1982; Maccoby & Jacklin, 1974; Parker & Parker, 1979), then it seems more useful to consider that the answer to the first question lies, at least in part, in the realm of biology.[21] Men are more likely to respond aggressively to frustration than women, and when they do, they are likely to "win" a fight with a woman, which reinforces the aggressive response. When women do start a fight they are likely to get hurt, and this tends to inhibit them from overt violence the next time they are angry. This may be linked to the folk observation that women are more likely to use verbal than physical aggression.[22]

There are hints in the studies of domestic violence that something more complex is also occurring; that men may regularly inhibit the urge to hit out at their wives when angry – perhaps because they sense the injury this might cause (Adler, 1981, quoted in Pagelow, 1984; Gayford, 1983). However, when a dispute escalates, perhaps with an exchange of verbal attacks, a man's inhibition may fail, leading him to "release his full physical force without inhibition and even resort to weapons, [when] few women stand a chance" (Gayford, 1983).

If this pattern were to prove general it would support the suggestion that there is a premise of male physical dominance in conjugal relations. But it would also indicate that we should focus on the psychological and social mechanisms of inhibition which prevent male force being "released without inhibition" in most marriages, most of the time. For it must be emphasized that in any given society the level of physical force used by men within marriage is a result of the interplay between social norms and social structural pressures and constraints on the one hand, and male biology, on the other. Psychological mechanisms of inhibition presumably emerge from the interaction of these two types of constraint.

When norms, social structural pressures, and failure of inhibition do act together in our society to produce recurrent violence by a man, how can the wife manage this situation? The more obvious possible modes of response would seem to be:

1. **Withdrawal** – she may leave the situation. In socio-cultural terms this means conjugal separation or divorce.
2. **Submission**
   (a) This may lead to established male dominance, but avoid conjugal violence.

(b) Or it may lead to routinization of male violence, with the woman remaining in the situation "because of the children" or "because it is up to her to make the marriage work," or because she lacks the resources and confidence to leave. Probably the single most consistent finding in study after study of conjugal violence is that women who are subject to regular physical attack remain, often for many years, in this situation. It is this which leads to the view that in some way they must "like it" and even encourage it.

3. **Fighting back** – this is likely to lead to chronic fighting, since sources of conflict are endemic in the domestic situation.

(a) In a situation of chronic violence every index indicates that it is the women who are most likely to be hurt. Where this happens repeatedly the women may become cowed and demoralized, and adopt the submissive mode (2a) above.

(b) Some women refuse either to leave or to submit, and perhaps as a means of self-respect, try to fight back. They may do this verbally (with taunts and arguments) and they may risk physical combat. If, as Pizzey argues, women find this confrontation exhilarating as well as painful, are they so different in this from boxers or soldiers? Yet we celebrate the courage of these male roles, but denigrate women who defend themselves. It is also likely that a woman's failure to be submissive stimulates her husband to further aggression, and she is again likely to get hurt, but now we can see that she has indeed "brought it on herself."

It is important in considering how these different alternatives might affect women's domestic strategies to be aware of their variable consequences. Submission does not guarantee the avoidance of male violence, but it may achieve this goal. Fighting back may not save a woman from getting beaten up, but she may have self-confidence in addition to the bruises. While there is probably a strong tendency towards routinization of one mode of response (Dobash & Dobash, 1979), there can also be a shift from one mode to another, as when the consequences of fighting back become too painful, and a woman becomes submissive; or when a woman who has passively put up with violence for years finally decides to leave. I am not arguing that one mode of response is "better" or "worse" and indeed the only "correct" response is to engage external social support against male violence, simply because it is physically dangerous to women. But the different modes of response have interesting implications for the problem of institutionalization of beliefs about the illegitimacy of female power. If one looks at the societies already discussed in this paper, certain patterns emerge.

Withdrawal from violent conjugal relationships. Sometimes women are allowed to initiate divorce, but this is relatively uncommon. Among Amazonian Indians men may forceably keep their wives from returning home, a situation sometimes related to exchange marriages. Some African societies permit women to divorce, others do not. Judaism and Christianity have fought keenly against divorce. But even where divorce is legally available the importance of the roles of wife and mother, and the absence of resources for maintaining the household apart from the husband, force many women to remain in a violent marriage (Dobash & Dobash, 1979; Freeman, 1979; Homer, Leonard & Taylor, 1985; Martin, 1979; Pagelow, 1984). The difficulty and importance of being able to withdraw from a violent marriage are reflected in the high level of demand for refuges (UK)/shelters (USA) in which women can live while trying to establish an alternative life.

Submission. If all women are defined as "naturally" subordinate to all men, then the dominance hierarchy is fixed and not subject to contest. This may in fact support male inhibition of the use of force against women. It is by far the most common solution on a cross-cultural basis. This fact is reflected not only in the belief systems described here, but in the many legal systems in which women are jural minors. While the institutionalization of submission, and the elaboration of belief systems which validate submission, do not prevent male violence against wives, they do remove one source of challenge, fighting back, which clearly sometimes elicits violence. Thus the institutionalization of submission is one kind of society-level response to male physical strength as this affects the domestic situation.

Fighting back. Very few societies treat it as legitimate for a woman to "fight back" against a husband. This prohibition is achieved in many ways: by the community closing ranks against any woman who does so;

by legal rules; by norms which hold that a man has the right to "chastise" his wife for disobedience; and by belief systems which deny the legitimacy of female power. Our society is highly ambivalent on this score. While we claim that men and women are equal, representatives of the normative order – police and social workers – frequently consider that if a woman fights back, or even tries to escape a violent home, she is in some way morally at fault.

There is a third aspect of women's sense of guilt and lack of self-confidence arising from the very fact that in the violent domestic situation, Might is Right. If a woman knows that she is likely to be hit for doing what her husband says is "wrong," then she will inevitably try to avoid the pain which follows if she does "wrong." This creates a situation in which her husband comes to define what is "right" and what is "wrong" for her in a purely pragmatic sense. Here I would recall the finding that men explain their violence as a response to their wives' faults (inedible food, failure to prepare meals on time, failure to keep the children from crying and flirting or promiscuity). A woman in this situation will attempt to have a hot meal ready for her husband at whatever hour he chooses to return; taking it as her responsibility to make the marriage work, and seeing her domestic role as central, she can believe that it is perfectly reasonable for her husband to demand this. In other words, violent men in part use their physical power to enforce their definitions of right and wrong, and their wives may come to accept this situation. Such a physically constructed definition comes to be used as a criterion for the wife's behavior, both by her husband and by the wife herself. Have we here a model for the shaping of belief and myth? In any case we have one model for the formation of consensus within the domestic group. (There are clearly others, and of course only a small minority of couples live in a violent relationship.) But where domestic groups are open (see Goody, 1973) and domestic life is closely keyed to external political and ritual forms (Fortes, 1958; Goody, 1973; Hugh-Jones, 1979; La Fontaine, 1981) domestic consensus tends quickly to generalize and become group consensus. Thus it is in the very preliterate societies I have described that such a model would also apply to the construction of group norms about definition of right and wrong.

But why do men trouble to justify the beating of a wife if indeed a man is free to do as he pleases in his own home? Obviously male freedom to behave as they choose is not complete, and it is by invoking norms which he believes are shared by the wider society (a wife should not be promiscuous, a wife should cook for her husband) that a man seeks approval for his actions. So there is a further twist. These husbands want both the power to define what is right within the family, and they want it to be recognized that they are *right* to do so. They want to be approved of, and to feel that they are behaving as a husband should. Case material also makes it plain that despite their violent behaviour, most of them want to retain the affection of their wives. So they need to convince themselves, their wives, and others that what they do is right.

Hinde has argued (1985) that this pattern of behavior is best explained by the constraints of the optimal male reproductive strategy. This conclusion requires that men make sure that their wives are not unfaithful, since although there is no doubt as to the genetic mother of a child, a husband cannot be sure he is the father of his wife's children. A husband who suspects that his wife might have an interest in other men will thus seek to restrain her and punish any infidelity severely. Male sexual jealousy clearly is adaptive in this sense over the long-evolutionary term; adaptive for men. But it is hard to see that it is adaptive *for women* either to be denied legitimate power in small-scale societies or to be subjected to regular physical violence in some traditional societies and a small proportion of households in our own society. The only way in which institutionalized subordination might be adaptive for women is if it acted to reduce male violence (which may indeed by the case). Subordination only helps women achieve their own goals of support and protection while rearing their children because men are in a position to enforce their demands of male control. If one were to speculate on the origins of the moderately greater strength and aggressiveness of human males compared to females, one possibility would be that the pressure for these attributes from male hunting and warfare (Divale & Harris, 1976; van den Berge & Barash, 1977) was balanced for women by an advantage for those who, being smaller and passive, did not elicit violence by challenging their men. If women were physically stronger than men, would the Barasana myth tell of the overthrow of women, who for the good of the society were deprived of their sacred flutes, punished and returned to their rightful place as cultivators of manioc, and the ones who menstruate and bear and rear children?

Notes

This paper was originally written for the History and Anthropology Round Table III, *Domination as Social Practice*, although I was unable at the last minute to be present. I would like to thank particularly the discussant, Barbara Duden, for the time she took over her thoughtful comments, and in corresponding about them. The notes of the discussion, and comments from Alf Ludtke and Hans Medick also gave me much food for thought. Realizing that the points I wanted to make raised other, much debated, issues, I also prevailed on a number of other colleagues to look at the paper critically. Several of the comments have led to substantial changes. The various critics will no doubt recognize the points they raised; if they have not been satisfactorily dealt with, the responsibility is mine, not theirs, but for their time and ideas I would like to thank Michael Cole, Robert Hinde, Jack Goody, Stephen Hugh-Jones, Jean La Fontaine, Penelope Roberts, Joan Stevenson-Hinde and Marilyn Strathern. Some of the points apparently ignored really deserve separate papers of their own; others have been definitively handled by published work, to which I can add nothing.

1. See R. A. Hinde, 1979, pp. 193–210 for an overview of learning theory from a perspective which seeks to set the individual processes of learning in the context of social relationships. There is increasing evidence that substantial learning takes place independently of direct reward or punishment. Hinde calls this "exposure learning" but notes that this covers several different forms. Much shaping of behaviour occurs through subliminal cues (Bruner, 1974, 1975; Trevarthan, 1974; Goody, 1978). Indeed attention itself may serve as a reward (Chance, 1975). If the reward/punishment format is extended in this way, as seems necessary in looking at social relationships, then it seems to underlie a good deal of human learning, as well as to have been picked up and built on in the social institutions of every society.

2. The universality of male dominance is of course a function of the way in which dominance is defined. I am specifically concerned here with the holding of positions of legitimate authority and control in the political and economic system; with those who formally organize and manage political and economic activities. This form of domination is widely acknowledged to be virtually universal, even by those who argue that women hold other kinds of power (e.g., Ardener, 1975; Rogers, 1975; Sanday, 1993). If women hold other, informal types of power – as they often do – this raises for me the question of why it is women (not men) for whom power is "muted," "masked," "informal," etc. As I shall argue in the body of this paper, the view of Divale and Harris seems difficult to dispute: "The most obvious explanation (for the male supremacist complex) is that institutionalized male supremacy is the direct product of genetically determined human sexual dimorphism which endows males with taller stature, heavier musculature, and more of the hormones that are useful for aggression." (1976, p. 526). However, like others who have come to this conclusion (e.g., Parker & Parker, 1979) they go on to consider other questions instead of asking what are the implications for institutions and relationships of this fact.

3. This may be racial or ethnic or based on the supposed inheritance of lower intelligence or inferior skills or moral constitution.

4. Since Warner's early publication (1937), Berndt (1951) and others have recorded other versions, and many scholars have commented on the corpus, among whom Meggitt (1967), Hiatt (1975) and Knight (1983) are particularly useful.

5. They might almost be seen as a sort of Anthropological Rorschak, allowing projection of the preoccupations of a wide range of scholars: Radcliffe-Brown (1926, 1930) pointed to the ubiquity of the rainbow serpent in Australian myths linked with initiation rites; Warner stressed the close association between the myth and the initiation ritual; Levi-Strauss argues that the double division of society into male/female and initiated males/uninitiated males is, throughout Australia, a solution to the contradictions of social organization (1966); and Hiatt sees the symbolism of swallowing and regurgitating (by serpents or women) as providing an idiom for male control of initiation on the model of normal parturition (1975).

6. There is not the space to consider this material here, but M. Strathern's work, for instance, describes the fear and distrust with which women in Mt. Hagen are regarded, as expressed in the belief that a woman can kill her husband by polluting his food with her menstrual fluids, and that wives may indeed do this because of loyalty to their natal clan (Strathern, 1972). Here again women are inherently dangerous and evil, though Strathern's work makes clear that attitudes towards women are complex, and also contain strong positive elements (1981).

7. This distinction between "bad" and "good" witches is an analytic one that is not necessarily reflected in the terminology used in a given society. Rather it is based on whether or not the community treats the verdict of witchcraft in a particular instance as a cause for direct accusation and counteraction, or on the contrary, the reputation for witchcraft power adds to the political or ritual stature of the "witch." This is argued fully in E. N. Goody, 1970. In *Gbanyito* there is a single word, *egbe*, for "witch" which refers to any person using certain kinds of mystical aggressive power, whether male or female, and whether for social, or anti-social ends. Other African languages distinguish between mystical aggression using powers internal to the attacker (witchcraft) and that which employs external weapons (sorcery). The English popular usage that makes witches female and sorcerers male has elements of the associations: female = illegitimate, evil power; male = legitimate, good power – which are reflected in the Gonja tolerance for male witchcraft.

8. European Colonial authorities forbade the execution of witches, which placed great strain on communities in which people "knew" that a witch was killing them. A variety of new forms of counteraction have evolved generally referred to as "witchfinding cults." These focus on identifying the witch and providing some form of purification ritual by which her witchcraft powers are destroyed and she is made safe to live with. (See for instance Douglas, 1963.)

9. It has been argued that women are seen as witches in patrilineal societies because, due to rules of exogamy, they are married into their husband's lineage from other descent groups. Such "foreign" wives are potentially hostile strangers with dangerous access to secrets of their husband's descent group and enduring loyalties to their

natal lineage. However, evil witches are also mainly women among the matrilineal Ashanti and the non-unilineal Gonja. This suggests that while the divided loyalties of a wife may lead to fear and hostility, there are other factors beside descent group affiliation involved.

10. The prototype of heat-seeking missiles?

11. Even 50 years after the legal ending of executions people graphically described a variety of forms of execution for female witches: sealing the witch into a room filled with the smoke of burning red peppers; placing the witch's head in a red-hot cast iron pot filled with red peppers; placing her on a fire in a deep pit; stabbing her with a sharpened stick of a special wood. Part of the elaborateness of these executions was due to the belief that witches were difficult to really kill. But there is a strong element also of sadism. I concluded that when a woman killed a close relative, everyone – kin and neighbors – felt a fear and revulsion based on the intrusion of lethal aggression into a relationship of supposed trust (see E. N. Goody, 1970).

12. The Gonja word, *egbe*, refers to both good and evil witches. (See Middleton, 1963.)

13. Details of these cases are given in E. N. Goody, 1970.

14. Sanday (1981) and Rosaldo (1974) have discussed the difference between power and authority in the context of sex roles. I do not completely agree with the focus on decision making, but the issue is a difficult one. Sanday, by including informal power, avoids what is for me a critical distinction between power and authority, i.e., the legitimacy of the latter, but not the former. It is the very non-formality of much of the power exercised by women which makes it difficult for men to be sure of their control. Where male power is the legitimate authority, this makes female power at best non-legitimate. If men are operating as they often do, on an implicit premise of male control, then it is very threatening not to be able to control women's informal power. It may well be that this is the dynamic behind the male perception of women's power as somehow illegitimate or evil.

15. Other studies generating intermediate figures (e.g., Walker, 1979, 50%; Frieze, 1980, 35%) have either been based on counseling, work with women in refuges, or studies with small samples and matched controls.

16. In fact this view is an atypical one, in the sense that in most societies there are strong norms which limit the harm which one individual is free to do to another, and which are enforced within the community, either at the level of the extended kin group or the local neighborhood. If, indeed, domestic violence is more prevalent today in the West than in many other societies, it is almost certainly because of the extraordinary isolation of the family from anchorage in such local level constraints.

17. The police and the courts tend to see it as their duty "to sustain the sanctity of marriage." by reconciling a quarreling couple and reinforcing the authority of the husband to "chastise" his wife (see particularly Freeman, 1979, 1985; Pahl, 1982; Paterson, 1979). The only person a woman in this situation may feel able to talk to is her doctor. A recent study showed that very few doctors feel able to advise them, and that the regular response is a prescription for tranquilizers. While from the

doctor's point of view this may be intended to allow the woman to keep going in a difficult situation, women tend to see this as further proof of their own inadequacy (Borkowski, Murch, & Walker, 1983; Johnson, 1985).

18. Walker (1979) has suggested that this inability to find a way out of the violent situation may be due to what Seligman has called "learned helplessness" (Seligman, 1976). Seligman found that animals who were repeatedly punished in a situation from which they could not escape later failed to leave the painful situation when there was nothing preventing them. He links the lethargy and maladaptive behavior of these animals to the human syndrome of depression in a provocative and much cited study. Morgan (1982) and Pagelow (1984) make this same association.

19. This suggestion has been made on the basis of case material, so it does sometimes happen. However, a recent review of studies relevant to the possible intergenerational transmission of violence concluded: "The vast majority of woman batterers do not come from homes where they were beaten, and the vast majority of men who were beaten as children do not beat their wives." (Stark & Flitcraft, 1985) Straus et al. concluded from their U.S. national interview survey that "the majority of today's violent couples are those who were brought up by parents who were violent to each other" (1980). However, serious difficulties have been found with this study (Dobash & Dobash, 1979) and Stark & Flitcraft point out that the same data shows that while a boy who witnessed wife-battering is three times as likely to beat his wife now, a current batterer is more than twice as likely to have had a non-violent as a violent home in childhood. One of the difficulties in assessing the extent of modeling of wife-battering from a violent family is the lack of longitudinal studies. Such modeling in all probability does occur sometimes.

20. Hinde suggests that this is probably true in all human societies (personal communication). However, in many tribal societies men must marry and show that they can manage and support a household before they can participate in the external politico-jural domain. Here the simple male conjugal role is a requirement for valued male political and economic roles. A man who repeatedly fails to keep a wife will experience social as well as personal failure (E. Goody, 1973 and fieldnotes; La Fontaine, 1981). In other societies the sexual division of labor is so linked to marriage that it is not possible to function in adult economic roles unless also married. These are cases in which for men the conjugal role is a prerequisite to core adult male roles: It is not actually being a husband and father which is central in itself. In this sense Hinde is probably correct.

21. Recent reviews and analyses of the literature on sex differences (Maccoby, 1966; Maccoby & Jacklin, 1974; Parker & Parker, 1979) have convincingly argued the basic dimorphism characteristics of size, strength, and aggression-enhancing hormones. Analyses reaching such different conclusions as Sanday (1981) and Divale & Harris (1976) agree in seeing males as dominant in hunting and warfare in the long period when homo sapiens survived as hunters and gatherers. The latter conclude that "central to the sexual distribution of power is the fact that almost everywhere men

monopolize the weapons of war as well as weapons of the hunt" (1976, p. 524). They further argue that it is only by assuming the advantage to preindustrial societies of rearing the largest number of fierce and aggressive warriors that the widespread imbalance in sex ratios in favor of males can be explained.

A very different sort of evidence occurs in the totally different way in which homosexuality is structured in men's and women's prisons. In men's prisons males challenge each other with aggressive demands for homosexual services. The only possible responses (Toch, 1977) are (a) to fight the man who demands sex, (b) to flee and seek protection from the prison guards, (c) to give in and provide homosexual service. This leads to a high level of violence, a very high level of anxiety about being caught and raped (by a single inmate or by several) and a situation in which every gesture is scanned for sexual and aggressive implications. Giving in leads to a crisis of sexual identity, and of self-worth and ability to function outside the prison. Giving in also leads to being labeled as a homosexual which is closely linked to being weak and powerless, and so carries the risk of further attacks, both aggressive and sexual.

Gialombardo also found a preoccupation with homosexuality in women's prisons (1966, 1974). However, there is virtually no aggression associated with homosexual soliciting in women's prisons. Instead there is an elaborate culture of courtship, marriage ritual, in some prisons there are rules for divorce, and kinship systems which include incest rules prohibiting sexual relationships between "brother" and "sister," "father" and "daughter," "mother" and "son." Incest rules "had" to be invented because of the sexual jealousy between women over the same "man." If two individuals of opposite prison gender were seen alone together, it was likely to be assumed that there was a sexual relationship involved. The only way to avoid jealousy was to define the relationship in close kinship terms which rendered a sexual relationship impossible.

However, there is clearly tremendous variation among members of each sex in their adaptation to biology and the cultural institutions which it generates. There is presumably variability among both males and females in strength, stature, and hormonal levels as with other physiological characteristics. Both developmental interactions and social norms (cultural, sub-cultural and familial) will differentially reinforce aggressive responses on this initially variable base. Thus individual men must vary greatly in readiness to express aggression and this is further differentiated by the response pattern of the spouse. In addition to this complex individual variation, the relationship between external stress – in work finances, unemployment, peer conflicts, etc. – and aggressive responses in the conjugal relationship need to be understood.

22. The analysis of projective material in boys' and girls' stories in a study in northern Ghana showed boys significantly more aggressive on measures of extreme aggression, physical aggression and mystical aggression, but the girls were higher on measures of verbal aggression. (Goody, 1982). Where males are likely to win an open fight and it is illegitimate for females to physically confront males (as in Gonja) verbal aggression may be the only safe form for females.

References

Adler, E. S. (1981). The underside of married life: Power, influence and violence. In L. H. Bowker (Ed.), *Women and crime in America*. New York.

Ardener, E. (1975). Belief and the problem of women. In S. Ardener (Ed.), *Perceiving women*. New York.

Bamberger, J. (1974). The myth of matriarchy: Why men rule in primitive society. In M. Z. Rosaldo & L. Lamphere (Eds.), *Women, culture and society*. Stanford.

van den Berge, P. L., & Barash, D. P. (1977). Inclusive fitness and human family structure. *American Anthropologist, 72*, 1073–1078.

Berndt, R. M. (1951). *Kunapipi: A study of an Australian aboriginal religious cult*. Melbourne.

Beteille, A. (1983). *The idea of natural inequality and other essays*. Delhi.

Blau, P. (1968). Social exchange. *International Encyclopedia of the Social Sciences, 7*, 452–457.

Bohannan, L., & Bohannan, P. (1953). *The Tiv of Central Nigeria*. London.

Borkowski, M. M., Murch, M., & Walker, V. (1983). *Marital violence: The community response*. London.

Bridges, S. L. (1948). *Uttermost ends of the earth*. London.

Brown, J. K. (1970). A note on the division of labour by sex. *American Anthropologist, 72*, 1073–1078.

Bruner, J. S. (1974, 1975). From communication to language: A psychological perspective. *Cognition, 3*, 255–287.

Chagnon, N. (1968). *Yanomamo: The fierce people*. New York.

Chance, M. R. A. (1975) Social cohesion and the structure of attention. In R. Fox (Ed.), *Biosocial anthropology*. London.

Divale, W. T., & Harris, M. (1976). Population, warfare and the male supremecist complex. *American Anthropologist, 78*, 521–528.

Dobash, R. E., & Dobash, R. P. (1978). Wives: The "appropriate victims" of marital violence. *Victimology, 2* (3–4), 426–442.

Dobash, R.E., & Dobash, R. P. (1979). *Violence against wives*. New York.

Douglas, M. (1963). Techniques of sorcery control in Central Africa. In J. Middleton & E. H. Winter (Eds.), *Witchcraft and sorcery in East Africa*. London.

Evans-Pritchard, E. E. (1940). *The Nuer*. Oxford.

Farragher, T. (1985). The police response to violence against women in the home. In J. Pahl (Ed.), *Private violence and public policy*. London.

Fortes, M. F. (1958). Introduction. In J. R. Goody (Ed.), *The developmental cycle in domestic groups*. Cambridge.

Frankenberg, R. (1977). *Battered women's project: Interim Report*. Keele.

Freeman, M. D. A. (1979). *Violence in the home*. Westmead, Hants.

Freeman, M. D. A. (1985). Doing his best to sustain the sanctity of marriage. In N. Johnson (Ed.), *Marital violence*. London.

Friedl, E. (1975). *Women and men*. New York.

Frieze, I. H. (1980). *Causes and consequences of marital rape.* Paper presented to the annual meeting of the American Psychological Association, Montreal.

Gayford, J. J. (1983). Battered wives. In R. J. Gelles & C. P. Cornell (Eds.), *International perspectives on family violence.* Lexington, MA.

Gelles, R. J. (1972). *The violent home: A study of physical aggression between husbands and wives.* London.

Gelles, R. J., & Cornell, P. C. (Eds.). (1983). *International perspectives on family violence.* Lexington, MA.

Gialombardo, R. (1966). *Society of women: A study of a women's prison.* New York.

Gialombardo, R. (1974). *The social world of imprisoned girls.* London.

Goody, E. N. (1970). Legitimate and illegitimate aggression in a West African state. In M. Douglas (Ed.), *Witchcraft confessions and accusations.* London.

Goody, E. N. (1973). *Contexts of kinship.* Cambridge.

Goody, E. N. (1978). Introduction. In E. Goody (Ed.), *Questions and politeness.* Cambridge.

Goody, E. N. (1982). *Parenthood and social reproduction.* Cambridge.

Goody, J. R., & Tambiah, S. J. (1973). *Bridewealth and dowry.* Cambridge.

Hart, C., & Pilling, A. (1960). *The Tiwi of Northern Australia.* New York.

Hiatt, L. R. (1975). Swallowing and regurgitation in Australian myth and rite. In L. R. Hiatt (Ed.), *Australian aboriginal mythology.* Sidney.

Hinde, R. A. (1979). *Towards understanding relationships.* London.

Hinde, R. A. (1984). Why do the sexes behave differently in close relationships? *Journal of Social and Personal Relationships, 1,* 471–501.

Hinde, R. A. (1985). (Personal communication).

Homans, G. C. (1958). Social behavior as exchange. *American Journal of Sociology. 63,* 597–606.

Homer, M., Leonard, A., & Taylor, P. (1985). The burden of dependency. In N. Johnson (Ed.), *Marital violence.* London.

Hugh-Jones, C. (1979). *From the milk river.* Cambridge.

Hugh-Jones, S. (1979). *The palm and the Pleiades.* Cambridge.

Hugh-Jones, S. (1985). (Personal communication).

Johnson, N. (Ed.) (1985). *Marital violence.* London.

Johnson, N. (1985). Police, social work and medical response to battered women. In N. Johnson (Ed.), *Marital violence.* London.

Kaberry, P. (1952). *Women of the grasslands.* London.

Keiser, R. L. (1969). *The vice lords: Warriors of the streets.* New York.

Knight, C. (1983). Levi-Strauss and the dragon: Mythologiques reconsidered in light of an Australian myth. *Manual of Natural Sciences, 18* (1), 21–50.

Konner, M. (1982). *The tangled wing: Biological constraints on the human spirit.* London.

La Fontaine, J. S. (1981). The domestication of the savage mind. *Manual of Natural Sciences, 16,* 333–349.

La Fontaine, J. S. (1985). (Personal communication).

Lee, R. B. (1968). What hunters do for a living, or how to make out on scarce resources. In R. B. Lee & I. DeVore (Eds.), *Man the hunter.* Chicago.

Levinger, G. (1966). Sources of marital dissatisfaction among applicants for divorce. *American Journal of Orthopsychiatry*, *36*.

Levi-Strauss, C. (1966). *The savage mind*. London.

Levi-Strauss, C. (1969). *The elementary structures of kinship*. R. Needham (Ed.). J. H. Bell & J. R. von Sturmer (Trans.). Boston.

Loizos, P. (1978). Violence and the family: Some Mediterranean examples. In J. Martin (Ed.), *Violence and the family*. Chester.

Maccoby, E. E. (Ed.) (1966). *The development of sex differences*. Stanford.

Maccoby, E. E., & Jacklin, C. N. (1974). *The psychology of sex differences*. Stanford.

Martin, D. (1979). What keeps a woman captive in a violent relationship? In D. D. Moore (Ed.), *Battered women*. London.

Meggitt, M. J. (1967). *Gadjari among the Walbiri aborigines of central Australia*. Sidney.

Middleton, J. (1960). *Lugbara religion*. London.

Middleton, J. (1963). Witchcraft and sorcery in Lugbara. In J. Middleton & E. H. Winter (Eds.), *Witchcraft and sorcery in east Africa*. London.

Moore, D. M. (Ed.). (1979). Introduction. *Battered women*. London.

Morgan, E. S. (1944). *The Puritan family*. Boston.

Morgan, S. M. (1982). *Conjugal terrorism: A psychological and community treatment model of wife abuse*. R. & E. Research, Palo Alto.

Murphy, R. (1958). *Mundurucu religion*. Berkeley.

Murphy, Y., & Murphy, R. (1974). *Women of the forest*. New York.

Nadelson, L. (1981). Pigs, women and the men's house in Amazonia: An analysis of six Mundurucu myths. In S. B. Ortner & H. Whitehead (Eds.), *Sexual meanings*. Cambridge.

Ortner, S. (1974). Is female to male as nature is to culture? In M. Z. Rosaldo & L. Lamphere (Eds.), *Women, culture and society*. Stanford.

Ortner, S., & Whitehead, H. (Eds.). (1981). *Sexual meanings*. Cambridge.

Ortner, S., & Whitehead, H. (Eds.). (1981). Introduction. In S. Ortner & H. Whitehead (Eds.), *Sexual meanings*. Cambridge.

Pagelow, M. D. (1984). *Family violence*. New York.

Pagelow, M. D. (1985). The battered husband syndrome: Social problem or much about little? In N. Johnson (Ed.), *Marital violence*. London.

Pagels, E. H. (1979). *The Gnostic gospels*. New York.

Pahl, J. (1978). *A refuge for battered women*. London.

Pahl, J. (1982, November). The police response to marital violence. *Journal of Social Welfare Law*.

Parker, S., & Parker, H. (1979). The myth of male superiority: Rise and demise. *American Anthropologist*, *81*, 289–309.

Paterson, E. J. (1979). How the legal system responds to battered women. In D. M. Moore (Ed.), *Battered women*. London.

Pizzey, E. (1974). *Scream quietly or the neighbours will hear you*. London.

Pizzey, E., & Shapiro, J. (1982). *Prone to violence*. Feltham, Middlesex.

Radcliffe-Brown, A. R. (1926). The rainbow-serpent myth of Australia. *J.R.A.I.*, *56*, 19–25.

Radcliffe-Brown, A. R. (1930). The rainbow-serpent myth in south-east Australia. *Oceania*, *1* (3), 342–347.

Reiter, R. (Ed.) (1975). *Towards an anthropology of women*. New York.

Rogers, S. C. (1975). Female forms of power and the myth of male dominance: A model of female/male interaction in peasant society. *American Ethnologist*, *2*, 727–756.

Rosaldo, M. Z. (1974). Woman, culture and society. A theoretical overview. In M. Z. Rosaldo & L. Lamphere (Eds.), *Woman, culture and society*. Stanford.

Rosaldo, M. Z., & Lamphere, L. (Eds.) (1974). *Woman, culture and society*. Stanford.

Russell, E. H. (1982). *Rape in marriage*. New York.

Sanday, P. R. (1973). Toward a theory of the status of women. *American Anthropologist*, *75*, 1682–1700.

Sanday, P. R. (1981). *Female power and male dominance*. Cambridge.

Seligman, M. P. (1976). *Learned helplessness and depression in animals and men*. Morristown, NY.

Stanner, W. E. H. (1959–1963). *On aboriginal religion*. Sydney.

Stark, E., & Flitcraft, A. (1985). Woman-battering, child abuse and social heredity: What is the relationship? In N. Johnson (Ed.), *Marital violence*. London.

Steinmetz, S. K. (1977). Wife-beating, husband-beating: A comparison of the use of physical violence between spouses to resolve marital fights. In M. Roy (Ed.), *Battered women*. New York.

Steinmetz, S. K. (1978). The battered husband syndrome. *Victimology*, *2* (3/4), 499–509.

Strathern, M. (1972). *Women in between*. London.

Strathern, M. (1981). Self-interest and the social good: Some implications of Hagen gender imagery. In S. Ortner & H. Whitehead (Eds.), *Sexual meanings*. Cambridge.

Straus, M. A., Gelles, R. J., & Steinmetz, S. K. (1980). *Behind closed doors*. Garden City. NY.

Straus, M. A., & Hotaling, G. J. (Eds.). (1980). *The social causes of husband-wife violence*. Minneapolis.

Toch, H. (1977). *Living in prison: The ecology of survival*. New York.

Trevarthan, C. (1974). Conversations with a two-month-old. *New Scientist*, *62*, 230–235.

Walker, L. E. (1979). *The battered woman*. New York.

Warner, W. L. (1937). *A black civilization*. New York.

Whiting, B. B. (1965). Sex identity conflict and physical violence: A comparative study. *American Anthropologist*, *67*, (6. Part 2), 123–140. (Special publication).

Whiting, J. W. M., & Whiting, B. B. (1975). Aloofness and intimacy of husbands and wives. *Ethos*, *3*, 183–207.

33   Just say no: Responsibility and resistance

Bonnie E. Litowitz

Ever since Vygotsky (1978) we take it as axiomatic that all development appears twice or on two planes, first interpsychically (i.e., between two people) and then, intraphysically (i.e., within one person). The process by which inter- becomes intra- is called internalization or interiorization: what was once external becomes internal; for example, other-regulation becomes self-regulation.

Since the zone of proximal development is the difference between what the learners can do on their own and that which they can do in collaboration with a more knowledgeable other, the zone defines the space or range where learning takes place and internalization describes the process of learning that takes place there. Examples illustrating how this learning process works require two persons, one more knowledgeable than the other; usually a mother and child, but also a teacher and a student or an expert and a novice. These two persons working as a dyad approach a task or problem organized (sometimes called "scaffolded") in steps by the knowledgeable partner. The novice is directed through the steps in such a way that s/he can ultimately take over the whole sequence.

At first the novice will be carried in the task, given just one part to carry out and guided with questions. Gradually, however, more and more of the steps will be turned over to the novice until the novice shares the same organizational plan as the once-more-knowledgeable partner (Bruner, 1978). In the end, the unequal members of the dyad become equal participants. The non-knower becomes knower as well, able to take over responsibility for solving problems and completing tasks. Several

473

authors note that the movement from being carried in a task to becoming a full participant is capped by "taking responsibility" for a task. Nelson and Gruendel (1986) illustrate this point in a common occurrence in child development.

Getting dressed was relatively low for the younger children and high order for the older. It may be that, although both groups of children had had considerable experience with this routine, the 4-year-olds were *only beginning to take responsibility* for it themselves and thus to have to predict its details. To the extent that a person must plan ahead, the script must become much more reliably established and automatic. The younger children presumably had not yet reached this point (Nelson & Gruendel, 1986, p. 36; italics added).

Kaye (1982) also notes the gradual process of taking responsibility:

While the infant *takes on a slowly increasing share of the responsibility for the interaction*, other parts of his role are performed for him, or the parents merely pretend he is performing them. In effect, then, he never really achieves autonomy until he has become a member of the system, taking over functions that had been performed by the parent (Kaye, 1982, p. 226; italics added).

Bruner (1983) describes the earlier appearance of reciprocity in interactions between caretaker and child, who enter into formats or routines "contain[ing] demarcated roles that eventually become reversible" (p. 120). The distinction, however, between the reciprocity of equal partnership and the reversibility of equal responsibility has not been clarified. I will return to it below.

This scenario of sociocultural learning rests on two important presuppositions and raises two interesting questions: (1) The more knowledgeable member of the dyad is always performing two functions: solving the specific problem and teaching the novice how to solve the problem. Is there an innate pedagogical impulse in us?[1] (2) A child wants gradually to take on more and more of the adult's role in structuring tasks rather than just being carried or directed by another in them. Is there an innate need to master problems and perform tasks in just the ways more knowledgeable others do?

The unspoken acceptance of these presuppositions leads to descriptions of perfectly orchestrated dyads, moving smoothly through the stages of adult-teaching and child-learning with few exceptions. The positive intent of both participants is only rarely questioned (cf.: Henriques, Holloway, Urwin, Venn & Walkerdine, 1984, who confront the "voluntarism" of this approach); and similarly, the smooth efficiency is rarely doubted.[2] However, Goodnow (1987) is one writer who does so:

> My disappointment with the picture usually presented is that once again the world is benign and relatively neutral. To be more specific, the standard picture is one of willing teachers on the one hand and eager learners on the other. Where are the parents who do not see their role as one of imparting information and encouraging understanding? Where are the children who do not wish to learn or perform in the first place, or who regard as useless what the teaching adult is presenting (p. 15)?

When, as often happens, learning does not take place, we are left with two possible causes: either the adult did not create the right scaffold or the child was not able/did not choose to use the scaffolding provided. Such a child may be seen as deviant or even deficient in her or his ability to learn, requiring special structuring of tasks by an expert (e.g., a special educator). In the paper quoted above, Goodnow goes on to mention her own inability to learn how to type. Proficiency in such a skill would have identified her with a group of "girls who were expected not to do well academically" (Goodnow, 1987, p. 17). The cause of her inability was neither poor teaching methods nor lack of ability to use those methods. Rather she claims that "areas of knowledge and skill are differentially linked to one's social identity, and that the linkings can help account for both acceptance and resistance to learning" (ibid.).

This example points out two elements missing from discussions of the zone of proximal development and the learning theory based on internalization: identification and resistance. What motivates the children to master tasks is not the mastery itself but the desire to be the adult and/or to be the one whom the adult wants her or him to be. Such desires constitute identification with another person as described initially by Freud (1917, 1923) and elaborated more recently by Lacan (1977; see Henriques et al., 1984). Making the same point but from a sociological perspective Goodnow concludes:

> A link to social identity seems essential also in any Vygotskian account of negotiations toward a transfer of skill or a shared definition of a task. The negotiations one is willing to work on are likely to be those with people one perceives as similar, wishes to be like, or wishes to impress (1987, p. 18).

One assumes that Vygotsky would concur as he concludes *Thought and Language* with the following challenge:

To understand another's speech, it is not sufficient to understand his words – we must understand his thought. But even that is not enough – we must also know its motivation. No psychological analysis of an utterance is complete until that plane is reached (1986, p. 253).

The transfer of a skill or learning takes place through the process of internalization, exemplified in Vygotsky's insights concerning egocentric and inner speech (1986). The language of an other becomes our own when we speak to ourselves as others first spoke to us. Thus, as the child internalizes the language that structures the task, he becomes the one who speaks in that manner.[3] We know, following Vygotsky, that language as internalized social mediation changes not only the content but creates new processes and forms of thinking; indeed changes all high mental functioning (e.g., perception, memory). But not just cognitive structure is altered; psychosocial structure or *lichnost* (personality) becomes altered as well. We may say that as our inner speech is the internalized speech of others, our self is constituted by the internalized others who speak.

For this reason, however, we cannot assume a uniform internalized voice or only one way to transfer a skill. In an example of apprenticeship in skill learning, illustrating the zone of proximal development, Kaye observes:

The parental role . . . is [to] pose manageable subtasks one step at a time, and gradually pull that support away from [children] as their competence grows . . . When my father taught me to swim he backed away as I paddled toward him. I can remember crying that it was unfair – but 25 years later I did the same thing to my son . . . (1982, pp. 55–56).

Although Kaye offers this anecdote as an example of an innate pedagogical impulse, an identification with his own father and thus with how fathers behave is an alternate interpretation. I would argue that it is a preferable interpretation because there are so many counterexamples. What can we say about the father who pushes his son off into deep water with: "Swim! Your cousin Helene is a year younger than you and she already knows how to swim!" Was this father's goal to teach or to compete with his brother through their respective children? Yet children do learn via the sink or swim method, and there are undoubtedly a variety of preferred methods depending upon skill to be transferred as well as intercultural, intracultural and personal styles (Wertsch, Minick & Arns, 1984).

Ever since Bakhtin (1973, 1981) we take it as axiomatic that speech is heteroglossic or polyphonic; that is, speech is dialogic within itself. We are born into a language and internalize speech that has a history; it has its sources in many voices from many dialogues, making our speech in turn equally multiple. Bakhtin notes that "the ideological becoming of a human being . . . is the process of selectively assimilating the words of others" (1981, p. 341). Contradictions and conflicts arise among these internalized voices, not just inter-sociologically and ideologically, but also interpersonally. Speaking of the "intense interaction and struggle" within each utterance, Bakhtin states: "The utterance so conceived is a considerably more complex and dynamic organism than it appears when construed simply as a thing that articulates the intention of the person uttering it, which is to see the utterance as a direct, single-voiced vehicle for expression" (1981, p. 354). Such a view makes every speech act not only indirect but contradictory and conflictual.

Since these multiple voices are the source of our subjectivity, we are fractured and split ultrasubjectively, unable to speak with one voice (Lacan, 1977). In Goodnow's example above, the speech that structures learning how to type and the speech of the person who knows how to type, i.e., the one you will become if you internalize that knowledge, may contradict one another. And these contradictions do not yield so easily to sublation!

The zone of proximal development addresses how the child can alter her/his behavior by copying my behavior to become more like me. As such, its use can come perilously close to a description of learning as a neo-behavioristic shaping of behavior (viz: Nelson, 1986, p. 237). This is especially true when the adult's role is described as a series of care-fully arranged steps, teaching skill (e.g., "raise the ante," "communica-tive ratchet," "extension"), and when the child's contribution as tabula rasa is to absorb the language and structure input from the adult.

I have noted elsewhere (Litowitz, 1988) that the zone of proximal development is an adultocentric view of the child's behavior. As Good-now observes: "It is too exclusively concerned with what is being done by the dispensers of knowledge" (1987, p. 16). The child's perspective, I have suggested, can be captured by another spatial metaphor: Winnicott's potential space (1971). The potential space is the area that is neither what the child nor the mother knows. It is the range of the child's grandiosity and omnipotence. In that space the child sees her/himself as more capable than s/he really is. Like Vygotsky and the zone of proximal development, Winnicott connects the potential space to play, the use of symbols and creativity. Unlike Vygotsky, Winnicott notes its connection to fantasy and illusion. One could say that a child performing in the zone of proximal development with an adult feels her/himself to be accomplishing the task and that the adult's organizations of the task (what Winnicott calls the "holding environment") permits that illusion or fantasy.

A child psychoanalyst once asked me how psycholinguists explain why young children continue speaking when so much of what they produce is phonologically, grammatically and semantically in error: Don't they hear that they're wrong a lot of the time and don't they get discouraged? One answer is that the force of the innate preprogram of a universal grammar (LAD) will prevail and needs only minimal practice. Another is that errors are patterned and show rule acquisition; the child as little linguist must feel as positive about acquiring those rules as linguists are about positing them. Still another answer is that, by speaking, children feel like adults and hear themselves as more competent speakers. Children may tolerate their lack of structural competence as long as pragmatically they are using language as adults do, and thus using language to be adults. In fact, children do not feel incompetent unless adults interfere with their grandiose fantasy of enhanced performance.

Does the adult create the potential for that illusion through a pedagogical impulse or because s/he also has a fantasy? I think the latter: s/he believes that the child can be/is becoming just like her/him. Thus, identification defined as the process of *making similar* or *being like* (L. *idem*: same) goes in both directions, from child to adult as well as from adult to child. The role of parental fantasies is seldom noted (but see Kaye, 1982, pp. 189–203). The use of fantasy in creating goals for activities is inexplicably underappreciated in Vygotsky's theory of learning since it was Marx (in *Capital*) who claimed that the difference between the most talented bees and even inept architects is one of imagination and fantasy. So we might say that mothers are as grandiose and omnipotent in their expectations for their children as children are for themselves. One could even go further to state that fantasy will need to be better understood if the concept of a dyad is ever to transcend the personhood boundaries of its two separate participants. That is, only a distortion of reality (fantasy) allows one to treat another person as performing a function for oneself or as performing a function s/he is incapable of (cf.: Kohut, 1971).

Some theorists have called attention to the child's contribution to the learning process by suggesting that the child may bring a different definition of the task to the dyadic process (e.g., Rogoff & Wertsch, 1984). It is important, they remind us, for adults to understand where the child is coming from so that they can more finely attune their assistance in the ZPD, making the interiorization process easier for the child and avoiding resistances or obstacles to a smooth transition of knowledge, inter- to intra-. However, redefinition of the task to include the learner's perspective should not only involve a reexamination of what we are asking the learner to do but whom we are asking the learner to be. One encounters the same deficiency in discussions of language functions or pragmatics, which, following Austin, emphasize what one can do by means of language neglecting who one can *be* through speech.

There are causes of resistance other than those based on contrasting definitions of the task or even conflicting identifications. Sometimes, I would suggest, resistance is an early or primitive form of identification. That is, the very process that motivates internalization of knowledge can be manifested as a resistance to cooperation in the smooth functioning of that process. For example, in a study of interactions between mothers and their preschool children, dyads were asked to engage in any free-play activity of their choice. In spite of her child's objections, one mother insisted on reading a story with her child (perhaps to impress the videotapers?).

This mother tried several different ways into book-reading as an activity: "we do this all the time"; "you know you love to read books." But the child always refused: saying "no"; turning away; refusing to sit still; grabbing the book from her mother, etc. The mother tried to establish a routine in which the child would be forced to participate: "Oh, look, a little dog. What's he doing?" Refusing to be carried in the activity, the child gave only absurd answers; for example, reducing the task beyond even picture descriptions, the mother asked how many eyes the dog had, to which the child responded, "five!" Such rejections of activities can signal early attempts to perform the adult's functions of choosing and structuring activities.

In another example, a 3+-year-old child with Down's Syndrome who is mainstreamed in a 2+-year-old nursery school class had learned over the course of the year how to participate with the other children in group action-songs at rug time. Checking the teacher's and other children's actions, he would follow the record's instructions to touch the floor and point to the door, touch your head and point to something red, and so forth. Wanting to enhance his performance (perhaps for the university team videotaping in the classroom?), a teacher took over his actions by holding his hands and dancing with him, twirling him to the music. He collapsed on the floor, totally dependent, so that she had to take over all direction of his actions, even holding him upright. His drop in performance from equal participation to being carried in the task was in response to the teacher's refusal to relinquish functions to him.

Once again we can look to language development for insights into these phenomena; specifically, the acquisition of negation. Pea (1980) demonstrated that the earliest expressions of negation by the child are refusal and rejection. (Self-prohibitive use of "no" is also relatively early; that is, using negation to oneself as others had used it previously to regulate one's behavior.) In contrast, commenting on the non-existence or disappearance of things or persons, and especially denying the truth of a proposition are later acquisitions. The earlier forms of negation are tied to interpersonal relationships (Spitz, 1957). In comparing the child's and mother's uses of the contexts of child-rearing practices, Pea demonstrates that the use of negation reflects negotiations in interpersonal relationships between self and other. Early forms of negation serve to separate self from other in a primitive way: I am not you; I refuse to participate. In contrast, denial places negation within a proposition which must be spoken by someone taking up a position within a dialogue, and is therefore negation *within* participation: I am like you; I am participating but I disagree with what you assert.

Just as the refusal to participate in scaffolded activities may be an early stage in the identification-with-the-adult process, taking responsibility for an activity is an acceptance of identification which would permit the child to alter it by denial. In the following example, this exchange transpires midway in a study on the transfer from mother to a 2+-year-old child of a novel script involving a circus game (Lucariello, Kyratzis & Engel, 1986, p. 158). Transmission of scriptal knowledge was to be accomplished by repeated joint-action with the circus toys, noting at different points how the child was internalizing the mother's sequence of events, uses of objects, roles of persons such as ringmaster, lion tamer, and so forth.

C: (Scoops the lions up off the floor and throws them into cage.) They not going to do tricks today.
M: No tricks today! Oh, the children are going to be so disappointed!
C: (Scoops lions out of cage and puts them into ring.) The which lion's performing.
M: What kind of tricks will they do?
C: No lion man!
(Picks up tamer and puts it into ring with lions.)
C: (Cracks the tamer's whip against floor of ring.)
M: What do the lions do?
C: He doesn't want to do the hoops today.
(Throws the lions back in the cage.)
He's going to sleep; he's resting.
C: No one's performing today.

In this case the child demonstrates the internalization of event knowledge by staying within the framed activity, but he negates the mother's acts for framed objects, thereby taking over her role as the one who decides what happens and how objects will be used. Clearly, this child is not just learning script structure any more than children are *just* learning the forms and rules of negation in English.[4]

I have made a similar point about the acquisition of pronouns (Litowitz & Litowitz, 1983). The child's progress from personal name or "me" to "I" in self-reference signals a shift from the child as object for an other to her/his position as subject. Children are not simply learning the forms of expression and rules of use for the pronominal system in English; they are learning how to participate reciprocally and then reversibly in discourses with others. Pronoun acquisition concretely reflects Vygotsky's maxim that "all development consists in the fact that the development of a function goes from *me* to I" (1989, p. 64). Being able to establish oneself as an equal "I" is to accept a shift from reciprocity to reversibility, an important step towards responsibility.

In the following examples, the 3+-year-old child (mentioned above) takes responsibility for his actions and even takes on some of his teacher's functions. Following the above exchange when he collapsed with over-assistance, he joined in a game where everyone sits in a circle with their feet in the center. The teacher acts frightened, exclaiming: "Oh dear, there's a boa constrictor!" She instructs the children to act frightened, whereupon this little boy adds, "We'd better hide!" heightening the atmosphere of mock-terror that sets the scene for the actions to follow (Oh no, he's up to my toes; oh gee, he's up to my knees; oh my, he's up to my thighs . . . oh heck, he's up to my neck). In another game, all the children pretend to lie sleeping on the floor while the teacher steals into the rug area as a monster and scares them. After several repetitions, this little boy, pointing to himself, goes outside the rug area to imitate the teacher-as-monster. Thus, he takes over her role in the game, going from reciprocity (the scared one to her scarer) to reversibility (the scarer to her scared one) in their roles.[5]

The desire to move beyond participation to responsibility is in itself an act of resistance, a resistance to being dependent and controlled by another. The motivation cannot be mastery of the other's skill but to be the other *by means of* mastery of the skill. Language plays a crucial role, not just as a social sign system (e.g., shared referent labels and denotative meanings) or as the means to do things (e.g., organize activities, regulate others and oneself), but as a means to be a human subject – that subject lying hidden in the syntax of "cogito ergo sum" who has been lost to linguistics and objectified as "experimental subject" in psychology.

Notes

1. "We see this kind of behavior in any adult, even in children . . . it is a basic birthright of the human species [with] adaptive value, directly related neither to the individual's survival nor to reproduction. Instead, its raison d'etre is education, bringing up the young" (Kaye, 1982, p. 68).
2. The smoothness may have its roots in Hegelian (and Fichtean) dialectics, albeit reinterpreted by Marx, in which conflict and contradiction are cancelled out and overcome (*aufhebung*), always in a positive and progressive direction. The negation of the dialectical process, however, ignores the fact that there are different kinds of negation (Wilden, 1984; Pea, 1980).
3. Kaye quotes Delgado: "We cannot be free from parents, teachers, and society because they are the extracerebral sources of our minds" (1982, p. 237).
4. Certainly, issues of power and control are at work here but not in any simplistic sense (Verdonik, Flapan, Schmit & Weinstock, 1988; Henriques, et al., 1984).
5. The role of turn-taking in reciprocal games such as peek-a-boo is obvious (Bruner, 1983). Here I wish to stress that step beyond which is responsibility.

References

Bakhtin, M. (1973). *Problems of Dostoevsky's poetics.* Ann Arbor, MI: Ardis.

Bakhtin, M. (1981). *The dialogic imagination: Four essays by M. M. Bakhtin.* M. Holquist (Ed.). Austin: University of Texas Press.

Bruner, J. (1978). The role of dialogue in language acquisition. In A. Sinclair, R. J. Jarvella, & W. J. M. Levelt (Eds.), *The child's conception of language* (pp. 241–256). New York: Springer-Verlag.

Bruner, J. (1983). *Child's talk: Learning to use language.* New York: Norton.

Freud, S. (1971). Mourning and melancholia. *S.E. 14.* London: Hogarth Press.

Freud, S. (1923). The ego and the id. *S.E. 19.* London: Hogarth Press.

Goodnow, J. (1987). *The socialization of cognition. What's involved?* Paper presented at Conference on Culture and Human Development. University of Chicago.

Henriques, J., Holloway, W., Urwin, C., Venn, C., & Walkerdine, V. (1984). *Changing the subject: Psychology, social regulation and subjectivity.* New York: Methuen.

Kaye, K. (1982). *The mental and social life of babies.* Chicago: University of Chicago Press.

Kohut, H. (1971). *The analysis of the self.* New York: I.U.P.

Lacan, J. (1977). *Ecrits: A selection.* New York: Norton.

Litowitz, B. (1988). Early writing as transitional phenomena. In P. C. Horton, H. Gewirtz, & K. J. Kreutter (Eds.), *The solace paradigm: An eclectic search for psychological immunity* (pp. 321–338). New York: I.U.P.

Litowitz, B., & Litowitz, N. S. (1983). Development of verbal self-expression. In A. Goldberg (Ed.), *The future of psychoanalysis* (pp. 397–427). New York: I.U.P.

Lucariello, J., Kyratzis, A., & Engle, S. (1986). Event representation, context and language. In K. Nelson (Ed.), *Event knowledge: Structure and function in development* (pp. 137–159). Hillsdale, NJ: Lawrence Erlbaum.

Nelson, K. (1986). *Event knowledge: Structure and function in development.* Hillsdale, NJ: Lawrence Erlbaum.

Nelson, K., & Gruendel, J. (1986). Children's scripts. In K. Nelson (Ed.), *Event knowledge: Structure and function in development* (pp. 21–46). Hillsdale, NJ: Lawrence Erlbaum.

Pea, R. (1980). The development of negation in early child language. In D. Olson (Ed.), *The social foundations of language and thought* (pp. 156–186). New York: Norton.

Rogoff, B., & Wertsch, J. (Eds.). (1984). *Children's learning in the "zone of proximal development."* San Francisco: Jossey Bass.

Spitz, R. (1957). *No and yes: On the genesis of human communication.* New York: I.U.P.

Verdonik, F., Flapan, V., Schmit, C., & Weinstock, J. (1988). The role of power relationships in children's cognition: Its significance for research on cognitive development. *Quarterly Newsletter of the Laboratory of Comparative Human Cognition, 10* (3), 80–85.

Vygotsky, L. S. (1978). *Mind in society.* Cambridge, MA: Harvard University Press.

Vygotsky, L. S. (1986). *Thought and language.* Cambridge, MA: M.I.T. Press.

Vygotsky, L. S. (1989). [Concrete human psychology] *Soviet Psychology*, *27* (2), 53–77.

Wertsch, J., Minick, N., & Arns, F. (1984). The creation of context in joint problem-solving. In B. Rogoff & J. Lave (Eds.), *Everyday cognition: Its development in social contexts* (pp. 151–167). Cambridge, MA: Harvard University Press.

Wilden, A. (1984). Montage, analytic and dialectic. *American Journal of Semiotics*, *3* (1), 25–47.

Winnicott, D. W. (1971). *Playing and reality*. New York: Basic Books.

Author index

485

Subject index

490

498   *Subject index*

preschool children
    literacy experiences, naturalistic study,
        313–29
    object location memory, 7–8, 79–89
    self-regulatory skills, 81–7
        age differences, 85–7
presentants, 193–9
primary representation, 219
primitive mentality problem, 412, 416n5
problem-solving activities
    experience-based performance, 365–6
    factory work tasks, 355–68
        simulations, 361–4
    laboratory versus everyday settings, 57–68,
        355
    Liberian tailors study, 57–68
pronoun acquisition, 481
pronunciation skills, 263–7
proxemic shifts
    postural kinesics relationship, 23, 27
    videotape study, classroom, 27
purity of sound, 174–8

quantitative analysis, 317–18
queries, context dependence, 36
question–answer format
    bilingual program, 258–60
    and discourse development, 303–9
    in frame methodology, 34–6
    white-room ethnography, 36

reading comprehension
    background knowledge role, 321
    in bilingual instruction, 258–63
    minority children instruction, 249–51
    versus phonics strategies, 249–51, 263–7
reading skills
    affective factors, preschoolers, 321–2, 326–7
    behavior sampling, preschoolers, 324–7
    bilingual instruction, 254–68
    experience-related instruction, 246–8
    Hawaiian children, KEEP program, 241–53
    home–school mismatch issue, 327–8
    and low-income preschoolers, home
        experiences, 313–29
    phonics programs, 244, 249–51, 263–7
        versus comprehension strategies, 249–51,
        263–7
    top-down versus bottom-up instruction,
        246–8
rebec, 167
reciprocity of interaction, 474, 481–2
reductionism
    activity theorists objections to, 156–7
    as alternative to Cartesianism, 156

referent structures, 193–9
reflexivity, 25
representational medium, *see* mediating
    representations/structures
Rescue Mission game, 286–7
research funding
    and normativity assumptions, 107–10
    paradigm prejudice, 100–14
    peer review, 112–13
resistance
    in children, 475–82
    identification role in, 479–80
responsibility, 473–83
reward/punishment format, 432–3, 464n1
risk assessment, 43
role learning, 348
rotated figure tasks
    body analogies in solving of, 90–9
    and mental rotation, 95–9

Saussurianism, 390
scaffolding, 475
    in bilingual instruction, 258
    resistance to, 480
"scenes"
    dramatic metaphor, 44–5
    as object of study, 41–4
schemas, embodied cognition in, 90–9
school performance
    home environment relationship, 241–53
    minority children, reading program, 241–53
    teacher versus child-led groups, 238–40
scripts
    in coordinated interactions, 372
    in courtroom interactions, 372–4, 378
    dramatic metaphor, 44–5
    as object of study, 41–4
SE number system, 212–13
secondary representations, 219, 223
self-blame, women, 455–7
self-regulatory skills
    as meta-cognition, 81–2
    preschool children, 81–9
        age differences, 85–7
    transsituational properties, 81
self-report, 322–3
semantic learning, 249–50
semiotics, 185–202
    ecological application, 185–202
    function circle in, 193–200
    Leont'ev's view, 227
    Peirce's theory, 192–200
    in Vygotskian theory, 121, 227
sentence-bound semantics, 34
sequential context